ESSAYS ON HISTORY, PEOPLE, AND PLACE

MONTANA LEGACY

Edited by

Harry W. Fritz, Mary Murphy, Robert R. Swartout, Jr.

MONTANA
HISTORICAL
SOCIETY
PRESS

D1042817

Cover image: *Indians Watching Crow Fair at Crow Agency, Montana*
Photograph by Marian Post Wolcott, 1941,
Farm Security Administration Collection, Library of Congress.
Colored by Kathryn Fehlig.
Book design by DD Dowden, Helena
Typeset in Berkeley Book and Eras

10 11   9 8 7 6 5 4

ISBN 10: 0-917298-90-X   ISBN 13: 978-0-917298-90-5

Library of Congress Cataloging-in-Publication Data
    Montana legacy : essays on history, people, and place / [selected by]
    Harry W. Fritz, Mary Murphy, Robert R. Swartout, Jr.
        p. cm.
Includes bibliographical references and index.

    1. Montana—History. 2. Montana—History, Local. 3. Montana—
    Social conditions. I. Fritz, Harry W., 1937– II. Murphy, Mary, 1953–
    III. Swartout, Robert R., 1946–
F731.5 .M655 2002
978.6—dc21   2002006808

Contents

Maps and Illustrations

Preface

TEN YEARS AGO ROBERT R. SWARTOUT, JR., AND HARRY W. FRITZ ISSUED
The Montana Heritage: An Anthology of Historical Essays (Helena: Montana
Historical Society Press, *1992*). Intended for use by both general readers
and students taking Montana history classes, the book contained sixteen
articles chronologically arranged from the period of Lewis and Clark to
the present. Designed to offer the latest insights into Montana history,
Montana Heritage's obsolescence was assured by the simple fact that one
decade's latest insight is the next's conventional wisdom. Hence, *Montana
Legacy: Essays on History, People, and Place.*

Like *Montana Heritage, Montana Legacy* is designed for both students
and general readers. Organized chronologically, its articles were
consciously chosen to touch on major themes in Montana history as well
as for readability and the quality of their scholarship. With a few exceptions
we selected recently published essays for inclusion, ones that reflect current
interpretations and approaches. For history is not the same today as it
was ten years ago. Perspectives have changed. A new generation of
historians has reinterpreted the past in light of their own concerns. They
have discovered new sources, introduced new topics, and revised
traditional understandings. Today's past is not yesterday's past; our
understanding is constantly changing, ever more cumulative, always richer
and subtler.

Ten years ago we noted that the scope of historical inquiry had
widened considerably, that scholars had begun to investigate people and
topics that received little attention previously, in particular women, Native
Americans, ethnicity, and the environment. That trend has continued.
Race, class, gender, and ethnicity provide new ways of organizing

information, and historians have increasingly turned to these categories of analysis to explore the past. A glance at our table of contents reveals how much these concepts have influenced our understanding of history in the last decade.

One problem peculiar to Montana history has been a focus on the nineteenth and early twentieth centuries. From Lewis and Clark to the War of the Copper Kings, the state's nineteenth-century past has been studied and restudied, written and rewritten. Current scholarship often offers new insights into traditional topics—see Colin Calloway's essay on the Little Bighorn in this anthology, for example—but for a variety of reasons the twentieth century has had less attention paid it than it deserves. This anthology seeks to adjust that imbalance.

We claim timeliness, not timelessness. Other historians a decade hence will find this collection dated and commonplace. We will probably find it a bit passé ourselves. The frontiers of history are continually expanding, capturing new subjects, and experimenting with new methodologies. We eagerly await the new findings. For now, we hope you enjoy and learn from these.

Harry W. Fritz
The University of Montana, Missoula

Mary Murphy
Montana State University, Bozeman

Robert R. Swartout, Jr.
Carroll College, Helena

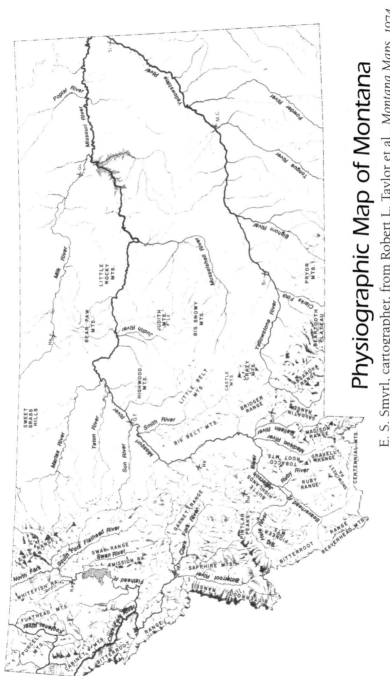

Physiographic Map of Montana

E. S. Smyrl, cartographer, from Robert L. Taylor et al., *Montana Maps*, 1974,
Montana State University Foundation

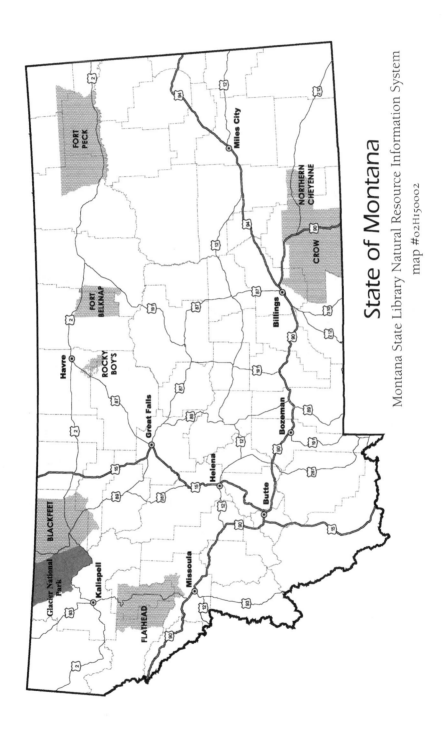

State of Montana

Montana State Library Natural Resource Information System

map #o2H5ooo2

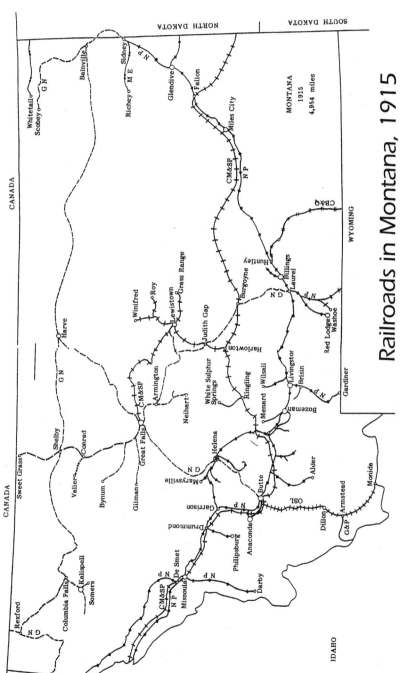

Railroads in Montana, 1915

From Donald B. Robertson, *Encyclopedia of Western Railroad History*, vol. 2

Karl Bodmer illustrated the topography that Maximilian described in his journals. Both men were captivated by the Stone Walls, depicted here in Bodmer's aquatint, View of the Stone Walls on the Upper Missouri.

REUBEN G. THWAITES, ED., *TRAVELS IN THE INTERIOR OF NORTH AMERICA*, VOL. 4

Marvelous Figures, Astonished Travelers

The Montana Expedition of Maximilian, Prince of Wied

JOSEPH C. PORTER

The fur trade initiated the first sustained contact between Native Americans and Euro-Americans in what would become Montana. As Joseph Porter, chief curator of the North Carolina Museum of History in Raleigh, illustrates in this article, the fur trade was a vastly complex enterprise. Intermarriage between Indians and non-Indians fostered trade relations, international companies fiercely competed for furs provided by Native Americans, and tribes warred against each other for access to trade goods. Alcohol, a wildly profitable commodity for Euro-Americans, had a devastating effect on the tribes and, as some traders noted, on the quality of furs themselves.

Much information about the fur trade on the upper Missouri River in the 1830s and the Native Americans who inhabited the region comes from the journals of Prince Maximilian of Wied and the paintings of the artist Karl Bodmer, who, accompanied by the hunter and taxidermist David Dreidoppel, traveled with a trading party of the American Fur Company to Fort McKenzie near present day Fort Benton in 1833. Maximilian, whose Montana experiences are recounted here, was a product of the Enlightenment as were his predecessors, Meriwether Lewis and William Clark. Like Lewis and Clark, Maximilian was an empiricist dedicated to scientific observation and the gathering of data upon which he and others would make rational analyses about the natural world, including its human inhabitants. Porter's essay demonstrates the close connections between exploration, science, and commerce in the nineteenth-century West, a pattern that continues into the present day.

"LIKE A DREAM THESE MARVELOUS FIGURES STREAK PAST THE EYES OF THE ASTONISHED traveler, and only through direct sketches of the most striking ones do these later still survive in the rewarding recollection of the remote, forgotten, marvelous world of nature."

—*Maximilian journal entry, September 17, 1833,*
concerning the Stone Walls region of the Missouri River in Montana[1]

Exploration and the fur trade often were closely related in North American history because traders and trappers were occasionally explorers, and other times they followed explorers. In 1833 exploration and the fur trade merged during the expedition of Prince Maximilian of Wied. Maximilian joined the traders of the Upper Missouri Outfit of the American Fur Company on July 6, 1833, and departed Fort Union on the keelboat *Flora* for what would prove to be a difficult voyage up the Missouri River to Fort McKenzie near the mouth of the Marias River. Although in the company of men who primarily sought economic reward, Maximilian represented the Enlightenment and the Second Great Age of Discovery, a mind-set he shared with Meriwether Lewis and William Clark, his predecessors in the exploration of Montana and the northern West.

The journals of Lewis and Clark and of Maximilian reveal how fully they accepted similar assumptions about exploration, natural history, geography, and human cultures. They shared attitudes typical of the late eighteenth and early nineteenth centuries. Lewis, Clark, and Maximilian were explorers devoted to the exact observation and recording of details, the raison d'etre for their expeditions.[2]

Coming almost thirty years later, Maximilian benefited from Lewis and Clark's pioneering efforts. In authorizing the Lewis and Clark expedition President Thomas Jefferson had ordered his explorers to acquire knowledge to assist Americans in governing and exploiting the resources of their newly acquired Louisiana Purchase. They sought details about natural history and Native American cultures because such information was essential to the American fur trade. The president knew the flag followed the fur trade, and he wanted Americans to counter the British trading companies in Canada. Lewis and Clark provided a preliminary geographical, ethnographical, and natural history survey of the Missouri River valley, and others soon followed in their footsteps.

In addition to the work of Lewis and Clark and other explorers, Maximilian also depended upon the American Fur Company, then extending its operations into what would become Montana. Lewis and Clark's desire to collect, observe, and record infused Maximilian, but in part because he accompanied American Fur Company personnel, the prince was spared the burdens of command and the geopolitical and diplomatic obligations of Lewis and Clark. Thus the prince had more time to pursue detailed investigations and become a candid chronicler. Indeed one could call Maximilian the first historian of the upper Missouri fur trade.

After 1500 Europeans explored and mapped oceans and continents and studied, described, and classified a multitude of new flora and fauna. They pondered the existence of what was to them an unexpected variety of human cultures. By 1800 Johann Friedreich Blumenbach (1752–1840) and other European thinkers had developed methodologies to organize the information then inundating European centers of learning. Savants like Blumenbach and Jefferson and their explorers in the field—Lewis, Clark, Maximilian—based their investigations upon ideas derived from Francis Bacon, Isaac Newton, and John Locke.

Bacon emphasized that knowledge could be gained by disciplined observation of the physical world. Newton and Locke elaborated upon a philosophy that emphasized description and classification. Thus the research strategies of explorers like Maximilian were based upon "both the Newtonian world machine, running according to law, and the empiricism of John Locke [which] stressed the need for first discovering the external facts and then arranging them in an orderly manner so that the structure of the natural law underlying them might be revealed."[3] Amassing details would allow explorers and savants to discern "patterns of terrestrial distribution for rocks, minerals, fossils, plants, animals, and men . . . [because] everything in nature had its proper place and nothing was superfluous."[4]

The intellectual roots of Maximilian's explorations therefore lay in the cultural ferment in Europe before and during his childhood and in his studies as a young man. Born on September 23, 1782, Maximilian was the eighth of ten children of the ruling Prince of Wied. Natural history fascinated the prince, and only military service interrupted his lifelong studies. While a student at Göttingen, Maximilian was exposed to distinct notions about exploration especially those of his mentor, Professor Blumenbach. As a student Maximilian learned that rationalistic empiricism was the philosophic foundation for natural history and the study of man, and this view influenced his response to the environment and peoples of the Western Hemisphere. Moreover the example of Alexander von Humbolt, the noted explorer of Latin America, so impressed Maximilian that in 1815 he and two companions (one was hunter-taxidermist David Dreidoppel, who also accompanied the prince to North America) began a two-year study of Brazil's flora, fauna, and indigenous peoples. Returning to Germany in 1817 Maximilian published his findings on Brazil and prepared for his North American expedition.[5]

Maximilian was especially interested in American Indians because his mentor, Blumenbach, was a leading Enlightenment theorist about the development of the human races. Of great concern to Blumenbach was the issue of human "varieties," which was at the heart of the question of whether human races were "separate species or . . . varieties of a single species." Debate over the issue held significant theological, political, and scientific implications for Europeans because it directly challenged the Christian belief in the common descent of all humankind from Adam and compelled Europeans to confront their growing colonial relationship to indigenous peoples around the world.[6]

Blumenbach and Maximilian believed in the biological equality of all peoples, that is, that there was one species of mankind. As monogenists they rejected arguments that inherent racial differences caused "variations" in cultures. Instead they believed natural environment to be the key factor. Blumenbach taught his students that climate, habitat, diet, and the means of human subsistence within a locale affected the development of races and cultures. In concentrating on the relationship between humans and nature, Blumenbach demanded close observation and the collection of plant, animal, and even human specimens.

Also essential to the anthropology of Blumenbach and Maximilian was visual documentation of peoples and their natural habitat, and it was in this context that Swiss artist Karl Bodmer contributed so much to Maximilian's expedition. The fervent belief of Blumenbach and his contemporaries in painstaking empiricism demanded that field-workers and collectors have great skill in observation and description.

For Blumenbach, Jefferson, and their explorers, discrete fact was the bedrock of science.[7]

Polymaths like Blumenbach and Jefferson were the generals of Enlightenment science, and they required foot soldiers to go to distant lands to observe, document, and collect. Exploration was Blumenbach's most important research tool, and since he rarely left Göttingen he relied upon field illustrations and explorers' narratives as his primary sources. Such information was essential to the vexing debate about human races, and Blumenbach made Göttingen an important European center for exploration studies. Indeed, one of the courses at Göttingen was "apodemics" or the art of traveling.[8]

Maximilian, then, was one of the Göttingen "school" of explorers. At Göttingen he saw the collections gathered by British expeditions, including items from Captain James Cook's last Pacific voyage of 1776–80, and stored at the university museum. Blumenbach acquired his material directly from expeditions, and he maintained extensive global contacts to provide him with portraits, artifacts, specimens, and human anatomical parts. Blumenbach compiled one of the largest collections of anthropology in Europe, consisting by 1795 of eighty-two skulls, samples of human hair, and "first hand portraits of representatives of the different human varieties."[9] To Blumenbach, Maximilian, and their peers these massive collections were essential to description and classification. Thus, in Montana and the northern West, Maximilian collected plant and animal specimens, cultural artifacts, and human anatomical remains while Karl Bodmer, his field illustrator, provided a visual record.

Beyond a research strategy, an explorer required tact, tenacity, and a determined sense of purpose to gain cooperation from peoples quite different from himself. Maximilian's expedition was not a simple meeting of Indians and Europeans, but an ongoing exchange among several cultures. Maximilian, Bodmer, and Dreidoppel had forceful, empathetic personalities that gained the respect and cooperation of Indians and frontiersmen. Along the Missouri River, for example, Bodmer and Dreidoppel frequently served as armed bodyguards for the woodcutters, which represented a significant vote of the frontiersmen's faith and acceptance of the two men. During dangerous times at Fort McKenzie, Maximilian, Bodmer, and Dreidoppel served as officers of the guard during the night watch.

Before leaving St. Louis in April 1833 Maximilian befriended explorer and Superintendent of Indian Affairs William Clark; Clark's nephew, ex-Indian agent and trader Benjamin O'Fallon; and hard-bitten frontier capitalists Kenneth McKenzie and Pierre Chouteau, Jr. The four men were crucial to Maximilian's Missouri River journey. They helped him determine his final itinerary on the Missouri River, and Clark and O'Fallon gave the prince a copy of route maps that Clark had made during the Lewis and Clark expedition. O'Fallon shared his frontier experiences, showing the prince and Bodmer the artwork of George Catlin, who had gone upriver as far as Fort Union in 1832. O'Fallon, an amateur botanist and backyard gardener who raised specimen of frontier flora at his home near St. Louis, asked the prince to gather seeds for him on the upper Missouri.[10]

Chouteau, superintendent of business and director of affairs in Indian country for the American Fur Company, and McKenzie actually made Maximilian's journey possible. In 1827 Chouteau was instrumental in the American Fur Company's absorption of its fierce and ruthless rival, the Columbia Fur Company, which included such men as McKenzie and James Kipp. The Columbia Fur Company became the American Fur Company's Upper Missouri Outfit, and the outfit and its personnel were crucial to Maximilian's efforts on the Missouri River in 1833–34. Chouteau would have had to approve the arrangement made by McKenzie and Maximilian for the prince and his entourage to travel on American Fur Company steamboats as far as they were "able to forge ahead." Chouteau and McKenzie advised Maximilian to take no money because he would have nowhere to spend it on the river. The prince deposited $2,500 with the American Fur Company in St. Louis, and the company kept an account of Maximilian's expenses on the river, then deducted the total from his deposit when he returned to St. Louis in 1834.[11]

The men on board the humble *Flora* carried two grand strategies when the keelboat departed Fort Union for Fort McKenzie: Maximilian's Enlightenment paradigm for exploration; and the Upper Missouri Outfit's plan to wrest the lucrative Blackfeet and Gros Ventre trade away from the Hudson's Bay Company. In his typically thorough fashion Maximilian began his Montana journal by listing all fifty-two crew and passengers on the *Flora*. Over the next five grueling weeks he came to know all of these people well, including David D. Mitchell, who was in charge of the *Flora* and supervised Fort McKenzie once the group arrived there. Mitchell had operated several trading posts and had joined the Upper Missouri Outfit in 1830. He began constructing Fort McKenzie in 1832 to replace the short-lived Fort Piegan at the mouth of the Marias River. Mitchell selected a new site seven miles upstream, and Fort McKenzie operated there until it was abandoned in 1844. The prince also came to know Mitchell's Métis wife, a daughter of Deschamps, a hunter for the company, and Alexander Culbertson, who joined the Upper Missouri Outfit in 1833 and was making his first trip up the Missouri River with Maximilian.[12]

Working in two-hour shifts groups of sixteen to eighteen men, using towlines, pulled the *Flora,* loaded with people and cargo, upstream against the current. Occasionally they stood on the deck and propelled the keelboat by pushing poles against the river bottom. If lucky they hoisted a sail to catch the wind. Most of those on board lived and slept in the open on the boat or ashore in the evenings. Maximilian shared the tiny cabin (eight of his paces in length) with Bodmer, Dreidoppel, Mitchell, Mitchell's wife, and one other, probably either Culbertson or a Blackfeet woman who was returning to her people. Maximilian and the Mitchells used the two beds while the rest slept on the cabin floor. "Guns hung on the ceiling and walls; the traveling bags and chests had been suitably distributed and moved to the side," Maximilian noted, adding, "we had slept very well on our buffalo hides with blankets."[13]

The slow passage of the *Flora* usually allowed Maximilian, Bodmer, and Dreidoppel ample time to observe, sketch, and collect. Frequently the prince, his men, and the hunters walked on the shore, keeping pace with the *Flora.* In addition to sketching, Bodmer, an accomplished hunter, collected bird and animal specimens. The prince and Dreidoppel also hunted daily, and fur company hunters often contributed specimens.

Approximately 504 river miles separated Fort Union from Fort McKenzie, and in 1833 the forts were the only notable Euro-American incursions in Montana's Indian country. The Missouri River presented a formidable challenge to the heavily laden keelboats, which meant hard, backbreaking labor from the *engagés,* who pushed and pulled the boats against the current. Sandbars stopped the *Flora* occasionally, and the crew unloaded hundreds of pounds of cargo to lighten and refloat the boat.

Once the keelboat was afloat they reloaded the cargo. Terrible wind and rainstorms and voracious swarms of mosquitoes frequently tormented the boat's occupants.

Sometimes Maximilian found the upper Missouri River valley desolate and forbidding. At other times it struck him as stark and hauntingly beautiful. The region captured the prince's imagination and kept Bodmer busy sketching and painting, but the *mauvaise terre* and the Stone Walls area inspired them both the most.[14] Terrain and topography were of special concern because their features held the key to understanding the elemental processes of nature. The scenery challenged Bodmer, and he drew scenes in pencil and watercolor while the prince described topographic formations and features in his journal, noting where he saw them. He then keyed his journal entries to specific Bodmer sketches, occasionally noting the exact location, using his route maps from William Clark. On August 1, 1833, for example, Maximilian wrote, "We reach an island, Lewis and Clark's Ibex Island.... Somewhat about the island, behind the prairie and along the left bank, rose hills, on which unusual formations stood. One of them looked like a house with a pair of gables (see sketch U)." Bodmer did sixteen sketches of the area's formations.[15] Continuing upstream and passing the mouth of the Judith River, the *Flora* entered the region of the Stone Walls, of which Maximilian noted the "Jagged peaks like figures and old ruins, and again one saw the strangest figures like pillars, which on top support a stone slab, as noted earlier." A panorama of marvelous figures and intricate stone shapes unfolded as the *Flora* made its way upriver. Entranced, Maximilian wrote: "Isolated, free-standing ledges like walls extend horizontally; they contain caves, perpendicular and horizontal ledges; and on top of them stand rows of strange figures, partly pillars with stone slabs like tables, then figures like organs, pulpits, small towers, even like men."[16]

Maximilian and his men did not work in isolation. Throughout their North American expedition they were members of distinct communities. On the Missouri River they were paying guests of the American Fur Company, but they became a part of the world of fur traders and Indians and occasionally there was friction. At the beginning Maximilian disdained what he regarded as crude and vulgar behavior among the men of the Upper Missouri Outfit. He was not an inflexible, unthinking man, however, and eventually relinquished his early impressions and even befriended individuals who he scorned initially.

The engagés were predominately of French or Métis descent, and they performed the hard labor. They functioned as boatmen, hunters, winterers, interpreters, and in such specialized trades as carpenters, cooks, and blacksmiths. Once they had signed on with the company and left St. Louis, they might be upriver for years. When Maximilian first met the fur company's "rough, wild army of Canadian engagés," they were holding one last raucous celebration prior to shipping out. "The engagés or trappers continued making a loud noise; they shouted, fired their guns, drank. They are just as coarse as the Indians, speak French, are partly half-breed Indians and dark brown," Maximilian wrote. "One such small fellow was very unpleasant; on his back he carried an Indian scalp, stretched on a circular frame. All of them keep their big scalping knives in a sheath in the belt on their backs." Forever a collector Maximilian never let personal penchant impede science, and from "the young engagé, who had been so rowdy lately, I bought the Blackfeet scalp he was wearing."[17]

If the prince sometimes disapproved of the engagés, some of them wearied of him and his endless collecting of animal specimens. Grumbling in his journal, Maximilian wrote,

> The skulls had been prepared with great effort and other objects had been deliberately thrown into the river. I had already lost two bear's heads, an antelope head, a white wolf, and several other things in this manner; even though Mr. Mitchell had threatened to punish such transgressions severely, they still occurred. Therefore it is hardly possible to make any kind of collection on this keel boat. And despite all the interesting objects we acquired, my collection has, as a result, remained quite insignificant.[18]

Maximilian's frustration is understandable, but so, too, is the irritation of the engagés, who were pushing and pulling the *Flora* upstream and could not have appreciated the extra dead weight in animal specimens.

Despite differences, Maximilian and the engagés breached their cultural barriers. Some of the engagés voluntarily gave him animal and bird specimens. Others shared with him their extensive knowledge of Indian cultures and languages, and they introduced Maximilian to the families of their Indian wives. Because of the engagés the French language was probably the primary bridge between the prince and Native Americans.

Maximilian and nearly all of the Upper Missouri Outfit personnel spoke French. When Maximilian asked a question in French, an engagé translated it into the appropriate Indian language. The Indians responded in their native language, and the engagé translated the responses into French. Indeed the Upper Missouri Outfit had such a French aura that the Blackfeet collectively referred to it as the "French."[19]

Like Blumenbach, Maximilian studied racial differences, and he was most interested in Native Americans and their cultures. There had been signs of Indians since leaving Fort Union, but the prince was anxious to actually see Indians. Then, as the *Flora* edged past the Judith River, he saw an entire Gros Ventre village on the right or south bank of the Missouri River. "Everywhere, under single shady trees along the bank, one saw groups of Indians sitting, who were resting. They enlivened the whole region. . . . [They] sat everywhere in the grass on the hills to the left. Their big wolf-like dogs ran around them. . . ." The traders and Maximilian were unnerved to learn that the entire Gros Ventre tribe was camped just ahead. The prince noted that "a keel boat cannot easily escape them. If an exchange of words or dissatisfaction arises among them, 800-900 Indians can easily massacre the fifty men on our boat." His anxiety increased when the *Flora* encountered the Gros Ventre village of more than two hundred tepees.[20]

Soon eight Gros Ventre chiefs boarded the keelboat. Lack of a Gros Ventre speaker among the crew made communicating difficult, so engagé Charles Doucette addressed them in Blackfeet, which some of the Gros Ventre understood. Doucette, Mitchell, Maximilian, and the eight chiefs crowded into the tiny cabin of the *Flora* for a council. The chiefs were "big, strong men with expressive faces." One of them, Mex-keh-mah-uastan, had threatened to shoot Mitchell a year earlier, but in 1833 he was cordial to the trader. Their talks had barely begun when many of the Gros Ventre men and younger people swam the river and boarded the *Flora*. The Gros Ventre greatly outnumbered the crew, and the keelboat became so dangerously overloaded that it floundered in the river. They "all wanted tobacco, powder, bullets, but particularly whiskey and brought along whatever they owned in the way of furs, tanned hides, dried meat, and the like," Maximilian wrote. "Those who had nothing to exchange begged." The chiefs ordered the *Flora* to stop and commence trading, but Mitchell, speaking through Doucette, convinced them to postpone trading until they reached Fort McKenzie. With gifts of tobacco and whiskey the Gros Ventre left the *Flora*, much to the relief of Maximilian and the crew.[21]

This brief encounter demonstrated how such upper Missouri tribes as the Gros Ventre pitted the competing trading companies against each other. Not only did the Gros Ventre want to control trading in their domain, they also sought the best advantage for themselves with the company of their choice. In 1833 the Gros Ventre preferred the American Fur Company to their only alternative, the Hudson's Bay Company. "Now, however, they are compelled to be on good terms with the American traders for in all other respects they have completely forfeited the good will of the whites." Mitchell informed Maximilian that, "Actually they live north near the English frontiers; there they destroyed a fort and killed a clerk and eighteen men of the Hudson's Bay Company, and in the Rocky Mountains they have slain a number of whites, so that no one wanted to have any more dealings with them."[22]

When the Gros Ventre and Blackfeet killed trappers found in their tribal lands, Americans blamed it on "meanness," but in fact the tribes had a vested economic interest in doing their own trapping and hunting because they traded hides and pelts at the trading posts they allowed in their territory. Permitting trappers in their hunting grounds amounted to giving away valuable tribal resources. Moreover American trading practices exacerbated the vehemently anti-American attitudes of the Blackfeet, Gros Ventre, and their allies because, as one historian explains, "American companies engaged large numbers of white or mixed-blood trappers to hunt and trap in Indian territory," while the "Hudson's Bay Company and North West companies wisely avoided competing with the Indians for furs and game," depending instead on the Indians for furs.[23] His exciting encounter with the Gros Ventre was Maximilian's first glimpse of such complex relationships.

On August 9, 1833, four months after Maximilian departed St. Louis, and thirty-four days after leaving Fort Union, the *Flora* reached Fort McKenzie, the outermost post of the American Fur Company and what would be the westernmost extent of Maximilian's expedition. Of the scene Maximilian wrote: "the whole region was filled with groups of the brown and brownish-red (the hides covering them are painted yellowish-red or reddish-brown) mass of humanity, who, some on foot, some on horse-back, some spread in groups along the bank, awaited us. Closely surrounding the fort were the men, about 806 Piegans or Piekani, in a densely compact multitude, drawn up like a well-ordered battalion."[24]

The three Blackfeet tribes—the Piegan, the Blood, and the Blackfeet or Siksika—and their allies the Gros Ventre and Sarsi permitted Fort McKenzie to exist because it was a market for their buffalo hides, beaver pelts, and wolf skins. In exchange they received firearms, knives, a variety of utensils, European-style clothing, blankets, and such items as paint, glass beads, jewelry, and other finery that had been incorporated into their culture and economy.

Among the first Indians the prince met was a warrior "who works for the company, with several more of his people. These people are called soldiers, and at Fort McKenzie there are several from all the nations and tribes living nearby, the Piegan, Blood Indians, Blackfeet, and Gros Ventre des Prairies," Maximilian wrote. "These people," he continued, "are dressed half in the European manner and serve as a sort of guard; they are also employed for various kinds of dealings with the Indians."[25]

Fort McKenzie held both opportunities and obstacles for Maximilian's science. Such forts were excellent places to meet Native Americans and learn about their cultures. The prince met distinguished chiefs, medicine men, and warriors who were the acknowledged leaders of their people. His journal entries provided specific details about the individuals who sat for Bodmer, and the prince often commented on the clothing and artifacts they wore. The combination of Bodmer's visual documentation and Maximilian's text provides an additional dimension to their fieldwork at Fort McKenzie. The Bodmer portraits approach clinical accuracy, but alone they might portray anonymous individuals. When paired with Maximilian's journals, Bodmer's portraits present the subjects as a part of their flourishing cultures with distinct personalities and personal histories. One such drawing shows Chief of the Bears, the imperious Piegan chief, and some of his relatives in grief for the chief's murdered nephew.

Iron Shirt was one of the first chiefs Maximilian met, and his name demonstrated the extensive geographic range of Piegan war parties. He became "Iron Shirt" after he captured a chain mail shirt during a Piegan raid against a Hispanic settlement in the Southwest. Iron Shirt, recognized by the Americans and the Hudson's Bay Company as a significant leader, died in the 1850s, his prized chain mail shirt buried with him.[26]

Occasionally Bodmer and Maximilian met the same Indians that artist George Catlin had sketched at Fort Union in 1832, providing additional insight to these individuals. On September 11 Maximilian met Bull's Back Fat, a chief of the Buffalo Followers band of the Blood. In 1832 Bull's Back Fat had impressed George Catlin, and Catlin and Bodmer both painted portraits of the chief, described by Maximilian as a "very good man, who saved Mr. Mitchell's life last year when an Indian wanted to kill him with a lance. He is the chief of the small band of Blood Indians, which for some time now has been living near the Piegan, and he wants to remain loyal to the fort here. On his chest the chief wore a medal from President Jefferson. His face had a very pleasant, calm expression." Bull's Back Fat was a deliberate, thoughtful leader who tried to calm the growing tension between the Blood and Piegan bands.[27]

Chief of the Bears was perhaps the most forceful personality Maximilian encountered at Fort McKenzie, "the most highly regarded" among the Piegan. The chief's prestige was based on the consensus of his followers, which required continual demonstrations of a chief's ability. "He is now held in such esteem," Maximilian wrote, "because just a short time ago he did battle with the Flatheads, in which forty-seven of the latter were killed." Chief of the Bear's victory over the Flatheads occurred in May 1833 in the Rocky Mountains. The chief and five hundred Piegan attacked about forty-eight Flatheads and two French Canadians, killing all but one Flathead who escaped. The Piegan took forty-seven scalps, but the Flathead fought with valiant desperation before their annihilation. After his battle with the Flatheads, Chief of the Bears "changed his name, something they always do when they have accomplished a remarkable feat." Before the fight his name was Spotted Elk.[28]

Traders of the Upper Missouri Outfit were Maximilian's hosts, and they introduced the prince to the important Indian men. Consequently most of Maximilian's observations were based on the perspective of male informants, and most of Bodmer's portraits are of men. Only seven Bodmer portraits of Indian women are extant from his more than two years in North America. Bodmer did two of these portraits at Fort McKenzie—a Shoshone woman married to an engagé and a Piegan woman whose beauty impressed both the prince and the artist. At Fort Union Bodmer sketched a Blackfeet girl who apparently had been captured by the Assiniboin, and he did two portraits of a Cree woman who was married to the hunter Deschamps.[29]

Maximilian collected artifacts from women, commissioning a fully functional model tepee from two Piegan women and paying them in blue glass trade beads. Their handiwork, "completely accurate on a small scale," delighted the prince. Some of the miniature lodge poles were as "thin as a finger," and their length ranged from 5 feet 8 1/2 inches to 4 feet 4 1/2 inches.[30] Maximilian also hired women to tan hides for him and purchased other objects, paying them or their husbands in trade goods. His frequent visits to the lodges of Indians near the fort gave him ample opportunity to witness the domestic side of Blackfeet life. He noted Blackfeet marriage customs and child rearing practices and watched the women erect tepees, dye feather and porcupine quills to embroider "attractive patterns in beautiful colors," brain-tan buffalo hides, and do the myriad tasks of Plains Indian women. He watched them at their games, and he saw women die in battle.

The traders and engagés married Indian women, and at Fort McKenzie Maximilian witnessed the marriage, "according to local custom," of Alexander Culbertson to a Piegan woman. Culbertson "had paid a price of 100 dollars, and his Piegan wife had brought him a rifle, and a horse was to follow."[31] A good marriage was advantageous to both the trader and the bride's family. A shrewd trader used the influence of his wife's relatives on behalf of himself and the fur company while an ambitious chief or warrior assured himself and his family access to trade goods through a son-in-law or brother-in-law. Culbertson's bride was from the family of White Buffalo, a fur company soldier at the fort.

Maximilian observed such marriages all along the Missouri River. Many "whites—indeed, most of them at the trading posts in Indian country— have Indian womens whom they purchase," he wrote. "They often pay one, two, or even three hundred dollars for them and offer two, three, or more horses, fine costumes, glass beads, knives, powder, lead, rifles, and the like for them." The prince did not entirely approve of the practice, however. "[W]omen here along the Missouri are left in the lurch as soon as [the trader or engagé] is transferred, often after only a short period, to another place, and most employees have women of this kind, often with children, at several trading posts simultaneously."[32]

Although Maximilian had accepted Blumenbach's theories, which tended to prejudge peoples, he saw through the cultural differences that separated him from frontiersmen and the Indians. He earned their friendship, and frequently they volunteered information. Knowing the prince's desire for specimens, they made him gifts of animals and birds they had killed. The son of one chief gave Maximilian a beaver pelt and thanked the prince for having come such a great distance to visit his people.[33]

The fur trade dominated Maximilian's visit to Montana for both good and bad. It made possible his survey of Blackfeet and Gros Ventre cultures, but it crippled Maximilian's natural history research. Rivalries among Indian bands at Fort McKenzie created volatile tensions that prevented Maximilian from collecting natural history specimens. Bodmer could not leave the fort to paint without armed guards. The situation grew so grave that the prince abandoned his plans to travel farther upriver to the Rocky Mountains. Meanwhile the trade itself became a topic for Maximilian's observation. He noted the history of the fort and its physical descriptions, and his notes provided a detailed look at the personnel who worked for the Upper Missouri Outfit. He described the devastating impact of traders' whiskey on the Indians. He witnessed murderous intratribal vendettas between the Piegan and the Blood, and he fought in a battle between the Piegan and attacking Assiniboin and Cree warriors.

Maximilian, Bodmer, and Dreidoppel remained at Fort McKenzie, where they shared a humble room with engagé Charles Doucette from August 9 until September 14. The fort was a microcosm of the Missouri River fur trade. "The supplies at Fort McKenzie, both merchandise as well as other necessities, were replenished by our arrival. Clerks were placed in charge of the stores; special hunters provided our food; workers, woodcutters, fishermen, all were here together." Maximilian observed, "now there were people from all nations: Americans, Englishmen, Frenchmen, Germans, Spaniards; several of the latter were hunters." If Maximilian had his opinions and impressions of the fur trade, the traders had their own of him. Kenneth McKenzie, king of the upper Missouri, called Maximilian a "fine old gentleman" and praised the prince's natural history and ethnological research and the fidelity of Bodmer's work. Culbertson described the prince as

> nearly seventy years of age [he was actually 51], but well preserved, and able to endure considerable fatigue. He was a man of medium height, rather slender, sans teeth, passionately fond of his pipe, unostentatious, and speaking a very broken English. His favorite dress was a white slouch hat, a black velvet coat, rather rusty from long service, and probably the greasiest pair of trousers that ever encased princely legs. The Prince was a bachelor and a man of science, and it was in this latter capacity that he had roamed so far from his ancestral home on the Rhine.

Culbertson added that Maximilian's companions, Bodmer and Dreidoppel, had a gift for "putting their princely employer into a frequent passion, till there is hardly a bluff or a valley on the whole upper Missouri that has not repeated in an angry tone, and with a strong Teutonic accent, the names of Boadman and Tritripel."[34]

Maximilian's first contact with the Piegan came during formalities that opened the trading sessions at Fort McKenzie. Iron Shirt invited Mitchell, called "Black Thunder" by the Piegan, and Maximilian to "a so-called festivity." After feeding his guest Iron Shirt exchanged gifts with Mitchell, including what Maximilian described as "a scarlet-red uniform with blue lapels, collar, and yellow braid, made in the manner of an overcoat, which he had received from the English." In addition, Maximilian noted, the chief offered "six red and black plumes, a dagger with sheath, a colorful handkerchief, and finally several beaver pelts."[35] Iron Shirt's presentation to Mitchell was the first step in an elaborate etiquette that governed the trade.

The following day, August 10, 1833, the personnel of the fort prepared to trade with the Piegan bands of Iron Shirt and Chief of the Bears. The crew in the fort fired a cannon, the roaring boom informing the Indians that "they could now make their visit to commence trading." After half an hour Maximilian "heard singing and shooting and saw the throng of Indians advancing from all sides." More cannon fire welcomed the chiefs at the gates. "Mr. Mitchell had wanted to dispense with the petty formalities and the welcoming cannonade last year," Maximilian noted, "but the Indians seemed to place great value upon them and even wanted to withdraw if sufficient honors were not bestowed upon them."[36]

Once in the fort the chiefs and about thirty of the leading warriors sat on buffalo robes that had been spread on the ground. The assemblage of chiefs and warriors fascinated the prince with their "interesting, characteristically Indian physiognomies painted in every possible way, beautifully adorned, and in martial attire."[37] Maximilian was mildly disappointed because many of the Indians purposely wore European-style clothing and hats to celebrate the advent of trading.

At least thirty chiefs were in the fort, Maximilian noted, when "whiskey was passed around, and they smoked their pipes." Mitchell presented Chief of the Bears with a magnificent red and green greatcoat with impressive epaulets and silver braid, a red flat hat, and a new double-barreled percussion lock gun; "all in all a complete outfit," the prince noted, adding, "This Chief had always shown himself to be loyal to the American Fur Company and had never gone to trade with the English posts in the North, for which reason they wanted to show him special honor."[38]

While Chief of the Bears strode about in his new finery Mitchell bluntly told the other chiefs that the American Fur Company favored its friends. "Could anyone say that they had ever received such fine clothes from the English?" Mitchell demanded, adding that some "of them had gone to trade with the English and had sold them their beaver skins; for this reason he could not give them big gifts."[39] Resplendent in his new clothes, Chief of the Bears mounted a horse and rode about, while Blood warriors, jealous of the Piegan chief, talked openly of shooting him.

The chiefs made more speeches while fur company personnel served Indians whiskey diluted with water and presented small kegs of whiskey to the chiefs. The formal ceremonies lasted until about six o'clock that evening when frantic trading began. Shocked and dismayed, Maximilian watched the whiskey's effect. "They brought their beaver pelts, buffalo blankets, and other objects; and whiskey, their idol, was always the main thing for which they traded them." Maximilian continued, "Now a tumultuous scene began. Our French engagés, who had drunk too much whiskey, began fighting. There were bloody noses. Harvey, the clerk intervened, became involved in the fight, struck someone in the head with his tomahawk after he had been struck, and the fight became very serious."[40] Trading and drinking among the Indians and drinking and brawling among the employees lasted until late in the night.

Maximilian had already seen the use of alcohol at Fort Union, and the demoralization it caused deeply troubled him. "We witnessed indescribable scenes," he wrote, of "barter and bacchanalia." He learned how profitable whiskey was for the fur company at Fort Union, where the price the Indians paid in hides and pelts for whiskey represented a 3,000 percent markup over the fur company's cost of the alcohol. The Upper Missouri Outfit traders insisted that they could not stop using whiskey at Forts Union and McKenzie because the competing Hudson's Bay Company provided it at rival posts.[41]

Like Maximilian, the traders saw the cultural disruption that alcohol caused. Mitchell admitted to "the abuse of selling whiskey to the Indians," which he said made them become "bad, dissolute, lazy, as well as dangerous." In fact Mitchell insisted that alcohol was a serious impediment to the trade because it caused Indians to "neglect to sell the whites good hides and goods." He added: "The women, who know only too well that they will get nothing for their work because the men immediately buy whiskey and bring nothing substantial home, tan the hides only partially and poorly." Mitchell told Maximilian, "the men neglect beaver trapping and become totally dissolute and bad."[42]

Maximilian blamed the Indian agents for not keeping alcohol out of Indian country. The United States government banned the sale of alcohol to Indians, but enforcement was nonexistent. The prince predicted a continued lack of enforcement because "all the Indians living up here can obtain as much whiskey as they want from the English. . . . If they were not given any by the American Fur Company, trade would totally withdraw from here and turn to the English." Maximilian added, "Among the Mandans and the Minitaris there is no whiskey at all; Mr. McKenzie has no supply of it there at all."[43]

Fierce competition for hunting and trapping grounds, for access to trade goods, for horses—a crucial asset and resource—all contributed to warfare among northern plains tribes. The demand for furs and hides also exacerbated intertribal warfare because it increased competition for hunting grounds. Although the trade spurred warfare the fur traders tried to stop fighting among tribes because it hurt the trade itself. "Warfare," notes one historian, "prevented concerted hunting and trapping by the companies' customers."[44]

Karl Bodmer, Fort McKenzie, August 28th 1833, *shows Assiniboin and Cree warriors attacking a Piegan village outside the fort.*

REUBEN G. THWAITES, ED., *TRAVELS IN THE INTERIOR OF NORTH AMERICA,* VOL. 4

On August 28, 1833, 480 Assiniboin and 100 Cree attacked the Piegan camp outside the walls of Fort McKenzie, and Maximilian, Bodmer, and Dreidoppel were thrust suddenly into a deadly battle. The Assiniboin and Cree struck at daybreak, causing panic among the Piegan and chaos within the fort. Maximilian and his men were asleep when their roommate Doucette "ran for his weapons, and shouted that we had to fight." Maximilian, Bodmer, and Dreidoppel rushed to the ramparts of the fort, and the prince beheld the full striking force of an attacking Plains Indian war party. He "saw, on the hills behind the fort, everywhere red with Indians on foot and on horseback. They quickly descended, all 580 of them, into the plain and fell upon the Piegan in their tents." Piegan men tried to rally while their women and children fled to the gates of the fort, only to find the attackers there ahead of them.[45]

The engagés were shooting at the Assiniboin and Cree, and Culbertson recalled that the prince quickly joined the fight, seizing his loaded rifle, and, in the excitement of the moment, loading it again. Taking dead aim on an Assiniboin, he fired. The recoil from the double load was so great that it knocked the prince backwards and almost senseless.[46] Heavy gunfire from the fort finally forced back the Assiniboin and Cree, who also had attacked outlying Piegan camps.

Sporadic and frequently intense fighting lasted until noon. At times Assiniboin and Cree warriors dismounted, advanced, and fought on foot. "One heard the latter [Assiniboin and Cree] calling out to one another to advance and attack," Maximilian observed, "and in twenties and thirties they did advance, something which the Blackfeet did not dare to do." Despite the horror of combat, the faces of the dead, the agonized cries of the wounded, and the spectacle of war parties colliding in battle, the warriors "in their finest attire" held an eerie, thrilling, magnificence for Maximilian, who wondered at the warriors who prepared themselves so elegantly before fighting and possibly dying.[47]

The battle ceased fitfully, and the prince watched as the relatives and medicine men attended to the dead and wounded. Dying horses and dogs, struck with bullets or arrows, lay pitiably among wretched human casualties. Anguished shrieks from the wounded and keening wails from mourners were the epilogue to the terrible fight. The attackers had killed ten Piegan, and they had warriors killed. The prince saw mutilation when the body of an Assiniboin warrior fell into Piegan hands. Maximilian's disgust was not altogether humanitarian for he wanted the head of the Assiniboin corpse for Blumenbach's skull collection. It was soon so "completely destroyed," however, that the prince rejected the idea.[48] Maximilian, Bodmer, and Dreidoppel had been participant observers in a most fundamental, yet unique way: they had watched and fought in a battle between two great war parties and had taken part in the entire course of a Plains Indian battle from the first shots to final care of wounded and mourning for the dead.

Maximilian had three perspectives on the fight. He fought for the Piegan and afterwards interviewed Piegans and traders who experienced the battle. Remarkably, later at Fort Union, he met the Assiniboin warriors, including Chief Antelope, who attacked the Piegan at Fort McKenzie. Antelope was an extraordinary and powerful Assiniboin chief for many decades. In 1831, acting as principal chief of all the Assiniboin, he had signed a treaty with the Blackfeet and the American Fur Company.[49]

Antelope told of Assiniboin perceptions of the battle, and Bodmer later depicted the Fort McKenzie battle in an aquatint engraving with Antelope as the central figure. The engraving is further confirmation of Bodmer's accuracy. Antelope had several names including Left Handed or the Left Handed Man, and, in the central foreground of Bodmer's work, the leader of the Assiniboin is holding what appears to be a Bear Society knife in his primary or left hand and the scalp of a fallen Piegan warrior in his right hand. Bodmer's work graphically interprets the violent fury of the battle. Many artists of the American West (not to speak of filmmakers) have represented scenes of Indian warfare, but only Karl Bodmer and Indian warrior artists apparently ever in fact witnessed or participated in an Indian battle.[50]

The battle emphasized the unstable situation at Fort McKenzie. Tensions between the Piegan and Blood and the dangers presented by war parties from other tribes made the area too hazardous for observing, documenting, and collecting. Even before the battle Maximilian complained that it was virtually impossible to collect. On August 30 Mitchell sent a trading expedition to the Kutenai tribe. The expedition included seven engagés, whom Maximilian regarded as exceptionally good men. The prince believed their absence further jeopardized the security of the fort, and Mitchell was compelled to maintain a constant night watch. Maximilian, Bodmer, and Dreidoppel took their turns at sentry duty, even serving as officers of the guard.

Maximilian wanted to go upstream as far as the Great Falls of the Missouri River, but a Piegan chief warned him against it. The Piegan would do the prince no harm, but the chief "could not vouch for the Blood Indians and the Blackfeet." Armed escorts accompanied Bodmer whenever he left the fort to sketch and paint. As the summer trading season ended, fewer Indians would come to Fort McKenzie, removing another reason to remain there. By September 6 Maximilian abandoned his plans to visit the Great Falls and told Mitchell to hurry construction on a boat to carry him, his men, and his collections downstream to Fort Union. Mitchell also ordered cages built for the prince's two newly acquired young live bears, and Mitchell assigned four engagés to man the prince's boat.[51]

Maximilian left Fort McKenzie on the clear, beautiful morning of September 14. His collections, especially the large crate containing the bears, nearly crowded the men out of the boat. The bears complained loudly, and a driving rain soon overtook them, soaking the men and the precious collections.

> We took all the crates and trunks on shore, but how horrible! None of our things was dry; all the Indian and natural history collections, articles of clothing, mathematical instruments, books, in short everything was completely soaked and drenched; one trunk was completely open at every joint and had become useless . . . [b]ut what grieved me most of all was that my entire botanical collection, which I had assembled with effort and persistence during a journey of five to six months on the Missouri now seemed completely lost.

The prince attempted to dry his botanical specimens in the sun, but his effort failed.[52] Despite crowded conditions on their little boat Maximilian still observed and described as he went downstream. The group traveled quickly and as quietly as the complaining bears would allow. Anxious to avoid Assiniboin war parties who might remember their defense of the Piegan at Fort McKenzie, they often traveled at night. Their difficulties did not prevent Maximilian from being impressed again by the rugged, stark beauty of Stone Walls and the mauvaise terre and immense herds of buffalo numbering in the thousands. On September 29, two weeks after leaving Fort McKenzie, Maximilian's boat pulled into view of Fort Union. "Renewed zeal seizes our crew; at 1 o'clock we reached the fort," Maximilian entered in his journal.[53]

Although forced to leave Montana behind, Maximilian had captured much of a sense of it in his journals, in Bodmer's art, and in his collections. Like his Enlightenment predecessors Lewis and Clark, the prince had served his science as he best knew how. In his work he labored to preserve something of that time and place. In the 1830s the traders came and went, seemingly ephemeral in their passage. Others came later with agendas to change the land and alter the lives of its indigenous peoples. Maximilian, Bodmer, and Dreidoppel, too, had their purpose. They came to see, to learn, and to record. With the legacy of Maximilian's journals and Bodmer's art, we today can glimpse something of those people, that time, and that place.

NOTES

1. Maximilian journal entry, September 17, 1833, concerning the Stone Walls region of the Missouri River in Montana in "The American Journals, 1832–1834 of Maximilian, Prince of Wied," Joslyn Art Museum, Omaha, Nebraska (hereafter "American Journals"). Volumes 1 and 2 of "American Journals," featured in this essay, have been translated from Maximilian's German-language journals by Paul Schach, professor emeritus, Department of Modern Languages, University of Nebraska, Lincoln.

2. Brooke Hindle, *The Pursuit of Science in Revolutionary America* (1956; reprint, New York, 1974), 11–30; William H. Goetzmann, *New Lands, New Men: America and the Second Great Age of Discovery* (New York, 1986), 1–60; Gary E. Moulton, ed., *Journals of the Lewis and Clark Expedition,* vol. 2 (Lincoln, Neb., 1986), 8.

3. On Francis Bacon see Barbara Maria Stafford, *Voyage into Substance: Art, Science, Nature, and the Illustrated Travel Account* (Cambridge, Mass., 1984), 31–32; Hindle, *Pursuit of Science,* 12.

4. Goetzmann, *New Lands, New Men,* 2. See also John C. Greene, *American Science in the Age of Jefferson* (Ames, Iowa, 1984), 3–59. On the evolution of scientific fields of inquiry see Thomas S. Kuhn, *The Structure of Scientific Revolutions,* 2d ed. (Chicago, 1970), 66–91.

5. Wied was a Prussian principality on the Rhine River. On Maximilian see Philip Wirtgen, *Zum Andenken an Prinz Maximilian zu Wid seine Umgebung* (Neuwied, Germany, 1902), 242–49; Karl Vikto, "Maximilian Prince of Wied: A Biographical Survey," in *Proceedings of the Thirtieth International Congress of Americanists Held at Cambridge, 1952* (London, n.d.), 193–94. On Maximilian in Brazil see Maximilian, Prinz zu Wied, *Reise nach Brasilien in den Jahren 1815–1817,* 2 vols. (Frankfurt, Germany, 1820–1821), translated into a one-volume English edition, Prince Maximilian of Wied-Neuwied, *Travels in Brazil in the Years 1815, 1816, 1817* (London, 1820); and Maximilian, Prinzen zu Wied-Neuwied, *Abbildungen zur Naturgeschichte Brasiliens* (Weimar, Germany, 1822).

6. Blumenbach derived his racial classifications in part from Swedish naturalist Carolus Linnaeus, although he believed explorers had disproved Linnaeus's ideas about human races. See "Introductory Letter to Sir Joseph Banks," in J. F. Blumenbach, *De Generis Humani Varietae Nativa* (1795), in *The Anthropological Treatise of Johann Friedrich Blumenbach* (1865; reprint, Boston, 1973), 150; and John C. Greene, *The Death of Adam: Evolution and its Impact on Western Thought* (Ames, Iowa, 1959), 221. On Blumenbach and ethnology see Marvin Harris, *The Rise of Anthropological Theory: A History of Theories of Culture* (New York, 1968), 84–87; and Fred W. Voget, *A History of Ethnology* (New York, 1975), 58–61. Also on Blumenbach see F. W. P. Dougherty, "The Correspondence of Johann Friedrich Blumenbach," *History of Anthropology Newsletter,* 10, no. 2 (1983), 6–7; and Timothy Lenoir, "Kant, Blumenbach, and Vital Materialism in German Biology," *Isis,* 71, no. 256 (1980), 77–108; and Timothy Lenoir, "Johann Friedrich Blumenbach's Research Program for Natural History and the Biological Thought of the Naturphilosophen," *Studies in the History of Biology* (1981), 5.

7. Donald Jackson, *Letters of the Lewis and Clark Expedition with Related Documents, 1783–1854*, 2d ed. (Urbana, Ill., 1978), 61–62; Goetzmann, *New Lands, New Men*, 1–110; Stafford, *Voyage into Substance*, 31–64.

8. M. Flourens, "Memoir of Blumenbach," in *The Anthropological Treatises of Johann Friedreich Blumenbach*, trans. Thomas Bendyshe (London, 1865), 58; Erwin H. Ackernecht, "George Forster, Alexander von Humboldt, and Ethnology," *Isis*, 46 (1955), 83–84. See also Hans Plischke, *Die Ethnographic Sammlung der Universitat Göttingen, Ihre Geschichte und Ihre Bedeutung* (Göttingen, Germany, 1931); Hans Plischke *Johann Friedreich Blumenbachs Einfuss auf die Entdeckungsreisenden seiner Zeit* (Göttingen, Germany, 1937); and Gloria Flaherty, "Goethe and Shamanism," *Modern Language Notes*, 104 (April 1989), 584–88.

9. Vogert, *History of Ethnology*, 105–6.

10. "American Journals," 1:231–32. On Catlin see Brian W. Dippie, *Catlin and His Contemporaries* (Lincoln, Neb., 1990), 22–27; and William H. Truettner, *The Natural Man Observed: A Study of Catlin's Indian Gallery* (Washington, D.C., 1979).

11. "American Journals," 1:228, 232, 235; Ray H. Mattison, "James Kipp," in *The Mountain Men and the Fur Trade of the Far West*, ed. LeRoy Hafen, (Glendale, Calif., 1965–1972), 2:201–5.

12. David Smythe, "The Struggle for the Piegan Trade: The Saskatchewan versus the Missouri," *Montana The Magazine of Western History*, 34 (Spring 1984), 3–15; David Smythe, "Jacques Berger, Fur Trader," *The Beaver*, 63 (June-July 1987), 39–50; "American Journals," 2:164; Charles Larpenteur, *Forty Years A Fur Trader*, ed. Elliott Coues, vol. 1, pt. 4 (New York, 1898), 109–11; Ray H. Mattison, "David Dawson Mitchell," in Hafen, ed., *Mountain Men*, 2:241–46; Ray H. Mattison, "Alexander Culbertson," in Hafen, ed., *Mountain Men*, 1:253–56; James H. Bradley, "Affairs at Fort Benton from 1831 to 1869," in *Contributions to the Historical Society of Montana*, vol. 2 (1900; reprint, Boston, 1966), 206–10.

13. "American Journals," 2:163, 164.

14. The French term *mauvaise terre* "applied to any district cut up into deep and intricate chasms." John F. McDermott, *A Glossary of Mississippi Valley French 1673–1850* (St. Louis, 1941), 102. This area is upstream from the Judith River. "Maps of the Missouri River" (Missouri River Commission, 1895), maps 70 and 71. The Stone Walls or White Cliffs area begins about 2.5 river miles upstream from the mouth of Arrow River, continuing on both banks of the Missouri River for the next 25 river miles. "Maps of the Missouri River," maps 73 and 74; Joseph C. Porter on-site survey, 1983, 1984, 1987.

15. "American Journals," 2:201; David C. Hunt and Marsha V. Gallagher, annotators, *Karl Bodmer's America* (Lincoln, Neb., 1984), nn. 220–24.

16. "American Journals," 2:209–11. Maximilian drew some of these formations in his journal, cross-referencing his text to Bodmer's sketches. See Hunt and Gallagher, *Karl Bodmer's America*, nn. 223–37.

17. "American Journals," 2:2, 7. Maximilian also collected the scalp of the Arikara Indian who killed the famous mountain man Hugh Glass. Employee contracts, lists, and accounts are in the Chouteau-Maffitt Collection at the Missouri Historical Society,

St. Louis. William Hunt, Midwest Archeological Center, National Park Service, Lincoln, Nebraska, assisted with his comprehensive census of employees of the American Fur Company and its successor, the Pierre Chouteau, Jr. and Company, for years 1826–65.

18. "American Journals," 2:193.

19. "American Journals," 2:249, 255. Maximilian could read English and speak broken English.

20. "American Journals," 2:206–8; Elliott Coues, ed., *The History of the Lewis and Clark Expedition*, vol 1: (1893; reprint, New York, [1965?]), 335–36, n. 22; "Maps of the Missouri River," map 73; Porter on-site survey.

21. "American Journals," 2:209. Maximilian translated *Mex-keh-mah-uastan* as Stirring Iron or *Le fer qui remue.* See Hunt and Gallagher, *Karl Bodmer's America,* n. 241; and *Bodmer's America: Karl Bodmer's Illustrations to Prince Maximilian of Wied-Neuwied's Travels in the Interior of North America* (Omaha, Neb., 1991), tableau 20 (hereafter *Bodmer's America*). The hairstyle worn by the chief in the Bodmer portrait indicates that he was also a medicine man. See also Hunt and Gallagher, *Karl Bodmer's America,* n. 240; and *Bodmer's America,* tableau 38. Karl Bodmer used his field sketches and objects and artifacts collected by Maximilian as the basis of a series of eighty-one aquatint images. These eighty-one aquatints (forty-eight folio-size tableau and thirty-three vignettes) were to serve as the illustrations for Maximilian's publication about his North American expedition. For an index to the eighty-one Bodmer aquatints see *Bodmer's America.*

22. Gros Ventre attacked and looted the Hudsons Bay Company post at Manchester House—de l'Isle site in October 1793. In 1794 Gros Ventre and some Blackfeet attacked the company's South Branch House, destroying the post and killing all but two of the Hudson's Bay Company personnel and their families. South Branch House was on the Lower South Saskatchewan River near its confluence with the North Saskatchewan River. Arthur S. Morton, *A History of the Canadian West to 1870–71,* 2d ed. (Toronto, 1973), 456–57; E. E. Rich, *The History of Hudson's Bay Company 1670–1870* (London, 1959), 2:171–73; David Smythe, "The Fur Trade of the Northern Plains and Rocky Mountain House," MS, pp. 37–44.

23. Smythe, "Struggle for the Piegan Trade," 5–6.

24. "American Journals," 2:219.

25. Ibid.

26. Dale L. Morgan, ed., *The West of William Ashley, 1822–1838* (Denver, 1968), 42–43; James W. Schultz, *Signposts of Adventure* (Boston, 1926), 41–42. See also Hunt and Gallagher, *Karl Bodmer's America,* n. 248; and *Bodmer's America,* tableau 45.

27. "American Journals," 2:255, 220. Maximilian translated his name as Bull's Hide, but Stomick-Sosack (ca. 1782–1848) is best known as Bull's Back Fat. John C. Ewers to Joseph C. Porter, June 4, 1984; George Catlin, *Letters and Notes on the Manners, Customs, and Condition of the North American Indians,* vol. 1 (London, 1841), 29–31, plate 11; Truettner, *The Natural Man Observed,* 184, fig. 15; Hunt and Gallagher, *Karl Bodmer's America,* n. 264; *Bodmer's America,* tableau 46.

28. "American Journals," 2:220.

29. Hunt and Gallagher, *Karl Bodmer's America,* nn. 205, 258, 259, 267, 268.

30. "American Journals," 2:233–34.

31. Ibid., 2:243.

32. Ibid., 2:271.

33. Ibid., 2:227.

34. Ibid., 2:223; Annie H. Abel, ed., *Chardon's Journal at Fort Clark 1834–1839* (Pierre, S.Dak., 1932), 353, 366; Bradley, "Affairs at Fort Benton," 3:206–7.

35. "American Journals," 2:223.

36. Ibid., 2:224.

37. Ibid.

38. Ibid.

39. Ibid.

40. Ibid. "Harvey" was the volatile and notorious Alexander Harvey (died 1854). Roy H. Mattison, "Alexander Harvey," in Hafen, ed., *Mountain Men,* 4:119–23.

41. "American Journals," 2:227, 160.

42. Ibid., 2:240.

43. Ibid. On regulation of Indian trade and sale of alcohol see Francis Paul Prucha, *The Great Father: The United States Government and the American Indians,* vol. 1 (Lincoln, Neb., 1984), 88–102.

44. Smythe, "Struggle for the Piegan Trade," 10–11.

45. "American Journals," 2:274–76.

46. Bradley, "Affairs at Fort Benton," 3:208.

47. "American Journals," 2:276.

48. Ibid.

49. Ibid., 2:244, 316.

50. *Bodmer's America,* tableau 42.

51. "American Journals," 2:258.

52. Ibid., 2:286–88.

53. Ibid., 2:301.

Army Allies or Tribal Survival?

The "Other Indians" in the 1876 Campaign

COLIN G. CALLOWAY

During the first seventy years of the nineteenth century the expansion of the fur trade, discovery of massive gold deposits, and the building of transcontinental railroads all posed a direct threat to the traditional economic and social order of native communities on the northern plains. In time the competition between native and non-native peoples over the resources of the land led to violence and bloodshed. Of all of the conflicts that arose in the mid-nineteenth century, none has received more attention by historians than the Great Sioux War of 1876–77.

That war, including the famed Battle of the Little Bighorn on June 25, 1876, has often been portrayed in both academic history and popular culture as a classic example of "white" versus "red." Yet as Colin G. Calloway, a professor of history and Native American studies at Dartmouth College in Hanover, New Hampshire, effectively illustrates in the following essay, "simple stories distort human realities." Long before Euro-Americans had arrived on the Great Plains, intertribal warfare had been a common feature of Native American societies. These conflicts were often based on shifting military alliances, competition over natural resources, and specific cultural values within individual tribes. As readers shall see all of these factors came into play during the Great Sioux War of 1876–77.

IN THE LATE 1750S, AS FRANCE BATTLED TO SAVE HER CRUMBLING NORTH AMERICAN empire, the army of the Marquis de Montcalm was a polyglot crew, composed of regular troops, Canadian militia, volunteers, and Indians.

The Indian contingent comprised, at one time or another, warriors from various Iroquois tribes, Indians from Catholic mission villages on the St. Lawrence River, Hurons, Algonkins, Nipissings, Penobscots, Abenakis, Maliseets, Ottawas, Chippewas, Menominees, Mississaugas, Potawatomis, Delawares, Shawnees, Sauks, and Mesquakies. The diplomacy and expense of keeping together such a coalition, most of whose members spoke mutually unintelligible languages and many of whom harbored ancient hostilities, taxed French resources and resilience to the limit. The French devoted considerable effort to cultivating and maintaining their Indian alliances—they had to: their North American empire depended on it.[1] The British likewise employed Indian allies—mainly Mohawks, Mahicans, and Mohegans. In some campaigns Indians constituted as much as one-seventh or one-eighth of New England's colonial armies.[2] The British developed the administration, personnel, and expertise to deal with their Indian allies.

Nevertheless the Indians who participated in the so-called "French and Indian Wars" were neither mercenaries nor pawns. They fought by their own rules and mostly for their own reasons, as indicated by the frequent frustrations of their European allies, who were never quite sure what they were up to. In some cases the prime motive for going to war was to strike enemy Indians in traditional patterns of culturally motivated war, not to fight European troops in imperially driven conflicts. Some of Montcalm's Indian allies canoed a thousand miles to fight, then paddled home after a brief skirmish had netted them a few scalps. Others perpetrated the slaughter of the English garrison at Fort William Henry in 1757, an event made infamous by *The Last of the Mohicans*. The French had secured their objective when they took possession of the fort, but the Indians felt betrayed that their objectives had been frustrated. They took matters into their own hands to secure the scalps and plunder they felt their services warranted.[3] These people fought for their own reasons.

Looking back at the wars in the eastern woodlands, most of us can jettison the racist views of writers like Francis Parkman and Theodore Roosevelt that this was a simple story of conflict between natural enemies, with Anglo-Saxon "civilization" destined to defeat Indian "savages" and French Catholics. The "French and Indian Wars" were complex and messy affairs, in which international rivalries, intercolonial disputes, intertribal foreign policies, and intratribal politics overlapped in a kaleidoscope of conflicts and competitions.

More than a hundred years later and a thousand miles west, we rarely see such confusion. Instead we often still get simple stories. European rivals have long since fallen out of the picture, and the United States alone engages in a straightforward campaign of whites against Indians. What is more, you do not have all those trees to obscure your vision: Indian war parties and United States cavalry units move across an uncluttered canvas, like easily distinguishable teams on an open playing field. Add to that star quarterbacks like Custer and Crazy Horse, whose "parallel lives" as representatives of cultures in inevitable conflict culminate in the encounter, and it is easy to see why the Little Bighorn has captured our imagination as an epic, an elemental struggle with clear life-and-death issues and obvious resolution.[4]

But simple stories distort human realities. Serving as scouts and soldiers for the United States Army was a fairly common practice among Plains Indians.[5] Other Indian peoples besides the Sioux and Cheyenne participated in the Battle of the Little Bighorn, which, after all, was fought on the Crow reservation. On the day after the battle, as Lieutenant James Bradley's column approached the scene of the fight, the Crow scouts he had sent ahead met three Crow scouts who had been with Custer. They came back singing a mourning song and in tears. As the Crow scout Little Face struggled to tell Bradley his story, the other Crows went off a ways and "sat down alone, weeping and chanting that dreadful mourning song, and rocking their bodies to and fro. They were the first listeners to the horrid story of the Custer massacre, and, outside of the relatives and personal friends of the fallen, there were none in this whole horrified nation of forty millions of people to whom the tidings brought greater grief."[6]

Why? I doubt it was for love of Custer. What Native American interests and foreign policies caused Crows—and Arikaras, and Shoshones, and Pawnees—to be involved on the "wrong side" in the 1876 campaign, and what caused them to be so mortified at the outcome of this classic Indian-white encounter? These people were not lost, they were not confused, and they had not "sold out" to the Americans. We think we know what the soldiers and the Sioux were doing at the Little Bighorn and, of course, they were the main protagonists. But unless we include as actors in their own right the other Indians who were there as allies of the United States we cannot appreciate the different meanings that this "Indian victory" had for different Indian peoples. The Little Bighorn was a battle between cavalry and Sioux, but it was also an Indian-Indian conflict and occurred in the context of competing strategies for survival.

I thought of calling this essay "Oh, and by the way, Custer was there as well." Thankfully I thought better of it, but perhaps we can move Custer aside for a moment and pay some attention to those Indian participants whose stories have been rather forgotten. If we leave the lens of our historical camera focused squarely on Indian-white conflict, with Little Bighorn as its dramatic culmination, we see these people but faintly, off to the side, and their actions make no sense to us. But if we move our lens half a turn, or better still put these people center screen, things fall into place. Crow tears become understandable as a response to a perceived Crow tragedy and not as the paean of "faithful allies" to a departed American hero.

Let us muddy the picture somewhat. Indians are usually the victims in American history. At the Battle of the Little Bighorn we see them in the unaccustomed role of victors, but we know the end of the story and we know, as they knew, that this was a late-in-the-game rally, not a final result. In a broader sense, however, everyone at the Little Bighorn was a victim. Industrializing America, with immigrant factory workers to feed in the East, demanded that cattle and settlers replace buffalo and Indians in the West. The instrument of this policy, the frontier army, was manned in large part by people from the margins of American society, casualties of similar economic and demographic changes. For many of the soldiers who died there the Little Bighorn was the final stage in a journey of economic victimization that drove them from Europe or the East to death at the hands of other peoples fighting to escape their victimization. Charles Windolph, who was with Reno, had fled Prussia six years before to avoid being drafted to fight in the Franco-Prussian war. Unable to find steady work in New York he joined the United States Army and got the kind of life he had come to America to escape.[7] I am not suggesting we should see American soldiers and American Indians as class allies, sacrificed to the capitalist goals of eastern elites, but it is worth a thought to break up some of the racial battle lines so deeply impressed in our historical memory.

The actions and motivations of the Indians involved in the 1876 campaigns poke additional holes in those racial battle lines. In August, about six weeks after the battle, Crow and Arikara scouts with General Alfred Terry came racing back to the main command, occasionally running their ponies in circles to signify they had sighted the enemy. They galloped through the columns to the rear, stripped to their loincloths, painted their faces, mounted fresh ponies, and dashed back to the front, ready to fight the Sioux. In this event the "enemy" Indians turned out to be General George Crook's Shoshone scouts.[8] But notice that in this incident the United States Army is irrelevant: Indian warriors prepare, Indian fashion, to fight Indian enemies. Four months later these Crows killed five Minneconjou chiefs who came in under a flag of truce. General Nelson Miles was furious at an act that threatened to prolong the war. He confiscated the Crows' horses and sent them to the relatives of the slain chiefs with a message "that no white man had any part in the affair." A month after that, when the army had rounded up a group of Sioux women, the Crows took turns counting coup on them.[9] American concerns and objectives did not govern the actions of Crow warriors.

On close examination the lines of tribal conflict can become as fuzzy as those of racial conflict. When the Sioux smashed in the head of a fallen Arikara scout and thrust a willow branch into his chest, the mutilation had as much to do with old tribal enmities as with participation on different sides of a United States Army campaign, and stories of a vendetta between the Hunkpapa Gall and Custer's Arikara scout Bloody Knife have become part of Little Bighorn lore.[10] But five Sioux rode with Custer's Arikara scouts, apparently Hunkpapas who had married Arikara women. One of them returned to the Sioux in the course of the campaign and was killed, evidently fighting the soldiers he had previously scouted for.[11] According to Chief Plenty Coups the only Crow death at the Battle of the Rosebud "was a Cree who had lived with us for years, so that we looked upon him as a Crow."[12] Mitch Boyer, Custer's scout, was of mixed Sioux-white parentage but a Crow by choice and adoption. He went to his death with Custer, and his body was found "in the middle of the troopers."[13]

The series of scattered skirmishes, charges, and retreats we know as the Battle of the Rosebud was so much a battle between Indians that American troops were afraid of confusing Crow and Shoshone allies with Sioux and

Cheyenne enemies. Some Sioux remembered it not as the day they turned back Crook's force but as "the battle with our Indian enemies."[14] Before the "Sioux War" of 1876–77 was over, Crows, Shoshones, Arikaras, Utes, Bannocks, Pawnees, Northern Arapahos, Cheyennes, and Sioux had all served with the United States Army, and one hundred Winnebagoes even offered their services.[15] The comparison with Montcalm's coalition of tribes 120 years earlier begins to seem less farfetched.

The reasons for the presence of Arikaras, Pawnees, Crows, and Shoshones in this war are not hard to find. The westward expansion of the Sioux in the late eighteenth and early nineteenth century placed them all on the defensive.[16] Not dependent for their supplies of guns and ammunition on the trade network that centered on the upper Missouri River, and growing in population while other peoples declined, the Sioux reduced trade systems and power balances on the northern and central plains to a shambles.[17]

By 1804 smallpox and Sioux attacks had reduced the once-powerful Arikaras (four thousand warriors in thirty-two villages, according to fur trader Jean Baptiste Truteau; eighteen villages, according to trader Pierre Antoine Tabeau) to five hundred warriors in a couple of villages. The Sioux pushed them upriver, blocked their trade routes with the Kiowas, stole horses, curtailed their hunting expeditions, kept the buffalo away from Arikara villages, and evidently browbeat the Arikaras into trading on Sioux terms.[18] Americans contributed to the Arikara misfortune. In 1823, in a reversal of the situation half a century later, United States troops and fifteen hundred Sioux launched a united assault on the Arikara villages. The Americans performed poorly in Sioux eyes, and the Sioux finished the removal of the Arikaras themselves, forcing them out of their Missouri River villages. The Yanktonai Sioux took over the old Arikara territory.[19] In response to the 1831 smallpox epidemic on the central plains, the United States initiated a vaccination program. The most heavily vaccinated groups were the Yankton, Yanktonai, and Teton Sioux, and they escaped relatively lightly from the massive smallpox epidemic of 1837. Lack of funds meant that tribes farther up the Missouri River remained unvaccinated and hence susceptible to mass destruction in 1837.[20]

The surviving Mandans, Hidatsas, and Arikaras congregated in Like-a-Fishhook village on the Fort Berthold reservation. Cholera struck Fort

Berthold in 1851 and 1853, smallpox returned in 1856, and periodic crop failures increased the Indians' dependence on the Americans. Sioux attacks contributed to the steady attrition of their population. In December 1862 a Sioux war party burned much of Like-a-Fishhook village. Arikaras could continue to fight old Sioux enemies only if they had strong allies. The United States fulfilled that role. In 1868 Arikaras enlisted as scouts with the American army to fight the Sioux.[21]

The Arikaras still faced insurmountable odds, however, in confronting the Sioux. The Arikara scouts at the Little Bighorn, many of them young and inexperienced, spat on clay they had brought from their homeland and rubbed it on their chests as good medicine. But the thin line of Arikaras extending on the left of Reno's men was overwhelmed by a mass of Sioux horsemen. A bullet blew out Bloody Knife's brains and Bob-tailed Bull, who as leader wore three stripes on his sleeves, was killed, "a solitary horseman facing scores of circling warriors."[22]

The fact that Arikaras supplied scouts for American campaigns into Sioux country and fought and died at the Little Bighorn did not mean they were any more enthusiastic than their Sioux enemies to accept white American attempts to "civilize" them and to reeducate their children.[23] Like their enemies, the Arikaras were struggling on several fronts to survive as a people.

The Arikaras' relatives, the Pawnees from the Loup and Platte rivers in Nebraska, had experienced similar calamities. Brulé Sioux winter counts record skirmishes with the Pawnees in the first decade of the nineteenth century; by the 1830s Pawnee conflicts with Sioux, Cheyennes, and Arapahos were becoming a common occurrence.[24] Decimated by disease, the Pawnees were in no position to withstand the growing Sioux assaults. In 1839 they lost 180 warriors in a pitched battle. American missionaries John Dunbar and Samuel Allis witnessed a major attack by several hundred Sioux on a Pawnee village just a mile from their mission in June 1843. The Pawnees defended themselves as well as they could, but the Sioux were all mounted and nearly all had guns. The Sioux drove off two hundred horses, killed or captured sixty-eight people, and burned half the lodges in the village. Allis said the Sioux shot down women and children as they fled from the burning lodges. The burning homes, mutilated bodies, and cries of women and children made a desolate sight. The Pawnees hastily buried their dead and departed the village, leaving some of their cornfields unhoed. The Sioux boasted that they would exterminate them, and the Pawnees were constantly on the lookout for enemy war parties. Hunting and horticulture were disrupted. That spring alone the Pawnees lost four hundred horses and more than two hundred people to Sioux attacks. The missionaries despaired of what they could do for "the perishing Pawnees," who were "at the entire mercy of the Sioux." Three years later they closed their mission.[25] In 1873, just three years before the Battle of the Little Bighorn, the Sioux killed one hundred Pawnees on the Republican River. In 1875–76 the Pawnees abandoned their Nebraska homelands and moved to Indian Territory (now Oklahoma).[26] Pawnees had good reason to fight the Sioux in 1876.

So had Shoshones. Having been pushed off the plains in the late eighteenth century by more powerful and better-armed enemies, especially the Blackfeet, the Shoshones welcomed American trade and allied themselves with growing American power in the West.[27] As competition for diminishing hunting grounds increased in the second half of the nineteenth century, Shoshones went less often to war with longtime Crow enemies and more often confronted new threats from Sioux, Cheyennes, and Arapahos. According to the Shoshone chief Washakie, the Sioux troubled them, "but when the Sioux are taken care of, we can do well."[28] Eighty-six Shoshone warriors led by Wisha, Naaki, and a French-Shoshone mixed-blood named Luisant or Luishaw, joined Crook's command in June 1876, making a striking impression as they galloped into camp.[29] Some writers believe that the Shoshone charge at the Battle of the Rosebud saved the day for the Americans by preventing the Sioux from splitting the command in two. Captain John Bourke characterized the behavior of his Shoshone and Crow allies in the battle as "excellent."[30] Shoshones also served with United States troops in the assault on Dull Knife's Northern Cheyenne village in November 1876. Shoshone soldier scouts scalped Crow Split Nose, the chief of the Elk Scraper society, and carried off his sacred shield in triumph.[31]

But the Shoshones were motivated by more than just traditional enmity in turning out on campaign. At a time when United States agents on the Shoshone agency were pressuring the tribe to give up the old ways and accept a sedentary farming life, going to war against the Sioux and Cheyennes offered young Shoshone men a chance to pursue traditional activities, to avoid becoming farmers. Not only did they get to fight old enemies, the United States Army provided them with soldiers' rations while they were on campaign and arranged for their wives and children to be fed. Bourke noted that they were also armed with the latest model .45 caliber rifles.[32]

When the Shoshone contingent reached Crook's command prior to the Battle of the Rosebud, they galloped into camp in what John Bourke described as a "barbaric array" of feathers, beads, bells, scarlet cloth, and flashing lances. The Shoshone chief charged into the battle on a fiery pony with an eagle feather headdress sweeping the ground behind him. The Crows were just as flamboyantly attired. Bourke said Medicine Crow "looked like a devil in his war-bonnet of feathers, fur, and buffalo horns." After the battle the Crows and Shoshones each held a scalp dance.[33] Back on the reservations this was exactly the kind of behavior the United States government was intent on eradicating. The American need for Indian allies gave the Crows and Shoshones the opportunity to fight old enemies, celebrate their warrior culture, and get paid for doing it. These people were hardly the white man's fools.

In the past Shoshones and Crows had fought each other, but in 1876 they made common cause against the Sioux and Cheyennes. From time immemorial, it seemed, the Crows had battled to defend the Yellowstone valley. Few in number, they fought off predatory tribes who encroached on their rich hunting lands. By the mid-nineteenth century American traders and travelers predicted the Crows were on the verge of extermination, and Sioux pressure was increasing steadily. "Look at our country, and look at our enemies," Crow chiefs declared in 1870, "they are all around it; the Sioux, Blackfeet, Cheyennes, Arapahos, and Flatheads, all want our country, and kill us when they can." In such circumstances it is a tad misleading to speak of the United States employing Crow allies; the Crows employed the United States as allies in their war for survival.[34]

The Crows faced a difficult situation in 1876. The year before President Ulysses S. Grant had placed them on a reduced reservation south of the Yellowstone, opening traditional hunting grounds in the Judith Basin in the north to white farmers and stockmen, and opening the upper Yellowstone to miners. The Crows moved eastward from the Yellowstone to a new agency at the junction of the Stillwater River and Rosebud

Creek. There, in 1876, "temptingly closer" to the Sioux, they were starting over again.[35]

When Colonel John Gibbon came that spring to ask for Crow scouts to serve as his eyes because "[t]he white man goes through the country with his head down and sees nothing," there was no rush to enlist. The chiefs sat silent with bowed heads. When Gibbon pressed them for an answer, Old Crow retorted angrily, "You have said what you had to say; don't be too fast! We are studying within ourselves and will talk after awhile." Mountain Pocket declined the request. "I have fought the Sioux till I am tired," he said. "You want to fight now—I'll let you go alone." The chiefs tried to explain to Gibbon that it was up to each Crow to make his own decision. Twenty-three young warriors and two "squaw men" did enlist as "wolves for the blue soldiers," swearing allegiance on the point of a knife and placing red bands on their left arms to distinguish them from the enemy. Blackfoot said the Crows did not understand the white man's ways, but he explained their reasons for enlisting: "The land we tread belongs to us, and we want our children always to dwell in it. All other Indian tribes do evil to the whites, but I and my people hold fast to them with love. We want our reservation to be large, we want to go on eating buffalo, and so we hold fast to the whites."[36]

According to *Chicago Times* war correspondent John Finerty, Old Crow later reviewed his people's sufferings at the hands of the Sioux and declared his support for the United States. The Great Spirit had given the Crows their lands, he said,

> but the Sioux stole them from us. They hunt upon our mountains. They fish in our streams. They have stolen our horses. They have murdered our squaws, our children. What white man has done these things to us? The face of the Sioux is red but his heart is black. But the heart of the pale face has ever been red to the Crow. . . . Our war is with the Sioux and only them. . . . The Sioux have trampled upon our hearts. We shall spit upon their scalps.[37]

The Crows made invaluable scouts. James Bradley recorded: "Crows scouted excellently today, scouring the country for a breadth of ten or twelve miles and holding themselves well in front." Charles Varnum, Custer's chief of scouts, recalled they "were in their own country and knew it thoroughly."[38]

Crow scout White Man Runs Him, circa 1913,
was one of six Crow scouts from Colonel John Gibbon's
column selected to accompany Custer.

One hundred and seventy-six Crows eventually joined General Crook and, according to John Bourke who was impressed by them, "they were soon on terms of easy familiarity with the soldiers."[39] Medicine Crow and Alligator Stands Up led the warriors at the Battle of the Rosebud where, according to Pretty Shield, a Crow woman and a berdache participated in the fighting. The woman, Other Magpie, rode into battle with her forehead painted yellow and wearing a stuffed woodpecker on her head. Determined to avenge her brother's death at the hands of the Sioux, she counted coup, taunted her enemies, and spat on them. This was not exactly the kind of ally the United States Army had in mind when it recruited the Crows for the campaign.[40] Like her male counterparts, Other Magpie turned an American campaign into an occasion for Crow warfare.

Six Crow scouts from Gibbon's column were selected to accompany Custer: Half Yellow Face, White Swan, Curley, Goes Ahead, White Man Runs Him, and Hairy Moccasin. Five days before his death Custer wrote his wife:

> I now have some Crow scouts with me, as they are familiar with the country. They are magnificent looking men, so much handsomer and more Indian-like than any we have ever seen, and so jolly and sporting, nothing of the gloomy, silent redman about them. They have formally given themselves to me after the usual talk. In their speech they have heard that I never abandon a trail; that when my food gave out, I ate mule. That was the kind of man they wanted to fight under; they were willing to eat mule too.[41]

As the Seventh Cavalry started up the Rosebud, Custer had thirty-five Indian scouts: twenty-five Arikaras; six Crows; and four Sioux. At the Little Bighorn all the Indian scouts except four Crows served with Reno.[42]

Reporting what her husband Goes Ahead had told her, Pretty Shield said that while White Swan and Half Yellow Face went with Reno, Goes Ahead, White Man Runs Him, Hairy Moccasin, and Curley led Custer to the Little Bighorn, telling him several times there were more Sioux and Cheyennes than soldiers' bullets. But, said Pretty Shield, Custer "was like a feather blown by the wind, and had to go." She said that Goes Ahead, White Man Runs Him, and Hairy Moccasin saw Custer fall at the river and then left, but Goes Ahead himself denied seeing any part of Custer's battle. John Gray, who appears to have followed

*Fred E. Miller photographed Crow scout Curley, circa 1900.
Curley, also one of the scouts from Gibbon's column,
reported Custer's defeat to the steamer* Far West *on June 28.*

MONTANA HISTORICAL SOCIETY PHOTOGRAPH ARCHIVES, HELENA

everyone's movements around the Little Bighorn battlefield with a
stopwatch, found the claim "impossible."[43] Nevertheless, the Crows knew
what was happening to Custer. On reaching Reno's command they told
the Arikara scouts "the Dakotas kill the soldiers easy." On June 28 Curley
brought news of the defeat to the steamer *Far West* at the mouth of the
Little Bighorn River.[44]

Crows continued to serve in the mopping up operations the following
year. On one occasion in the winter they brought corn to the Americans'
suffering livestock; on another they brought news, inaccurate as it turned
out, of the presidential election results.[45]

When Plenty Coups was a boy the Sioux had killed his brother, and
he had sought a vision to avenge the death.[46] But, like Blackfoot, Plenty

Coups in later life explained the Crows' allegiance to the United States as motivated by love of homeland, not blind revenge or misplaced loyalty: "Our decision was reached, not because we loved the white man who was already crowding other tribes into our country, or because we hated the Sioux, Cheyenne, and Arapaho, but because we plainly saw that this course was the only one which might save our beautiful country for us. When I think back my heart sings because we acted as we did. It was the only way open to us."[47] Tribal historian Joe Medicine Crow echoes Plenty Coups's sentiments: "We were looking for our survival and I think we played it smart."[48] Like the Shoshones, the Crows held onto a reservation in their precious homeland. They used the United States as allies to secure their survival as a people, and it paid off.

But an American alliance was a mixed blessing. Fighting alongside American soldiers did not protect the Crows from steadily mounting assaults on their culture. Nor did it guarantee them the boundaries of the reservation they had fought so hard to secure. Plenty Coups's recollection of his visit to President Rutherford B. Hayes in Washington in 1880, along with Old Crow, Pretty Eagle, Long Elk, and Medicine Crow, aptly conveys the point:

> The President asked how we had treated the soldiers, and I said that we had been friendly to them. When their horses feet were sore, so were ours. When they had to drink alkali, we shared their misfortune. When they suffered, we suffered, and I said we would continue to have friendly relations. Then the President said that he would grant our requests to remain in the country where we lived, but in return he expected us to let them build a railroad through the valley of the Yellowstone.[49]

After the delegation returned from Washington, the Crows ceded a four-hundred-foot right-of-way through the reservation to the Northern Pacific Railroad. They also ceded the extreme western portion of their reservation, which the Great Father thought it "might be better for you to dispose of" because it contained mines. Adding insult to injury an executive order in 1886 set aside land from the Crow Reservation for a national cemetery and the "Custer Battlefield."[50] "We helped the white men so we could own our land in peace. Our blood is mixed in the ground with the blood of white soldiers," said Crow warrior Two Leggings. "We did not know they were going to take our land. That is what they gave us for our friendship."[51]

History, like popular trends, tends to go in cycles. Today's heroes often become tomorrow's villains and vice versa. Most of us now recognize the Sioux and Cheyennes not as the killers of a great American hero but as people fighting to defend their lands, their families, and their way of life against alien aggression. But if in this post–*Dances with Wolves* era the Sioux and Cheyennes are today's heroes, where does that put the people who used to be "good Indians" because they fought against them? Was the struggle of the Crows, Shoshones, and Arikaras any less heroic because they sided with those whose historical reputation has taken a beating lately? These "other Indians" knew as well as anyone the threat the Americans posed to their way of life. The Crow struggle to preserve their culture would continue long after the Battle of the Little Bighorn and all that happened there. But in 1876 Crows were fighting an old battle of simply surviving against the odds.

In the long view of Indian relations with Euro-Americans, the foreign policies of the Crows, Arikaras, Shoshones, and Pawnees were more typical than we have acknowledged. Open resistance was only one strategy for survival and few Indian peoples resisted constantly. All across America and across the centuries, capable Indian leaders tried policies of accommodation at one time or another: Squanto of the Patuxets; the Pennacook Wanalancet; Hagler of the Catawbas; Red Shoes of the Choctaws; Keokuk of the Sauks; the Miami war chief turned government chief Little Turtle; Cornstalk and Black Hoof, chiefs of the Maquachake division of the Shawnees; White Eyes of the Delawares; Little Carpenter of the Cherokees; Sioux chiefs Little Crow and Red Cloud; the Arapahos Black Coal and Sharp Nose; Washakie and Plenty Coups. The world created by white invasion was not a simple world with rigid battle lines fixed along racial lines. If it had been, the story would have been very different, and the Battle of the Little Bighorn would have been very different as well.

NOTES

1. Edward P. Hamilton, ed. and trans., *Adventure in the Wilderness: The American Journals of Louis Antoine de Bougainville, 1756–1760* (1964; reprint, Norman, Okla., 1990), passim; Richard White, *The Middle Ground: Indians, Empires and Republics in the Great Lakes Region, 1650–1815* (New York, 1991), chaps. 1–6.

42 Colin G. Calloway

2. Richard R. Johnson, "The Search for a Usable Indian: An Aspect of the Defense of Colonial New England," *Journal of American History,* 64 (December 1977), 640.

3. Ian K. Steele, *Betrayals: Fort William Henry and the "Massacre"* (New York, 1990).

4. Stephen E. Ambrose, *Crazy Horse and Custer: The Parallel Lives of Two American Warriors* (Garden City, N.Y., 1975).

5. Thomas W. Dunlay, *Wolves for the Blue Soldiers: Indian Scouts and Auxiliaries with the United States Army, 1860–1890* (Lincoln, Neb., 1982); Registers of Enlistments in the United States Army, vols. 150–51, 1866–1877: Indian Scouts, roll 70, National Archives Microfilm Publication M233, National Archives, Washington, D.C. (hereafter NA).

6. James H. Bradley, *The March of the Montana Column,* ed. Edgar I. Stewart (1961; reprint, Norman, Okla., 1991), 153–54.

7. Charles Windolph, *I Fought with Custer: The Story of Sergeant Windolph, Last Survivor of the Battle of the Little Big Horn,* by Frazier Hunt and Robert Hunt (1947; reprint, Lincoln, Neb., 1987).

8. Jerome A. Greene, *Yellowstone Command: Colonel Nelson A. Miles and the Great Sioux War, 1876–1877* (Lincoln, Neb., 1991), 41–42.

9. Colonel Nelson A. Miles to Assistant Adjutant General, December 17, 1876, Letters Received by the Adjutant General's Office, roll 280, National Archives Microfilm Publication M666, NA; Greene, *Yellowstone Command,* 150–52, 164; Thomas B. Marquis, ed., *Memoirs of a White Crow Indian by Thomas H. Leforge* (1928; reprint, Lincoln, Neb., 1974), 270.

10. O. G. Libby, "The Arikara Narrative of the Campaign against the Hostile Dakotas, June 1876," *Collections of the State Historical Society of North Dakota,* vol. 6 (Bismarck, N.Dak., 1920), 110; Joseph Henry Taylor, "Bloody Knife and Gall," *North Dakota Historical Quarterly,* 4 (April 1930), 165–73; Edgar I. Stewart, *Custer's Luck* (Norman, Okla., 1955), 180.

11. Dunlay, *Wolves for the Blue Soldiers,* 140–41.

12. Frank B. Linderman, *Plenty-Coups, Chief of the Crows* (1930; reprint, Lincoln, Neb., 1962), 170.

13. John S. Gray, *Custer's Last Campaign: Mitch Boyer and the Little Bighorn Reconstructed* (Lincoln, Neb., 1991).

14. John G. Bourke, *On the Border with Crook* (New York, 1891), 313; Dunlay, *Wolves for the Blue Soldiers,* 116.

15. Bourke, *On the Border with Crook,* 357, 391–92, 395.

16. Richard White, "The Winning of the West: The Expansion of the Western Sioux in the Eighteenth and Nineteenth Centuries," *Journal of American History,* 65 (September 1978), 319–43.

17. Colin G. Calloway, "The Intertribal Balance of Powers on the Great Plains, 1760–1850," *Journal of American Studies,* 16 (April 1982), 44–46.

18. White, "Winning of the West," 325–26, 331–32; J. Daniel Rogers, *Objects of Change: The Archaeology and History of Arikara Contact with Europeans* (Washington, D.C., 1990), 44, 87–88; Annie Heloise Abel, ed., *Tabeau's Narrative of Loisel's Expedition to the Upper Missouri* (Norman, Okla., 1939), 123–25, 131–33; Douglas W. Owsley, "Demography of Prehistoric and Early Historic Northern Plains Populations," in *Disease and Demography*

in the Americas, ed. John W. Verano and Douglas H. Ubelaker (Washington, D.C., 1992), 75. George A. Dorsey, comp., *Traditions of the Arikara* (Washington, D.C., 1904), 159–71, recounts instances of hostilities with the Sioux.

19. Roger L. Nichols, "Backdrop for Disaster: Causes of the Arikara War of 1823," *South Dakota History,* 14 (Summer 1984), 93–113; Edwin Thompson Denig, *Five Indian Tribes of the Upper Missouri,* ed. John C. Ewers (Norman, Okla., 1961), 54–59; White, "Winning of the West," 332–33.

20. White, "Winning of the West," 329; Michael K. Trimble, "The 1832 Inoculation Program on the Missouri River," in Verano and Ubelaker, eds., *Disease and Demography in the Americas,* 260–63.

21. Roy W. Meyer, *The Village Indians of the Upper Missouri: The Mandans, Hidatsas, and Arikaras* (Lincoln, Neb., 1977), 104–8, 119, 127.

22. Libby, "The Arikara Narrative of the Campaign against the Hostile Dakotas," 11–12, 84. The names of the Arikara scouts are given in ibid., 49–51; in David Humphreys Miller, *Custer's Fall: The Indian Side of the Story* (1957; reprint, London, 1965), 202–3; and W. A. Graham, comp., *The Custer Myth: A Source Book of Custeriana* (New York, 1953), 27–28. Biographies of some of the scouts are in Libby, "Arikara Narrative of the Campaign," 177–209, together with photographs of survivors taken in old age.

23. Meyer, *Village Indians of the Upper Missouri,* 143, 145.

24. George E. Hyde, *The Pawnee Indians* (new ed., Norman, Okla., 1974), 157, 180–87, 197, 199–201.

25. White, "Winning of the West," 337–38; Waldo R. Wedel, ed., *The Dunbar-Allis Letters on the Pawnee* (New York, 1985), x, 656–60, 663, 730–31.

26. White, "Winning of the West," 339.

27. Colin G. Calloway, "Snake Frontiers: The Eastern Shoshones in the Eighteenth Century," *Annals of Wyoming,* 63 (Summer 1991), 82–92.

28. Quoted in Dunlay, *Wolves for the Blue Soldiers,* 115.

29. Bourke, *On the Border with Crook,* 303, 306, 312; John F. Finerty, *War-Path and Bivouac: The Bighorn and Yellowstone Expedition,* ed. Milo Milton Quaife (Chicago, 1955), 103.

30. Dunlay, *Wolves for the Blue Soldiers,* 116; Bourke, *On the Border with Crook,* 312–13, 316.

31. Peter J. Powell, "High Bull's Victory Roster," in *The Great Sioux War, 1876–77: The Best from Montana The Magazine of Western History,* ed. Paul L. Hedren (Helena, Mont., 1991), 160.

32. Agents on the Shoshone reservation no doubt encouraged young men to enlist: army rations reduced the demand on agency beef. Henry E. Stamm IV, "Community, Economy, Policy and Spirituality: A History of Shoshones, Arapahoes, and Settlers in the Wind River Valley, Wyoming, 1868–1885," (Ph.D. diss., University of Wyoming, 1994); Bourke, *On the Border with Crook,* 305.

33. Bourke, *On the Border with Crook,* 303, 316, 318; Quaife, ed., *War-Path and Bivouac,* 101.

34. Colin G. Calloway, "'The Only Way Open to Us': The Crow Struggle for Survival in the Nineteenth Century," *North Dakota History*, 53 (Summer 1986), 25–34, quote on 33. See also, Katherine M. Weist, "An Ethnohistorical Analysis of Crow Political Alliances," *Western Canadian Journal of Anthropology*, 7, no. 4 (1977), 34–54.

35. Michael P. Malone and Richard B. Roeder, "1876 on the Reservations: The Indian Question," in Hedren, ed., *Great Sioux War*, 56–57; Gray, *Custer's Last Campaign*, 118.

36. Gibbon's council with the Crows is reported in Stewart, ed., *The March of the Montana Column*, 39–46, see, especially, 40–43, 48. See also Bourke, *On the Border with Crook*, 300–301; and Marquis, ed., *Memoirs of a White Crow Indian*, 206–8. Pretty Shield used the term "wolves for the blue soldiers." Frank B. Linderman, *Pretty-Shield, Medicine Woman of the Crows* (1932; reprint, Lincoln, Neb., 1972), 225.

37. The speech was attributed to Old Crow by John Finerty of the *Chicago Times*, one of five correspondents with Crook. Quaife, ed., *War-Path and Bivouac*, 104.

38. Stewart, ed., *March of the Montana Column*, 52; John M. Carroll, ed., *Custer's Chief of Scouts: The Reminiscences of Charles A. Varnum, Including His Testimony and the Reno Court of Inquiry* (Lincoln, Neb., 1982), 60.

39. Bourke, *On the Border with Crook*, 300–302.

40. Joseph Medicine Crow, *From the Heart of the Crow Country: The Crow Indians' Own Stories* (New York, 1992), 47; Linderman, *Plenty-Coups*, 166–69; Linderman, *Pretty-Shield*, 228–31. The medicine power of the woodpecker is discussed in Peter Nabokov, *Two Leggings: The Making of a Crow Warrior* (1967; reprint, Lincoln, Neb., 1982), 110.

41. Gray, *Custer's Last Campaign*, 202.

42. Ibid., 204, 296–97.

43. Miller, *Custer's Fall*, lists Custer's Crow scouts but says only White Swan was present at the battle that day, 157, 203; compare Linderman, *Pretty-Shield*, 236–39; and Gray, *Custer's Last Campaign*, 348–49.

44. Gray, *Custer's Last Campaign*, 351. According to Pretty Shield, Curley said he was sick and ran away. John Gray, however, using maps and time-motion analysis to check Curley's accounts, believed the much-maligned scout to have been a reliable informant. Ibid., 373–82.

45. Greene, *Yellowstone Command*, 45, 131, 219.

46. Linderman, *Plenty-Coups*, 34.

47. Ibid., 154.

48. Film interview with Joseph Medicine Crow, Hardin, Montana, March 1, 1991, quoted in Paul Stekler, "Custer and Crazy Horse Ride Again . . . and Again, and Again: Filmmaking and History at Little Bighorn," *Montana The Magazine of Western History*, 42 (Autumn 1992), 68.

49. Peter Nabokov, ed., *Native American Testimony* (New York, 1979), 180–81.

50. Burton M. Smith, "Politics and the Crow Indian Land Cessions," *Montana The Magazine of Western History*, 36 (Autumn 1986), 30–34.

51. Nabokov, *Two Leggings*, 187.

From Kwangtung to the Big Sky
The Chinese Experience in Frontier Montana

ROBERT R. SWARTOUT, JR.

The discovery of major gold deposits in the northern Rockies in the early 1860s dramatically altered the landscape that became known as Montana. It seemed as though almost overnight rough-hewed urban communities sprang up in the high mountain valleys—Bannack along Grasshopper Creek on the upper reaches of the Jefferson River in 1862, Virginia City in Alder Gulch in 1863, and Helena in a place called Last Chance Gulch in 1864. Almost as quickly transportation routes such as the Mullan Road, the Bozeman Trail, and James Liberty Fisk's Northern Overland Route began linking the region to outside national and international forces. The sudden explosion of the non-Indian population also led directly to territorial status for Montana in 1864.

As mining activities and other related economic enterprises spread throughout the region, an amazingly broad mix of peoples appeared in Montana from across the country and, indeed, from around the world. Ethnic diversity, in fact, was one of the most important characteristics of early Montana society. Among these groups were Chinese pioneers, many of whom had come to Montana by way of California. The following essay by Robert R. Swartout, Jr., a professor of history at Carroll College in Helena, shows how these Chinese played a vital role in the development of nineteenth-century Montana. Too often popular accounts of western history have either ignored the contributions of Asian Americans or have used them as a backdrop for "Chinatown" adventures. Fortunately historians in recent years have begun to focus much more of their attention on the richness and importance of the Asian experience in America.

INTO THE EARLY TWENTIETH CENTURY MONTANA CONTAINED A REMARKABLY heterogeneous society, with significant numbers of Native Americans, Irish, black Americans, Scandinavians, Jews, and Slavs—to name only a few of the many groups living and working in the region. Among the racial and ethnic minorities that contributed to this fascinating mix, the Chinese were certainly one of the most important. Yet for far too long many of the historical studies about Chinese immigration to the American West have tended to use these Chinese pioneers simply as a backdrop for analyzing the thinking and behavior of non-Chinese groups.[1] It is time that we begin to focus more of our attention on the Chinese themselves.[2]

By focusing more directly on the Chinese experience, we may better appreciate the valuable economic and cultural contributions that these Asian pioneers made to the development of early Montana society. To understand the extent of the Chinese involvement in Montana's history, we must move beyond the retelling of "colorful and humorous" accounts. The Chinese struggle—and it was a struggle—to achieve social and economic security in Montana was demanding, and it deserves serious historical attention.[3]

The Chinese immigrants arriving in America in the mid-nineteenth century overwhelmingly came from the delta region surrounding Canton in Kwangtung Province. The general reasons behind the desire of certain Chinese to emigrate during the nineteenth century are not too difficult to identify. The great population explosion in China between roughly 1700 and 1850 had placed tremendous pressures on China's traditional agrarian production, and in many parts of China the population had outstripped the land's ability to produce adequate foodstuffs. Another factor contributing to emigration was the gradual decline of the Ch'ing dynasty. The dynasty's inability to rule effectively had resulted in a series of rebellions, the largest and most famous of which was the Taiping Rebellion of 1850–64. In a broader sense the decline of the dynasty also led to a rise in both government corruption and banditry, problems that created special burdens for the peasantry.[4] Finally there was the American factor itself. Between the 1840s and the 1890s the resource-rich, labor-poor American West offered opportunities to foreign workers searching for financial and material security. In many important respects Montana was a perfect microcosm of these forces at work within the developing American West.[5]

Why the Chinese immigrants would come almost exclusively from Kwangtung Province—in fact from just three major regions within the province—is more difficult to pinpoint.[6] One factor might have been the influence of the West on and around Canton during the first half of the nineteenth century. The penetration of imperialist powers during the era certainly led to considerable social and economic dislocation for the Chinese.[7] Another factor might have been the maritime traditions of the southeastern China coast. The story of Chinese emigration to America during the nineteenth century is just part of a much larger movement. For decades people of this area had traveled abroad in search of wealth and adventure. Between 1850 and 1900 roughly five million Chinese from the southern coast area would leave the country, only a half-million of whom would go to the United States.[8] Perhaps one of the most critical local forces leading to emigration was that many of these people were "have-nots" with only limited ties to the traditional Chinese order. Some were members of an ethnic minority known as the Hakka while many others were locally oriented rural poor who viewed emigration simply as a "means of survival" for themselves and their familes.[9]

Large-scale Chinese immigration to America began in the late 1840s and early 1850s. Spurred on initially by the great gold discoveries in California, first hundreds and then thousands of Chinese headed east across the Pacific Ocean.[10] With the gradual decline in the placer fields, Chinese workers entered other lines of employment and moved on to other regions of the western United States and Canada. By the 1860s and 1870s, important Chinese communities had been established all along the West Coast—in Oregon, Washington, British Columbia, and California—and within the interior West—in places like Nevada, Idaho, Colorado, Wyoming, and Montana.[11] Of all these Chinese, few have received less attention from historians than those found in the isolated Rocky Mountain state of Montana.[12]

By 1870 census surveyors counted 1,949 Chinese in the first official census taken for the Territory of Montana. This may not appear to be an impressive figure, but those 1,949 Chinese represented approximately 10 percent of Montana's official population in 1870. Moreover, because census records were often notorious for underestimating the Chinese population in any given community, the actual Chinese population may have been much higher—by perhaps 50 percent or more. In 1880 the official figure for the Chinese population in Montana dipped to 1,765; but by 1890 it was back up to 2,532. From that point on the number of Chinese in the state, and in the United States as a whole, steadily declined. This decline was due partly to local factors as well as to various Chinese exclusion acts passed by the United States Congress during the 1880s and 1890s. By 1920 there were fewer than 900 Chinese residents left in Montana out of a total state population of 548,889.[13] It is clear, then, that the major period for Chinese influence in Montana was roughly the last third of the nineteenth century. This period not only represented the largest number of Chinese immigrants within the region, but it was also a time when those Chinese made up a large percentage of Montana's total population.

As was true in so many other regions of the West, the discovery of major gold deposits during the early 1860s had a profound effect on the history of Montana. The great gold-mining boom in the high mountain valleys of the northern Rockies would attract thousands of American miners and would-be miners almost overnight and would lead directly to the creation of the Territory of Montana in 1864.[14] And as was the pattern in many other western states and territories, the development of the goldfields also resulted in the arrival of the first Chinese pioneers in Montana.

As placer camps like Bannack, Virginia City, and Last Chance Gulch built up across western Montana, word went out to the older mining districts of the new opportunities in Montana Territory. Chinese miners—many with extensive mining experience in California, Oregon, Idaho, or elsewhere—began moving into Montana. An 1870 federal government study on mining in the American West reported that "some 2,000 to 3,000 Chinese are domiciled in the Territory of Montana. . . . It is reasonable to expect that their numbers will rapidly increase." The same report commented on the techniques of Chinese miners: "The Chinese work their own placer claims, either taking up abandoned ground or purchasing claims too low in yield to be worked profitably by white labor. The ground thus obtained sometimes turns out to be very valuable, but usually they work or rework only what would otherwise remain untouched. . . . They are frugal, skillful, and extremely industrious. Frequently maltreated by evil-disposed whites, they rarely, if ever, retaliate." The author of this valuable report had the insight to note that, contrary to much popular opinion, the Chinese miners working in Montana "are not coolies or living in a state of slavery. . . . They seem to be their own masters, only associating together for mutual assistance."[15]

By the early 1870s there were dozens of Chinese mining operations in western Montana. The 1880 census listed 149 Chinese in Missoula County, 710 in Deer Lodge County (which included Butte), 265 in Madison County (Alder Gulch), and 359 in Lewis and Clark County (Helena). Many mining camps that are almost forgotten today, such as the small community of Pioneer located southwest of present-day Garrison, were the site of widespread Chinese activities. Unfortunately the very success of these Chinese miners helped create a backlash among many members of Montana's white population. For example, in 1872 the territorial legislature passed a bill prohibiting aliens (that is, Chinese) from holding titles to any placer mine or claim. Even though this law was later struck down by the territorial supreme court, it was typical of much of the popular sentiment of the day.[16]

Because the passage of such laws was, at least in part, racially motivated, supporters of the legislation consistently overlooked the contributions that Chinese miners made to the development of Montana. As one outsider commented at the time, the law concerning Chinese mining titles "is certainly destructive of the interests of the community, as may be shown in numerous instances where the Chinese have purchased, for cash, claims which white men could no longer afford to work, and have proceeded to make them productive, at a smaller profit to themselves than to the Territory. Besides being bad policy, this course toward the Chinese is rank dishonesty." [17] The notion that Chinese miners competed directly against white miners and thus "stole" badly needed work from them is largely untrue. In fact Chinese miners generally complemented the work being done by white miners and played a vital role in helping to develop the mineral and commercial resources of the territory.[18]

As placer mining began to fade from the scene during the late 1870s and 1880s, the role of the Chinese immigrants in Montana also began to change.[19] Chinese railroad workers in America had first been used on a large scale in the construction of the Central Pacific Railroad during the 1860s. In fact roughly four-fifths of all the grading done from Sacramento, California, to Ogden, Utah, was completed by Chinese laborers. Of the

13,500 workers on the Central Pacific payroll at the time of construction, 12,000 were Chinese.[20]

It is not too surprising, then, that Chinese railroad workers found their way to Montana. During the early 1880s the first transcontinental railroad to pass through Montana—the Northern Pacific—was being constructed at a frantic pace under the leadership of Henry Villard. Because of the critical shortage of skilled labor at the western end of the project and the reputation of the Chinese as experienced and dependable workers, Villard and his associates hired 15,000 Chinese to work on the Northern Pacific line through Washington, Idaho, and Montana.[21]

The press often referred to these Chinese workers, especially those constructing the Northern Pacific along the Clark Fork River in northern Idaho and western Montana, as "Hallett's Army" after construction manager J. L. Hallett. This region of the Clark Fork contained some of the most

The labor of Chinese workers, such as those in this section gang photographed on the Clark Fork River, was essential to completion of the Northern Pacific Railroad through Montana.

rugged terrain found anywhere along the Northern Pacific line. One newspaper reported on October 28, 1882:

> One must ride over the completed track, or watch the thousands of men at work in these rock-ribbed hills, see the deep cuttings, the immense fillings, count the bridges and miles of trestle-work that carry the trains safely over streams and arms of lakes and inlets, to fairly realize the expenditure of muscle . . . necessary for such a work as building a great railway route through this mountainous country. At places, for instance, a point near Cabinet Landing, to the men who do the labor, and even to subordinate leaders, the passage seemed closed against them. The mountain towers like a prop to the sky, and from the water's edge it rises like a wall, presenting no break or crevice for a foothold.[22]

> The special skills, dedication, and perseverance of the Chinese workers were critical in overcoming these tremendous obstacles. The same reporter took note of this Chinese contribution, although in somewhat condescending terms. To conquer nature's "insurmountable barrier . . . cable ropes holding a plank staging go down the precipitous sides of the mountain. Down rope ladders, to this staging clamber Chinamen armed with drills, and soon the rock sides are filled with Giant powder. Then they clamber up, the blast is fired, and the foothold made by the explosives soon swarms with Celestials; the 'can't be done' has been done. . . ."[23]

Chinese workmen not only had to overcome great physical obstructions, but they also had to contend with bitter winter weather: "It was terrible work last winter," one source noted, "with deep snow to clear away at every step, the thermometer registering on an average ten and twelve degrees below zero [Fahrenheit], abetted by razor-like winds."[24]

The Chinese also played a crucial role in constructing the Mullan Tunnel, which enabled the Northern Pacific to cross over the Continental Divide not far from Helena, Montana. Chinese workers built the critical stretch of line leading to Stampede Pass in Washington Territory's North Cascade Mountains, which allowed the Northern Pacific to reach Puget Sound. For all of these remarkable efforts the average Chinese worker was paid about one dollar per day, approximately half of what white workers received.[25] This disparity was but another indication of the racial attitudes that permitted white employers to exploit Chinese laborers because of their "inferiority."

Once the Northern Pacific Railroad reached Puget Sound in 1887, the railroad dismissed most of its Chinese workers, retaining only a few Chinese as section hands. The Great Northern Railway, which also built a transcontinental line across Montana (it was completed in 1893), employed very few Chinese workers. Both railroads turned increasingly to an even cheaper source of labor, Japanese workers.

The contributions of Chinese railroad workers to the development of Montana are of significant historical importance. Their expertise in grading, drilling, masonry, and demolition was vital to the construction of the Northern Pacific, which opened Montana to settlement, particularly during the homestead era of the early twentieth century. Thousands of pioneer homesteaders would move into the state and transport their bountiful farm products to market outside the state along tracks laid by the forgotten pioneers of another sort—the Chinese.

The arrival of Chinese miners and railroad workers during the 1860s, 1870s, and 1880s helped to create other economic opportunities for Chinese pioneers. Local Chinese communities began to develop through much of western Montana. For example the 1890 census listed 602 Chinese living in Lewis and Clark County (Helena) and another 584 living in Silver Bow County (Butte).[26] Throughout the late nineteenth and early twentieth centuries the state's largest "Chinatowns" were in Helena and Butte.

These urban residents came from a variety of backgrounds. Some were former miners and railroad workers who had been in Montana for some time while others were recent arrivals from the West Coast who brought with them particular skills and trades. A few came directly from China, enticed to Montana by relatives and friends already living in the state.

Once the Chinese settled in Montana communities, they pursued a variety of occupations. They owned and operated restaurants, grocery stores, tailor shops, mercantile stores, vegetable gardens, and laundries. In 1890 Helena alone had twenty-six Chinese-owned laundries.[27] Laundry businesses were common because some Chinese had experience in this area but also because it took little capital to start up such a business and, at least for a while, Chinese laundries posed little threat to established white businesses.[28] In addition to commercial activities many Chinese provided important social and professional services. In 1900 Butte had at least seven Chinese physicians, some of them serving white as well as Chinese patrons.[29]

Chinese skills and diligence were such that their movement into new fields of work was limited only by the willingness of the larger white community to accept the Chinese as equal members of society.

Despite intermittent white hostility, Chinese entrepreneurs were valuable to the general community. For instance they operated pharmacies, laundries, restaurants, mercantile stores, and vegetable gardens that might have otherwise been absent in Montana's early frontier towns. Less well known is the contribution that Chinese businessmen made to the community by paying local taxes, which helped to support community growth not commonly associated with the Chinese. The 1870 tax lists for Lewis and Clark County, for instance, reveal a total assessment of Chinese taxpayers of $38,900. By 1890, the figure had climbed to $80,905. Similar statistics can be found for other Montana communities that had significant Chinese populations.[30] At the pre-inflation prices of nineteenth-century America, these figures represented a sizable amount of taxable property.

Longtime resident and physician Dr. Huie Pock sold merchandise and goods to the Chinese community. His shop at 227 S. Main Street established a respected Chinese presence in Butte's business community.

These figures also indicate that many Chinese were not "day laborers" simply passing through the state. Nor were they all sojourners planning to return immediately to China. Although large numbers did return to their homeland, still others decided to remain in the United States to establish what they hoped would be permanent livelihoods for themselves and their families. Perhaps most impressive of all, these self-reliant entrepreneurs were often forced to struggle against significant odds in their efforts to create businesses that would become an integral part of their local communities.

The Chinese pioneers in Montana created a vibrant and complex social network. As was true for many other immigrant groups in nineteenth-century America, the recent arrivals from China organized themselves to perpetuate many of their traditional social and cultural practices. Such activities were important in helping the immigrants maintain a sense of identity, particularly when they were confronted by a rather hostile social climate in America.

American conditions alone, however, were not the only factors influencing the unique structure of Chinese immigrant society. Because the overwhelming majority of these people came from one part of China, Chinese immigrants were often able to maintain or to create new social organizations based along traditional clan or district lines. This was especially important because local districts in China, even at the village level, had their own distinct lineages and dialects. Place of origin thus played a critical role in the development of Chinese social relationships in America.[31]

Another important feature of Chinese society in America was the general absence of women. The 1870 census listed only 123 females out of a total Chinese population of 1,949. In 1880 the figures were 80 women out of 1,765; in 1890, 59 out of 2,532; and in 1900, 39 out of 1,739. Chinese women made up no more than 7 percent, and sometimes as little as 2 percent, of the total Chinese population in Montana during the nineteenth century.[32]

The absence of women in the Chinese community had a clear effect on the nature of Chinese society in America. To begin with it helps explain the difficulty the Chinese had in producing future generations in America after the passage of the Chinese exclusion acts. Moreover Chinese men could not depend on a traditional family dwelling to provide all their social and cultural needs. Consequently Chinese communities in this country worked to establish institutions that would help to bind people together as they attempted to adjust to the difficulties of living in a new and sometimes hostile country.[33]

One of the most important institutions within Montana's Chinese communities was the local temple, or joss house. Sometimes this institution was contained within a store or private dwelling; other times, particularly in Butte, it was a separate structure entirely. The joss house was a focal point for both social and religious activities within the Chinese community. "The great Chinese Joss," a November 1882 Butte newspaper reported, "arrived last night by express from California, and is being feasted to-day with all the delicacies of the season. . . . The room in which he has taken up his quarters is gaily decorated with flags, roast hogs, chickens, drums, and a thousand and one articles which defy description. [The Chinese] will wind up with a grand free lunch to-night, at which at least three hundred will be present."[34] Butte's Chinatown had two separate temples, one of which was not torn down until 1945.[35]

Another institution that sometimes played an important role in the lives of early Montana settlers was the Chinese masonic temple. In addition to providing its members with an opportunity for relaxation and entertainment, this institution, with its emphasis on brotherhood, also reinforced Chinese social and cultural values.

In an effort to maintain a sense of order and group identification, members of the Chinese Masonic Temple in Virginia City compiled a list of twenty-one regulations. Some were designed to protect the group from outside interference and threats. For example members were required to defend the secrecy of the lodge, and if a member were arrested, he "may not compromise any other brother" of the lodge.[36] Members were also prohibited from assisting Chinese who might belong to rival organizations.

Other regulations were guidelines for ethical social behavior. For instance, members were not to "covet the wife or sisters of brethren because of their beauty." They were warned: "do not occupy by force the property of your brethren" nor "deceive your brethren through fast talking." Members were prohibited from quarreling or feuding in public for fear of damaging the reputation of the brotherhood. More powerful members of the lodge were reminded not to "bully your brethren because of your might." Finally the regulations established rules for the proper handling of such important social occasions as weddings and funerals.[37] To ensure obedience specific punishments—such as 306 strokes with a cane—were enumerated.

Taken as a whole these regulations indicate that Chinese pioneers were often concerned about maintaining order within their communities. Moreover the masonic temple, like other Chinese institutions, provided its members with a sense of belonging and a feeling of camaraderie in an apparently harsh and frequently intimidating world.

In the case of Butte a council of elders representing the four-clan associations eventually formed to provide valuable leadership for the Chinese community. The council, generally made up of leading businessmen, also attempted to resolve conflicts that might flair up among the Chinese.[38] One early Chinese resident in Butte recalled:

> When I first came to Butte about fifty years ago [1890s], there were about thirty-two laundries in the city. About twenty belonged to our clan cousins, while the others belonged to the members of the opposite four-clan association. There were then two large four-clan associations, but the members were not friendly toward each other. Many disputes arose between associations.
>
> In case of a dispute within our own association, it would be settled here. The elders—businessmen and those men who have lived in Butte longest—would hear the facts from the parties in dispute. The council of elders would decide who was right and who was wrong.[39]

When a dispute could not be resolved locally, the case was sent to association headquarters in San Francisco for final settlement. The Chinese communities in Montana, although geographically isolated, were still able to maintain important social, economic, and cultural ties with the outside world.

The celebration of traditional festivals was also an important feature of Chinese social life. Celebrations included the Ching Ming, Dragon Boat, Moon, and Winter Solstice festivals, but most important of all was the New Year festival.[40] The February 15, 1872, *Helena Weekly Herald* began its story on the Chinese New Year by declaring: "One of the most interesting days we have ever spent in the Territory was on yesterday, during a visit which we made to Chinatown. When we went there, we put ourselves under the care of Tong Hing, and Tong, with his usual urbanity and courtesy, put us through the more prominent of the Celestials." The reporter described in detailed, if rather patronizing, terms the local arrangements made to celebrate this most famous of Chinese festivals.[41]

Ancestor worship, a product of China's strong Confucian heritage, was reinforced through funeral rites and special days of commemoration.[42] The *Herald* reported on April 8, 1869, that

> to-day is the [Chinese] annual Josh Day, on which occasion their custom is to visit the burial places—as our China men and women have done, closing their ceremonies about 2 p.m.—burn incense and innumerable small wax candles about the head stones or boards of the graves, deposit a liberal lunch of choice eatables and drinkables, designed for the spirits of the departed; recite propitiatory prayers to their savior (Josh), and otherwise show themselves sacredly mindful of the welfare of their dead.[43]

While reflecting certain religious duties, these activities served another important purpose. They enabled Chinese pioneers in Montana to maintain a cultural and spiritual link with family and clan members in China. It was unfortunate that various Sinophobic groups in the country would use the very strength of these enduring Chinese customs as a weapon against the immigrants. All too often Americans viewed Chinese social and cultural practices as "proof" that these immigrants could never be assimilated into American society. Some critics even claimed that because of their different ways and values Chinese immigrants posed a direct threat to the traditional social order in America.

White Montana's response to Chinese immigration largely reflected contemporary regional and national attitudes. Although Chinese settlers in Montana were never the victims of the kind of mass violence that erupted in Rock Springs, Wyoming, in 1885 and along the Snake River in 1887, they were physically and mentally abused and politically exploited well into the early twentieth century.[44] It was not unusual to hear about individual Chinese being harassed or beaten in many nineteenth-century Montana communities.[45] Moreover, even before Montana became a state in 1889, lawmakers in the territory passed and attempted to pass laws discriminating against Chinese residents, including one aimed at ownership of mining properties.

A typical example of these anti-Chinese sentiments was expressed in an 1872 law that established a special tax, or "license," on Chinese laundries. In one form or another this law remained on the books well into the twentieth century.[46] Discrimination against the Chinese became even more pronounced once Montana achieved statehood. In the decade or so after 1889 Montana judicial decisions systematically upheld a number of anti-Chinese laws. "By 1902," writes historian John R. Wunder, "the doors to economic opportunity and cultural equality for Chinese Montanans had been closed with appropriate legal fanfare." On March 3, 1909, the final insult was added when the state legislature passed an anti-miscegenation law prohibiting interracial marriage—a law directed against black Americans and Japanese immigrants as well as against the Chinese.[47]

Why was such animosity directed toward the Chinese, especially when they represented one of the most peaceful and diligent groups in Montana? Nineteenth-century critics of Chinese immigration often emphasized that the Chinese introduced tremendous social evils into Montana. Yet as a group the Chinese were much more law-abiding than many whites were. Between 1900 and 1918 only six Chinese residents of Montana were sent to the state penitentiary, four of them for the same crime. This does not necessarily indicate that Montana's Chinese communities were crime-free, but the evidence does argue against the stereotypical view of Chinese communities as places "teeming" with "tong wars" and "hatchetmen."[48] Some Chinese did have an opium habit (partly because of the Western world's role in expanding the opium trade during the early nineteenth century), but "authorities generally agree that the Chinese were able to exercise better control over opium than most white miners could over whiskey and that they seemed no better or worse for the habit."[49]

Opponents of Chinese immigration also cited the "economic" threat posed by Chinese workers. During the citywide boycott against Chinese merchants and laborers in Butte from 1897 to 1899, union leaders in the mining city frequently referred to unfair labor competition. Such notions, however, were largely fictitious.[50] To begin with, the Chinese often did the kind of work that many white workers refused to do. Moreover, when the two groups did compete for the same job, the Chinese, who were usually excluded from most white-controlled labor unions, were often forced to accept lower wages. The few times when Chinese workers did attempt to strike for higher wages, they found themselves caught between a hostile management and an indifferent general public.[51]

Ultimately the overriding reason behind the anti-Chinese sentiment in Montana and the rest of the American West was racism—a racism based on cultural stereotypes as well as skin color. It was unfortunate for these Chinese pioneers that their migration to America occurred at a time when racism was especially fashionable in the United States. In fact the animosity directed toward the Chinese coincided with similar attitudes and acts of violence against black Americans. As the country became increasingly industrialized and urbanized, minorities often became convenient scapegoats for other groups who felt "victimized" by rapid economic and social changes.[52]

An 1893 editorial published in a Butte newspaper gave voice to this racism: "The Chinaman is no more a citizen than a coyote is a citizen, and never can be." After making obligatory references to cheap labor and opium, the scathing editorial continued:

> The Chinaman's life is not our life, his religion is not our religion. His habits, superstitions, and modes of life are disgusting. He is a parasite, floating across the Pacific and thence penetrating into the interior towns and cities, there to settle down for a brief space and absorb the substance of those with whom he comes into competition. His one object in life is to make all the money he can and return again to his native land, dead or alive. His very existence in our midst is an insult to our intelligence. Pestilence and disease follow in his wake, no matter what sentimentalists say to the contrary. Let him go hence. He belongs not in Butte.[53]

These racist and stereotypical attitudes were not confined to Butte, but were prevalent in many Montana communities during the late nineteenth century.[54] The power and popularity of such racial sentiments help to explain the ease with which the Montana legislature and the federal government could pass so many discriminatory laws aimed at the Chinese. These laws not only limited economic opportunities and cultural equality for Chinese pioneers, but they also effectively shut off the flow of new arrivals from China. Without new, especially female, emigrants the once-vibrant Chinese communities of the intermountain states were bound to disappear.

Several important observations can be made from this rather brief description of the Chinese experience in nineteenth-century Montana. First of all one is struck by the great diversity of occupations that the Chinese pioneers pursued in Montana. They did not limit themselves to placer mining or railroad building, but were willing to try almost any occupation that might allow them to achieve financial security and independence. Ultimately the ability of the Chinese to branch out into new lines of work was limited not so much by their own prejudices and cultural habits as by the prejudices of the larger white community.

One of the most important aspects of the Chinese experience was their contribution to the economic development of nineteenth-century Montana. Chinese pioneers were an integral part of the infant mining industry in the territory helping to pump thousands of dollars into the local economy while exploiting resources that other miners often ignored. The Chinese role in building the Northern Pacific Railroad was of tremendous value to the future development of the state, as the railroad made possible the greatest growth in the state's history, from 1890 to 1920. In Montana's budding urban communities Chinese entrepreneurs provided valuable services to non-Chinese as well as Chinese patrons. Taken as a whole these contributions played a crucial part in transforming Montana from a primitive, isolated patchwork of localities into an increasingly sophisticated, urbanized, and economically prosperous society.

As these Chinese pioneers contributed to Montana's economic development, they also built a complex and semipermanent subcommunity of their own. This subcommunity often stressed traditional ties of clan and region, which were reinforced through participation in various cultural and religious acitivities. Unfortunately the same customs that gave Chinese pioneers a sense of identity and purpose were used by critics to "prove" that Chinese immigrants were "polluting" America's cultural values and social order. Such attacks made it difficult for non-Chinese Americans to comprehend the richness and subtleties of Chinese customs and traditions.

This inability or unwillingness to appreciate the value of Chinese contributions was a direct result of the racial attitudes of the day. In that sense the reaction of many white Montanans to the presence of Chinese settlers was all too typical of broader national and regional patterns.

Montanans generally supported the passage of federal laws prohibiting Chinese immigration to America. At the local level Montanans passed a series of state laws, which were upheld by the state supreme court, that intentionally discriminated against Chinese Montanans. These prejudices were so pervasive that recognition of the Chinese role in the development of modern Montana would come only after most of the Chinese pioneers and their descendants had left the state.

NOTES

1. See Elmer Clarence Sandmeyer, *The Anti-Chinese Movement in California* (Urbana, Ill., 1939); Alexander Saxton, *The Indispensable Enemy: Labor and the Anti-Chinese Movement in California* (Berkeley, Calif., 1971); Stuart Creighton Miller, *The Unwelcome Immigrant: The American Image of the Chinese, 1785–1882* (Berkeley, Calif., 1969); Robert Edward Wynne, *Reaction to the Chinese in the Pacific Northwest and British Columbia, 1850–1910* (New York, 1979). In calling for greater attention to the Chinese experience itself, it is not my intention to dismiss the valuable contributions that works such as these have made to our understanding of United States history. The American response to Chinese migration is clearly an important historical issue and will be dealt with later in this essay.

2. An excellent example is the recent book by Sucheng Chan, *This Bittersweet Soil: The Chinese in California Agriculture, 1860–1910* (Berkeley, Calif., 1986).

3. To see how the Montana experience fits into a broader, international context, see Michael H. Hunt, *The Making of a Special Relationship: The United States and China to 1914* (New York, 1983), especially chaps. 2, 3, 7; Shih-shan Henry Tsai, *China and the Overseas Chinese in the United States, 1868–1911* (Fayetteville, Ark., 1983).

4. Hunt, *Making of a Special Relationship*, 63–64; Jack Chen, *The Chinese of America: From the Beginnings to the Present* (San Francisco, 1981), 6–9; Frederic Wakeman, Jr., *Strangers at the Gate: Social Disorder in South China, 1839–1861* (Berkeley, Calif., 1966).

5. Chen, *Chinese of America*, 35–124; Gunther Barth, *Bitter Strength: A History of the Chinese in the United States, 1850–1870* (Cambridge, Mass., 1964), 32–49; Kil Young Zo, *Chinese Emigration into the United States, 1850–1880* (New York, 1978), 81–92.

6. The three regions were San-i (Sam Yup in Cantonese), Ssu-i (Sze Yup in Cantonese), and Hsiang-shan (Hueng-shan in Cantonese; later renamed Chung-shan). See Hunt, *Making of a Special Relationship*, 61–62.

7. See June Mei, "Socioeconomic Origins of Emigration: Guangdong to California, 1850–1882," in *Labor Immigration under Capitalism: Asian Workers in the United States before World War II,* ed. Lucie Cheng and Edna Bonacich (Berkeley, Calif., 1984), 219–47.

8. Hunt, *Making of a Special Relationship*, 61; Chen, *Chinese of America*, 10–13.

9. Hunt, *Making of a Special Relationship*, 63.

10. Chen, *Chinese of America*, 15–29; Barth, *Bitter Strength*, 50–76; Zo, *Chinese Emigration into the United States*, 114–45.

11. See Ping Chiu, *Chinese Labor in California, 1850–1880: An Economic Study* (Madison, Wis., 1963); Saxton, *Indispensable Enemy;* Chan, *This Bittersweet Soil;* Wynne, *Reaction to the Chinese;* James Morton, *In the Sea of Sterile Mountains: The Chinese in British Columbia* (Vancouver, British Columbia, 1974); Jeffrey Barlow and Christine Richardson, *China Doctor of John Day* (Portland, Ore., 1979); John R. Wunder, "Chinese in Trouble: Criminal Law and Race on the Trans-Mississippi West Frontier," *Western Historical Quarterly,* 17 (January 1986), 25–41.

12. To date, only three scholarly articles have been published on the Chinese historical presence in Montana: Larry D. Quinn, "'Chink Chink Chinaman': The Beginnings of Nativism in Montana," *Pacific Northwest Quarterly,* 58 (April 1967), 82–89; John R. Wunder, "Law and Chinese in Frontier Montana," *Montana The Magazine of Western History,* 30 (Summer 1980), 18–30; Stacy A. Flaherty, "Boycott in Butte: Organized Labor and the Chinese Community, 1896–1897," *Montana The Magazine of Western History,* 37 (Winter 1987), 34–47. Moreover, these articles deal primarily with the reaction of white Montanans to Chinese rather than with the experiences of the Chinese themselves.

13. Census Office, *Eleventh Census of the United States, 1890: Population, Part 1* (Washington, D.C., 1895), 29, 439; Bureau of the Census, *Fourteenth Census of the United States, 1920: Population,* vol. 3 (Washington, D.C., 1922), 574, 577.

14. Michael P. Malone and Richard B. Roeder, *Montana: A History of Two Centuries* (Seattle, 1976), 50–55.

15. Rossiter W. Raymond, *Statistics of Mines and Mining in the States and Territories West of the Rocky Mountains,* 41st Cong., 2d sess., 1870, H. Doc. 207, serial 1424, 260.

16. *Laws, Memorials, and Resolutions of the Territory of Montana, Seventh Session* (Deer Lodge, Mont., 1872), 593–96; *Laws, Memorials, and Resolutions of the Territory of Montana, Eighth Session* (Helena, Mont., 1874), 97; Wunder, "Law and Chinese in Frontier Montana," 24–25. The original law stated: "No aliens shall be allowed to acquire any title, interest, or possessory or other right to any placer mine or claim, or to the profits or proceeds thereof, in this territory."

17. Rossister W. Raymond, *Statistics of Mines and Mining in the States and Territories West of the Rocky Mountains,* 42d Cong., 2d sess., 1872, H. Doc. 211, serial 1513, 292.

18. See Randall E. Rohe, "After the Gold Rush: Chinese Mining in the Far West, 1850–1890," *Montana The Magazine of Western History,* 32 (Autumn 1982), 18.

19. Most Chinese miners in Montana worked small placer claims, either individually or with various partners. Generally speaking, the Chinese did not play an important role in the development of industrial mining in Montana, partly because employers were reluctant to hire them and partly because there were fewer Chinese left in the state by the time industrial mining came into its own around the turn of the century.

20. Chen, *Chinese of America,* 65–77; Tzu Kuei Yen, "Chinese Workers and the First Transcontinental Railroad of the United States of America," (Ph.D. diss., St. John's University, 1977).

21. "First Across the Northwest—The Northern Pacific," MS, p. 5, box 515, President's Subject files, Northern Pacific Railway Company Records (hereafter NP Records), Minnesota Historical Society Archives, St. Paul, Minnesota (hereafter MNHS).

22. Newspaper clipping, October 28, 1882, Secretary Scrapbooks, 1866–1896, vol. 25, box 4, NP Records, MNHS.

23. Ibid.

24. Ibid.

25. Anderson to Harris, August 7, 31, 1886, Letters Received, Registered: President and Vice President (1882–1893), President's Department, box 19, NP Records, MNHS; *Weekly Missoula (Mont.) Missoulian,* February 16, 1883.

26. *Eleventh Census of the United States, 1890,* 439.

27. *Helena City Directory, 1890,* 465–66.

28. See Paul Ong, "An Ethnic Trade: The Chinese Laundries in Early California," *Journal of Ethnic Studies,* 8 (Winter 1981), 95–113. Although laundries were labor-intensive businesses, they did require some capital. In California, "investments ranged from $400 to $1,600, with the average being about $800" (101).

29. *Butte City Directory, 1900,* 689–90.

30. Lewis and Clark County Tax Lists, 1870, 1890, Montana Historical Society Archives, Helena (hereafter MHS); Rose Hum Lee, *The Growth and Decline of Chinese Communities in the Rocky Mountain Region* (New York, 1978), 155–65.

31. Hunt, *Making of a Special Relationship,* 65–73; Zo, *Chinese Emigration into the United States,* 131–39.

32. Census Office, *Ninth Census of the United States, 1870,: Population,* vol. 1 (Washington, D.C., 1872), 609; Census Office, *Tenth Census of the United States, 1880,: Population* (Washington, D.C., 1883), 545; *Eleventh Census of the United States, 1890,* 488; Census Office, *Twelfth Census of the United States, 1900, Population, Part 1* (Washington, D.C., 1901), 492.

33. Normal male-female relations were skewed even further because an unusually large percentage of the Chinese women in the American West in the nineteenth century were employed as prostitutes. See Lucie Cheng, "Free, Indentured, Enslaved: Chinese Prostitutes in Nineteenth-Century America," in Cheng and Bonacich, eds., *Labor Immigration under Capitalism,* 402–34.

34. *Butte (Mont.) Weekly Inter Mountain,* November 23, 1882.

35. Lee, *Growth and Decline of Chinese Communities,* 263.

36. Virginia City Chinese Masonic temple banner, March 3, 1876, Montana Historical Society Museum, Helena. Regulations translated by John Wang of Missoula.

37. Ibid.

38. Lee, *Growth and Decline of Chinese Communities,* 226–32.

39. Quoted in ibid., 229.

40. See ibid., 273–80.

41. *Helena (Mont.) Weekly Herald,* February 15, 1872.

42. See *Weekly Missoula (Mont.) Missoulian,* June 17, 1881.

43. *Helena (Mont.) Weekly Herald,* April 8, 1869.

44. See Robert R. Swartout, Jr., "In Defense of the West's Chinese," *Oregon Historical Quarterly,* 83 (Spring 1982), 25–36; David H. Stratton, "The Snake River Massacre of Chinese Miners, 1887," in *A Taste of the West: Essays in Honor of Robert G. Athearn,* ed. Duane E. Smith (Boulder, Colo., 1983), 109–29.

45. See *Helena (Mont.) Weekly Herald,* May 31, 1883, September 24, 1885; *Helena (Mont.) Daily Herald,* January 26, 1870; *Butte (Mont.) Tribune Review,* August 4, 1906; *Great Falls (Mont.) Daily Tribune,* December 20, 1903; *Livingston (Mont.) Post,* December 6, 1906; *Miles City (Mont.) Yellowstone Journal,* April 5, 1884; *Quigley (Mont.) Rock Creek Record,* June 13, 1896; *Deer Lodge (Mont.) New North-West,* December 23, 1881; *Butte (Mont.) Weekly Miner,* December 27, 1881, August 7, 1891; *Butte (Mont.) Semi-Weekly Miner,* October 3, 1885; *Butte (Mont.) Daily Miner,* October 2, 3, 1893; *Butte (Mont.) Daily Inter Mountain,* August 24, 1901; and *Anaconda (Mont.) Standard,* January 21, March 8, 1892, January 8, 1893, September 5, 1899.

46. *Laws, Memorials, and Resolutions . . . Seventh Session,* 589; *Codes and Statutes of Montana 1895,* (Butte, Mont., 1895), 562; *Revised Codes of Montana, 1907,* vol.1 (Helena, Mont., 1908), 807. Although Chinese were not specifically named in the law, female-operated laundries and, later, steam-type laundries were exempt from paying the tax. These descriptions were synonymous with white-operated laundries. The intent of the law was obviously discriminatory.

47. Wunder, "Law and Chinese in Frontier Montana," 30; William L. Lang, "The Nearly Forgotten Blacks on Last Chance Gulch, 1900–1912," *Pacific Northwest Quarterly,* 70 (April 1979), 57.

48. Records of the Montana State Board of Prison Commissioners, 1887–1962, Record Series 197, Montana State Prison Records, MHS.

49. W. Eugene Hollon, *Frontier Violence: Another Look* (New York, 1974), 89.

50. Members of the Butte Chinese community eventually took the boycott leaders to court. See *Hum Fay et al. v. Frank Baldwin et al.* Records, Manuscript Collection 43, MHS. Local newspapers gave the case extensive coverage, especially the *Anaconda Standard, Butte Inter Mountain,* and *Butte Miner.* The Chinese won the case in the federal courts in May 1900, but they received no damages to cover their financial losses. See *Butte (Mont.) Miner,* April 4, 1899; *Butte (Mont.) Daily Inter Mountain,* May 19, 1900; Final Record, Case 40, United States District Court, Montana, Record Group 21, National Archives, Pacific Northwest Region, Seattle, Washington. For an outstanding study of the entire affair see Flaherty, "Boycott in Butte," 34–47.

51. See Yen, "Chinese Workers and the First Transcontinental Railroad," 129–31; Chen, *Chinese of America,* 74–75.

52. See, especially, Saxton, *Indispensable Enemy;* and Luther W. Spoehr, "Sambo and the Heathen Chinee: Californians' Racial Stereotypes in the Late 1870s," *Pacific Historical Review,* 42 (May 1973), 185–204.

53. *Butte (Mont.) Bystander,* February 11, 1893.

54. As early as 1871, a Missoula reporter declared: "The Chinaman lands upon our shores a serf, and remains so. He clings to his idolatry and heathenism with the tenacity of life; lives upon less than the refuse from the table of a civilized man, and devotes his sister to the basest lusts of humanity." *Missoula (Mont.) Pioneer,* June 22, 1871. For similar comments see, for example, *Miles City (Mont.) Yellowstone Journal,* April 5, 1884; *Livingston (Mont.) Post,* December 6, 1906; and *Anaconda (Mont.) Standard,* January 4, 1903.

Hogan's Army
"A Petition with Boots on"

Dave Walter

At the core of America's industrial revolution during the post–Civil War years was the construction of a nationwide railroad network. By 1893 five transcontinental railroads had been completed; two of those five, the Northern Pacific and the Great Northern, ran across the state of Montana. The coming of the railroads provided access to national and international markets for Montana beef and wheat. The railroads also made possible the development of industrial mining, especially of silver and copper, in the northern Rockies. The arrival of the first railroads into Montana in the early 1880s led to a dramatic growth in the territory's economy and population and thus paved the way for attainment of statehood in 1889.

But the industrialization of the Montana economy also left the newly created state and its people increasingly susceptible to the twists and turns of economic forces beyond their direct control. The Panic of 1893, which produced the second worst economic crisis in American history, brought silver mining to a standstill, forced many of the nation's railroads—including the Northern Pacific— into bankruptcy, and gave added impetus to a recently established political reform movement known as the Populist, or People's, Party.

One of the most intriguing characters of this tumultuous era was a crusader by the name of Jacob Coxey. His impact on Montana is colorfully captured in the following essay by Dave Walter, a research historian at the Montana Historical Society in Helena and author of numerous accounts in Montana history.

BY JUST ABOUT ANYONE'S STANDARDS JACOB SECHLER COXEY STOOD APART—
a different sort of fellow. Whether you considered him a crank or a
visionary depended upon your perspective. The wealthy Ohio quarry
owner certainly had proposed some outlandish programs to Congress.
Further, he brazenly had named his newborn son "Legal Tender" Coxey!
Maybe he was exactly what his critics charged: "the most dangerous man
since the Civil War." Yet if that were so, why did tens of thousands of
Montanans rally to Coxey's cause?[1]

In the early 1890s Jacob Coxey offered a voice of reform to a most
receptive audience. During that Age of Industrialization popular wisdom
held that the federal government existed primarily to assist big business.
Yet Coxey's "Good Roads Bill" (1892) asked Congress to ease national
unemployment by funding road-building projects and other local
improvements that would create jobs. In effect Coxey argued that the
federal government should move proactively to provide its citizens with
the means for self-help. And that was a radical idea in the heart of the
Gilded Age.[2] Only the agrarian Populists—albeit a valid third-party
movement at the time—advocated such progressive solutions to
America's problems.

Then in 1893 a financial crisis struck, devastating the nation's economy.
During that year thousands of factories and businesses closed while others
drastically reduced the number of their employees. In addition hundreds
of banks closed their doors, railroad construction ceased, and dozens of
railroads declared bankruptcy and fell into receivership. More than 2.5
million men found themselves without jobs. Many of them roamed the
country, hitching rides on freight trains, seeking work. The economic
and social dislocation of the Panic of 1893 gripped the entire country while
the administration of President Grover Cleveland failed to respond.

In Montana the national panic hit hard. The Northern Pacific Railroad
Company declared bankruptcy, and the federal court in Helena placed its
operations in the hands of receivers. At least a dozen of the state's most
prominent banks closed. Investment capital for transportation, livestock,
and mining projects disappeared overnight.

When the federal government finally reacted to the depression, it
repealed (November 1, 1893) the Sherman Silver Purchase Act of 1890—
legislation that had sparked scores of silver-mining operations in the state.

Immediately, laid-off miners abandoned high-mountain camps to seek work in Montana's cities. Through the winter of 1893–94 almost twenty thousand unemployed Montanans struggled to survive in a world of few jobs and deflated wages. With no hope of relief another eight thousand left the state.[3]

Into this breach jumped Jacob Coxey with his earlier request to Congress: fund local-improvement programs that will employ the jobless millions across the nation. When rebuffed again by the federal government, Coxey revealed his alternative. Unemployed workers would organize into industrial armies (which he called "commonweals") to form the Commonweal of Christ. These contingents would march on Washington, D.C., during spring 1894 to demonstrate their plight.[4]

Coxey believed that his "petition with boots on" would convince Congress of the need for action. He frequently cited the First Amendment right to petition the government for a redress of grievances—in this case on a personal basis.

In spring 1894 few Montanans knew Coxey or understood his reform proposals. Yet to the state's unemployed any solution that promised jobs and relief offered possibilities. So in Montana, as elsewhere, Coxey became a symbol of hope to thousands of clerks, teamsters, accountants, railroad workers, lumbermen, salesmen, miners, and day laborers. In March 1894— about the time that Coxey's own army left Massillon, Ohio, on its four-hundred-mile march to Washington, D.C.—the Montana contingent of the Commonweal Army began to gather in Butte.[5]

Throughout the West similar armies of the unemployed organized to carry their demands to the nation's capital. From such divergent points as Los Angeles, San Francisco, Portland, Seattle, Spokane, Yakima, and Denver, the tightly knit groups charted their routes across the country. Although they received massive public support and donations for their crusade, all of the armies faced treks of thousands of miles. The transcontinental railroads offered the logical means of travel. And from some West Coast locations railroad companies already had hauled the Coxeyites either without charge or for nominal fares.[6]

In Butte by early April the Montana contingent had formed under the leadership of an out-of-work teamster from the Moulton Mine, William Hogan. A self-educated, thirty-four-year-old Irishman who liberally quoted

Shakespeare, Hogan was of medium height and slim. He was altogether an unassuming leader.[7] His group of several hundred Coxeyites—soon called "Hogan's Army" by the press—established a camp near the Northern Pacific yards on the flats south of town. The protesters received demonstrative support from workaday Montanans across the state.[8]

While the Montana army acknowledged Coxey's general program, it emphasized the free coinage of silver at sixteen-to-one, an obvious reflection of the mining situation in the state. Hogan led not a mob of unruly anarchists, but a well-structured organization of frustrated, determined workers who saw a march on Washington as their last hope of relief. Above all, Montana's "Industrials" committed themselves to a peaceful demonstration, a constitutionally guaranteed "redress of grievances." By April 12 Hogan's camp had grown to almost five hundred Coxeyites.[9]

Hogan and his two elected lieutenants, William Cunningham and John Edwards, met with the Butte mayor and the Silver Bow County commissioners to arrange train transportation east. The complete support of these public officials reflected the sentiments of their constituents, who daily donated wagonloads of foodstuffs and clothing to the protestors. Nevertheless Hogan's request for a special train met with ambiguous replies from Northern Pacific officials.[10]

Yet the railroad's own situation was confused. During fall 1893 the Northern Pacific had declared bankruptcy. The federal court in Helena had assumed jurisdiction over the company and placed it in the hands of receivers responsible for its operation. So officially Northern Pacific executives *could not* grant the request of Hogan's "Wealers," even if they had been so inclined.

The Northern Pacific receivers watched a rapidly growing camp of Hogan's men beside their yards in Butte, and they panicked. On April 20, 1894, they petitioned Helena federal court judge Hiram Knowles to restrain the Coxeyites from hijacking Northern Pacific property. A violation of this order would place the men in contempt of court. Although Judge Knowles ruled in the receivers' behalf, United States Marshal William McDermott never personally served the injunction on Hogan. Rather he wired it via telegram to Butte on April 21—a telegram which may or may not ever have been delivered to Hogan.[11]

With such widespread support for Hogan's men and their cause in Montana, the Wealers interpreted Marshal McDermott's action as "implied noninterference." Butte officials also had concluded that noninterference represented the position of local Northern Pacific executives. That is, should Hogan and his army commandeer a train in the Butte yards, they would be allowed to run east without opposition. Such "unofficial" runs had been arranged for other armies of Coxey's crusaders in the West.

Meanwhile Hogan continued to negotiate transportation with the recalcitrant J. D. Finn, superintendent of the Northern Pacific's Montana Division, based in Livingston. Again Hogan's impression of these talks pointed to the railroad's implied noninterference—particularly since such prominent mine owners as Marcus Daly and William Clark had tried to pay for the Commonwealers' special train, and Northern Pacific executives had refused their offers. Finally the situation peaked on

L. A. Huffman photographed members of Hogan's Army in Forsyth, Montana, in front of their "borrowed" Northern Pacific train.

MONTANA HISTORICAL SOCIETY PHOTOGRAPH ARCHIVES, HELENA

Monday, April 23, 1894—an occasion in Butte that combined St. George's Day celebrations with Industrial Army speeches and rallies.[12]

Shortly after midnight on Tuesday, April 24, out-of-work railroad men from Hogan's camp entered the Northern Pacific roundhouse and commandeered Engine #542. They attached a boxcar for their provisions and six coal cars to carry the men. After a short stop at the nearby camp to load, almost 250 Montana Wealers began their trek east, heading for Bismarck, St. Paul, and ultimately Washington, D.C. The Butte dispatcher telegraphed that he had a "wild train" coming down the line—that is an unscheduled run for which all other trains must clear the track.[13]

The Hogan special sped east and switched onto the Northern Pacific mainline at Logan where it picked up about fifty more Industrials. At five-thirty in the morning the train pulled into Bozeman greeted by a cheering crowd of hundreds of townsmen. Here Hogan exchanged the coal cars for seven boxcars and coupled on another boxcar full of provisions donated by the people of Bozeman. With flags flying the special steamed out shortly after ten, now carrying about four hundred Coxeyites.[14]

The first trouble that Hogan's Army encountered involved a cave-in that covered the tracks near the east end of the Muir Tunnel between Bozeman and Livingston. After several hours of digging with picks and shovels, the Wealers cleared the rails. The special rolled into Livingston at five o'clock that afternoon to be met by another enthusiastic crowd.[15]

At the depot "Lieutenant" William Cunningham climbed atop a boxcar and delivered a rousing speech. The people of Livingston responded with generous donations of food, clothing, and blankets. Meanwhile Hogan's crew exchanged engines and added a tool car from the Northern Pacific shops. A raucous, carnival atmosphere prevailed until the train departed at dusk.

Unfortunately the reliance of Hogan and his lieutenants on "implied noninterference" proved unfounded. Upon learning that the Montana Army had commandeered Engine #542, United States Marshal McDermott ordered Deputy Marshal M. J. Haley to assemble a posse of deputies in Butte and to pursue the Industrials' train with a fistful of contempt-of-court orders.

However Haley found that the popular support for the Wealers ran so deeply in Butte that he could deputize only eighty men, fifteen of whom deserted before the posse's train could leave town. The *Butte Bystander,* a Populist weekly, characterized the members of this posse as "the scum of Butte." Finally at six in the evening on Tuesday—sixteen hours after Hogan's men had steamed out—Haley's pursuit train left Butte.[16]

As Hogan's special rolled east, Northern Pacific Superintendent Finn began his own delaying tactics. Since Finn was already east of Hogan's Army, ahead of the Wealers on the line, he dynamited a rock slide onto the tracks near Livingston. He then spiked switches at Reedpoint and Columbus, and he drained trackside water tanks to delay the Wealers' progress.

Finn also telegraphed Yellowstone County Sheriff James Ramsey in Billings, asking him to stop Hogan's Army there. However, Finn earlier had lost an election to that sheriff, and Ramsey's undersheriff thought that the wire was a prank. He wired in reply, "COUNTY ATTORNEY AND SHERIFF OUT IN THE BULL MOUNTAINS, LAYING OUT ADDITIONS TO BILLINGS. EVERY ABLE-BODIED MAN IS SELLING REAL ESTATE. STOP COXEY'S ARMY YOURSELF IN LIVINGSTON."[17]

Hogan's 450 Wealers halted east of Livingston and removed the rock slide from the rails—then carefully replaced much of the rubble on the tracks. When they needed water at Reedpoint but found the water tank dry, the Coxeyites filled the boiler using a bucket brigade from the Yellowstone River. On Wednesday morning they chugged into Columbus and made camp to the cheers of the townspeople.[18]

While Cunningham was delivering another rousing speech, Marshal Haley's train pulled into Columbus behind the renegade special. Hogan averted a confrontation by ordering his engineer to open the throttle, leaving the deputies standing at trackside. The two trains then raced down the line toward Billings.

At a quarter to eleven on Wednesday morning, Billings received Hogan's Army. More than five hundred men, women, and children surrounded the special while almost one hundred men climbed into the boxcars to join the crusade. The people of Billings had gathered 400 pounds of beef, 250 loaves of bread, and 400 pounds of potatoes, which they loaded into the provisions cars. Cunningham was addressing the crowd from atop a boxcar when Haley and about two dozen of his deputies approached the crowd from the rear.[19]

To the jeers of the crowd, Haley demanded that Hogan and his men surrender—when suddenly one of the deputies discharged his rifle. In the ensuing melee about thirty shots were fired by the lawmen. The bullets wounded several Coxeyites, and they fatally wounded Charles Hardy, a Billings tinsmith standing on the platform.

The crowd immediately surrounded the Butte deputies and disarmed them. They smashed their rifles on the rails and then chased them back to their train. Cooler heads among the Industrials dissuaded both the crowd and some of Hogan's men from pursuing the frightened lawmen—although Billings officials later detained ten deputies for the shooting of Hardy.

Quickly the Wealers' train crews shoveled in a load of coal and coupled on Engine #464, "the Hog of the Rocky Fork Branch." A subdued army of five hundred protesters then switched back onto the mainline to steam down into the Northern Pacific's Yellowstone Division. Ultimately Hogan's men did gain some time, because the Billings crowd purposefully delayed Haley's departure for another seven hours.

Meanwhile Marshal McDermott and Judge Knowles had wired to President Cleveland requesting the use of federal troops. Cleveland ordered soldiers at Fort Keogh to intercept Montana's Army of the Commonweal as quickly as possible near Miles City. To this end Superintendent Finn had pushed his engine down the line to Miles City to confer with the military.

By Wednesday evening, April 25, Hogan's crusaders had pitched camp at Forsyth, and Colonel John B. Page had issued field rations to six companies of the Twenty-second United States Infantry. Maintaining his pacifistic approach to "the petition with boots on," William Hogan telegraphed down the line that, if faced with federal troops, his Industrialists would offer no resistance.

Superintendent Finn received this wire and immediately checked to see if the Wealers had departed their Forsyth camp. When he learned that they had not, he and Colonel Page loaded the troops on a Northern Pacific special and raced the forty-five miles up the line to Forsyth.

Early on the morning of April 26—two full days after Hogan's Army had commandeered the train in Butte—250 infantrymen surrounded the

*Hogan's Army captured by United States infantry troops at
Forsyth, Montana, April 26, 1894.*

Industrials' overnight camp. Hogan peacefully surrendered to Colonel
Page although scores of his men escaped into the sagebrush in the dark.
Ultimately the soldiers captured about 330 Coxeyites at Forsyth. On
Thursday morning the Montana contingent's dash to Washington officially
ended, about 325 miles from where it had begun.[20]

Yet simply stopping Hogan's run and arresting the Industrials did not
solve the problem of Coxey's Army in Montana. Federal officers still needed
to handle these hundreds of peaceful protesters in the face of massive
public support for their crusade.[21] Furthermore the authorities faced real
difficulty portraying Hogan's men as raving anarchists bent on rampant
violence. One state newspaper reported, "When Hogan's addition to
Coxey's Army was searched at Forsyth, three guns were found. One was
broken; one was a .22 caliber; one was made back in the 1860s, for which
no cartridges can today be secured. On the other hand, forty-three copies
of the Bible were found. The Army didn't seem to be composed of such
desperate characters after all."[22]

Following several days of deliberation, federal officials ordered Hogan and his men to Helena so Judge Knowles could try them for contempt of court. Three companies of soldiers accompanied the nine boxcars of Wealers in a special train that departed Forsyth at six in the evening on Saturday, April 28, and reached Helena at eight the next morning. Here the men formed ranks at the Northern Pacific depot and marched out to create "Camp Cunningham" at the county fairgrounds. The Montana detachment then numbered 320 men, with about 110 soldiers guarding them. Relations between the two armies had remained cordial from their initial encounter at Forsyth. The Industrials even cooked hot meals for the troops in Helena.[23]

After a couple of weeks Judge Knowles's calendar allowed him to address Hogan and his men. He found all of the Wealers guilty of contempt of court for violating his Northern Pacific property injunction, but the sentences varied. William Hogan received six months in the Lewis and Clark County jail; Hogan's engineer and fireman, plus about forty "officers," earned sixty-day terms; and the other 275 men gained their freedom after they swore to honor Northern Pacific property. Judge Knowles dismissed charges against "Lieutenant" William Cunningham after he revealed that he was not really a Coxeyite at all. Rather, he was a reporter hired by the *Anaconda Standard* to cover Hogan's campaign![24]

By May 20, 1894, the soldiers of the Twenty-second United States Infantry had returned to Fort Keogh, and about two hundred of the freed Coxeyites had established a new camp at the Helena fairgrounds—still determined to reach Washington, D.C. The people of Helena continued to donate substantial amounts of clothing, blankets, and food to the Industrials, but the protestors became eager to restart their pilgrimage. Finally Helena's mayor and the city council devised a plan that would "save face" for a city caught in the furor of the 1894 "Capital Fight" with Anaconda.[25]

An experienced boat-builder, William Sprague, would be granted a letter of credit and sent to Fort Benton. Here he would direct a small crew of Hoganites in constructing flatboats on which to float down the Missouri River to Omaha, where they could join other Coxey contingents. The "Helena Relief Committee for Coxeyites" would purchase supplies for the trip as well as provide five wagons to transport the Wealers' gear from Helena to Fort Benton. So on May 27, amid much fanfare, about 250 men broke camp, formed ranks, and marched out of Helena behind the wagons, beginning the 130-mile hike to Fort Benton.[26]

Hogan's men straggled into that river town all through the next week. Here they found ten large flatboats bedecked in flags and bunting as well as a forty-eight-foot cook boat complete with brick oven and stacks of foodstuffs. The men named eight of the flatboats: *Butte; Helena; Livingston; Bozeman; Great Falls; Free Silver; Hogan; Fort Benton.* Sprague had performed well, and he added considerable capital to Fort Benton's economy.

After some training from seasoned rivermen almost four hundred Coxeyites pushed off into the bank-high waters of the Missouri on June 6, 1894. The Wealers obviously learned the rudiments of flatboat navigation quickly, for by June 28 the flotilla had reached Yankton, South Dakota. By July 9 it landed even beyond Omaha, at St. Joseph, Missouri. Here the remnants of Hogan's Montana Army joined other Coxeyites working their way east.

In the end the Coxeyite movement in Montana proved more a harbinger of social change than it did an effective protest. Montana Coxeyism, personified by William Hogan's Army, enjoyed close ties to Populism and to the Rocky Mountain demand for the free coinage of silver at sixteen-to-one. More important it recognized human rights over property rights.

Finally the Coxey movement in Montana emphasized that the federal government must acknowledge workers' concerns and must assume an active role in managing the national economy. Jacob S. Coxey's solutions to the national Panic of 1893 simply had surfaced forty years too early: President Franklin D. Roosevelt's New Deal programs incorporated Coxey's ideas to combat the Great Depression in the 1930s.

With the exception of the shooting incident at the Billings depot, the Coxey movement in Montana proved remarkably peaceful—in the best sense it was a "petition with boots on." It derived from legitimate frustration with an economic system unresponsive to its workers. For that reason other Montanans widely supported it.

One can argue with William Hogan's tactics, but his concept of a peaceful demonstration to redress grievances finds deep roots in the American heritage. In Montana that demonstration entailed a wild, forty-eight-hour run across the state, which ended alongside the Northern Pacific tracks in Forsyth. Without doubt this remarkable protest created one of the more curious and instructive incidents in Montana's past.

NOTES

1. A version of this piece ran as "Montana's Gentle Protestors: Coxey's Army, 1894," *Montana Magazine,* March-April 1991, 25–29. The best overall work on Coxey's Army in the Northwest is Carlos A. Schwantes, *Coxey's Army: An American Odyssey* (Lincoln, Neb., 1985). See also Henry Vincent, The Story of the Commonweal (1894; reprint, New York, 1969); and Donald L. McMurray, *Coxey's Army, A Study in the Industrial Army Movement of 1894* (1929; reprint, Seattle, 1968). For information on the Montana episode of Coxey's movement, see Schwantes, *Coxey's Army,* 150–65; and Thomas A. Clinch, "Coxey's Army in Montana," *Montana The Magazine of Western History,* 15 (October 1965), 2–11.

2. See Embry Bernard Howson, "Jacob Sechler Coxey: A Biography of a Monetary Reformer, 1854–1951" (Ph.D. diss., Ohio State University, 1973).

3. *Second Annual Report of the Bureau of Labor and Industry of Montana* (Helena, Mont., 1895), 10–13; *Third Annual Report of the Bureau of Labor and Industry of Montana* (Helena, Mont., 1896), 97. See also Michael P. Malone, *The Battle for Butte: Mining and Politics on the Northern Frontier, 1864–1906* (Seattle, 1981), 53–56 and Thomas A. Clinch, *Urban Populism and Free Silver in Montana: A Narrative of Ideology in Political Action* (Missoula, Mont., 1970).

4. Schwantes, *Coxey's Army,* ix–82.

5. See the *Butte (Mont.) Weekly Miner,* April 19, 1894. See also *Anaconda (Mont.) Standard,* April 5, 1894.

6. Schwantes, *Coxey's Army,* 83–230. One can follow news of the various Coxey contingents across the West in the *Butte (Mont.) Weekly Miner,* April 26–May 24, 1894. For the story of the Coxeyites in Idaho, see Schwantes, "Law and Disorder: The Suppression of Coxey's Army in Idaho," *Idaho Yesterdays,* 25 (Summer 1981), 10–26.

7. *Anaconda (Mont.) Standard,* April 8, 1894; Census Office, *Twelfth Census of the United States, 1900: Silver Bow County, Silver Bow Township,* line 50, enumeration district 128, sheet A; ibid., line 2, enumeration district 128, sheet B; "Hogan," in *Butte City Directories, 1889–1912.*

8. *Anaconda (Mont.) Standard,* April 11, 1894. See also the *Butte (Mont.) Bystander,* a Populist weekly sympathetic to the Coxeyites, April 21–May 19, 1894.

For a taste of the widespread public support for the Hoganites, see *Miles City (Mont.) Yellowstone Journal,* April 28, 1894. Anti-Coxey arguments can be found in the *Miles City (Mont.) Stock Growers Journal,* April 28–May 26, 1894.

9. The most complete statement of the beliefs of the Montana Coxeyites can be found in the single issue of their self-published newspaper: Northwest Industrial Army, *Keep Off the Grass,* June 1, 1894, copy in Montana Historical Society Library, Helena (hereafter MHS). This issue was printed in the *Anaconda Standard* print shop. See also Joel Overholser, "Coxey's Army in Montana," Montana Newspaper Association (hereafter MNA), "News Inserts," April 29, 1940. Other MNA "News Inserts" addressing the movement include May 10, 1926, May 11, 1931, and February 1, 1937.

10. *Anaconda (Mont.) Standard,* April 11–13, 15, 18, 20–21, 1894; *Helena (Mont.) Daily Herald,* April 23, 1894.

11. Schwantes, *Coxey's Army,* 150–53. See also *Anaconda (Mont.) Standard,* April 21–22, 1894; *Butte (Mont.) Daily Inter Mountain,* April 20, 1894; *Billings (Mont.) Gazette,* April 21, 1894.

12. *Anaconda (Mont.) Standard,* April 22–24, 1894.

13. Self-contained, contemporary summaries of "the Montana run" can be found in *Marysville (Mont.) Mountaineer,* May 3, 1894; *White Sulphur Springs (Mont.) Rocky Mountain Husbandman,* May 3, 1894; *Billings (Mont.) Gazette,* April 28, 1894; *Helena (Mont.) Daily Independent,* April 25, 1894; *Butte (Mont.) Weekly Miner,* April 26, May 3, 1894; *Fort Benton (Mont.) River Press,* April 25, 1894; *Bozeman (Mont.) Avant Courier,* April 28, 1894; *Helena (Mont.) Daily Herald,* April 24, 1894; and *Anaconda (Mont.) Standard,* April 25, 27, 29, 1894.

14. *Anaconda (Mont.) Standard,* April 25, 1894; *Bozeman (Mont.) Avant Courier,* April 28, 1894.

15. *Anaconda (Mont.) Standard,* April 25, 1894; *Livingston (Mont.) Enterprise,* April 21, 28, May 5, 1894.

16. *Anaconda (Mont.) Standard,* April 25, 1894; *Butte (Mont.) Bystander,* April 28, 1894.

17. *Anaconda (Mont.) Standard,* April 25, 1894; Schwantes, *Coxey's Army,* 155–59.

18. For a useful local-history look at Hogan's Army reaching Columbus, see James T. Annin, *They Gazed on the Beartooths,* vol. 2 (Billings, Mont., 1964), 104–6.

19. Ibid., 2:108–9; *Billings (Mont.) Gazette,* April 28, 1894; *Anaconda (Mont.) Standard,* April 26, 1894; *Helena (Mont.) Daily Herald,* April 25, 28, 1894; *Missoula (Mont.) Evening Missoulian,* April 25, 1894; *Helena (Mont.) Daily Independent,* April 26, 1894; *Butte (Mont.) Daily Inter Mountain,* April 25–26, 1894.

20. *Anaconda (Mont.) Standard,* April 26, 1894; *Helena (Mont.) Daily Independent,* April 26–27, 1894; *Butte (Mont.) Daily Inter Mountain,* April 26, 1894; *Miles City (Mont.) Yellowstone Journal,* April 28, May 5, 1894; *Missoula (Mont.) Evening Missoulian,* April 26, 1894; *Helena (Mont.) Daily Herald,* April 26, 1894.

21. *Anaconda (Mont.) Standard,* April 27, 29–30, 1894; *Butte (Mont.) Daily Inter Mountain,* April 26, 1894; *Helena (Mont.) Daily Independent,* April 27, 1894; *Helena (Mont.) Daily Herald,* April 27, 1894.

22. *Big Timber (Mont.) Pioneer,* as reported in the *Butte (Mont.) Bystander,* May 5, 1894.

23. *Anaconda (Mont.) Standard,* May 1, 5, 1894; *Helena (Mont.) Daily Herald,* April 30, May 3, 5, 1894; *Miles City (Mont.) Yellowstone Journal,* April 28, May 5, 1894; *Helena (Mont.) Daily Independent,* April 28–30, May 23, 1894; *Butte (Mont.) Daily Inter Mountain,* April 30, 1894.

24. The full legal file on the Hogan case can be found in *United States v. William Hogan,* Circuit Court of the United States, Ninth Circuit, District of Montana, microfilm 354, MHS. See also *Anaconda (Mont.) Standard,* May 11, 14–15, 1894; *Helena (Mont.) Daily Independent,* May 2, 15, 20, 1894; and *Helena (Mont.) Daily Herald,* May 1, 10–11, 14–18, 1894.

25. *Anaconda (Mont.) Standard,* May 20, 1894; *Helena (Mont.) Daily Independent,* May 17, 24, 26, 1894; *Helena (Mont.) Daily Herald,* May 24, 1894.

26. The story of the Coxeyites in Fort Benton is addressed in Marilyn Ritland, "Coxey's Army and the Merchants of Fort Benton," *Montana Historian,* 2 (Winter 1972), 22–24; Schwantes, *Coxey's Army,* 219–21. See also *Fort Benton (Mont.) River Press,* May 30, June 6, 1894; *Anaconda (Mont.) Standard,* May 22, 27, 1894; *Helena (Mont.) Daily Independent,* May 27–28, 31, 1894; and *Helena (Mont.) Daily Herald,* May 28, June 4, 11, 1894.

The Orange and the Green in Montana

A Reconsideration of the Clark-Daly Feud

DAVID EMMONS

U ntil David Emmons, professor emeritus of history at the University of
Montana, Missoula, pointed out its significance, no one really knew or
cared that William A. Clark ate barbecued beef on an October Friday in 1888.
But evidence like this has enabled the author of the award-winning The Butte
Irish: Class and Ethnicity in an American Mining Town, 1875–1925 (1990) to
reinterpret one of the pivotal events in the history of Montana—the struggle
between William Clark and Marcus Daly for power and political spoils. Traditional
interpretations of the Clark-Daly feud by K. Ross Toole and Michael P. Malone
emphasized economic factors. No one denies the importance of economics,
but Emmons's reconstruction restores ethnic politics to the primal position it
once apparently held. If the Clark-Daly feud "affected almost every aspect of the
political and economic life" of early Montana, and if Emmons is right, then
clearly "almost every aspect" of the fabled "War of the Copper Kings" is subject
to reevaluation.

This article has more far-reaching implications than a simple revision of a specific
historical circumstance. Much of Montana history undoubtedly would look different
if considered from an ethnic perspective. One cannot help but wonder as well:
Does the clash between the Orange and the Green affect contemporary politics?

IN MONTANA'S SHORT HISTORY FEW EVENTS HAVE CAPTURED AS MUCH ATTENTION
as the bitter feud between Marcus Daly and William Andrews Clark. The
two men, "copper kings" in the preferred phrase, fought one another

Marcus Daly

W. H. HOOVER, PHOTOGRAPHER,
MONTANA HISTORICAL SOCIETY
PHOTOGRAPH ARCHIVES, HELENA

William Andrews Clark

MONTANA HISTORICAL SOCIETY
PHOTOGRAPH ARCHIVES, HELENA

from 1888 until Daly's death in 1900. There was an epic quality to their rivalry. Both men were from Silver Bow County (Butte), both were Democrats. Both were also fiercely stubborn, politically ambitious, though in different ways, and, even as their hostility to one another began, monumentally rich. Their fight consumed the better part of twelve years, and it does not stretch its significance to say that it affected almost every aspect of the political and economic life of the territory and state of Montana. Gigantic corporate mergers, the location of the state capital, and the election of United States senators and congressmen all were influenced if not determined by the Clark-Daly feud.[1]

Of the two Clark appeared to be far more affected by the rivalry, at least publicly. He could scarcely speak Daly's name without venom. The man was a "veritable czar," the leader of an "infamous gang," a gang so "despotic that it would not be tolerated in Russia or anywhere else in the civilized or uncivilized world." Daly was guilty of "insolent domination," and "political debauchery." He was a "perversion of wealth," an "envious . . . and diabolical" plotter who was responsible for the "financial and moral ruin of men, the misery of women and children." Only with God's help was Clark able to "break . . . this great tyrant . . . and remove the heel of the despot forever from the necks of our people." Curiously, since Clark also described him as a "victim of his own bile . . . the most ill-tempered man I've ever known," Daly did not reply in kind. But his hatred, if the amount of money he spent trying to defeat Clark is any indication, was at least as deep.[2]

Both sides to the controversy agree that it began, or at least first manifested itself, in fall 1888. The issue is simply explained. Clark was the nominee of the Democratic Party for the election of territorial delegate to the national Congress. The nomination, which Clark had apparently not sought, was thought tantamount to election in the overwhelmingly Democratic territory. More significantly, Montana was on the threshold of statehood and it was assumed that its last territorial delegate would be its first United States senator. Clark cannot have cared much about the office of delegate, but his subsequent career indicates how very much he cared about the United States Senate. It was to that latter office that Montana's huge Democratic majority was, in fact, expected to send him.[3]

There were internal rifts in the territory's democracy, divisions between its two principal components: Southerners (Missourians, as they were known) and Irish Catholics, most of them employed in the mines in and around Butte City and on the railroads. But no one doubted that both groups were solidly Democratic. Careful students of ethno-cultural voting habits have asserted that 75 to a remarkable 95 percent of the Irish Catholic vote, from New York to the mines of California, went to the Democratic Party. Montana's history confirmed that the young territory's significant Irish population was not likely to break the habit in 1888. For this reason Clark's Republican challenger, the young and relatively unknown Thomas H. Carter of Helena, was accorded little chance. It was assumed, not without cause, that the Irish-born Daly and the thousands of Irishmen in his employ would support both the party and its candidate. Indeed Daly had promised as much. There had been no open disagreements between the two men and no reason to assume that the Irish vote would be defected away from the Democratic Party.[4]

Balloting took place on November 6; Carter won by 5,126 votes, carrying Silver Bow County, Clark's home territory and consistently Democratic, by 1,537 votes. Analysis of the upset began immediately. Clark's forces noted the strong support for Carter in those parts of the territory where Daly's Anaconda Company had its greatest influence. These included parts of far western Montana near Missoula, where Daly and/or his business associates had timber interests, those sections of the territory served by the Northern Pacific Railroad, and most particularly, those wards in Butte and Silver Bow County where Anaconda miners congregated. In every instance these were thought to be safely Democratic districts, in considerable measure because they were overwhelmingly Irish districts. It required, then, no political wizardry to figure out that the Irish, Daly included, had defected and thrown their support to Carter. Less easily determined was whether they had done so on Daly's instruction.[5]

Rumors that Daly's support for Clark's candidacy might be slipping had began as early as October, but his final "betrayal" of Clark did not become clear until after the election. Clark, obviously, never forgave him. But historians have used language only scarcely less heated than Clark's to describe Daly's presumed disloyalty. "Behind the scenes," writes one recent historian of the feud, "Marcus Daly and his allies secretly plotted Clark's defeat." "Allies" later became "cohorts" and "henchmen," the plot became a "clandestine campaign" on which Daly "put the finishing touches." Another student of the rivalry, writing in 1941, noted that Daly employed ten men for every one employed by Clark and that he used his disproportionate influence with clumsy if telling effect, ordering his men to vote for Carter or risk their jobs. It was the kind of cynical and corrupt act expected of robber barons and copper kings.[6]

Speculation has centered on Daly's motives. The majority verdict is that Daly thought the Republican Carter would have greater leverage with what Daly and his advisors presumed would be a Republican administration in 1889 and that his leverage could and would be used to squash or at least slow the prosecution of the indictments filed by Democratic President Grover Cleveland's administration against Daly and his associates' illegal timber cutting operations. It is an explanation that certainly does nothing to diminish the sinister aspect the incident has always worn.[7]

The historian most responsible for this explanation of Daly's motives was K. Ross Toole. His arguments are presented in his article, "The Genesis of the Clark-Daly Feud," written in 1951. They had, and still have, some credibility. The latest account of the feud in Michael Malone's *The Battle for Butte* is based almost entirely on Toole's account. Toole began by pointing out the obvious flaws in the earlier efforts to account for Daly's political apostasy. There were stories that Clark had treated Daly disrespectfully, that he had attempted to block Daly's acquisition of certain key water rights, or that he had insulted one of Daly's business partners. Toole convincingly disposes of each of these, choosing to accept the account of Daly's good friend, John Branagan, that the feud owed nothing to business or business-related matters. Instead Toole found evidence linking Daly and other prominent Montana Democrats in what can charitably be labeled a political sting operation, a well-conceived and carefully disguised plan to block any effort to interfere with their plunder of federal forest reserves. It could be argued that this was a "business" motive; in fact Toole specifically states that Daly supported Carter "for economic reasons," an argument which, at the very least, confuses the issue of Branagan's explanation. But there are other and more compelling reasons for a reappraisal of Toole's interpretation.[8]

Clark, a man adjudged uncommonly shrewd by all, was strangely oblivious to what in time should have seemed a transparent case of influence peddling and graft. As late as 1900, however, though the memories of 1888 still seared, Clark did not accuse Daly of that form of corruption. Neither did he or his newspaper, the *Butte Miner*, raise the issue of timber lands to explain the election of 1888. It could be that Clark was no happier with the Cleveland administration's indictments than was Daly and that this explains his silence on the issue. But that begs an obvious question: why would Clark not then have been an even more effective advocate of unrestricted timber cutting than Carter? The point here is not that Clark was sure of Daly's motives; only that he did not consider this one to have been among them.

There are other problems with Toole's explanation. Perhaps the most obvious is that it simply assumes that far the greater percentage of Daly's employees would follow his lead, even if it meant supporting the representative of a party whose anti-Irish and anti-Catholic roots were deep and well known. It can be countered, indeed Toole and Malone in essence argue, that Daly's control of his men was absolute and that nothing, including nostalgia for the "old rock" and loyalty to its Butte facsimile, could get in the way of the "boss Irishman's" timber predations. The election returns from Silver Bow County as well as from those areas where Northern Pacific influence was greatest do indicate considerable Irish support for Carter. But if reasons other than Daly's command could be found to explain that vote, the charge that Daly was autocratic and corrupt and the Irish meekly submissive would at least have to be reconsidered. This is particularly the case since the only hard evidence that Daly coerced his employees in 1888 was provided fourteen years later by John Caplice, then as later a strong Clark supporter and the proprietor of what many believed was the "company store" for Clark's employees.[9]

There is another and related issue. Irish fidelity to the Democratic Party was never entirely witless. Among Clark's many criticisms of Daly, in fact, was that the Irishman was a party "irregular," that "although claiming to be a Democrat, he really had no politics." Rather "he elected men whom he knew would subserve his purpose . . . giving the preference often times to Republicans." Obviously Clark intended this as further criticism of Daly and his tactics. Inadvertently, however, it absolves Daly of the charge of betrayal. The point is that Irish support for the Democratic Party was always based on the party's support of the Irish. In fact one of the times when Daly gave his preference to a Republican occurred in a Butte mayoralty campaign when he supported Lee Mantle's candidacy because Mantle had opposed anti-Irish bills during his tenure in the state legislature.[10]

There were other prominent Butte Irishmen during these years who were also convinced that the Democratic Party was not honoring its part of the unstated agreement with Irish voters. For example Pat Boland and Maurice O'Connor, both Irish and both presidents of the Butte Miners Union, joined the Republicans. So did the journalist John Kirby and, on the national level, John Devoy, head of the militantly Irish nationalist organization, the Clan-na-Gael. This hardly constitutes a groundswell but it does indicate that by 1888 Irish Catholic and/or working-class support for Democrats was not automatic. The national Republican platform in 1888, moreover, played to this growing disaffection with spirited defenses of Irish Home Rule, the remonetization of silver, and the beauties of tariff protection for the working class.[11]

Another flaw in the Toole interpretation is that it does not account for Daly's continuing hostility to Clark's political ambitions except, of course, as Daly was responding to Clark's unrelenting hatred of him. But that leaves unanswered the question of Clark's motives. A good case could be made that Carter's usefulness was over once the timber suits had been derailed and that Daly, along with his dutiful Irish retainers, should then have rejoined the forces of Clark. One can even imagine Clark, described by one historian as "coldly practical in finance and politics," understanding Daly's temporary alliance with a Republican. After all the stakes were high, the office was not a particularly important one except as it influenced Senate elections, and Daly had plenty of time to return to the Democratic Party before the next senatorial election. Daly, in fact, did return to the party, but he continued in the absence of any substantial political or economic differences with Clark to oppose and frustrate his senatorial hopes. As for Daly's partners in the conspiracy, the timber and railroad barons, their "conversion" to Republicanism was permanent—and explicable by simple reference to the thousands of others in the United States who made the same switch at about the same time and for the same reasons: They were attracted to the Republican's high tariff policy.[12]

Central also to Toole's explanation is the assumption that Harrison would defeat Cleveland and that a Republican delegate would be more welcome in a Republican court. Given the narrowness of Harrison's final margin and Cleveland's clear majority in the popular vote, predications of a Republican victory border on the miraculous—or were based on a coin-flip—and elaborate political schemes to take advantage of that victory were risky at best. Put simply, what could Carter have done for Daly and his timber raiders should Cleveland win that the far better situated Clark could not have done should Harrison be elected? This is a particularly troublesome point since Harrison and the Republicans were running on a platform that promised a revision of Cleveland's land and timber cutting policies and condemned the indictments as "harassment" by "prosecutions under the false pretense of exposing frauds and vindicating the law." They hardly figured to break that promise because of the election of a Democratic delegate from Montana.[13]

Moreover, of the two parties in Montana, the Democratic platform favored "legislation to allow free use . . . of all timber on the public land."

There was no mention of timber lands in the territorial Republican platform. Clark by his own admission was a "large consumer" of lumber and later, as senator, urged that the forests be turned over to the states in which they were located. The fact that some of the indictments were dropped or at least slowed after Carter's election, a point Toole emphasized, does not mean that the Harrison administration was following Carter's lead. Thirty-four-year-old territorial delegates did not wield that kind of power, and only because federal policy corresponded to territorial need was anyone able to claim it for him. In sum, a Harrison administration was no threat to the timber cutters regardless of the political coloration of Montana's delegate, and the threats from a Cleveland administration might at least be parried by the election of an interested Democrat.[14]

There is one other problem with Toole's interpretation. In his master's thesis, on which his article on the genesis of the feud is based, Toole wrote that "Clark was a second generation Irishman, so was Carter." He does not repeat this phrase in his article, but there is no reason to think that he was not still operating on the assumption that there were no politically relevant ethnic differences between the two. This was not the case. Carter was a second-generation Irish Catholic, a favorite of the Montana hierarchy and the brother-in-law of Irish-born Thomas Cruse, a man whose fortune built the Helena Catholic cathedral. In other words, among the prominent Irish Catholic Republicans of Montana must be counted Thomas H. Carter.[15]

Clark, on the other hand, was quintessentially Orange, i.e., Scotch-Irish Presbyterian. Daniel J. Hennessy, admittedly a Daly friend and business associate as well as an Irish Catholic, even referred to Clark as a member of the intensely anti-Irish and anti-Catholic American Protective Association (APA). There is no corroborating evidence of APA affiliation, but the general point does not require any. Clark's family and that of his wife were all from the Ulster County of Tyrone in the "north of Ireland"; Clark was an elder in the Presbyterian Church and a Grand Master Mason. Indeed one of the most curious aspects of Clark's story is his affiliation with the Democratic Party. The same historians who found Irish Catholics voting for the Democrats found "Irish" Protestants voting 75 to 95 percent for the GOP. Perhaps Clark's brief stay in Missouri explains his political preference; more likely, the always politically ambitious Clark looked around him when he arrived in Montana in 1863 and did the obvious. But whether he was initially a Democrat by convenience rather than conviction is less important than the fact that more divided him from the Irish Catholic world than united him with it. Certainly no modern reader needs to be reminded of the bitter enmity between Northern Ireland Protestants and Irish Catholics.[16]

Neither would any Butte Irishman in 1888 have needed a reminder. For example, Michael Davitt, a leader of the Irish Home Rule fight, spoke in Butte in 1886. He can only have confirmed what the large Irish-born population of the camp already knew from experience both in Ireland and in the United States: Orange hostility to Irish Catholics and, more particularly, Irish Home Rule was intense and growing. Among his listeners that evening was Marcus Daly. Daly knew both Davitt and Charles Stewart Parnell, Davitt's partner in the fight for Home Rule. In fact Davitt stayed at Daly's home during his visit to Butte.[17]

Daly wore his Irish Catholicism like a badge—or a shield. Born in Ballyjamesduff, County Cavan, he was a member of the Ancient Order of Hibernians, an Irish Catholic organization whose origins went back to the often violent and always bitterly anti-British Whiteboys and Ribbonmen of Ireland. He was proposed for membership, which attested to his sympathy with its goals, in the Robert Emmet Literary Association (RELA), the Butte camp of the openly revolutionary Clan-na-Gael, the American equivalent of the Irish Republican Brotherhood. His good friend, John Branagan, the same who denied that the Clark-Daly feud had anything to do with business, also remembered that Daly was a regular reader of Patrick Ford's newspaper, the *Irish World and American Industrial Liberator,* a most uncommon journal for a copper king, filled as it was with advanced ideas of Irish nationalism, the rights of working classes, and the significance of a protective tariff to both.[18]

Daly's friends and closest business associates tended to be drawn from the community of Irish patriots. Branagan, for example, was conspicuous in his support of the cause of Ireland, arguing privately in 1883 that "revenge be taken for the persecution of our countrymen in the old country" and that Butte's Irish seek "retribution, an eye for an eye and a tooth for a tooth in whatever country or clime an English tyrant . . . be found." Dan Hennessy was another staunch Irish-American nationalist, as was Hugh

O'Daly, Marcus Daly's "biographer." Daly's successors in the top management of the Anaconda properties, William Scallon, John Ryan, and Con Kelley, were all Irishmen and members of the AOH; two of them, Scallon and Ryan, were also affiliated with the Robert Emmets. The managers and foreman of Daly's properties included such Irish nationalists as Ed O'Bannon, Michael Moran, Michael Carroll, Patrick Kane, James Brennan, "Rimmer" O'Neill, John J. O'Farell, and James Higgins. Each was an active member of both Irish associations.[19]

There is no evidence, other than that he read Pat Ford's *Irish World,* to indicate that Daly shared Branagan's and the others' zeal. There is incontrovertible evidence, however, that he gave preferential treatment to Irishmen in hiring. From his legal department to his smelting and mining engineers, from the managing editor of his newspaper to the lowliest mucker in his mines, Marcus Daly sought out and hired Irishmen. Both his alleged company store and his avowedly company boardinghouse

Members of the Ancient Order of Hibernians, an Irish Catholic organization with roots in anti-British societies, pose outside St. Patrick's Church in Butte, circa 1910.

were owned and managed by Irishmen. According to one member of the territorial legislature, it was a "matter of common report that the laborers of the Anaconda were almost exclusively Irish . . . that of two men equally competent to fill a position, the Irishman invariable got it." The APA even argued that "'NO MAN OF ENGLISH BIRTH NEED APPLY' was virtually posted on the doors of the Anaconda syndicate of mines"—a revealing variation on the conventional theme—while even the "suspicion of APA affiliation" led to immediate discharge. It was Marcus Daly, said Father Patrick Brosnan in a letter to his father in Ireland, who "made Butte an Irish town . . . he did not care for any man but an Irishman and . . . did not give a job to anyone else."[20]

The population of the place and the ethnic disposition of the Anaconda's work force reflected Daly's preference. By 1900 first- and second-generation Irish made up 36 percent of the town's population, making Butte, 2,500 miles from the nearest eastern port, the most overwhelmingly Irish town in the United States. By 1887 an Irishman could get a Guiness Stout or a Dublin porter on draught and smoke a Home Rule cigar. In 1889 St. Patrick's Catholic parish numbered 7,000 members; the Mountain View Methodists had the city's second highest membership with 145. As early as 1893 the place had its first Irish Catholic mayor; it would have eight more between then and 1919. Of the first thirty-six presidents of the Butte Miners' Union, thirty-two were Irishmen. These numbers reflected Irish dominance at Daly's mines. By 1894 there were 1,251 native Irish and approximately as many second-generation Irish among the Anaconda Company's 5,500 member work force; by way of striking contrast, only 365 English-born worked for Daly, and this at a time when the English outnumbered the Irish in Silver Bow County. Daly's mines even closed on such exclusively Irish holidays as St. Patrick's Day, Robert Emmet's birthday, and the day of the all Irish Societies Picnic.[21]

Few politicians, particularly Democrats, could ignore or affront this Irish constituency. One of the papers supporting Clark in 1888 reported that he was "the grandson of Irish exiles," a fluent Gaelic speaker and a direct descendent of Robert Emmet, the Protestant Irish nationalist executed by the English in 1803. The claims were untrue, but that they were made is revealing. They indicate that the party, if not necessarily Clark, felt the candidate had ethnic fences to mend. It had not escaped notice, for example, that Clark gave hiring preference to Cornishmen. The work force of one of his mines, the Mountain View, was so predominantly Cornish that it was called the Saffron Bun. And when the Parrot Mine, another Clark property, was sold to the Anaconda Company a Cornishman was heard to lament, "Good bye birdie, savage [Irish] got thee; no more place for we."[22]

The problem for Clark was that Cornish Democrats were as rare as Irish Republicans—rare, but not unknown. Among Clark's most enthusiastic supporters was William J. Penrose, Cornish born and editor of the *Butte Mining Journal*. It became Penrose's self-appointed responsibility to ally Cornish and Irish miners around the banner of Clark's Democratic candidacy, a tactic that required a simultaneous courtship of both. He was almost sycophantic in the effort. Penrose "remembered the time when I was a strict Republican and the only reason I had for it was because Irishmen were Democrats." He had long since recanted. By 1887 the Catholic church was a "wondrous religious organization"; St. Patrick was described in language that would have embarrassed the most fervent Hibernian; the conquest of Ireland was "England's disgrace and shame." As for the Cornish, the Republicans had badly mistreated them in 1886 and intended to use them as "vote fodder" in 1888. Fortunately, however, "That time has gone . . . when the men who hail from the west of England will vote one ticket" because "some idiot" tells them that Catholicism was "in direct opposition to the religious trainings of his youth." That was less a prophesy than a devout hope.[23]

It was a hope shared by all Democrats. If the Irish could be held to the Democratic Party and the Cornish converted to it, the party's dominance would be assured. Clark's reputed lineal descent from Robert Emmet is a case in point. The party's reminder that the Republican presidential candidate, Benjamin Harrison, had once accused the Irish of being "good only to shovel dirt and grade railroads" was another. Clark personally concentrated his energies on converting the Cornish, perhaps assuming that the Irish vote needed little tending. The columns of his paper, the *Butte Miner,* were filled with stories on the "men from the land of tin and fog." One of them listed the accomplishments of more than two hundred Cornishmen; another asked: "our 1200 Cornish Friends . . . what has the Republican Party ever given you? . . . who knifed [you] in 1886?" Some

Irish Democrats may have thought this harmless campaign talk. But those with memories of the bitter rivalries between the Irish and the Cornish, whether in the mines of Ireland or Colorado, can only have wondered what was implied by these overtures to English Protestant Republicans.[24]

Clark may have given them an answer in the campaign. On September 29 in Missoula Clark delivered the first speech in his bid for the office of territorial delegate. Most of it was taken up with a defense of tariff reform. He also made reference to statehood for Montana and, interestingly, the importance of new timber cutting policies. It was, in other words, the kind of speech expected of a Democratic candidate—except for one remarkable lapse. During his defense of lower import duties he referred to the statements of certain critics of tariff reform including those "made in the *Irish World* by a prominent deserter from the federal army in the civil war." The alleged deserter was Patrick Ford, a venerated leader of the Irish-American nationalist movement, especially among working-class Irish. Clark's reckless charge against him was false and easily shown to be such. The *Helena Independent,* a strong Clark supporter, made the matter worse by writing that "Pat Ford . . . was using his power and influence in deceiving his countrymen," and that this was a "thousand times worse than his desertion." This was five weeks before the election. Toole called this reference to Ford "a silly mistake." It was a good deal more than that.[25]

Neither Clark nor his newspaper, the *Butte Miner,* ever retracted or apologized for the statement. Lee Mantle, editor of the Republican *Butte Inter Mountain,* thought he knew why. "For fear of offending Mr. Clark," he wrote, the *Miner* "dare not deny the story; and for fear of offending the Irish-American voters of Montana, it dare not affirm it." The issue, however, would not go away, in part because Mantle and the *Inter Mountain* would not let it. The paper gave full coverage to Ford's heated denial of the charge of desertion, then pointed out that another "sour and virulent Orangeman," the New York journalist E. L. Godkin, had called Ford a "dynamiter and deserter . . . and a cowardly cow." Linking Clark to Godkin was like linking him to Cromwell.[26]

Penrose was in no position to retract the story, so he dissembled. Clark's "sympathies," he wrote, "have ever been enlisted in [the Irish] struggle for independence." He was "too intelligent to insult the Celt"; the Republicans were "trying to poison the minds of the Irish people against"

Clark, and Carter was "trading on his nationality." Besides, "Pat Ford cuts no figure in the Montana campaign . . . [he] has no . . . claim to represent the Irish vote of the U.S." As for Daly, the boss Irishman, "he will in every legitimate way, exercise his influence in behalf of Mr. Clark. Mr. Daly is not an intimidator nor a bulldozer. . . . He has no possible personal interest in the coming contest."[27]

Penrose may not have known better. There was no public Irish response. Daly said nothing although it was about this time that rumors of his disaffection for Clark began. The Irish associations also made no reply though the RELA heard a speaker tell its members in September of a national revival of nativism; two years later the Emmets received instructions from their parent organization, the Clan-na-Gael, on how to "keep down the nativist element by electing . . . men . . . favorable to us." But with the exception of one man who wrote that all Irishmen should vote against Clark because "he is a Know Nothing," there was no public Irish response. This may have been because, as Democrats, they were without an effective forum in which to protest; perhaps they had already determined to avenge Ford and understood that an Irish protest would only serve to warn Clark. More likely, however, there was no organized Irish protest because they were waiting, individually not collectively, for Clark to retract the story or apologize for it.[28]

He did neither. In fact his insensitivity to the issue, or that of his advisors, seems almost calculated. For example, on October 19, less than three weeks before the election, the Democrats held a much-publicized barbecue in Anaconda, Montana. On the eighteenth a virulently anti-Catholic organization known as the Patriotic Order, Sons of America had a formal ball in that same city. Clark hoped that the "good Democrats" in the Patriotic Order would attend both functions. This was bad enough, but then a "son of Erin" pointed out that the nineteenth, the day of the barbecue, was a Friday, hardly the day for Irish Catholics to be eating "roasted bullock and fatted calf."[29]

The *Inter Mountain* began almost visibly to celebrate. The Democratic effort to convert the Cornish was failing, and it was beginning to appear that Clark's candidacy could cost it the Irish vote. The Friday barbecue, it noted with tongue firmly in cheek, had to have been a "studied attempt to curtail expenses." Then, more somberly, it noted that "dietary regulations are sacredly observed by a large portion of our most intelligent citizens." The Ford incident was a source of even greater pleasure. "We submit," said the *Inter Mountain,* "that the Irish-Americans of this country who read Patrick Ford's paper will not be slow to resent Mr. Clark's aspersion upon his loyalty." It is tempting to believe that the *Inter Mountain* knew that Marcus Daly was among those readers. "Verily," the paper continued, "it begins to look as though the Patrick Ford issue will side track Mr. Clark." Verily indeed.[30]

The Irish case against Clark could probably have rested on his background, his hiring practices, and his remarkable insensitivity. But there was another related issue. Both Toole and Malone point out that the stockmen of eastern Montana were strongly protectionist and that Carter's strength in that region came from his support for high protective duties. The Republicans also attempted, with mixed results, to convince the working class that protectionism kept production and wages high. One element of that working class, however, needed no convincing. For Irish nationalists, whether in the United States or in Ireland, free trade was one of the props supporting England's imperial domination of Ireland. Ireland's freedom required, among other things, a weakened England or an England at war. High protective tariffs, particularly for the United States and Germany, strengthened England's trade rivals and might produce that war. Moreover the independent Ireland that would emerge from the conflict would have to claim the small nation's right to protect its industries. The principle of protectionism thus became a litmus test of Irish nationalism, and Patrick Ford, among others, made it a featured part of the "Irish question."[31]

Mantle's *Butte Inter Mountain* turned the Irish/tariff issue into a kind of partisan incantation. Protectionist editorials reprinted from the *Irish World* appeared in almost every issue; joining them were Mantle-inspired articles playing more directly to a Butte audience. Clark's attack on Ford, as Mantle pointed out repeatedly, was not a gratuitous ethnic insult; Ford, according to Clark, was a protectionist as well as a deserter. Other stories extended the argument. In an "open letter to the Irish Americans of Montana," published before Clark's attack on Ford, the *Inter Mountain* reminded the Irish that "free trade ruined the industries and disrupted the homes of Ireland." The result was "wholesale immigration." To Irishmen, whose list of England's sins against them began with their own exile, this had to have been a powerful argument. So must have Mantle's story in which a "British peer" was quoted favoring Cleveland, the Democrats, and free trade because protectionism allowed American workers, many of them Irish, to afford "carpets and pianos."[32]

The point repeatedly made was that Cleveland and, by direct political association, Clark were pro-British. In addition to the substance of this argument there is considerable significance in the mere fact that it was made. The remarks of British peers were not the ordinary stuff of American territorial elections—unless, of course, those elections turned on ethnic issues. This one was beginning to appear that it might, and Mantle was relentless in his efforts to link Clark with England. Three weeks before the election he quoted from nine British newspapers, including the *London Times* and the *London Economist*. Each insisted that Britain would be "the chief beneficiary" of American tariff reform; each embraced Cleveland and the Democratic Party. Then, late in the campaign, Mantle was handed another issue. The English ambassador to the United States, the wonderfully named Sir Lionel Sackville-West, wrote that Cleveland was his and England's preferred candidate. Mantle wasted little time pointing out that Sir Lionel would probably like Clark, too.[33]

As noted, Irish Catholic support for the Democrats was always conditional; Irish Catholic Butte made that clear when it gave Carter his 1,500 vote majority. Penrose understood precisely what happened. It was in a "real estate and insurance office on West Broadway" that the decision to "inject religion into the campaign" was made. The only such office on West Broadway was co-owned by Lee Mantle. Obviously Mantle made a wise decision though it might have been argued that Clark had forced the issue with his attack on Ford. "The religious principles of both candidates . . . ," Penrose went on, "cut some figure in the contest," adding that Clark's invitation to the Patriotic Order, Sons of America alone cost him "1,500 votes." So persistent, in fact, were the rumors of religious influence that Father Van de Ven, pastor of St. Patrick's Church, publicly had to deny that he or his church had anything to do with the election. He denied specifically that he was "driving around . . . advising his congregation to vote for Mr. Carter." Those denials notwithstanding, Penrose reported in 1890 that Carter "claims that he owns the Irish vote," evidence enough that the Republican delegate-elect knew exactly the forces that had elected him.[34]

Penrose was a close and interested observer. But given the history—and historiography—of the Clark-Daly feud, Clark's own assessment of his loss is of greater significance. There is strong evidence that he also understood the nature of the "gigantic conspiracy" that defeated him. The *Miner*, a week after the election, noted that "at least 1,000 Democratic votes" in Silver Bow County were cast for Carter and not for "any tariff considerations, but solely as a result of potent influences which are well understood and deeply deplored by the best thinking citizens of this county, Democratic or Republican alike." Citizens were identified as "best thinking" precisely because they deplored the insinuation of ethnicity into politics, however routine that insinuation had become. But the *Miner* was not always so vague. Earlier it had labeled the "conspiracy" that defeated Clark as one "that originated in Republican circles to influence religious prejudice against" him. It then asked, and it was a most interesting and instructive question, if the tactics of 1888 were to become a permanent part of Montana politics. Specifically the *Miner* wanted to know, *"will religious feelings be worked upon and men employed in the mines be commanded to vote so and so or be dismissed?"* It made no references to any other motives.[35]

Thus did Clark explain his defeat. It was a most credible explanation—at least so far as it recognized the significance of the Irish factor. Its credibility is enhanced, moreover, by Clark's and, by inference at least, Penrose's later charges against Daly and the Irish. Among Daly's unpardonable sins was his use of the boycott, a peculiarly Irish tactic and one which aroused the rage of both Clark and Penrose. As Penrose put it, less than three years after the election of 1888, "the boycott is a foreign importation only a little less obnoxious to decent American citizens than nihilism, communism and kindred tenets of foreign cut throats and robbers." On another occasion he referred to the boycott as "the lowest, meanest, most despicable instrument of malice and revenge that was ever imported . . . , an un-American principle." Penrose's specific references are unclear. But given the close association of boycotting with the Irish—the word is of Irish derivation—it was obvious his courtship of Irish voters was over. He may have been talking about the boycotting of merchants, and he did not link the practice to the Irish—only to certain Irishmen, Daly *not* among them.[36]

Clark, however, was more direct. "The boycott," he said in 1900, "is another great weapon used by Daly and his associates." It was used, moreover, for very specific purposes. In language remarkably similar to that used by the *Miner* in 1888, Clark accused Daly of "boycotting all who don't vote as dictated to. They can not get a job or work." In other words Daly boycotted working men by refusing to buy the labor of those whose politics he could not control, a tacit acknowledgement, made explicit later by the APA, that Daly hired Irishmen because he wanted to assemble a work force he could control. Then, having boycotted non-Irish labor, Daly and the Irish were in a position to boycott Clark. Here was a conspiracy vaster by far than any described by Toole.[37]

Like all the conspiratorial explanations of the events of 1888, however, Clark's suffers from one obvious defect. It did not ask if the Irish had to be commanded to vote as they did. It did not take into account the possibility that Clark's impolitic remarks about Ford, among other indiscretions, might themselves be interpreted as a form of ethnic or religious prejudice and that the Irish needed no urging or threats from Daly or rebuke from Clark for them. It is certainly possible that the Irish, Daly included, boycotted Clark, and boycotting did require a certain discipline. But this is not the same as saying that Daly and his shift bosses choreographed the vote. It is unfortunate that so elementary a point needs to be made. However the possibility that Montana's Irishmen, including Marcus Daly, simply did not like or trust the Anglophilic Clark and voted accordingly was not considered—at the time or later. In fact it is plausible that Daly never forgave Clark for the latter's implied insult to the political independence of that community. This is, of course, a frankly speculative argument. Given the flaws in the story of the timber cutting plot, however, and the frank admission that ethnicity and religious feelings were enlisted in this campaign as they were in the later battles between the two men, it seems clear that the origins of the Clark-Daly feud are to be found not in the rascality of a copper king, but in the abiding tensions between the Orange and the Green.[38]

NOTES

1. For the feud, its origins, history, and significance see Michael P. Malone, *The Battle for Butte: Mining and Politics on the Northern Frontier, 1864–1906* (Seattle, 1981), 80–158; K. Ross Toole, *Montana: An Uncommon Land* (Norman, Okla., 1959), 161–62, 180–82; K. Ross Toole, "Marcus Daly: A Study of Business in Politics" (master's thesis, University of Montana, 1948), 56–113; K. Ross Toole, "The Genesis of the Clark-Daly Feud," reprinted from *The Montana Magazine of History*, 1 (April 1951), 21–33, in Michael P. Malone and Richard B. Roeder, eds., *Montana's Past: Selected Essays* (Missoula, Mont., 1973), 284–99; C. B. Glasscock, *The War of the Copper Kings* (New York, 1935), 64 ff; C. P. Connolly, *The Devil Learns to Vote: The Story of Montana* (New York, 1938), 93–104; Joseph Kinsey Howard, *Montana: High, Wide, and Handsome* (New Haven, Conn., 1943), 58–84; Forest L. Foor, "The Senatorial Aspirations of William Andrews Clark, 1898–1901: A Study in Montana Politics," (Ph.D. diss., University of California, 1941).

2. Clark's remarks are from United States Senate, *Report of the Committee on Privileges and Elections of the United States Senate Relative to the Right and Title of William A. Clark to a Seat as Senator from the State of Montana,* 56th Cong., 1st sess., 1900, S. Rept. 1052, 1838–41, 1849 (hereafter Senate, *Report of the Committee on Privileges*); *Congressional Record,* 56th Cong., 1st sess., 1900, 33, pt. 6:5531–36 (hereafter *Cong. Rec.*). The reference to Daly's "ill-temper" is from the *New York Herald,* September 23, 1900, in Foor, "Senatorial Aspirations," 223. Estimates of the amount of money Daly spent defeating Clark are necessarily inexact. See the testimony by and about Daly in Senate, *Report of the Committee on Privileges*; Malone, *Battle for Butte,* 80–110; Toole, "Marcus Daly," 56–191; Paul C. Phillips, "Marcus Daly," in *Dictionary of American Biography,* ed. Allen Johnson and Dumas Malone, vol. 5 (New York, 1930), 45.

3. Clark said in 1900 that he had "tried to avoid" nomination in 1888. Senate, *Report of the Committee on Privileges,* 1785. See also *Butte (Mont.) Semi Weekly Miner,* September 11, 1888. On Montana's territorial politics see Malone, *Battle for Butte,* 11–110; and Clark C. Spence, *Territorial Politics and Government in Montana, 1864–1889* (Urbana, Ill., 1975).

4. On the makeup of the Democratic party see Malone, *Battle for Butte,* 84–85; Spence, *Territorial Politics,* 20–22; George Lubick, "Introduction," from Symposium on Ethnic Groups: Butte, April 19, 1974, Oral History 15, Ethnic History Symposium (hereafter Ethnic History Symposium), Montana Historical Society Archives, Helena (hereafter MHS). For Irish Catholic support for the Democratic party see, among other sources, Lee Benson, *The Concept of Jacksonian Democracy: New York as a Test Case* (1961; reprint, New York, 1964), 185; Paul Kleppner, *The Cross of Culture: A Social Analysis of Midwestern Politics, 1850–1900* (New York, 1970), 70; Richard Jensen, *The Winning of the Midwest: Social and Political Conflict, 1888–1896* (Chicago, 1971), 60, 61, 97, 112, 297; Ronald Formisano, *The Birth of Mass Political Parties: Michigan, 1827–1861* (Princeton, N.J., 1971), 180–81, 304–6. Kevin Shannon, Butte born and a long-time resident, remembers there being two political parties in Butte: Catholics and Republicans. George Lubick, "Remarks," from Symposium on Ethnic Groups: Butte,

April 19, 1974, Ethnic History Symposium, MHS. For Daly's promise of support and the absence of any pre-election disagreements between Daly and Clark see *Anaconda (Mont.) Standard*, September 25, 1900; *Cong. Rec.*, 5533.

5. The November 14, 1888, *Butte (Mont.) Semi Weekly Miner* carried county returns. The November 14, 1888, *Butte (Mont.) Semi Weekly Inter Mountain* had a precinct-by-precinct breakdown of the vote in Silver Bow County. Clark's analysis of his defeat is from the *Helena (Mont.) Daily Herald*, November 22, 1888.

6. For the rumors that Daly was abandoning Clark see the *Butte (Mont.) Mining Journal*, October 31, 1888. The quotes are from Malone, *Battle for Butte*, 85–86; and Foor, "Senatorial Aspirations," 32. See also Senate, *Report of the Committee on Privileges*, 1624, 1627, 2237. There is a possibility that Clark was not above such tactics. For example, in 1888, at the precinct located at Clark's Parrot Smelter, eighteen Republican candidates for various offices averaged 109 votes; the lowest had 60. Carter got 10. *Butte (Mont.) Semi Weekly Inter Mountain*, November 14, 1888.

7. This was not simply a matter of corporate greed. The jobs and safety of thousands of miners also depended on a steady supply of timber. See *Butte (Mont.) Mining Journal*, June 13, 1888.

8. Toole, "Marcus Daly," 73. The Branagan story also appears in John Lindsay, *Amazing Experiences of a Judge* (Philadelphia, 1939), 72; K. Ross Toole and Edward Butcher, "Timber Depredations on the Montana Public Domain, 1885–1918," *Journal of the West*, 7 (July 1968), 351–62; and Malone, *Battle for Butte*, 83–87. Toole's reference to Daly's economic motives is from "Genesis of the Clark-Daly Feud," 299.

9. For Republican nativism see David Potter, *The Impending Crisis, 1848–1861* (New York, 1976), 241–65; John Higham, *Strangers in the Land: Patterns of American Nativism, 1860–1925* (1963; reprint, New York, 1981), 28–29, 56, 60, 79–84, 126–27; George W. Potter, *To the Golden Door: The Story of the Irish in Ireland and America* (Boston, 1960), 371–86; Formisano, *Birth of Mass Political Parties*, 304–6. The "boss Irishman" quote is from Samuel J. Hauser in Senate, *Report of the Committee on Privileges*, 1402. Toole used Caplice's testimony in "Marcus Daly," 96 n. 17, 99. That Caplice ran a company store for Clark was charged in the *Butte (Mont.) Reveille*, September 13, 1902. All other evidence of Daly's coercion was hearsay or came from Clark. For Daly's denial that he coerced anyone see Senate, *Report of the Committee on Privileges*, 2234. See also the remarks of John R. Toole, a Daly associate, ibid., 2147, 2167.

10. Clark's charges are from the *Cong. Rec.*, 5535. For Daly's support of Lee Mantle see Foor, "Senatorial Aspirations," 15. For an example of Mantle's opposition to nativist legislation see the *Helena (Mont.) Independent*, February 20, 1889.

11. *Butte (Mont.) Mining Journal*, September 22, 1888, September 10, 1890; Richard Lingenfelter, *The Hardrock Miners: A History of the Mining Labor Movement in the American West, 1863–1893* (Berkeley, Calif., 1974), 190–93; John Devoy, *Devoy's Post Bag, 1871–1928*, ed. William O'Brien and Desmond Ryan, vol. 2 (Dublin, 1948), 252–54. For Boland's and O'Connor's presidencies of the Butte Miners Union see the *Butte (Mont.) Bystander*, June 7, 1896; *Butte City Directory, 1886*; *Butte City Directory, 1889*. For the Republican platform see Donald B. Johnson and Kirk Porter, comps., *National Party*

Platforms, 1840–1972 (Urbana, Ill., 1973), 81–82. See also Jensen, *Winning of the Midwest,* 26–27, 298, 302, for a discussion of Irish Catholic Republicans.

12. The reference to Clark's "practicality" is from Paul C. Phillips, "William Andrews Clark," in *Dictionary of American Biography,* ed. Allen Johnson and Dumas Malone, vol. 4 (New York, 1930), 145. On the appeal of the Republican party in 1888 to men like Daly's associates see Jensen, *Winning of the Midwest,* 17–21.

13. Johnson and Porter, *National Party Platforms,* 81. Toole, "Genesis of the Clark-Daly Feud," 297, discusses the predictions of Harrison's victory.

14. The territorial Democrat's platform is from the September 11, 1888, *Butte (Mont.) Semi Weekly Miner.* The territorial Republican's platform is from the October 1, 1888, *Butte (Mont.) Daily Inter Mountain.* Toole, "Genesis of the Clark-Daly Feud," 298; Toole, "Marcus Daly," 95. For Clark's timber needs see Senate, *Report of the Committee on Privileges,* 822. Reference to Clark's efforts to have the forests turned over to the states is in Phillips, "Clark," 4:145.

15. Toole, "Marcus Daly," 98. Clark was actually a third-generation "Irishman." See *Progressive Men of the State of Montana* (Chicago, [1902]), 1104. For Carter see Paul C. Phillips, "Thomas Henry Carter," in *Dictionary of American Biography,* ed. Allen Johnson and Dumas Malone, vol. 3 (New York, 1929), 544; *Butte (Mont.) Mining Journal,* September 30, 1888; John O'Dea, *History of the Ancient Order of Hibernians and Ladies' Auxiliary,* vol. 3 (Philadelphia, 1923), 1206.

16. Hennessy's remark is from the September 20, 1902, *Butte (Mont.) Reveille.* Background information on Clark is from *Progressive Men of . . . Montana,* 1106. On "Irish Protestant" voting habits see, particularly, Kleppner, *Cross of Culture,* 70.

17. Hugh Daly, *Biography of Marcus Daly* (Butte, Mont., 1934), 10. That Davitt was Daly's guest is noted in the Robert Emmet Literary Association Minute Books (hereafter RELA Minute Books), October 14, 21, 1886, Irish Collection, K. Ross Toole Archives, University of Montana, Missoula (hereafter Irish Collection, UM).

18. Ancient Order of Hibernians, Division 1, Membership and Dues Ledger, April 1882–March 1887, Irish Collection, UM (hereafter AOH Membership and Dues Ledgers); Daly, *Marcus Daly,* 2–3; Lindsay, *Experiences of a Judge,* 17; Hugh O'Daly, "Autobiography," 1928, TS, n.p., copy in collection of author; Toole, "Marcus Daly," 1–3, 18. "Autobiography" is by the same Hugh Daly who wrote the short biography of Marcus Daly. He adopted the patronymic "O" only for his autobiography. I am indebted to Professor Kerby Miller of the University of Missouri for sending me a copy of the manuscript. For the origins of the Ancient Order of Hibernians see O'Dea, *History of the Ancient Order of Hibernians,* vols. 2 and 3; and Michael Davitt, *The Fall of Feudalism in Ireland* (1904; reprint, Dublin, 1972), 42–43. For the Ancient Order of Hibernians and the Clan-na-Gael see Michael Funchion, ed., *Irish American Voluntary Organizations* (Westport, Conn., 1983), 50–61, 74–93. For Daly's nomination for membership in the Robert Emmet Literary Association see RELA Minute Books, July 29, August 5, 1886, Irish Collection, UM. No one was nominated unless known to be sympathetic. H. B. C. Pollard, *The Secret Societies of Ireland: Their Rise and Progress* (London, 1922), 307–11. On the *Irish World* see Eric Foner, "Class, Ethnicity, and Radicalism in the Gilded Age: The Land League and Irish America," in *Politics and*

Ideology in the Age of the Civil War (New York, 1980), 157–62, 165–76. Daly was also a "benefactor" of the Catholic church. See, for example, Bishop John B. Brondel to Reverend Charles Brondel, January 25, 1902, Brondel Papers, Dioceses of Helena office, Helena, Montana; Reverend James Franchi, "History of the Catholic Schools of Butte," 1910, TS, St. Patrick's File, ibid.

19. Branagan's comments are from RELA Minute Books, December 4, 7, 1883, Irish Collection, UM. For Hennessy, O'Daly, Scallon, Ryan, Kelley, et al. see AOH Membership and Dues Ledgers, Irish Collection, UM; Ancient Order of Hibernians Minute Books, Irish Collection, UM (hereafter AOH Minute Books); Robert Emmet Literary Association Membership and Dues Ledgers, Irish Collection, UM (hereafter RELA Membership and Dues Ledgers); RELA Minute Books, Irish Collection, UM. The "Irishness" of the Anaconda Company, from top to bottom, is revealed in O'Daly, "Autobiography," n.p.; Work Projects Administration (WPA), *Copper Camp: Stories of the World's Greatest Mining Town, Butte, Montana* (New York, 1943), vii, 173, 200–202; Lindsay, *Experiences of a Judge,* 81–82; Isaac Marcosson, *Anaconda* (New York, 1957), 22, 41, 60, 65, 100–101; Wayland Hand, "The Folklore Customs, and Traditions of the Butte Miners," *California Folklore Quarterly,* 5 (January 1946), 159, 163, 177; Hand et al., "Songs of the Butte Miners," *Western Folklore,* 9 (1950), 9, 23–25, 29, 31, 33, 38, 40, 44, 46.

20. Glasscock, *War of the Copper Kings,* 74, 104, 133; O'Daly, "Autobiography," n.p. Dan Hennessy, of course, owned the so-called company store and Hugh Daly and P. J. Kenny were among the Irishmen who ran the Florence Hotel, the "Big Ship," as it was known, the ACM boarding house. O'Daly, "Autobiography," n.p.; *Butte City Directory, 1910.* In 1900 202 Irishmen, 180 of them miners, were staying at the Florence Hotel. Census Office, *Manuscript Census, Twelfth Census of the United States, 1900: Population Schedules,* Silver Bow County, rolls 914–15, microfilm 251, MHS (hereafter *Census . . . 1900*); *Helena (Mont.) Independent,* February 20, 1889. The APA charge was in the June 15, 1895, *Butte (Mont.) Examiner.* Father Patrick Brosnan to his father, February 18, 1917, Brosnan Letters. I am indebted, once again, to Professor Kerby Miller for sharing these letters with me.

21. *Census . . . 1900; Butte (Mont.) Mining Journal,* October 19, November 16, 1887; January 10, 1888; *Butte City Directory, 1889;* Donald James, *Butte's Memory Book* (1975; reprint, Caldwell, Idaho, 1980), 288–89. Polk's *Butte City Directories* list the BMU's officers. See also the *Butte (Mont.) Bystander,* June 7, 1896. General Office Subject file 522, folder 40, box 57, Manuscript Collection 169, Anaconda Copper Mining Company Records, MHS; *Census . . . 1900,* 798. There are repeated references in the minute books of the Irish association to the mines letting out on Irish holidays. See, e.g., RELA Minute Books, June 13, 1889, June 16, 1898, August 3, 1899, Irish Collection, UM; AOH Minute Books, July 7, 1886, March 14, 1889, March 3, 1898, July 10, 1901, Irish Collection, UM.

22. *Missoula (Mont.) Gazette* in *Butte (Mont.) Semi Weekly Miner,* September 26, 1888. On Clark's preference for Cornishmen see Glasscock, *War of the Copper Kings,* 74; *Butte (Mont.) Mining Journal,* November 2, 1887; WPA, *Copper Camp,* 210; Malone, *Battle for Butte,* 66; Foor, "Senatorial Aspirations," 34. For the Parrot story see Hand, "Folklore . . . of the Butte Miners," 178.

23. *Butte (Mont.) Mining Journal,* June 16, 1888, November 2, 1887, January 25, 1888, November 12, 1887. For examples of Penrose's courtship of the Irish see also *Butte (Mont.) Mining Journal,* September 17, 1887, March 17, 21, September 5, 1888.

24. *Butte (Mont.) Semi Weekly Miner,* August 25, 29, September 22, 1888. The other references are from *Butte (Mont.) Semi Weekly Miner,* September 11, 22, October 10, 1888. There is no history of the Irish copper mines in West Cork, but Daphne du Maurier's novel, *Hungry Hill* (1943; reprint, Cambridge, Mass., 1971) is based on the historical record and contains much useful information on the Irish-Cornish conflicts. For Irish-Cornish feuds in Colorado see Lingenfelter, *Hardrock Miners,* 103–5.

25. *Butte (Mont.) Semi Weekly Miner,* October 3, 1888. For Ford's standing among Irish-American workers see Foner, "Class, Ethnicity, and Radicalism." Ford's Massachusetts' regiment also answered the charge of desertion. See the *Butte (Mont.) Semi Weekly Inter Mountain,* October 10, 1888. The *Helena Independent's* remarks were reprinted in the *Butte (Mont.) Semi Weekly Inter Mountain,* October 7, 1888. Toole, "Marcus Daly," 98. The APA later argued that 72 percent of all Irish-American Catholics in the Union Army deserted. *Butte (Mont.) Examiner,* October 5, November 2, 1895.

26. *Butte (Mont.) Semi Weekly Inter Mountain,* October 10, 14, 1888. See also October 7, 17, 21, 28, 31, November 4, 1888.

27. *Butte (Mont.) Mining Journal,* October 17, 28, 331, November 4, 1888.

28. Ibid., October 31, 1888; *Butte (Mont.) Semi Weekly Miner,* October 31, 1888; RELA Minute Books, September 13, 1888, April 3, 1890, Irish Collection, UM.

29. *Butte (Mont.) Semi Weekly Miner,* October 17, 20, 24, 1888; *Butte (Mont.) Semi Weekly Inter Mountain,* October 21, 1888.

30. *Butte (Mont.) Semi Weekly Inter Mountain,* October 7, 21, 1888.

31. Toole, "Marcus Daly," 64, 98; Malone, *Battle for Butte,* 86; Thomas N. Brown, *Irish-American Nationalism, 1870–1890* (New York, 1966), 142. *Irish World and American Industrial Liberator,* September–November 1888, passim.

32. *Butte (Mont.) Semi Weekly Inter Mountain,* October 7, 17, 31, 1888. The "open letter" was in the edition of September 26, 1888. On the "exile mentality" of Irish immigrants see Kerby A. Miller, *Emigrants and Exiles: Ireland and the Irish Exodus to North America* (New York, 1985). The "carpets and pianos" story was from *Butte Semi Weekly Inter Mountain,* October 7, 1888.

33. *Butte (Mont.) Semi Weekly Inter Mountain,* October 17, 1888. On the Sackville-West affair see Charles S. Campbell, *The Transformation of American Foreign Relations, 1865–1900* (New York, 1976), 131; H. C. Allen, *Great Britain and the United States* (New York, 1955), 520–21; Charles C. Tansill, *America and the Fight for Irish Freedom, 1866–1922* (New York, 1957), 107–11.

34. *Butte (Mont.) Mining Journal,* November 11, 1888, October 30, 1890; *Butte City Directory, 1889.* Three years later Penrose was shot down and killed on a Butte street. No one was convicted of his murder, but three Irishmen, identified by some as "Molly Maguires," members of a secret and violent Irish society active in Pennsylvania in the 1860s and 1870s, were arrested. The English society, the Sons of St. George, offered a reward for the conviction of Penrose's murderers. This is further evidence of the tensions between the two ethnic communities at this time. Lingenfelter, *Hardrock*

Miners, 192–93; Malone, *Battle for Butte,* 77, says, without offering any evidence, that those who suspected "a Montana version of the Molly Maguires" were "probably right." Rowland Berthoff, *British Immigrants in Industrial America, 1790–1950* (Cambridge, Mass., 1953), 189–90.

35. Clark referred to the "gigantic conspiracy" in a private letter. Toole, "Marcus Daly," 58–59. *Butte (Mont.) Semi Weekly Miner,* November 10, 14, 1888.

36. *Butte (Mont.) Mining Journal,* April 19, May 10, 1891. See also the edition of June 17, 1891. The word came from the action of Irish Land Leaguers against the agent of their English landlord. The agent's name was Captain Charles S. Boycott. See, among many sources, Norman D. Palmer, *The Irish Land League Crisis* (1940; reprint, New York, 1978), chap. 10.

37. *Cong. Rec.,* 5535–36; Senate, *Report of the Committee on Privileges,* 1934, 2068–71.

38. On the discipline required of boycotting see Joseph Lee, *The Modernisation of Irish Society, 1848–1918* (Dublin, 1983), 94. Daly granted one post-election interview to Penrose. In it he denied coercing anyone, denied even he had the power to coerce. The interview appeared in the *Butte (Mont.) Mining Journal,* November 18, 1888. See also Daly's testimony regarding his role in the election of 1888 in Senate, *Report of the Committee on Privileges,* 2232–35. The next round in the feud, the struggle to determine the permanent site of the state capital, also had an ethno-religious dimension. Helena, Clark's choice and the eventual site, was identified by the APA as having been the "Protestant town." *Butte (Mont.) Examiner,* October 31, 1896. Anaconda, Daly's choice, was "the fiefdom" of "Pope Marcus." Ibid., September 3, 1896. Butte's and Anaconda's Irish Catholics responded to Helena's selection by raising money for a statue of the Irish hero Thomas Francis Meagher. The statue was placed on the capital's front lawn where the "APA's . . . must look in his face and salute his glorious memory for all ages." There can be little question that, had Meagher not been mounted, a different part of his anatomy would have been referred to. Daly was honorary chairman of the Thomas Francis Meagher Memorial Association. *Butte Montana Catholic,* July 15, 1899; RELA Minute Books, July 3, 10, 1899, Irish Collection, UM; quote from ibid., October 15, 1903.

Crown of the Continent, Backbone of the World

The American Wilderness Ideal and Blackfeet Exclusion from Glacier National Park

MARK DAVID SPENCE

L and and the potentially profitable uses of natural resources drew Euro-Americans to the West. However, by the late nineteenth century, some Americans became concerned by the reckless consumption of those resources. One response was a movement to conserve resources through scientific management. Laws, such as the Forest Reserve Act of 1891 and the Forest Management Act of 1897, implemented management of grazing, lumbering, and the development of hydroelectric sites on federal land. A second response was to preserve places of particular natural wonder and beauty through the national park system. National parks helped to institutionalize a concept of "wilderness," an idea that Mark David Spence, a professor of history at Knox College in Galesburg, Illinois, shows us is a very human creation.

This history of Glacier National Park examines the various ways in which peoples with different cultural practices and beliefs assign significance to the same piece of land. It forces us to question the meaning of terms such as "natural," "wilderness," and "virgin land." When Europeans first arrived in North America they saw a wilderness in lands that Native Americans had been farming and harvesting for centuries. That misconception was repeated over and over again as settlement pushed west. Highlighting the ironies and contradictions involved in removing Indians from national parks in order to preserve the parks' wilderness, Spence's essay points to the cultural, economic, and political consequences that removal had for the Blackfeet people.

THE CREATION AND EARLY MANAGEMENT OF GLACIER NATIONAL PARK IN THE
1910s and 1920s reflected the maturation of American ideas about wilderness
as scenic playground, national symbol, and sacred remnant of Nature's
original handiwork. These years also marked a heightened interest in the
"vanishing Indian," and the Blackfeet, whose reservation borders the park
on the east, became an important feature in early park promotions.
Although the presence of Indian dancers in front of the park's grand hotels
tantalized visitors who had come to "meet noble [Indians in] . . . their
native home," park officials vigorously enforced a series of programs that
excluded the Blackfeet from the rest of the park.[1] The importance of Indians
to the Glacier tourist experience seems odd when juxtaposed with policies
that banned Indians from the Glacier backcountry, but this apparent irony
holds an internal consistency when viewed in terms of early twentieth-
century ideas about Native Americans and wilderness. As "past tense"
Indians, those Blackfeet men and women who entertained tourists
appeared to be living museum specimens who no longer used the Glacier
wilderness—if, indeed, they ever had. On the other hand, those Indians
who continued to use the park illegally seemed simply un-American in
their lack of appreciation for the national park and almost barbaric in
their unwillingness to let go of traditional practices.

The eastern half of Glacier National Park once was part of the Blackfeet
reservation, and the tribe has long maintained that an 1895 agreement
with the United States reserves certain usufruct rights within the park.
Conversely, the Department of the Interior has argued repeatedly that the
Glacier National Park legislation of 1910 extinguished all Blackfeet claims
to the mountains on their reservation's western boundary.

The impasse stemmed from two very different conceptions of Glacier's
wilderness, both rooted in powerful ideas about national identity and
cultural persistence. For many Blackfeet, their "illegal" use of the Glacier
backcountry preserves a connection to places and items that have been
important to the tribe since time out of memory. Indeed, through the
surreptitious use of certain plants, animals, and religious sites within the
park, the Blackfeet have preserved a wealth of traditional knowledge that
otherwise might have been lost forever. Blackfeet use of park lands and
resources also illustrates *de facto* proof of the tribe's political sovereignty
as recognized in treaties with the United States. On the other hand, park

administrators view Glacier as one of the nation's most spectacular "crown jewels," and Blackfeet use of park lands threatens to tarnish their luster.[2]

Americans have long celebrated the uninhabited landscapes preserved in large national parks like Glacier as remnants of *a priori* Nature (with a very capital "N"), which they conflate with romantic visions of primordial America. Such an idea of wilderness conveniently neglects the fact that Indians profoundly shaped these landscapes; national parks are more representative of old fantasies about a continent awaiting "discovery" than actual conditions at the time of Columbus's voyage or Lewis and Clark's adventure. In many respects, the wilderness preserved in national parks is as much a fanciful product of American culture as the elaborate hotels built by the Great Northern Railway in the 1910s. Several scholars have argued recently that wilderness itself is a historical construct; they point to the fact that national parks "preserve" areas that did not become uninhabited until after the Indians who called them home had been confined to their reservations. The creation of the first national parks actually preceded efforts to remove Indians from prized "wilderness areas," and programs for Indian removal from Yellowstone, Yosemite, and the Grand Canyon, for example, did not begin until after these areas were "preserved."[3]

Although Blackfeet exclusion from Glacier National Park mirrors similar developments elsewhere, several factors distinguish the situation there from those in other parks. Most importantly, the Blackfeet possessed specifically designated rights to the Glacier area at the time of the park's establishment. Subsequent legal findings concluded that the 1910 Glacier National Park Act extinguished these rights, so Indian exclusion from park lands was explicitly linked to preservation itself. The persistent efforts of the Blackfeet to restore their rights to Glacier provide a well-documented illustration of the great significance that park lands have for many tribes in the Far West. Perhaps most poignantly, an examination of the different meanings that Glacier holds for tourists, park administrators, and the Blackfeet provides an important model for understanding similar issues that currently affect key management questions at other national parks. At Death Valley National Park, for example, the newly recognized Timbisha Shoshone have made claims on large portions of the park as part of an agreement with the United States government to provide the tribe with a reservation. Similar issues have cropped up at Yosemite, the Grand Canyon, and several Alaskan parks, and have once again come to the fore at Glacier. Ultimately the growing number of Indian claims on national parks may well lead to a profound reconsideration of long-cherished ideas about wilderness and its preservation.[4]

The idea of wilderness that informs the management of Glacier National Park is wholly foreign to Blackfeet culture. It would be absurd to think the Blackfeet could ever view their homeland as a place where they are "visitors" who only take photographs and leave footprints. For centuries the Blackfeet have regarded the area within Glacier National Park as part of the Backbone of the World, and though the mountains marked the outer edges of Blackfeet country, they did not stand at the periphery of the Blackfeet world. Within the mountains live such powerful spirits as Wind Maker, Cold Maker, Thunder, and Snow Shrinker (Chinook winds). One of the most important figures in Blackfeet mythology, a trickster called Napi, or Old Man, disappeared into the Rockies when he left the Blackfeet; many of the tribe's most important legends detail Napi's adventures in the mountains and foothills that rise abruptly out of the western plains. The Glacier area is the source of the Beaver Pipe bundle, one of the most venerated and powerful spiritual possessions of the tribe. Chief Mountain, standing at the border of the reservation and the national park, is by far the most distinct and spiritually charged land feature within the Blackfeet universe.[5]

Though deeply tied to the hunting of buffalo on the plains, pre-reservation-era Blackfeet based much of their livelihood on the resources of the mountains and eastern foothills.[6] The yearly cycle of the Blackfeet began in early spring as individual bands left their winter camps in the broken country east of the mountains to begin an intensive season of hunting and plant collecting. Women and youngsters headed to the mountains to dig for roots and collect other plant foods while small bands of hunters moved east seeking buffalo. Food gathering continued through the summer months until the annual Sun Dance celebration, when the various bands would convene for several weeks on the plains. At the conclusion of the Sun Dance ceremony, the various bands would disperse again; some returned to the buffalo grounds while others headed to the mountains to hunt elk, deer, big horn sheep, and mountain goats, to cut lodge poles, and to gather berries through the early autumn months. As fall arrived the buffalo moved west and north to their wintering grounds, and the Blackfeet bands would reassemble into larger groups for communal hunts. Some of this hunting occasionally took place within the present boundaries of the national park, where numerous buffalo skeletons could still be found as late as the 1890s. The annual cycle of hunt and harvest would end with the establishment of winter camps in heavily wooded river valleys near the mountains, sheltered from the severe northerly winds that swept the open plains and close to the winter foraging areas of elk and deer.[7]

The Blackfeet entered into their first treaty with the United States in 1855, but these official relations did little to change long-established patterns. Disease, war, famine, and the near-extinction of the buffalo reduced the Blackfeet to some two thousand individuals by the late 1880s and left them wholly subject to life on a reservation. At the same time a series of land cessions forced the tribe to establish semi-permanent communities along the foothills of the northern Rockies. Mismanagement and corruption within the Indian Service made this adjustment all the more difficult, but the Blackfeet persisted and, in the words of Chief White Calf, made the reservation their "last refuge."[8]

During the painful adjustment to reservation life, the Blackfeet developed a new dependence on the mountains that allowed them to maintain older traditions and ameliorate the loss of others. Although no longer able to hunt buffalo, young men still could prove their worth as they sought out deer, elk, sheep, and small game in the mountains. Women supplemented meager government rations with the traditional foods and herbs they gathered in the mountains, and healers collected and tended medicinal plants. In the midst of pervasive "Americanization" programs, the Blackfeet also turned to the shelter of the Backbone of the World to hold prohibited ceremonies. Young traditionalists maintained their connections with the past by fasting in the same mountain locales as their forebears. At the same time the mountains provided the resources that made the incorporation of new skills and livelihoods possible. Along with firewood and lodge poles, high-elevation forests provided timber for the construction of cabins, fences, and corrals. The foothills provided some of the best pastures for new herds of livestock, and the Indian Service tapped into lakes and streams to create a series of irrigation projects.[9]

George Bird Grinnell and the "Crown of the Continent"

As the Blackfeet struggled with life on the reservation, mid-nineteenth-century wilderness enthusiasts came to appreciate Glacier by a very different route. Euro-Americans had long conceived of wilderness as a defining characteristic of their nation, but until the late nineteenth century, at least, they regarded it generally as an Indian domain. Not surprisingly, the earliest proponents of a national park hoped to preserve what they called an "Indian wilderness." Preservationist efforts did not succeed until the latter half of the nineteenth century, when Euro-Americans began to conceive of wilderness as uninhabited and regarded reservations as the appropriate residence for Indians. These sentiments changed somewhat in the late 1880s as self-described "Friends of the Indian" sought to dismantle the reservations and assimilate Native Americans into mainstream society. Such "friends" argued that an Indian's place was not on the reservation, but they denied even more emphatically that Indians should remain in their former "wilderness haunts." These reformers saw wilderness as the depraved condition from which Indians needed "uplifting." Such uplifting also would benefit the wilderness since, as Helen Hunt Jackson noted during a visit to Yosemite valley, the presence of "filthy" Indians detracted from the sublimity of the scenery; the inability of their "uncouth" minds to appreciate the beauty that surrounded them was an affront to the Creator and His works.[10]

George Bird Grinnell perhaps best represents these new ideas about Indians and wilderness, and it is through him that preservationist ideals came into conflict with Blackfeet use of the Glacier area. Early in his career, Grinnell served as a government scientist on Lt. Col. George A. Custer's reconnaissance of the Black Hills in 1874 and the army's exploration of Yellowstone National Park in 1875. Despite his early connection to such famous people and places, Grinnell would become better known for his leading role in the effort to establish Glacier National Park and for his interest in the Blackfeet. As editor of *Forest and Stream* and author of numerous books on American Indians and the West, Grinnell was a leading voice for the preservation of wilderness landscapes and a respected advocate of Indian policy reform. His family background provided him with strong connections in Washington, D.C., where his views found a receptive audience among the nation's politic elite.[11]

On his first visit to northern Montana in 1885, Grinnell instantly became enamored of the mountains within the Blackfeet reservation. For the next several years he returned to the area to hunt and explore what he described as the last remaining "wild and unknown portion . . . of the country" and published several articles about his adventures. In search of untrodden, pristine landscapes, Grinnell relied on Blackfeet guides and followed countless Indian trails in order to discover areas that he described as "absolutely virgin ground . . . with no sign of previous passage." The irony of such statements was lost on Grinnell, however, and his enthusiasm for what he called the "Crown of the Continent" wholly supplanted Blackfeet concerns about the area. During a trip to the mountains in late summer 1891 Grinnell resolved "to start a movement to buy the [area] . . . from the Piegan [I]ndians at a fair valuation and turn it into a national reservation or park." As he noted in his diary, Grinnell assumed the "Great Northern R[ailway] would probably back the scheme and . . . all the Indians would like it." Grinnell believed that, as "primitive" Indians just setting out on the road to civilization, the Blackfeet would be only too happy to sell an area of little importance to their future social evolution. Although he correctly assumed the support of the Great Northern, then completing its rail line through the southern portion of the reservation, Grinnell could not have been more wrong about the importance of this region to the Blackfeet. His efforts to create Glacier National Park set in motion a series of acrimonious disputes between the Blackfeet and national park officials that continue to this day.[12]

Initially Grinnell came to the Rockies to partake of the outdoor life, but he also developed a great interest in his Blackfeet hosts. During each of his visits to northern Montana he recorded the stories and memories of tribal elders who had come to social prominence before the extinction of the buffalo. In addition he exposed corrupt agency personnel and successfully lobbied Washington to improve reservation conditions. The miserable state of the Blackfeet on their reservation was wholly divorced from concerns about his "beloved mountains," and Grinnell never tied the fate of the Blackfeet to his plans to preserve the Glacier area. While Grinnell linked the rapid exploitation of western lands with the destruction of native societies, his attempts to preserve some remnant of each epitomized late-nineteenth-century concepts of wilderness as uninhabited and of Indian culture as vanishing. As a result his efforts to preserve Blackfeet culture and some portion of the tribe's homeland took widely divergent courses: the Blackfeet would live on in his books and museum collections, but their mountain wilderness would persist within the boundaries of a national park. These concerns not only reflected a relatively new distinction between Indians and wilderness but also grew out of popular concerns about the place of each within late-nineteenth-century America. While he encouraged his countrymen to "uncivilize" themselves a bit and return to the mountains on a regular basis, Grinnell admonished his Blackfeet friends to "civilize" themselves and enter the mainstream of American society.[13]

In the early 1890s growing rumors of mineral wealth in Grinnell's favorite stomping grounds threatened to destroy his plans to convert the region into a nature preserve. Numerous prospectors invaded Blackfeet lands hoping to find a new bonanza, wreaking havoc on the reservation, and occupying most of the tribal police's time in a losing effort to evict trespassers and curb their abuses. Indian agents—who had a vested interest in keeping order on the reservation and hoped to stake claims of their own in the mountains—made common cause with mining interests and successfully petitioned the government to purchase the tribe's western lands. The commissioner of Indian affairs acted swiftly, and in summer 1895 he asked Grinnell to help negotiate a new land cession agreement with the Blackfeet. Grinnell almost declined since he hated to be a part of any efforts that might open up the mountains to destructive mining practices. He remained confident that the mountains possessed no great mineral wealth, however, and he must have viewed the cession of Indian lands as an important first step toward the creation of a national park. While on his way from New York to meet with the Blackfeet, Grinnell interrupted his trip in St. Paul to lobby Great Northern Railway officials for support of his plan to convert the western part of the reservation into a national park.[14]

The Blackfeet respected Grinnell and even requested that he be one of the three government commissioners, but negotiations were contentious and at one point broke down altogether. As Little Dog reminded the commissioners at the start of the proceedings, "[t]he Indians did not ask the government to come and buy their land" and "still felt bitter about previous treaty violations."[15] The tribe was negotiating from a weak position, however, and failure to reach an agreement with the government would have proven catastrophic. Tribal funds had nearly run out and the specter of another starvation winter like the one that claimed nearly a quarter of the Blackfeet just ten years earlier must have loomed large in the minds of their leaders. Nothing could prevent miners from invading the reservation; the tribe might eventually have to give up the land without any compensation.[16]

Despite the almost unavoidable necessity of selling land once again to the United States, a number of important Blackfeet leaders refused to come to any agreement with the commissioners. Moreover, as many as one-fifth of the eligible treaty signers stayed away from the most important tribal gathering of the year and hunted in the mountains instead. Ultimately such resistance had a profound effect on the final agreement between the commissioners and the Blackfeet. As he accepted the treaty agreement on behalf of his tribe, White Calf could not help but reflect on the mortal blow the entire process had dealt his people. Conjuring up the image of the reservation as the Blackfeet tribal body, he stated: "Chief Mountain is my head. Now my head is cut off. The mountains have been my last refuge." To alleviate some of the damage, and to insure that the Blackfeet would continue as a people, he stipulated that any agreement between the tribe and the United States must guarantee certain usufruct rights in the ceded area. Various tribal leaders seconded this last-minute addition to the agreement, and it received enthusiastic applause from all the assembled Indians. The commissioners acquiesced and the Blackfeet retained rights of access and use of the ceded mountains "so long as . . . they remain[ed] public lands of the United States." Although the "public lands" phrase was not part of the original negotiations, the Indians reasonably could expect to retain their rights to the mountains in perpetuity; the area had no agricultural value, and as Grinnell apparently reassured them, it never would support long-term mining.[17]

The Senate ratified the land cession agreement in June 1896, but the government could not complete a survey of the area and open it to mining claimants until April 1898. Prospectors trespassed on the reservation, and both Grinnell and his friends in the United States Geological Survey worried about the effects of miners' fires on the forests and watersheds of the Glacier area. Shortly after ratification of the Blackfeet agreement, Grinnell worked to have the "ceded strip" included in a proposed forest reserve that Gifford Pinchot, John Muir, Charles Sargent, and others were then surveying on the western side of the continental divide. Grinnell's efforts succeeded; on February 22, 1897, President Grover Cleveland signed a proclamation to establish the Lewis and Clark Forest Reserve at the headwaters of the Missouri, Columbia, and Saskatchewan rivers. In doing so the president made special note that Blackfeet "rights and privileges . . . respecting that portion of their reservation relinquished to the United States . . . shall be in no way infringed or modified." The Blackfeet already had become aware of the proposed forest reserve in summer 1896, but there is no record that any tribal leaders expressed concern over the new status of their recently ceded lands. If anything, such a reserve would have curtailed some of the damage wrought by prospectors, thus further preserving the resources upon which many Blackfeet families depended.[18]

As Grinnell predicted, the region held no great mineral wealth; the ephemeral boom busted in a few short years. By the turn of the century he had brought together a coalition of wilderness enthusiasts, senators, congressmen, and railroad magnates in a campaign to convert part of the Lewis and Clark Forest Reserve into a national park. After ten years of hard lobbying his efforts proved successful and on May 11, 1910, the Glacier National Park bill became law. Unlike the proclamations that established the forest reserve, the Glacier National Park act made no mention of the rights reserved to the Blackfeet in 1895. There is no evidence that any Indians opposed the creation of the national park; indeed a few Blackfeet strongly supported the effort, particularly members of the tribal business council who saw it as a potential boon to the reservation's economy. The new law stipulated that the area would be removed from "settlement, occupancy, or disposal . . . and set apart as a public park"; this must have seemed a solid guarantee of the ceded area's "public land" status, ensuring Blackfeet rights to the area would remain intact.[19]

The Call of the Mountains

In the first years after the creation of Glacier National Park, neither tourists nor park official seemed to trouble themselves about the Blackfeet, and early advertisements for Glacier closely identified the tribe with the new park. As the most influential force in developing and promoting Glacier, the Great Northern Railway used its vast public relations machinery to plant photographs and stories about the Blackfeet in magazines and newspapers throughout the country. The railroad also produced countless advertisements featuring Indians amidst spectacular alpine scenery; most of this advertising copy referred to the Blackfeet as the "Glacier Park Indians" and encouraged visitors to acquaint themselves with these "specimens of a Great Race soon to disappear." The "vanishing Indian" sentiment expressed in such advertisements was regaining popularity, and most visitors made the Blackfeet an important part of their vacations in Glacier National Park.[20]

Early tourists could hardly avoid associating the "Glacier Indians" with the park; from Indian art in the train cars to Blackfeet greeters at the Glacier Park station, from tepees and dances on the manicured lawns in front of the Great Northern's magnificent hotels to the veritable museum of Plains artifacts on display in hotel lobbies, they must have felt surrounded by Indians.[21] As early park promoter Edward Frank Allen wrote, Glacier seemed to preserve a place and a time when "there were no camps . . . and the Indians knew not the restrictions of the reservation." Consequently, "the majesty of the mountains is as undefiled and as poignant as [ever], and the region is still aloof from the desecrating hand of man." Blackfeet dancers at the hotels certainly imparted a sense of Indian "presence" to the mountains beyond, but their physical absence from the most heavily visited lakes, streams, and mountains of the park actually enhanced the tourist experience of Glacier. Allen reminded his readers that the Blackfeet may have "hunted in the mountains and fished in the lakes [but these] are now yours as an American citizen. That is a better thought as you glide over the surface of [a] lake than it possibly can be as drawn on a printed page. Glacier Park is yours and your children's!"[22]

Such a celebration of "non-Indian" wilderness did not stem from a latent fear of past Indian "atrocities." It reflected instead the deeply held values that shaped and defined how Americans experienced wilderness in Glacier National Park. Located in the northernmost stretch of the nation's grandest mountain range, Glacier was both figuratively and literally the crowning natural feature of the United States. It became a "sacred place" where tourists combined an experience of sublime nature with a

*Lawrence D. Lindsley, employed by the Great Northern Railway
to photograph Glacier National Park in 1914, photographed
(from left to right) Jack Big Moon, Medicine Owl, John Ground (Eagle Calf),
and Yellow Medicine (Phillip Wells) at the outlet of Ptarmigan Lake.*

Montana Historical Society Photograph Archives, Helena

deep sense of patriotism.[23] The Blackfeet may have used the Glacier area for many generations, but tourists and park managers believed that only citizens of an emerging world power could experience the mountains with appropriate awe and reverence. As undiscovered or rarely visited portions of Blackfeet territory, the northern Montana Rockies had intrinsic importance only for a few thousand Indians; but as the "Crown of the Continent," Glacier represented the power and grandeur of the entire country. Furthermore, the area's designation as a "public park or pleasuring ground for the benefit and enjoyment of the people" heartily reaffirmed the most cherished principles of democracy and equality. The Blackfeet also could enjoy the park once they had become sufficiently civilized and embraced all the prerogatives and benefits of citizenship. In the meantime Glacier National Park belonged to "the people" while the Blackfeet belonged on their reservation where they could best pursue the "white man's road."[24]

Although a visit to the new national park certainly appealed to the patriotic sensibilities of many tourists, particularly during the First World War, the idea of spending time in the Montana wilderness appealed to all visitors at a much more personal level. "The call of the mountains," as Mary Roberts Rinehart described it in an often reproduced promotional piece for the Great Northern Railway, offered the promise of throwing "off the impedimenta of civilization [and] the lies that pass for truth." In the mountains you could "throw out your chest and breathe; look across green valleys to wild peaks where mountain sheep stand impassive on the edge of space" and experience your "real" self.[25] For Rinehart and many others Glacier presented a fantasy realm where individuals could play out little frontier dramas and, like their European forebears, reinvigorate their lives through contact with the essential elements of the American wilderness. Although the Blackfeet inhabited the fringes of this frontier, standing at train stations or dancing in front of the hotels, they remained curiously absent from the tourist's experience of the Glacier backcountry—the "real" wilderness. Outside the hotels, the visitors were told, Glacier National Park preserved a vestige of the virgin continent where vacationing adventurers could experience the North American wilderness at the dawn of discovery.[26]

Naturalizing the Wilderness

If tourists viewed Glacier as a personal proving ground, a national symbol, and a pleasure resort, park officials were obligated to maintain this uninhabited wilderness preserve in order to meet two other significant objectives. The legislation that created Glacier took note of the region's scenic beauty and recreational potential but emphasized the area's importance as a game preserve and an arena of scientific inquiry as well. Consequently, the Glacier National Park Act stipulated that, in the interest of science and game protection, all must remain in an undisturbed "state of nature." An abundance of wild animals in the park also furthered the recreational appeal of Glacier since tourists expected to see wildlife near the roads and hotels and in the backcountry. Nevertheless Glacier required considerable management and manipulation to retain its "original" wilderness condition, and park officials implemented programs of predator reduction and winter feeding to increase populations of deer, mountain sheep, elk, and moose.[27]

During the first years of the park's administration, populations of game animals swelled after rangers and licensed hunters killed dozens of eagles and wolves and hundreds of coyotes. Glacier officials also worked to eliminate poaching, but their success against hunters from southern Alberta and communities west of the park could not be matched on the park's border with the Blackfeet reservation. No doubt chafing at any mention of the Great Northern's "Glacier Park Indians," park officials made repeated attempts to exclude Indians from the Glacier backcountry from the early 1910s onward. Problems with the Blackfeet involved more than just hunting, but concerns about game-protection framed the government's opposition to any native use of park lands. Because Blackfeet claims on Glacier challenged the authority of park officials and undermined the recreational, scientific, and symbolic significance of the national park, the "Indian threat" soon developed far beyond the bounds of a local dispute between hunters and rangers.[28]

Within a few years, the issue grew into a protracted battle between the tribe and the United States that involved various federal and state agencies, touched on key constitutional issues, led to a legal clarification of public lands, and captured the attention and energy of leading preservationists. The idealization of uninhabited wilderness affected others besides the Blackfeet; exclusion of Indians from Glacier's backcountry accompanied government efforts to extinguish all private inholdings in the park and mirrored a more successful anti-poaching program against white hunters. But the issue of Blackfeet rights in the park outlasted and far surpassed concerns about non-Indian hunters and private cabins on the west side of the park. The legal complexities of the conflict between park officials and the Blackfeet, the strength of tribal opposition to exclusion from the park, and the radically different meanings that Indians and non-Indians attached to the park landscape all created a unique and potent arena of contention that has so far defied resolution.

At least one-third of the Blackfeet depended to some extent on the resources of the Glacier region in the park's early years, and many supported the protests of an Indian named D. D. LaBreche to gain recognition of tribal rights in the park. In response to LaBreche's efforts on behalf of the tribe, Secretary of the Interior Franklin K. Lane sought to bolster his department's policies regarding Blackfeet hunting in the park.

‎The call of the Mountains

Vacations in

Glacier National Park

The Great Northern Railway used vivid images of Blackfeet Indians, such as the one in this 1925 brochure, to promote vacations in Glacier National Park.

He requested an opinion from Interior Department attorneys, eliciting from the government solicitors an eight-page report in which they concluded that Blackfeet rights ceased with the creation of the national park. The secretary directed that a copy of this report be sent to the Blackfeet agent and, hoping to wash his hands of the entire matter, tersely ordered him "to give due notice thereof to the Indians under his charge."[29]

Although the Glacier National Park act remained ambiguous on the question of Blackfeet rights, attorneys for the Interior Department concluded that park administrators had good legal grounds to exclude Indians from Glacier. Their argument rested on three key points: (1) since a national park is not subject to disposal or sale by the federal government, it can not be considered public land; (2) the Glacier Park Act of 1910 superseded the 1895 agreement because Blackfeet rights held only so long as the area remained "public land of the United States"; and (3) according to the 1903 Supreme Court decision in *Lonewolf v. Hitchcock*, Congress had plenary authority over Indian affairs, which gave it the right to abrogate an earlier agreement by unilaterally changing the "public" status of the lands on the western boundary of the Blackfeet reservation. Although these legal conclusions must have brought some comfort to park administrators and the secretary of the interior, the Blackfeet carried on their protests to government officials and continued to exercise their rights within Glacier as they interpreted them.[30]

Land War and Stalemate

Along with their concern about Indian hunters on the east side of the park, Glacier officials became deeply troubled about hunting on the reservation. Having taken great pains to increase the numbers of game animals through predator reduction and winter feeding programs, park managers felt a proprietary interest in the elk, deer, and moose that left the mountains and drifted onto the reservation during the fall and winter months. Beginning in summer 1917 the newly created National Park Service sought to prevent the Blackfeet from hunting any migratory animals that "originated" in the park. Park officials quickly appealed to the Bureau of Indian Affairs for help, but the commissioners informed them that all Indians possessed a sovereign right to hunt on their reservations free of outside regulation. Unable to restrict hunting on Blackfeet lands, park officials then proposed moving the park boundary further east—which would have involved removing hundreds of Indians from their homes—or at least extending their authority to the Many Glacier Highway that ran through the reservation. The commissioner of Indian affairs also balked at these proposals, but he could no longer withstand the increasing demands from the National Park Service for a resolution of the Blackfeet "problem."[31]

As director of the park service, Stephen Mather received strong support from national reservationist groups in his dealings with the Bureau of Indian Affairs. Hearing of Glacier's troubles with the Blackfeet, William T. Hornaday, the director of the New York Zoological Park and trustee for the Permanent Wild Life Protection Fund, complained to Secretary Lane about "Piegan Indians . . . openly slaughtering the game in the northern portion of Glacier Park"; he urged the secretary to force the Bureau of Indian Affairs "to remedy this abuse." Horace Albright, then assistant director of the National Park Service, shared Hornaday's concerns, noting that "anybody who knows anything about this feels that if the Indian office were drastic enough in its control the killings could be stopped." Even the venerable George Bird Grinnell lent his considerable weight to the issue, suggesting that "this matter may easily be remedied provided the Agent is willing to give orders to his Indians that the laws of the State of Montana are in operation on the Indian reservation." Although state laws had no authority on tribal lands, Grinnell felt that enough pressure from Secretary Lane would persuade the Indian agent to overlook such legal technicalities.[32]

The issue went well beyond game protection, as Hornaday made abundantly clear in a subsequent letter to Secretary Lane. "In view of the character of Glacier National Park and all that it stands for with the American people," he wrote ominously. "I think it would be deplorable for any of its winter-driven game to be killed for food contrary to the laws of the State of Montana." Although Lane complained of the difficulty in policing the western boundary of the reservation, he conceded "the importance of affording every protection to the game of our National Parks" and finally promised that "a special effort will be made to see that there is no further abuse by the Indians of the Blackfeet Reservation." Under the secretary's orders, the commissioner of Indian affairs then directed the Blackfeet agent to post notices throughout the reservation

unanimously rejected the proposal. Albright and park officials hoped the Indians could be swayed, but the tribe rebuffed his efforts again on several more occasions. In the spring of 1935 Superintendent Scoyen met with Blackfeet agent J. H. Brott and Tribal Business Council president Joseph W. Brown, and Scoyen learned first hand just how much bad blood ran among the Blackfeet in their opinions of the National Park Service. Much to his regret Scoyen informed his superiors that they would have to abandon their dream of extending the park eastward.[37]

By 1935 relations between the Blackfeet and the National Park Service had reached an impasse that remains in place to this day. On one side the park service, tourists, and preservationists largely made Glacier into the uninhabited wilderness that continues to inform potent ideas about Nature and national identity. Blackfeet use of park lands undermined this idealized notion of wilderness, and the tribe's resistance to Glacier's eastward expansion limited its physical expression. Tension between Indians and the park service subsided over the next few decades, but the issue of Blackfeet rights in the eastern half of Glacier never disappeared.[38]

By the 1960s few Blackfeet actually hunted near the park, and fewer still went to the mountains to gather traditional plant foods and medicines. But the continuing importance of the Backbone of the World never depended on how many people went to the mountains. Although the Glacier region provided the tribe with a large portion of its physical sustenance in the 1890s, the issue of Blackfeet rights in the area always had reflected concerns about cultural persistence and tribal sovereignty. In conjunction with the "Red Power" movement of the 1970s, these concerns arose again as Blackfeet leaders pushed for recognition of tribal rights in the park. Their efforts met with strong opposition from both park officials and environmentalists, who resisted the Blackfeet "threat" as fervently as they did plans to mine coal and explore for oil near the park.[39] The state of near-war that once characterized relations between the Blackfeet and park officials resurfaced in the early 1980s; the two sides only narrowly avoided armed conflict on several occasions. Ultimately, continued Indian protests, the ongoing risk of violence, and Blackfeet proposals for joint management of the eastern half of Glacier forced the National Park Service to revisit issues its leaders thought had been buried in the 1930s.[40]

Past, Present, and Future

At the height of efforts to extend Glacier's eastern boundary, Arthur E. Demaray, assistant director of the National Park Service, described the western portion of the Blackfeet reservation, "by topography and location, [as] a logical part of the park."[41] The unstated logic of his idea, which continues to inform park policy to this day, was that Indians must be excluded from this area in order for the ecosystem to operate "naturally." In recent years the park service has begun to see that Blackfeet use of the Glacier backcountry does not necessarily compromise the integrity of the park environment, which in turn has led to greater cooperation between park superintendents and the tribal council. Future progress depends on the park service's slow recognition that the Glacier wilderness is more a cultural construct than an absolute condition of nature, and that its construction came at the expense of the Blackfeet. At this writing the basic issue of Blackfeet claims on Glacier remains unresolved, but the tribe's increasingly successful efforts to exercise the rights reserved to them in 1895 could revolutionize the way all Americans experience the national parks. If fully recognized, Blackfeet claims would make plain that the American wilderness ideal is predicated on Indian dispossession. The notion of a usable or inhabitable wilderness implies that the status of human beings in Nature is something more than that of "visitors not to remain." More particularly, viewing the eastern half of Glacier as both the "head" of the Blackfeet people and the "Crown of the Continent" might lead tourists to see themselves as visitors in Indian country and not simply as pilgrims at an American shrine. Supporting rather than restricting Blackfeet use of the park would further tribal efforts to reclaim their traditions and, in the process, strengthen their ability to remain a politically and culturally distinct nation.[42]

NOTES

1. Quotation from advertisement in the *Saturday Evening Post,* May 15, 1926, reproduced in frame 40, roll 1, vol. 1, Great Northern Railway Company, Advertising and Publicity Department, Magazine and Newspaper Advertisements, 1884–1970 (hereafter GNRC Advertisements, 1884–1970), microfilm edition, Minnesota Historical Society, Minneapolis (hereafter MNHS).

2. Recent archaeological evidence suggests that Blackfeet use of the Glacier area stretches back more than a thousand years. See Brian Reeves and Sandy Peacock, "'Our Mountains Are Our Pillows': An Ethnographic Overview of Glacier National Park," May 1995, pp. 70–82, draft submitted to the National Park Service, Rocky Mountain Region, Denver. See also Clark Wissler, *Material Culture of the Blackfoot Indians,* vol. 5, *Anthropological Papers of the American Museum of Natural History* (New York, 1910), 11–20. The Blackfeet are not the only native group with a strong connection to the Glacier area; the confederated Salish and Kootenai tribes of the Flathead valley long used the mountains now contained within the national park, as did the Kalispell (Pend d'Oreille) and bands of Crow, Gros Ventre, Nakota, Cree, and Assiniboine. See Reeves and Peacock, "Our Mountains Are Our Pillows," 7–70; and James Sheire, *Glacier National Park: Historical Resource Study* (Washington, D.C., 1970), 3–47. Unlike other tribes, however, the Blackfeet were used extensively in park promotions from the 1910s through the 1930s, and only the Blackfeet had recognized treaty rights to the Glacier region at the time of the park's creation in 1910.

3. For discussion of the cultural and historical construction of wilderness see William Cronon, "The Trouble with Wilderness; or, Getting Back to the Wrong Nature," in *Uncommon Ground: Toward Reinventing Nature,* ed. William Cronon (New York, 1995), 78–79; Thomas C. Blackburn and Kat Anderson, eds., *Before the Wilderness: Environmental Management by Native Californians* (Menlo Park, Calif., 1993); and Gary Paul Nabhan, "Cultural Parallax in Viewing North American Habitats," in *Reinventing Nature?: Responses to Postmodern Deconstruction,* ed. Michael E. Soulé and Gary Lease (Washington, D.C., 1995), 87–101. For works that examine Indian removal from Yosemite and Grand Canyon National Parks see Mark Spence, "Dispossessing the Wilderness: Yosemite Indians and the National Park Ideal, 1864–1930," *Pacific Historical Review,* 65 (February 1996), 27–59; and Stephen Hirst, *Havsuw 'Baaja: People of the Green Water* (Supai, Ariz., 1985), 72–77.

4. See *Los Angeles Times,* October 29, 1995.

5. The term "Blackfeet" is confusing and deserves some clarification. I use it to refer to the Piik·ni or Piegan Indians residing on the Blackfeet Indian Reservation in northern Montana, who officially refer to themselves at the Blackfeet Nation. The Piik·ni are historically and culturally affiliated with the Siksik· (Blackfoot) and Kainaa (Bloods), and together they compromise the Nitsitapii. More commonly known as the "Blackfoot Confederacy," the Nitsitapii is made up of three bands that are divided between Canada and the United States. The Kainaa, Siksik·, and North Piik·ni live on three reserves in Alberta; the largest group within the confederacy, the South Piik·ni, live on their reservation in Montana. The Glacier area is important to all the Blackfoot tribes, but the Piik·ni have the strongest connection. For a comparative study of these three groups and their relations with the Canadian and United States governments see Hana Samek, *The Blackfoot Confederacy, 1880–1920: A Comparative Study of Canadian and U.S. Indian Policy* (Albuquerque, N.M., 1987). For a broader discussion of the sacred importance of the Glacier National Park area for the Blackfeet see J. Hansford C. Vest, "Traditional Blackfeet Religion and the Sacred Badger Two-Medicine Wildlands," *Journal of Law and Religion,* 6 (June 1988), 455–89.

The Blackfeet have a rich oral tradition; many of their stories concern the Glacier region. The most accessible written collection of stories is Percy Bullchild, *The Sun Came Down: The History of the World as My Blackfeet Elders Told It* (New York, 1985). As with all oral traditions, variations occur over time and between different storytellers, and much is altered in the process of transcription and translation. Nevertheless, the Napi stories have remained constant in nearly all of their geographic particulars since their first recording by an outsider in 1810. For comparison see Alexander Henry and David Thompson, *The Manuscript Journals of Alexander Henry, Fur Trader of the Northwest Fur Company, and of David Thompson, Official Geographer and Explorer of the Same Company, 1799–1814*, ed. Elliott Coues (New York, 1897); John Mason Brown, "Traditions of the Blackfeet," *Galaxy*, January 15, 1867, 157–64; Clark Wissler and D. C. Duvall, *Mythology of the Blackfoot Indians*, vol. 2, pt. 1, *Anthropological Papers of the American Museum of Natural History* (New York, 1908); and Jack Holterman, "Seven Blackfeet Stories," *Indian Historian*, 3 (September 1970), 39–43.

6. Alfred Runte's "worthless lands" thesis, which argues that only those scenic lands with no residential or economic value have ever become national parks, may serve well for European-American valuations of these areas; but his assertion that such lands were also worthless to Native Americans is unfounded. Even tribes greatly dependent on buffalo hunting spent a large part of every year in the foothills and high mountain areas of the Rockies. Far from "worthless," these places often were the most frequently inhabited areas since they provided shelter from winter storms and summer heat, sustained large seasonal herds of important game animals such as elk, and served as the locale for large tribal gatherings and important religious celebrations. See Alfred Runte, *National Parks: The American Experience*, 2d ed. (Lincoln, Neb., 1987), 48–64. For studies that examine native use of mountainous national park areas see Spence, "Dispossessing the Wilderness"; Ake Hultkrantz, "The Indians in Yellowstone Park," *Annals of Wyoming*, 29 (October 1957), 125–49; Ake Hultkrantz, *The Shoshones in the Rocky Mountain Area* (Salt Lake City, 1974); and D. B. Shimkin, "Wind River Shoshone Ethnogeography," in *Anthropological Records*, ed. A. L. Kroeber, vol. 5 (Berkeley, Calif., 1947), 245–88.

7. Vernon Bailey, *Wild Animals of Glacier National Park* (Washington, D.C., 1918); Walter McClintock, "Appendix: Medicinal and Useful Plants of the Blackfoot Indians," in *The Old North Trail, or Life, Legends, and Religion of the Blackfeet Indians* (London, 1910), 524–31; Alex Johnston, *Plants and the Blackfoot* (Lethbridge, Alberta, 1987); Karen Peacock, "Appendix II: Ethnobotanical Plant Descriptions" in Reeves and Peacock, "Our Mountains Are Our Pillows," 334–472; John C. Ewers, "The Horse in Blackfoot Indian Culture, with Comparative Material from Other Western Tribes," in *Bureau of American Ethnology: Bulletin 159* (Washington, D.C., 1955); Oscar Lewis, "The Effects of White Contact upon Blackfoot Culture with Special Reference to the Role of the Fur Trade," (Ph.D. diss., Columbia University, 1942); Jaqueline Biedl, "The Blackfeet and the Badger–Two Medicine: An Evaluation of Potential Traditional Cultural Significance Drawn from Archival Sources," January 1992, George C. Ruhle Library, Glacier National Park, West Glacier, Montana (hereafter Ruhle Library). Blackfeet movements in the nineteenth century closely followed seasonal patterns established in the

pre-equestrian era, when the Glacier region may have supplied an even larger portion of the tribe's material needs. See Reeves and Peacock, "Our Mountains Are Our Pillows," 70–82; and Wissler, *Material Culture of the Blackfoot Indians,* 11–20.

8. John C. Ewers, *The Blackfeet, Raiders on the Northwestern Plains* (Norman, Okla., 1958), 277–312; William E. Farr, *The Reservation Blackfeet, 1882–1945: A Photographic History of Cultural Survival* (Seattle, 1984); Thomas R. Wessel, *Historical Report on the Blackfeet Reservation in Northern Montana,* 1975, Indian Claims Commission Docket No. 279-D, PAM 3653, copy in Montana Historical Society Library, Helena (hereafter MHS); Michael F. Foley, *An Historical Analysis of the Administration of the Blackfeet Indian Reservation by the United States, 1855–1950s,* 1974, Indian Claims Commission Docket No. 279-D, copy in MHS. Chief White Calf's statement comes from "Proceedings of Councils of the Commissioners Appointed to Negotiate with Blackfeet Indians," in United States Senate, *Agreement with the Indians of the Blackfeet Reservation,* 54th Cong., 1st sess., 1896, S. Doc. 118 (hereafter Senate, *Agreement with the . . . Blackfeet*).

9. For contemporary accounts of Blackfeet hunting in the Glacier area see George Bird Grinnell's entries for November 7, 1888, and September 23–24, 1889, in "Journals," George Bird Grinnell Collection (hereafter GBGC), Southwest Museum, Los Angeles, California (hereafter Southwest Museum); McClintock, *Old North Trail,* 14–15, 24, 47; Walter McClintock, *The Tragedy of the Blackfoot* (Los Angeles, 1930), 8–13; and Warren L. Hanna, *The Life and Times of James Willard Schultz* (Apikuni) (Norman, Okla., 1986), 138–44. See also Farr, Reservation Blackfeet; and Foley, *An Historical Analysis of the . . . Blackfeet Indian Reservation,* passim. Blackfeet elder Mike Swimms Under recalls that his family depended upon the success of his father's hunting in the Rockies at the turn of the century. Mike Swimms Under, conversation with the author, August 1994, Heart Butte, Mont.

10. For the earliest proposal for a national park see George Catlin, *Letters and Notes on the Manners, Customs, and Conditions of the North American Indian,* 2 vols. (1844; reprint, New York, 1973), 1:261–62. For discussion of late nineteenth-century Indian policy see Frederick E. Hoxie, *A Final Promise: The Campaign to Assimilate the Indians, 1880–1920* (Lincoln, Neb., 1984), passim. The Helen Hunt Jackson quotes come from *Bits of Travel at Home and Abroad* (Boston, 1894), 106–8.

11. For a discussion of Grinnell's early career see John F. Reiger, *American Sportsmen and the Origins of Conservation* (New York, 1975).

12. See Gerald A. Diettert, *Grinnell's Glacier: George Bird Grinnell and Glacier National Park* (Missoula, Mont., 1992), 47–59. Quotations are from Grinnell, "Journals," September 11, 7, 1891, GBGC, Southwest Museum. Shortly after returning to New York, Grinnell penned an article titled "The Crown of the Continent," which he submitted to *Century Magazine.* While the article contained his first public appeal for the creation of Glacier National Park, it was not published until 1901. See George Bird Grinnell, "The Crown of the Continent," *Century Magazine,* 62 (September 1901), 660–72.

13. For a discussion of Grinnell's efforts to "preserve" Blackfeet culture see Wessell, *Historical Report on the Blackfeet Reservation,* 68. Grinnell wrote often about the importance of wilderness recreation for urban Americans and the importance of "civilization" programs for the Indians. See, for example, George Bird Grinnell,

Blackfoot Lodge Tales (New York, 1895), xiii–ix; George Bird Grinnell, *The Story of the Indian* (New York, 1895), ix–x; and Grinnell, "Crown of the Continent," 660–72.

14. Christopher S. Ashby, "The Blackfeet Agreement of 1895 and Glacier National Park: A Case History" (master's thesis, University of Montana, 1985), 20–21; Wessell, *Historical Report on the Blackfeet Reservation,* 90–95; Foley, *An Historical Analysis of the . . . Blackfeet Indian Reservation,* 181–87; Diettert, Grinnell's Glacier, 61–64.

15. Little Dog, quoted in Senate, *Agreement with the . . . Blackfeet,* 9.

16. The Blackfeet ultimately received $1.5 million for the land, half the amount they originally demanded. The tribe saw very little of this money. A large portion of the funds were used to pay the salaries of agency personnel and to construct their offices and homes. Much of the money also went to pay off debts that resulted from earlier shortfalls in promised government funding. See Foley, *An Historical Analysis of the . . . Blackfeet Indian Reservation,* 142, passim.

17. See Senate, *Agreement with the . . . Blackfeet,* 16–21. For numbers of absent Blackfeet see Grinnell, "Journals," September 28, 1895, GBGC, Southwest Museum. The Blackfeet may have been more amenable to selling the mountains since the land cession agreement amounted to little more than a short-term lease of mineral rights. Indeed, there is evidence that suggests the Blackfeet leaders may well have viewed the land cession agreement as a lease and not a sale. See Phillip E. Roy, "Position Paper of the Blackfeet Tribe of the Blackfeet Indian Reservation: Regarding that Portion of the Lewis and Clark National Forest which was in 1896 Divested from the Blackfeet Indian Reservation by an Act of Congress," September 19, 1979, copy in collection of author. I am grateful to the office of Chief Earl Old Person, chairman of the Blackfeet Tribal Council, for providing me with a copy of this document.

18. *U.S. Statutes at Large,* 29 (1897): 911. The origins of the Lewis and Clark Forest Reserve are discussed in Diettert, *Grinnell's Glacier,* 73–75; and Sheire, *Glacier National Park,* 143–44. Muir joined the survey as an ex officio member. For the early history of forest management in the northern Rocky Mountains see Hal K. Rothman, ed., *I'll Never Fight Fire with My Bare Hands Again: Recollections of the First Forest Rangers of the Inland Northwest* (Lawrence, Kans., 1994). The Blackfeet first learned of the proposed forest reserve from Walter McClintock, who had worked as the photographer for Pinchot's surveying party. See McClintock, *Old North Trail,* 20.

19. For political efforts that led to the creation of Glacier National Park see Diettert, *Grinnell's Glacier,* 80–95; and Michael G. Schene, "The Crown of the Continent: Private Enterprise and Public Interest in the Early Development of Glacier National Park, 1910–1917," *Forest and Conservation History,* 34 (April 1990), 69–75. For an example of Blackfeet support of the new national park see Robert J. Hamilton to Louis W. Hill, March 19, 1912, Roads—Indians Support file, Ruhle Library.

20. Quotes from various advertisements for the promotion of Glacier tourism come from rolls 1 and 6, vol. 1, GNRC Advertisements, MNHS.

21. For an excellent study of Great Northern's promotion of Glacier National Park see Marguerite S. Shaffer, "See America First: Tourism and National Identity, 1905–1930" (Ph.D. diss., Harvard University, 1994), 92–143. See also Ann T. Walton, John C. Ewers, and Royal B. Hassrick, *After the Buffalo Were Gone: The Louis Warren Hill, Sr., Collection of*

Indian Art (St. Paul, Minn., 1985); and Ann Regan, "The Blackfeet, The Bureaucrats, and Glacier National Park, 1910–1940" (paper presented at the Western History Association Conference, Billings, Montana, October 1986), copy in Ruhle Library.

22. Edward Frank Allen, ed., *A Guide to the National Parks of America* (New York, 1915), 93–94, 96. Robert Sterling Yard echoed these sentiments in a popular souvenir publication on the national parks in which he wrote, "Glacier [was] once the favorite hunting ground of the Blackfeet [but] . . . now . . . [it is] strictly preserved." See the *National Parks Portfolio* (New York, 1916).

23. John F. Sears, *Sacred Places: American Tourist Attractions in the Nineteenth Century* (New York, 1991). Robert "Bob" Marshall expressed these sentiments most succinctly when he wrote that anyone "who will . . . [visit] the glaciers and snow-capped peaks of the great Northwest will surely return with a burning determination to love and work for and if necessary to fight for and die for the glorious land which is his." See Robert Bradford Marshall, *Annual Report* of the *Superintendent of National Parks to the Secretary of the Interior* (Washington, D.C., 1916), 2.

24. Quotation from *An Act to Establish Glacier National Park, U.S. Statutes at Large,* 36, pt. 1 (1910): 354 (hereafter *An Act to Establish Glacier National Park*). For sentiments regarding Glacier as a "people's" national park see Mary Roberts Rinehart, *Tenting To-Night: A Chronicle of Sport and Adventure in Glacier Park and the Cascade Mountains* (New York, 1918), 98.

25. Though reprinted in countless promotional brochures, this originally comes from Mary Roberts Rinehart, *Through Glacier Park: Seeing America First with Howard Eaton* (New York, 1916), 24–25.

26. Kerwin Klein argues that public lands in the West have retained this appeal for at least a century. See "Frontier Products: Tourism, Consumerism, and the Southwestern Public Lands, 1890–1990," *Pacific Historical Review,* 62 (February 1993), 39–71.

27. The quotation is from *An Act to Establish Glacier National Park*. Some of the many scientific studies published by the government and sold to tourists included Bailey, *Wild Animals of Glacier National Park*; and Marius R. Campbell, *Origin of the Scenic Features of the Glacier National Park* (Washington, D.C., 1914). Game preservation was a key factor in winning support for the creation of Glacier and other national parks. See Reiger, *American Sportsmen and the Origins of Conservation,* 93–113.

28. For an overview of poaching on the western portions of Glacier National Park see Louis Samuel Warren, "The Hunter's Game: Poachers, Conservationists, and Twentieth-Century America" (Ph.D. diss., Yale University, 1993), 288–98. The park superintendent's annual reports and correspondence between government agencies detail the concerns and efforts of government officials to exclude the Blackfeet from Glacier National Park in the 1910s. For examples of park administration and interagency efforts as early as 1912 see James L. Galen, *Report of the Superintendent of the Glacier National Park to the Secretary of the Interior* (Washington, D.C., 1913), 15; Acting Superintendent to Glacier National Park Rangers, September 24, 1912, folder 95, box 15, Superintendent's Subject Files, 1908–1929, Record Group 75, Records of the Blackfeet Agency, Bureau of Indian Affairs, National Archives, Rocky Mountain Region, Denver, Colorado (hereafter RG 75, NA, RMR); and Ucker to Chapman,

August 1, 1912, Game Protection folder, box 23, Central Files, 1907–1939 (hereafter CF 1907–39), Record Group 79, General Records of the National Park Service, National Archives, Washington, D.C. (hereafter RG 79, NA).

29. Stephen Mather to Solicitor, September 4, 1915, Game Protection folder, box 23, CF 1907–39, RG 79, NA; D. D. LaBreche to Franklin K. Lane, November 1, 1915; Secretary of the Interior to Commissioner of Indian Affairs (hereafter CIA), January 6, 1916, file 119292-1916, Blackfeet 115, Central Classified Files, 1907–1939 (hereafter CCF 1907–39), Record Group 75, Records of the Bureau of Indian Affairs, National Archives, Washington, D.C. (hereafter RG 75, NA); Solicitor to the Secretary of the Interior, January 7, 1916, file 119292-1916, Blackfeet 115, CCF 1907–39, RG 75, NA; E. B. Meritt to Charles L. Ellis, January 14, 1916, file 119292-1916, Blackfeet 115, CCF 1907–39, RG 75, NA. See also Warren, "Hunter's Game," 298–300. Some 150 to 200 Blackfeet and their families hunted in the park area, and their efforts contributed to the livelihood of between 750 to 1,000 Indians out of an entire reservation population of approximately 2,300. See *Court of Claims for the United States, No. E-427: Blackfeet (et al.) Indians v. The United States, Evidence for Plaintiffs* (Washington, D.C., 1929), 119–27; and Ashby, "Blackfeet Agreement of 1895," 49–50. Blackfeet efforts to assert treaty rights to hunt off-reservation mirrored the concerns of other tribes throughout the West. The Wind River Shoshone, for instance, continued to hunt throughout western Wyoming long after court orders and agency regulations expressly prohibited such activity. See records in folder 208, Fishing and Hunting, box 4, General Correspondence Files, 1890–1960, Records of the Wind River Agency, RG 75, NA, RMR.

30. The Department of the Interior issued a number of inquiries and rulings on Blackfeet rights in Glacier National Park from the mid-1910s until the early 1930s. All are consistent with each other, but the clearest summary of the department's position comes from E. C. Finney, "Solicitor's Opinion of Blackfeet Rights on Glacier Park Land," June 21, 1932, copy in Ruhle Library.

31. CIA to Thomas Ferris, Superintendent, August 22, 1917, Blackfeet 115/66598, CCF 1907–39, RG 75, NA. A subsequent report from the Indian Field Service showed that some 338 Blackfeet owned land in the area between the park boundary and the highway. See O. A. Waetjen to F. L. Carter, Chief Ranger, Glacier National Park, April 11, 1928, Glacier National Park Archives, West Glacier, Montana (hereafter GNP); CIA to Thomas Ferris, Superintendent, July 30, 1917, Blackfeet 115/66548, CCF 1907–39, RG 75, NA; E. B. Meritt to Thomas Ferris, Superintendent, November 5, 1917, ibid.; Acting Director of the National Park Service to CIA, July 2, 1917, Blackfeet 115/66598, CCF 1907–39, RG 75, NA; Thomas Ferris, Superintendent, to CIA, November 19, 1917, ibid.; E. B. Meritt to Stephen Mather, December 3, 1917, ibid.; and CIA to Director of the National Park Service (hereafter Director, NPS), January 29, 1918, ibid. See also George E. Goodwin, "Glacier National Park," in *Report of the Director of the National Park Service to the Secretary of the Interior,* (Washington, D.C., 1917), 182–84; and Warren, "Hunter's Game," 301–5.

32. William T. Hornaday to Franklin K. Lane, April 7, 1919, Blackfeet 115/66548, CCF 1907–39, RG 75, NA; Horace Albright to Mr. Cotter, April 12, 1919, ibid.; George Bird Grinnell to William T. Hornaday, April 7, 1919, ibid.; William T. Hornaday to

Franklin K. Lane, April 9, 1919, ibid.; Franklin K. Lane to William T. Hornaday, April 16, 1919, ibid.; Horace G. Wilson to CIA, June 10, 1919, ibid.

33. William T. Hornaday to Franklin K. Lane, April 9, 1919, ibid.; Franklin K. Lane to William T. Hornaday, April 16, 1919, ibid.; Horace G. Wilson to CIA, June 10, 1919, ibid.

34. Chas. H. Burke to Fred C. Campbell, March 4, 1923, with enclosures, Blackfeet 115/17275, CCF 1907–39, RG 75, NA; J. Ross Eakin, "Superintendent's Monthly Reports to the Director, National Park Service," January 10, December 9, 1922, January 9, July 10, 1923, GNP. Little Chief to Senator Thomas Walsh, December 7, 1926, Blackfeet 115/7807, CCF 1907–39, RG 75, NA; Little Chief to Senator Thomas Walsh, January 23, 1928, with copy of 1924 petition attached, ibid.; CIA to Senator Thomas Walsh, March 21, 1928, ibid. See also Regan, "The Blackfeet, The Bureaucrats, and Glacier National Park, 1910–1940," 10–11; and Warren, "Hunter's Game," 318–22.

35. Daily reports for the Two-Medicine Ranger Station, November, December 1931, Ranger Station Log Books, GNP; E. T. Scoyen to Director, April 22, 1932, GNP. See also E. T. Scoyen to Director, NPS, May 26, 1931, enclosed in Scoyen to Director, April 22, 1932; Little Dog to CIA, December 4, 1909, vol. 22, Copies of Official Letters Sent, November 1878–June 1915, RG 75, NA, RMR; *An Act for the Relief of Certain Nations or Tribes of Indians in Montana, Idaho, and Washington, U.S. Statutes at Large,* 42 (1924): 21; *Court of Claims of the United States,* No. E-427: Evidence, 27–127.

36. See Finney, "Solicitor's Opinion"; and *Blackfeet (et al.) v. United States: Final Decision and Opinion* (Washington, D.C., 1935), 10–11.

37. Horace Albright to CIA, January 13, 1930, GNP; CIA to Horace Albright, January 24, 1930, ibid.; J. R. Eakin to Director, NPS, March 24, 1930, ibid.; E. T. Scoyen to Director, April 23, 1935, ibid.; A. E. Demaray to CIA, May 24, 1935, ibid.; E. T. Scoyen to Louis Glavis, Director of Investigations, United States Department of the Interior, June 27, 1935, ibid.; E. T. Scoyen to Director, NPS, June 29, 1935, ibid. The amount of correspondence generated by this subject over the years is enormous. The best summary of efforts to expand Glacier National Park eastward is an anonymous manuscript, "Glacier National Park, Montana: A History of Its Establishment and Revision of its Boundaries," n.d., pp. 6–19, copy in Ruhle Library. For early plans to extend the park's boundaries see Stephen Mather to Cato Sells, January 7, 1921, GNP. Along with their concerns about "park game" on the reservation, Stephen Mather and Horace Albright also hoped that extension of Glacier's boundaries would give the park service control over a number of lakes slated for development by the Bureau of Reclamation.

38. The Blackfeet still sought legal redress against the United States and the National Park Service in the 1950s and 1960s on at least three occasions. See Ashby, "Blackfeet Agreement of 1895," 52–60. Tension between the tribe and the NPS eased considerably in the 1940s as "surplus" game animals threatened to overgraze large areas of the park. By 1953 park officials even began to complain that Blackfeet hunters did not kill enough animals to keep the population of ungulates in check. See J. W. Emmert, Memorandum for Regional Director, April 3, 1953, GNP. For a thorough study of Glacier National Park management and changing attitudes about Blackfeet hunters in the 1940s and 1950s see Warren, "Hunter's Game," 344–50.

39. Thomas H. Watkins once criticized Blackfeet claims on Glacier with what might be called a "multiple conquest" thesis. The area did not morally belong to the tribe, he argued, because they had themselves conquered the Shoshone and taken the lands by force. Although the Blackfeet actually retook these lands from Shoshone "conquerors," who expanded into Blackfeet territory in the mid-eighteenth century, their legal claims on the park are not based on notions of ancient occupancy or "timeless" traditions. Indeed, the importance of the Glacier area to the Blackfeet in the twentieth century does not so much reflect the argument of "first in time [equals] first in right," as Watkins speciously put it, as it stems from ongoing efforts to maintain the social and political autonomy of the Blackfeet nation as recognized in treaties and agreements with the United States. For Watkins' argument see "Ancient Wrongs and Public Rights," *Sierra Club Bulletin,* 59 (September 1974), 15–16, 37–39. See also "Triple Jeopardy at Glacier National Park," *National Parks and Conservation Magazine* (September 1975), 20–22; and "Glacier: Beleaguered Park of 1975," ibid. (November 1975), 4–10.

40. For an overview of relations between the Blackfeet and the National Park Service in the 1980s see Kenneth P. Pitt, "The Ceded Strip: Blackfeet Treaty Rights in the 1980s," *American Indian Law Review,* 12 (September 1987), 18–43.

41. A. E. Demaray to Senator Burton K. Wheeler, February 17, 1930, GNP.

42. The phrase "visitors not to remain" comes from the so-called "Wilderness Act" of 1964. *U.S. Statutes at Large,* 78 (1964): 890–96.

*This photograph of Rankin family babies was taken some fifteen years
before Wellington decided his sister Edna's birth control campaign
embarrassed the family. Edna Rankin McKinnon,
standing to the right of Wellington, holds her baby, Dorothy.*

"Women's Matters"

Birth Control, Prenatal Care, and Childbirth in Rural Montana, 1910–1940

MARY MELCHER

In 1919 Belle Fligelman Winestine, a Montana woman suffrage activist and colleague of Jeannette Rankin, designed six maternity dresses for her pregnancy and decided to share her patterns with the nation's women. She sent them to Ladies' Home Journal. The editor sent her a formulaic rejection slip and a personal note: "The Ladies' Home Journal does not mention babies before they are born."

Silence surrounded matters of sex, contraception, pregnancy, and childbirth in the late nineteenth and early twentieth centuries. The women whom Mary Melcher, curator of history at the Arizona Historical Society Museum, discusses in this essay came of age in a period when information about reproduction and contraception was considered obscene, abortion was illegal, and prenatal care was rare. In 1873 Congress passed the "Act for the Suppression of Trade in, and Circulation of Obscene Literature and Articles of Immoral Use," commonly known as the Comstock Law after one of its sponsors, Anthony Comstock. The law made the distribution of information about birth control, which was widespread in the mid-nineteenth century, illegal and punishable by stiff fines and prison sentences.

Montana's own congresswoman Jeannette Rankin introduced legislation in 1918–19 to provide state and federal funds for health clinics, midwife education, and visiting nurse programs in an effort to reduce the nation's infant mortality. It was not enacted until 1921 and was repealed only eight years later. As Melcher concludes, women had little recourse but to depend upon each other when dealing with "women's matters."

IN APRIL 1920 DOVIE ZEHTNER OF LIVINGSTON, MONTANA, WENT INTO LABOR. It was "an awful year," she recalled, "and our lane . . . the mud was awful deep in it." When Dovie's brother-in-law asked if he should fetch the neighbor woman or the doctor, Dovie told him, "go get Betsy." Before Betsy could get to the Zehtner's home, Dovie's husband delivered the first of two babies. When the second arrived Betsy was there to help twins and mother while father tied both navels.[1]

Similar birth scenes were common among rural and working-class women in Montana well into the twentieth century. While women in northeastern cities were using doctors to aid with childbirth as early as the beginning of the eighteenth century, many Montana women, like other rural western women, relied on neighbors, midwives, and husbands to attend them in childbirth. Due to poverty, poor roads, a lack of trained physicians, isolation, extreme weather, or their own choice, women in the Rocky Mountain West often did not have qualified medical care and turned to each other for aid in giving birth, as a source for contraceptive information, and for help in aborting.[2]

Many women had little or no knowledge of proper prenatal care, and the advice they received was often misinformed. They were told, "don't hang clothes on the line or you'll tie a cord around the baby's neck" and "don't climb stairs." Dovie Zehtner said there were lots of things pregnant women avoided, but working was not one of them. She continued chopping wood and caring for animals when she was pregnant, as did Hazel Dorr, who worked throughout her pregnancies. Once, when she was pregnant, she was kicked in the stomach by a cow. She felt sick but recovered after a visit to her doctor. [3]

Zehtner's and Dorr's reminiscences are drawn from thirty-eight oral histories of elderly Montana women interviewed between 1976 and 1989. The women were born between 1890 and 1905, and their childbearing years roughly spanned the years from 1910 to 1950. About one-third of the women were born in Montana, while the others had moved into the area from other states or foreign countries. The interviewees were working-class and middle-class women whose families had originated in Germany, Norway, Yugoslavia, Canada, Ireland, and England. Of the thirty-eight, twenty-six lived in rural areas.[4]

The women's vivid descriptions of prenatal care, childbirth, and birth control practices show how the experiences of rural western women differed from those of their eastern counterparts as well as from upper-class women. Examining how issues of sexuality and childbirth were treated in the West increases our knowledge of women's reproductive lives and helps to clarify the relation of those experiences with other areas of activity—from family to community work.[5] Such candid discussions, usually absent from nineteenth-century written sources, were obtained years later through oral history interviews. In the course of the interviews, the women discussed issues they probably would not have touched upon otherwise in diaries or letters. The fact that such information became available through interviews demonstrates the significance of oral history as a means of collecting information related to personal and family matters.

In 1900, about the time the interviewees were born, Montana still qualified as a frontier with 243,000 people scattered over 146,000 square miles, or 1.7 persons per square mile. By 1910 the state's population had grown to 2.6 persons per square mile, largely as a result of Montana's homesteading boom. Only 23,000 miles of roads—long stretches of which were impassable much of year—crisscrossed the state. In this sparsely populated land, people made a living from three main sources—agriculture, mining, and lumber. In the western third of the state, the Rocky Mountains—rich in copper, silver, and lumber—were a pleasure to the eye and spirit but were difficult to cross. In eastern Montana rolling hills and plains, broken by river valleys, seemed to stretch to the sky. Surrounded by subtle beauty, people farmed and ranched or lived in small towns and provided services for ranchers and farmers who grew wheat and raised cattle or sheep. In this arid land at least 640 acres were needed for a family to survive.[6]

From 1910 to 1940 the state's economy was in flux as Montanans experienced severe drought, agricultural depression, bank failures, and the Great Depression. It has been estimated that between 1909 and 1918, seventy thousand to eighty thousand people came to eastern and central Montana, enticed by advertisements portraying the state as a land of plentiful rainfall. By 1922 at least sixty thousand had left, driven out by pitiful amounts of rainfall and a lack of knowledge about dryland farming.[7]

More than half of Montana's commercial banks failed from 1920 to 1926. Although banks throughout the country that had loaned money on war-inflated commodity and land values also were folding, the numbers were not as great as in Montana where eleven thousand farms were lost, farm mortgage indebtedness climbed to $175 million, and the bankruptcy rate was the highest in the country. By the time the rest of the nation felt the impact of the depression, Montanans were already accustomed to tough economic circumstances.[8] Women on farms and ranches affected by such economic conditions often could not afford professional medical care, and as noted, rural Montana women generally lacked knowledge about prenatal care or birth control. The availability of effective birth control elsewhere in the nation during this period was erratic. Margaret Sanger coined the term birth control in 1915 when she began her campaign to bring to American women information about limiting families. In fighting the Comstock Law, which banned discussion of the topic, mailing of information about it, or importation of contraceptive devices, Sanger risked arrest and ridicule to publicize her message. She lectured, distributed pamphlets and magazines, and, in 1916, opened a birth control clinic in Brooklyn, New York, for which she spent one month in jail after being indicted for violating the Comstock Law. At her trial in 1918 she achieved a modicum of success when the judge interpreted the law broadly enough to allow doctors to prescribe birth control methods in New York state.[9]

Sanger was unsuccessful in other states where she campaigned for "doctors only" legislation to permit physicians to prescribe birth control. Still, sympathetic physicians did prescribe birth control even as many legislators and other doctors were reluctant to support contraceptive use. Not until 1937 did the American Medical Association support birth control, and as late as 1936 the great majority of medical schools provided little or no training about contraception. Only in cities where birth control clinics existed could a small proportion of American women secure reliable, women-controlled contraceptives.[10]

In Montana Edna Rankin McKinnon, sister of Jeannette Rankin, the nation's first congresswoman, attempted to distribute contraceptive information in 1937. Newly converted to the cause of birth control, McKinnon enthusiastically began her campaign but soon encountered resistance to birth control among both ordinary women and medical professionals. She discussed the subject in public meetings and shocked her audience, but a few women did ask questions.

Most doctors in the state refused to support birth control publicly, and none was willing to establish a clinic. Stung by lack of support, McKinnon met even stronger resistance from her brother Wellington Rankin, a prominent attorney. He feared her work would embarrass the family and undermine his own prestige. The combined opposition of her brother and the medical community forced McKinnon to abandon the struggle in Montana after six months. She moved to Tennessee where she found greater support for her efforts.[11]

The lack of medical support for birth control, combined with a general belief that sex should not be discussed, prevented many Montana women from getting reliable birth control information. Those who were less inhibited learned of what frequently were questionable contraceptive methods from neighbors, relatives, friends, and helpful nurses and doctors. Women taught each other to use diaphragms, douches, and various spermicides, one of which was coal oil. Mary Schye's mother tried a "golden thimble," a pessary made of metal and inserted by a doctor, but developed a vaginal infection. Another woman learned from her sister-in-law to make a gummy mixture which served as a makeshift sponge. She succeeded with this mixture but discussed it very little because "it was tabooed" to limit one's family. Other women controlled reproduction through abstinence and the rhythm method. Some denied using any method and said they wanted as many children as the Good Lord gave them.[12]

One ranch woman, who had only two children, practiced a form of birth control that she could not or would not describe. She limited her family, she said, "because when you had so much work to do, you can't do all of it. So the children were the minor thing." Many women wanted birth control to make their homework easier rather than to escape it. They were not rebelling against the traditional female role, but they were attempting instead to perform better within it.[13]

Although they lacked competent medical help for using the best contraceptives such as diaphragms, Montana women generally were using most of the methods available throughout the country. Despite the unreliability of contraceptive methods, lack of medical help, and questionable information, most of the interviewees had five or fewer children, suggesting that they achieved some success with contraceptives while also practicing abstinence.[14]

For some women, abortion was a last resort. In both the nineteenth and twentieth centuries American women commonly used abortion to stop unwanted pregnancies. Abortion was legal until the 1870s when a coalition of medical doctors and religious authorities lobbied for legislation to limit the practice. Prior to that time ending a pregnancy before "quickening" (when the mother felt fetal movement) was commonly acceptable. In the mid-nineteenth century American women may well have aborted at least one of every five pregnancies.[15]

Abortions continued after anti-abortion laws were passed in the 1870s. Moreover the public was unwilling to prosecute and juries unwilling to convict either abortionists or the women who consciously ended their pregnancies. As contraceptives became more reliable, women used abortion less frequently until the 1930s when, it has been estimated, poverty drove women to abort as many as one in four pregnancies.[16] One woman who lived on a ranch in western Montana in the 1930s described how she ended two pregnancies because she and her husband had no money. Alice, a strong pro-choice advocate in her eighties when interviewed in Arizona, discussed her motivation for having abortions in 1930 and 1932 when she was a young ranchwife:

> I became pregnant when we were just wretchedly poor, not abjectly poor because there was plenty to eat but there was no money for clothes and so forth because you couldn't sell anything to bring in any money. So that was a great handicap—tragedy—to become pregnant. I was determined and my husband was with me on it, that we wouldn't bring in any children into the world unless they had a chance at a decent life. And we couldn't even begin to pay a doctor's bill, let alone [the] hospital and the rest of it.[17]

To find an abortionist Alice contacted a pharmacist in a mining town nearly one hundred miles from the couple's ranch. The pharmacist was a friend of her family, and Alice knew that prostitutes came to him for medicine. He assured Alice that a woman he knew performed safe, clean abortions. He made an appointment for her, and she went to what she later discovered was a brothel. The slim, older-looking prostitute inserted into her uterus sterile packing, which she expelled later along with the embryo. Alice suffered no side effects and visited the woman for a second abortion in 1932. Each operation cost a hundred dollars. Because of negative feelings toward abortion in her community, Alice discussed the situation only with her mother, who supported her because she, too, believed bringing children into impoverished homes was wrong. When Alice and her husband were established and secure in 1940, she became pregnant again and gave birth to a daughter. In 1942 she delivered a second baby girl.

In later years Alice heard of a rancher's wife in her community who had been a prostitute before marriage and had performed abortions. Occasionally she also had helped neighbor women end unwanted pregnancies. Midwives and a few doctors also performed abortions, while some women induced abortions themselves using crochet hooks, knitting needles, heavy lifting, coat hangers, turpentine drinks, and phisophex douches.[18]

In contrast to the liberal views of Alice and a few others toward abortion, several of the Montana women who were interviewed expressed disapproval. Although aware of abortion incidences, some who discussed the topic were unsympathetic toward women who interrupted pregnancies and toward people who helped them do it.[19]

In 1916 Viola Paradise and other members of the Children's Bureau, a federal agency established in 1912 to study maternal and infant care, surveyed an eastern Montana county to determine the health of mothers and infants before, during, and after delivery. Paradise did not name the county but said it was sparsely populated and isolated; had poor roads; a total lack of telephones; experienced hostile weather; and lacked physicians, nurses, and hospitals. Visiting 463 mothers in an area larger than the state of Connecticut, Paradise and a coworker found that three-fourths of the women had no prenatal care at all; eighty-six received inadequate care, and only twenty-two had "fair" prenatal care. One-third of the women surveyed had attempted to learn about prenatal care from books and magazines. Because of their isolation, the report concluded, rural Montana women received health care at times worse than that of urban poor.[20]

In addition to inadequate prenatal care the Montana women Paradise surveyed also frequently lacked professional or even competent care at the time of delivery. Summarizing the kind of care the women said they had received at childbirth during the five years preceding the survey, Paradise reported: "One hundred and four mothers left the area for childbirth. Of the 359 who remained only 129 were attended by a physician. In other words, almost two-thirds of these mothers had to meet the ordeal of childbirth without competent medical care. Forty-six, or more than one in eight, were delivered by their husbands. Three were quite alone." Many women suffered serious complications during pregnancy or delivery, and eight women died. Paradise concluded that compared to other rural areas not only the county surveyed but Montana generally "has a very bad record of maternal losses."[21]

All American women, not just those in western rural areas, commonly feared death in childbirth at the turn of the century. It was not an unrealistic fear. Deaths associated with childbirth occurred sixty-five times more often in 1900 than in 1980, with approximately one mother in every 154 dying in connection with live births. One historian has estimated that one of every thirty mothers delivering an average of five live babies could expect to die in childbirth during her fertile years.[22]

Like women throughout the country, women in Montana experienced difficult presentation, prolonged labor, and lacerations, but often contended with these crises without competent care. One mother was in labor for three days and then experienced fainting spells for an hour. Another woman suffered a bad laceration that was not repaired. For nearly three weeks she could not get out of bed, and it was many weeks before she could walk around the house. Many other women hemorrhaged severely following delivery.[23]

One woman, plagued with hemorrhages and weakness for several months of her pregnancy, also suffered from a severe, unrepaired laceration from a previous confinement. During the sixth month of her pregnancy she saw a doctor who said she needed hospital attention. Her husband, however, was unpersuaded that the natural function of childbirth could be dangerous. During her confinement she had no labor pains but hemorrhaged excessively. They sent for a doctor, who arrived after a twenty-four-hour journey of thirty-five miles. With instruments he delivered a stillborn baby that had been dead for at least four days. When the mother also died seven days later, the doctor said he believed her death was caused by blood poisoning from the dead fetus.[24]

Another mother labored for three days with a baby presenting in a breech position. Her doctor finally ordered her to travel by automobile over rough roads to the nearest hospital—115 miles away. Because of her weakened condition, a cesarean section could not be performed, and a very large stillborn baby was delivered with instruments. The mother died the following day of exhaustion.[25]

Considering the quality of available care, it is not surprising that women feared for themselves or their neighbors when pregnancy neared delivery. One hundred and eighty-one of the mothers in the Children's Bureau survey were attended by women, most of whom were untrained neighbors or relatives. Women cared for each other. Often they were afraid and full of misgivings, but as one woman remarked, "a woman can't be left alone at such a time," so "one neighbor does it for another out here."[26]

Because of poor roads, rugged geography, and severe winter weather, rural Montana women often had little opportunity to choose who would be on hand when they delivered. In other parts of the nation in the early twentieth century, many women surrounded themselves with chosen companions as labor and birth neared. Not so in Montana, where half of the twenty-six rural interviewees described having assistance from neighbors, husbands, and midwives at delivery. For many women, the person who performed the delivery was less a matter of choice than of expedience in an emergency.[27] Mary Schye's own birth illustrates how an early spring snowstorm could lay waste to the best-made birthing plans. She explained: "When I was born, they said there was a terrible storm, March 27 [1917], and my father rode the fenceline all night trying to get to town to the doctor. The neighbor, Mrs. Babrosky, she was the midwife. She delivered me."[28]

During times of great stress such as miscarriage or childbirth, western women sometimes turned to each other more than to physicians. Kristina, a Norwegian immigrant, had a doctor who she said was "more of a horse doctor." She hemorrhaged following the birth of a daughter, but the doctor did not care for her properly or sew her wound. Later she had to have an operation to repair the damage.[29] In her memoirs, published as *A Bride Goes West,* Nannie T. Alderson recalled miscarrying when the nearest doctor was one hundred miles away. One of her hired hands said she needed a doctor, and she replied, "I don't want a doctor. I want a woman."

Her neighbor, one of five women in the area who cared for each other in emergencies, came to her.[30]

Katherine Y. Sweeting, a trained nurse, moved with her new husband to homestead in northern Montana in 1917. During the 1920s and 1930s, she assisted many women in childbirth, and neighbor men commonly knocked on her door at all hours to ask for her services when their wives went into labor. Sometimes she received meat or vegetables for her efforts, but she usually worked without pay of any kind. Women helped in childbirth much as people assisted each other in building barns and digging wells.[31] "I delivered four babies, by myself . . . with God," Annie Knipfer remembered. "That was where we learned what neighbors meant."[32]

Unlike midwives in Europe, most American midwives were not professionally trained. A few schools for midwives existed in the Northeast and the Midwest at the beginning of the twentieth century, but their course of instruction was poor. Excellent schools in New York City, Chicago, and St. Louis trained only a small percentage of all midwives. Most midwives received only a smattering of education focusing on how to manage normal confinements and when to call a doctor. They were

Women in northern Montana were fortunate to have the trained nursing skills of Katherine Sweeting, shown here playing with her baby, Phyllis, in 1922.

Montana Historical Society Photograph Archives, Helena

unfamiliar with modern obstetric techniques and usually allowed nature to take its course. Despite their paucity of professional education, American midwives had lower mortality rates in the early twentieth century than general practitioners because they had more practical experience and did not use interventionist methods, a practice which often caused problems for physicians. Midwives' practices were generally limited to friends and relatives who paid a very small amount, usually less than half that collected by general practitioners. In addition to attending the expectant mother, midwives performed a variety of household services not required of a physician.[33]

Catherine Hayes Murphy was a midwife, whose only training was having had ten children herself. She was motivated by a strong Catholic faith and her belief that neighbors should be interdependent.[34] Most interviewees who were midwives came from farms and ranches, but Katie, who lived in Milltown near Missoula, also delivered babies for her friends and neighbors. Possessing an innate nursing skill, Katie said she gradually gained practical experience.

> You talk about it and you study and you learn as you go along. You feel the pulse in the cord and when it quits pulsating you tie it . . . You did the best you could when you were in a place where you had coal or wood stoves and the water had to be brought in. You tried to make it so there wouldn't be infection . . . you'd take a piece of cloth and iron it until it was scorched, sterile as you could make it, then put it around the navel.

Often Katie walked in hip-deep snow to deliver winter babies. She helped in the mothers' homes but had children of her own so could not stay away for long. She never received payment for her services. "Everyone was so desperately poor," she said. "You wouldn't have thought of pay. You helped one another." Once she assisted a pregnant woman who had been kicked in the stomach by her husband and had given birth prematurely. Katie wrapped the newborn girl in homespun woolen blankets and placed hot-water bottles nearby to keep her warm. Another woman said that a premature infant was placed in a shoebox and warmed by jars of hot water, methods used by trained physicians and lay people alike.[35]

As Katie's experiences demonstrate, some town women continued to use midwives well into the twentieth century. Barbara, of Anaconda, remembered calling on a Croatian midwife to assist her in five deliveries

A devout Catholic, Catherine Murphy, pictured here standing near her home in Jordan, Montana, in 1920, relied on her faith to sustain her during her ten deliveries and as she helped neighbors during childbirth.

MONTANA HISTORICAL SOCIETY PHOTOGRAPH ARCHIVES, HELENA

from 1925 to 1941. Due to choice or poverty some town women preferred the services of midwives, but the great majority of town informants used the services of a physician. Ten of the twelve interviewees who lived in towns from 1910 to 1940 had a doctor in attendance while giving birth, much like eastern women.[36]

While the majority of Montana midwives simply assisted their friends and neighbors when called, some operated maternity houses to serve women in a specific area. While many of these women worked with physicians, others were on their own. In the country near Jordan in east central Montana, a Mrs. Baker ran a maternity home where women stayed when ready to give birth. Following common practice of the time, the women stayed in bed for at least one week after giving birth. Other midwives worked with doctors in maternity homes in Montana cities and towns.[37]

The training and methods of Aino Hamalainen Puutio, a Finnish midwife, contrast with the limited practical experiences of many Montana midwives. Midwife Aino immigrated to America in 1911 and soon moved to Montana where she practiced midwifery in and around Butte and later in Red Lodge. Pregnant women contacted Aino during the middle of their pregnancies to reserve her services. She gave her patients instructions on diet, proper rest, and physical activity. Near the end of their pregnancies she examined the women externally and instructed them in preparing their beds for delivery: "Several layers of newspapers were to be placed directly on the mattress, if waterproof covers were not available. Clean sheets, including a draw sheet, and blankets were to be used in making the bed. The baby's bassinet was most often a wicker wash basket lined with clean soft blankets or sheets; a soft pillow was usually the baby's mattress."[38]

Midwife Aino packed her straw satchel a day or so before the expected delivery. She carried linen towels; sterilized instruments, including forceps, scalpel, scissors, catheter, and thermometers; linen cord; several rolls of cotton; a small alcohol lamp with a wick; sterile nurse's aprons; and a wooden hollowed-out instrument used as a stethoscope. She also took along silver nitrate to place in the newborn's eyes, rubbing alcohol, disinfectant, and birth certificates.[39] When Aino assisted a woman in delivery, other members of the family were not allowed in the room. The husband was available to call a physician if Aino needed assistance. Following the delivery, she stayed with the new mother as long as necessary, then visited each day of her patient's confinement, bathing the baby and providing bed care. Her fee for delivery was fourteen dollars. She sometimes collected a couple of lambs, chickens, or pigs in lieu of her fee.[40]

Half of the rural women interviewed used the services of a neighbor or midwife in labor and delivery while the remainder chose a doctor's care. Several women who chose doctors could afford to pay for their services and lived in areas where competent physicians were available. But some women who believed they were soliciting more experienced professional care were sadly surprised by the incompetence of rural "quacks." Training of physicians in the early twentieth century involved little or no practical experience and often taught physicians to rely too heavily on forceps and other forms of intervention.[41]

In addition to poorly trained physicians, nurses also could give poor care. Frieda, a German immigrant, lost her first child while being attended in a hospital by a nurse. "They just let me suffer it out," she said. "They told me to hold my breath when I had a pain." Her baby was stillborn.[42] Another woman, Sophie Guthrie, said a "quack" tried to deliver her baby too quickly. She ordered him out of the house because he told Mr. Guthrie not to listen to Sophie if she became hysterical. Having had other children, she felt experienced enough to rely on her own instincts. She had her baby with only her husband's assistance.[43]

Many other women reported that doctors provided good care. In the rural area near Willow Creek, Dr. James Bradbury attended many women in childbirth, none of whom died, although a few babies did not live. Describing her father's work, Helen Bradbury Murphy said, "Babies were the best crop that was around." Dr. Bradbury, who had been trained at Northwestern University in Chicago, provided no prenatal care, believing pregnancy was a natural experience that required no intervention. Frequently he was called at all hours to attend women in childbirth and often accepted payment in kind. Unlike most midwives in America, he used forceps and opium when necessary to ease in a delivery.[44]

Montana women who lived miles from experienced physicians sometimes traveled to their home states to be attended by familiar doctors. Sara O'Connor followed her husband from Missouri to northeastern Montana to homestead in 1917. After spending a winter in a one-room shack with her husband and two children, she decided to return home in the spring because she was pregnant. She considered the country too wild and did not believe any doctor could attend her. Sara remained in Missouri for over a year after giving birth, hoping her husband would give up homesteading life. Eventually she was the one to give in and return to him. Later she gave birth to another child in a hospital in Miles City.[45] Other rural women traveled to town several weeks or a month before their time of delivery. If a hospital was not available they stayed with friends and relatives until they gave birth and during their period of bed rest.

As demonstrated by some of the women's experiences, childbirth remained hazardous in the early twentieth century even for those served by professional caregivers. Hospital births, attended by nurses and doctors, became increasingly attractive to middle-class American women in the 1920s and 1930s. Many physicians and women believed by this time that hospitals provided superior birthing conditions. Hospitals could offer the newest technological and scientific methods to aid women giving birth while affording patients comfort and freedom from domestic duties. New ideas concerning germ transmission and the benefits of a sanitary environment also enhanced the appeal of hospitals.[46]

Despite the promise of a sanitary environment and trained physicians, maternal death rates did not decrease during the 1920s and 1930s. The rate of postpartum infection actually rose throughout the 1920s as more women gave birth in hospitals. Regulation of obstetric practices increased during the next decade, after the medical profession investigated the failure of physicians to provide safe, sanitary hospital environments. Physicians also began using antibiotics to treat infections and transfusions to replace blood lost by hemorrhaging. Fifty-five percent of American births took place in hospitals by 1940 and 88 percent by 1950.[47]

Childbirth history in America can be said to fall into three periods. In the earliest period, what has been termed the "social childbirth" era, which lasted until the late eighteenth century, women cared for each other and were attended by midwives and female relatives. In the second period—from the late eighteenth century through the early decades of the twentieth century—a long transition occurred from "social childbirth" to medically managed birth when physicians gradually replaced midwives. In the third period, during the remainder of the twentieth century, the medical profession consolidated management of the process.[48]

Because of Montana's isolation, rugged land, severe weather, and small population, women often were attended by midwives, husbands, and doctors at home until the 1940s. While the majority of mothers outside the Rocky Mountain West relied on physicians during this period, Montana women labored and delivered under conditions similar to those experienced by women elsewhere in the nineteenth century. Even those conditions were tempered for Montana women when bad weather or poor roads prevented them from gathering their friends around them for the birth of a child. Complications in childbirth also were more serious because of the great distances separating ranches and towns. Additionally, Montana women had no access to birth control clinics and only limited access to sympathetic physicians who might prescribe contraceptives.

Despite, or perhaps in response to, these difficulties, many Montana women, like other isolated western women, aided each other in various ways. They shared information about birth control, helped abort unwanted pregnancies, and provided care in labor and delivery. Rural women "learned what neighbors meant" when they gave birth or miscarried. Untrained women, serving as midwives with no thought of compensation, represented one more example of a frontier ethic in which neighbors assisted each other in difficult situations. Although doctors aided many women in childbirth, Montana women were extremely dependent upon each other in times of emergency, making sisterhood a powerful force in rural Montana.

NOTES

1. Dovie Zehtner, interview by Kathy White, October 26, 1976, Livingston, Mont., tapes 44 and 45, Collection 49, Montana Women's Oral History Collective (hereafter MWOHC), Mansfield Library, University of Montana, Missoula (hereafter UM).

2. Catherine M. Scholten, "On the Importance of the Obstetric Art: Changing Customs of Childbirth in America, 1750–1825," *William and Mary Quarterly*, 34 (July 1971), 426–46; Judith Walzer Leavitt, *Brought to Bed: Childbearing in America, 1750–1950* (New York, 1986). Because they encountered greater difficulties in trying to control how their deliveries occurred, the experiences of Montana women differed from the middle- and upper-class women Leavitt describes.

3. Zehtner, interview; Hazel Dorr, interview by author, June 25, 1981, Neihart, Mont., tape 24, MWOHC, UM.

4. Thirty-one of the interviews are in MWOHC, UM and were conducted by Mary Melcher, Kathy White, and Eleanor Wend between 1976 and 1981. Indexes for these interviews are available in the Mansfield Library. Seven interviews were conducted by Mary Melcher in Mesa and Phoenix, Arizona, in 1989 and are in her possession. Several interviewees requested anonymity and are identified by fictitious first names. Their interviews are in MWOHC, UM but cannot be identified by name or tape number. Women who released their interviews are referred to by their full names.

5. Since the early 1970s women's historians have argued that women's reproductive roles are highly significant in the female historical experience. See Juliet Mitchell, *Woman's Estate* (New York, 1973), 101; Gerda Lerner, *The Majority Finds Its Past* (New York, 1975), 155–56; Linda Gordon, *Woman's Body, Woman's Right: A Social History of Birth Control in America* (New York, 1976), xiii; John D'Emilio and Estelle B. Freedman, *Intimate Matters: A History of Sexuality in America* (New York, 1988).

6. K. Ross Toole, *Twentieth Century Montana: A State of Extremes* (Norman, Okla., 1972), 22. Montana's population dropped from 548,889 in 1920 to 537,606 in 1930, then gradually increased to 559,456 by 1940. Bureau of the Census, *Sixteenth Census of the United States, 1940: Population*, vol. 1 (Washington, D.C., 1942), 615.

7. Toole, *Twentieth Century Montana*, 26–30.

8. Ibid., 80–92.

9. Gordon, *Woman's Body, Woman's Right*, 220–36, 249–55.

10. Ibid., 267–70; D'Emilio and Freedman, *Intimate Matters*, 243–44.

11. Wilma Dykeman, *Too Many People, Too Little Love; Edna Rankin McKinnon: Pioneer for Birth Control* (New York, 1974), 45–50.

12. Dorothy Sweeting Stepper, interview by author, March 8, 1989, Mesa, Ariz., in collection of author; Mary Schye, interview by author, March 7, 1989, Mesa, Ariz., in collection of author; Dona Corr, interview by author, December 19, 1980, Missoula, Mont., tape 8, MWOHC, UM; Dorr, interview; Lettie Cook, interview by author, June 25, 1981, Neihart, Mont., tape 57, MWOHC, UM; anonymous interviews, MWOHC, UM.

13. Anonymous interview, MWOHC, UM; Gordon, *Woman's Body, Woman's Right*, 322–23; Sandra L. Myres, *Westering Women and the Frontier Experience, 1800–1915* (Albuquerque, N.M., 1982), 154. Myres found that nineteenth-century western women used a variety of contraceptive methods, including spermicidal douches, the vaginal sponge, condoms, and coitus interruptus.

14. Fertility rates of nineteenth-century farm women, like those of women in urban areas, dropped throughout the century. See Richard A. Easterlin, "Factors in the Decline of Family Fertility in the United States: Some Preliminary Research Results," *Journal of American History*, 63 (December 1976), 603.

15. James C. Mohr, "Patterns of Abortion and the Response of American Physicians, 1790–1930," in *Women and Health in America*, ed. Judith Walzer Leavitt (Madison, Wis., 1984), 117–19.

16. Ibid., 119–22.

17. Anonymous interview by author, Phoenix, Ariz., in collection of author.

18. Diane Sands, "Using Oral History to Chart the Course of Illegal Abortions in Montana," *Frontiers,* 7 (1983), 32–37.

19. Zehtner, interview; Corr, interview. Other women who had anonymous interviews stated the same view. MWOHC, UM.

20. Viola Isabel Paradise, *Maternity Care and the Welfare of Young Children in a Homesteading County in Montana* (Washington, D.C., 1919), 10, 12.

21. Ibid., 13–14.

22. Leavitt, *Brought to Bed,* 23–25.

23. Paradise, *Maternity Care and the Welfare of Young Children,* 40.

24. Ibid., 43.

25. Ibid., 44.

26. Ibid., 32. Katherine Harris, "Homesteading in Northeastern Colorado, 1873–1920: Sex Roles and Women's Experience," in *The Women's West,* ed. Susan Armitage and Elizabeth Jameson (Norman, Okla., 1987), 165–78; Julie Roy Jeffrey, *Frontier Women: The Trans-Mississippi West, 1840–1860* (New York, 1979), 69.

27. Leavitt, *Brought to Bed,* 206–7; Leavitt, *Women and Health in America,* 155. Leavitt stresses the importance of three main components in childbirth: assistance, choice, and safety.

28. Schye, interview.

29. Anonymous interview, MWOHC, UM.

30. Nannie T. Alderson and Helena Huntington Smith, *A Bride Goes West* (1942; reprint, Lincoln, Neb., 1971), 200–201.

31. Stepper, interview.

32. Annie Knipfer, interview by Kathy White, August 25, 1976, Broadus, Mont., tape 28, MWOHC, UM.

33. Judy Barrett Litoff, *American Midwives, 1860 to the Present* (Westport, Conn., 1978), 27–30.

34. Joe Murphy, interview by author, March 16, 1989, Mesa, Ariz., in collection of author.

35. Anonymous interview, MWOHC, UM; Helen Murphy, interview by author, March 16, 1989, Mesa, Ariz., in collection of author.

36. Anonymous interview, MWOHC, UM.

37. Joe Murphy, interview.

38. Arlene Harris, "An Early Day Montana Midwife" (n.d., n.p.), 1, 2.

39. Ibid., 3.

40. Ibid., 3–4.

41. Leavitt, *Brought to Bed,* 142–70.

42. Anonymous interview, MWOHC, UM.

43. Sophie Guthrie, interview by Kathy White, August 1976, Livingston, Mont., tapes 20 and 21, MWOHC, UM.

44. Helen Murphy, interview.

45. Ruth O'Connor Butz, interview by author, March 16, 1989, Mesa, Ariz., in collection of author.

46. Leavitt, *Brought to Bed,* 171.

47. Ibid., 180–94.

48. Nancy Schrom Dye, "History of Childbirth in America," *Signs: Journal of Women in Culture and Society,* 6 (Autumn 1980), 98.

Charles Taylor, the big man immediately to the right of the "Fight Eviction" sign, made Plentywood's Producers News *a powerful voice for radicalism in Montana's far northeastern "red corner."*

"A Paper of, by, and for the People"

The Producers News and the Farmers' Movement in Northeastern Montana, 1918–1937

Verlaine Stoner McDonald

In the early twentieth century, not all Americans embraced capitalism. In 1910 Americans elected Socialists to local offices in twenty-four states, and in 1912 Eugene V. Debs ran for president of the United States on the Socialist ticket, garnering 6 percent of the popular vote. Ordinary people, not sure that capitalism was the most beneficial economic system, talked, wrote about, and explored alternatives. The Nonpartisan League and its successor, the Farmer-Labor Party, was only one of many organizations that publicly debated the merits of the American capitalist system. Before the advent of radio and television, much of that discussion took place in newspapers.

Sheridan County, in the far northeastern corner of Montana, supported twenty newspapers in the 1920s. A professor of English at Berea College in Berea, Kentucky, Verlaine Stoner McDonald, who grew up in Sheridan County, analyzes one of the most influential of its papers, the Producers News. The rise and fall of the Producers News illustrates the way in which newspapers functioned in a community, providing news, entertainment, and a forum for political and economic campaigning. The owners and editors of papers such as the Producers News and the Plentywood Herald had clear political agendas, and they used powerful rhetoric as a means to advance their goals. McDonald's essay reminds us that newspapers are far more than objective reporters of the news and, like other historical sources, need to be read with a critical eye.

IN 1933 THE NATIONAL OFFICE OF THE COMMUNIST PARTY (CPUSA) PUBLISHED A position pamphlet on the farmers' movement. An advertisement on the back cover declared: "For complete accounts of all farmers' activities, read: the *Producers News* . . . the *Daily Worker* . . . the *Communist*." The *Worker* and the *Communist,* both produced in New York City, were the CPUSA's well-known newspaper and theoretical magazine, respectively. The *Producers News,* a weekly newspaper, was issued from the unlikely location of Plentywood, Montana. This Sheridan County newspaper, published far from any well-known center of working-class activity, had been the mouthpiece for a series of political organizations, including the Nonpartisan League (NPL), the Farmer-Labor Party (FLP), and the United Farmers League (UFL) since 1918.[1]

The farmers' movement was strong in northeastern Montana. Operating under the aegis of the Nonpartisan League and, later, the Farmer-Labor Party, Sheridan County radicals virtually ran local government during the 1920s. Voters sent *Producers News* editor Charles E. Taylor to the Montana state senate for two terms and cast more votes in 1928 and 1932 for William Z. Foster, the Communist candidate for president, than any other county in the state. Their success, however, was short-lived. Even before the reforms of the New Deal began to affect Montana farmers, the farmers' movement was in serious decline. By the time the CPUSA advertised the *Producers News* in 1933, the Reds in Sheridan County had begun to lose ground with the farmers and would never regain their strength of the 1920s.[2]

The odyssey of rural radicalism in Sheridan County has captured the interest of several historians, one of whom called northeastern Montana "one of the most class-conscious areas in the nation" and noted that it had the most successful rural party organization during the 1920s. The "red corner" of Montana has even appeared in fiction. The conditions that gave rise to the farmers' movement—drought, insect infestation, and low commodity prices—have been documented.[3] The role played by the *Producers News* and editor Taylor has remained more obscure. The rhetoric purveyed in the *News* from its inception in 1918 until it ceased publication in 1937 served as a powerful weapon of radicalism in northeastern Montana. The newspaper was crucial to help move the movement. Ultimately, however, it lost touch with the local community and became more an instrument of national and international organizations. The effect was decline and eventually cessation.[4]

Located in the northeastern corner of Montana, Sheridan County is an intemperate place. Carved out of a larger Valley County in 1913, the area suffers long, brutal winters with subzero temperatures and driving winds.[5] Summer can be mild, or it can bring drought, hail, and insect plagues. The region's history is similarly immoderate. Outlaws rode its hills, rum runners crossed its borders, and during the 1920s and 1930s, Communists held sway in Sheridan County government and published the *Producers News* in Plentywood, the county seat.

The *Producers News* originated with the Nonpartisan League, a farmers' organization launched in North Dakota by Arthur Townley in 1915.[6] The NPL sent Charles Taylor, who had offered his services, to edit the paper. Plentywood was a place he would later describe as a "Godforsaken little hole." In 1918, Taylor said, he began promoting the NPL in a town that was "hostile as hell to us." But the League had wisely chosen a man who was up to the task. When others have referred to Taylor it has usually been with such adjectives as "colorful," "volatile," and "impressive." Sheridan County historian Magnus Aasheim characterized him as "a personable individual with an impressive and handsome physique." Another writer described "a three-hundred pound giant of prodigious energy, who could use his fists in a political brawl but who preferred his acid pen."[7]

Born in 1884 in Dodge County, Wisconsin, Taylor was the second of twelve children and lived in what he later described as a "poor quality log cabin." A *Producers News* biographical sketch reported that he was raised by Republicans, "the most radical thing in the line of political parties then known."[8] His biography strategically associated him with the party of Lincoln, for Sheridan County voters had favored Republican candidates in the state and national elections of 1916 and 1918.[9] Curiously Taylor claimed in a 1965 interview to be the son of a man he described not as a Republican but rather as a Greenbacker, Farmers Alliance member, and populist. His father, he said, was a "rebel and contrary." Taylor himself remembered having always had an interest in progressive politics and debating the Republicans when he was only twelve years old. He described himself as "a Socialist in some terms" and a "great admirer of [Eugene] Debs" in 1907.[10]

Charles Taylor's career in journalism apparently began when he took an apprenticeship at a Minnesota newspaper in his early teens. Which Minnesota newspaper and his exact age at the time remain in dispute. Nonetheless his duties as press setter and cleaner often kept him busy for twelve hours a day. As an adult, he edited the *Port of Call,* a Socialist paper published in International Falls, Minnesota. Under his leadership, the paper became the most widely circulated in the county. "I was always a successful newspaper man" he observed years later. "People read my paper even when I wondered why they did it."[11] Taylor enjoyed success with the *Producers News* as well. Once established, the *News* quickly became the most widely read of the county's twenty newspapers. Lowell Dyson called the publication "the most important [Nonpartisan] league paper in Montana."[12]

Much of the popularity of the *Producers News*, and by extension the farmers' movement, is owed to Taylor's skill as a rhetorical tactician. His newspaper deliberately appealed to its agrarian readers by emphasizing that it was their paper and that it represented their interests. The *News* was also catalytic. It functioned in a manner that politicized the farmers. Yet editor Taylor never failed to make his paper readable and dramatic; it was consistently informal, humorous, and peppered with high adventure.

Taylor demonstrated a keen understanding for farmers and workers and their need for organization and representation. He claimed to have launched the *Producers News* to provide a "local paper" they owned and controlled. According to Taylor there were one thousand stockholders in the Peoples Publishing Company, many of whom purchased stock at five dollars per share. Taylor maintained that he never exercised complete control of the paper, but that it was "all in the hands of the farmers." In practical terms the paper was owned by the Nonpartisan League, and its editorial policy reflected the views of that organization. Rather than "handing everything down" to the farmers, however, Taylor said he and his associates "always worked on a policy of making it appear that everything came from the farmers. . . . We practiced basically the involving of the farmers themselves." Symbolically the paper was for the farmers. The *News* was the producers', it was a product of the Peoples Publishing Company, and its masthead reinforced that message by announcing that it was "a paper of the people, by the people, for the people."[13]

Consequently Taylor had to establish early on that he represented "the people." The editor bluntly announced in a 1918 article that he was from "old American stock," that several of his ancestors had defended the United States in wartime, and that he was a proud contributor to the Liberty Bond drive and the Red Cross. Later, when he ran for state senate, Taylor identified himself with farming. Writing in the third person, Taylor said that although he was not currently farming, "he was farming when he came here, grew up on a farm, came from parents who are farmers, and expects to be back on a farm just as soon as he can go back with the hopes of having half a chance to pay out on one, which no one can do at the present time." In fact Taylor had spent most of his adult life either teaching or working in the newspaper business.[14]

By establishing himself as an all-American man and fellow agrarian, Taylor gave local farmers a reason to identify with him. He also used the columns of his newspaper to distance himself and his rural cohort from those who he claimed were not truly "for the people," primarily business interests. Just as populists had done before him, Taylor distinguished producers from nonproducers in a way that politicized his audience. Sheridan County business people and their mouthpiece, the conservative *Plentywood Herald,* became the enemy. In a 1928 editorial titled "Farmers Support Your Paper" (probably written by Taylor, although it was not signed), the *Producers News* claimed that the *Herald* "stands for private gain and supports those who are fighting the farmers' movement." The editorial continued: "The *Producers News* is owned by 600 farmers . . . while the *Plentywood Herald* . . . [is] a catspaw for the old gang that has always fought the farmers' movement."[15]

An unceasing farmers' advocate, Taylor portrayed business people as meddlesome know-it-alls. He excoriated these opponents of the Nonpartisan League for trying to tell the farmer how to farm and for opposing the movement. "For years," Taylor wrote,

the farmer has been told what he should do to be successful, how much more he should raise, how he should diversify . . . how to "get down to business." And now he is getting down to business in real earnest and he wants to have a say in making the laws he has to do business under [and] he becomes a "sucker," a "traitor" and other vile things in the eyes of the same fellows who have so long been trying to teach him how to run his business.[16]

The *Producers News* often contrasted industry and business with a supposedly purer, more honest farm life. Occasionally the paper hinted that businessmen were waging war on farmers. The radicals made "farmer," "worker," and "organization" their god terms. Devil terms like "Main Streeters" and "small town kaisers" were among the names given to local merchants and business people. The Republicans, who had been preeminent in county politics until the late 1910s, were labeled "the old gang." Other enemies were "speculators," "food gamblers," "profiteers," "Wall Streeters," "money magnates," and, by 1926, "the capitalist class."[17]

To the *Producers News* business people sought only to take advantage of farmers. In 1923 the *News* described a "panic" among the "corrupt opponents" of the Farmer-Labor Party who sensed a growing farmers' rebellion. "These poor tit suckers dread the thought of the old cows drying up," the paper said. Another editorial, using a dubious metaphor, told readers that business people hated farmers just as "every parasite hates the carcass it lives on." The editorial was cautionary yet empowering: "We know these business men are not for us, that they want to destroy us and our party, and we know that when we quit patronizing them there will be more Closing-Out sales."[18]

The *Producers News* attacked not only business people, but all those who attempted to take advantage of farmers' vulnerability, including "crop-grabbers," "Ku Kluxers," and even western Montana mining companies. Politicians who advocated "anti-farm" legislation also were treated harshly. In 1922, for example, the paper reported on legislation called the American Valuation System, which was intended to change the method of levying ad valorem taxes. According to the *News*, the new system would be a "great [scheme] for the American manufacturer and profiteer, but a hell of a dose for the American farmer and consumer." President Warren G. Harding, the paper said, "is of course, heartily in favor of the scheme." When State Attorney General Le Roy Foot, a Republican, began investigating Sheridan County officials during Charles Taylor's tenure as state senator, the *Producers News* labeled members of the attorney general's office "frame up' artists" who were attempting to discredit Taylor and other leaders in the farmer's movement.[19]

Despite its attacks and indictments the *Producers News* was entertaining and rhetorically appealing during its early years. As one writer has suggested, the *News* seemed an embodiment of the Roaring Twenties, a "sort of party sheet" that was "fun to read." Part of the paper's fun was its earthy, colloquial editorial style and its use of humor. Although the *News* was a more professional publication than many other Sheridan County papers of the time, its news and editorial columns were informal by contemporary standards.[20] Contractions were acceptable, words such as "tho" for "though" were abbreviated, and colloquialisms, even malapropisms, were common. In one instance the paper reported that an unnamed source had been a "bird in the wall" at a secret meeting. In another case the paper noted that doctors at a local hospital "chewed the rag with the nurses" about a patient's condition. Opponents of the farmer's movement, the paper alleged, "howl[ed]" about the farmers' paper, and "start[ed] a rumpus about religion" to divert attention from the real issues.[21]

Humor in the *News* often came at the expense of local business people or other enemies of the farmers' movement. One often-repeated story about the newspaper describes a local attorney who had advertised himself to the predominantly Scandinavian community as a Norsk advokat or Norwegian lawyer. Editor Taylor, it is reported, began to refer to the counselor as the Norsk abekat or Norwegian monkey. Other humor in the newspaper carried more bite. A corpulent man who had fallen out of favor with Taylor went by the name of L. S. Olson. Taylor nicknamed the man "Lard S. Olson," knowing the public would make the derogatory connection.[22] The *News* victimized another Olson by accusing him of being an incompetent farmer. An opponent of the farmer's movement and a would-be county commissioner, A. J. Olson, the *News* claimed, thought he was above the menial labor involved in dirt farming and believed it a waste of his ability to throw "away his life farming dirt, or even farming in the dirt, or doing dirty farming, or getting himself dirty in the dirt, trying to farm when he can't farm, especially when he is heaven sent 'county commissioner timber'."[23]

While the *Producers News* used abundant earthiness and humor to make its message appealing, it also built a cult of personality around its editor to create interest and enthusiasm. When they reminisce about the 1920s and 1930s, Sheridan County residents describe Charles Taylor vividly. Ray Stoner, a Sheridan County farmer, explains that "the time was ripe for a leader with the personality, the talent, and the ability to practically hypnotize an audience" and that people in northeastern Montana were "looking for leadership." Part of this lasting impression may be due to the *Producers News*'s larger-than-life portrayal of the editor and the farmers' desire for a leader and hero.[24]

Stoner's view is supported by scholars who have noted that during the years of the Great Depression American farmers felt alienated and defeated. For the homesteaders of northeastern Montana, this frustration had begun well before the 1930s. Having labored for years with relatively little success, many farmers were desperate and had reason to question themselves and the wisdom of trying to farm. As Stoner recalls, many pioneers "came [to the area] with high hopes, sacrificed much, went through hardships and then either lost their land, sold it too soon, or died before they saw their dreams of a prosperous country come true."[25]

Into this milieu came Charles Taylor, a flamboyant, powerful, confident, and rather extraordinary individual by the standards of northeastern Montana at the time. Taylor possessed a clear sense of mission and a positive self-image. His confidence and spirit became a source of amusement and even intrigue for many of the region's farmers and workers. Local residents remember him as "a brilliant man" and "a real character." Said to be "a charming and brilliant conversationalist," he was not easily forgotten.[26]

Taylor built this persona in part on braggadocio. Early in his tenure the *Producers News* proclaimed him Sheridan County's "most distinguished citizen." His name appeared in the *New York Times* when the National Farmer-Labor Convention elected him chairman in 1924. Later, during his second term as Montana state senator, the *News* announced that "Senator Taylor is today one of the most respected public men in Montana."[27]

Taylor also entertained *News* readers with dramatic stories of his bravery, cunning, and, of course, commitment to farmers. Late in 1918, for example, the *Producers News* described an attack on its editor. A local businessman reportedly entered the newspaper office, punched Taylor, and "otherwise [made] a hoodlum out of himself." Taylor claimed the businessman "got the worst of the encounter and beat it out of the office." In the same issue, the editorialist, presumably Taylor, asserted that such shows of force failed to intimidate the editor who was not the dictator of editorial policy: "The *Producers News* is owned by the farmers of Sheridan

County. The editor, as he has announced many times, is only a hired man on the paper, the same as the printer."[28]

In 1922, when Taylor was vying for the position of state senator, the paper revealed an "intensive campaign against Charles E. Taylor" being conducted by one of his competitors for office. The editorialist, again probably Taylor himself, explained that the opponent was assailing him because he had "carried on an incessant fight against county robbers— many of whom are [the opponent's] close personal friends." The indictments continued during Taylor's tenure as state senator. While in office he accused Montana's attorney general and the Prohibition Department of conspiring against Sheridan County politicians as well as the people of the region, including himself, charging that the officials were "more interested in trying to discredit the farmers['] elected officials with a view of injuring their movement than they are in enforcing the law."[29]

The movement had become an extension of Taylor, and, consequently, its victories were his. He used the *Producers News* constantly to trumpet the achievements of his own political machine and its fight for the farmers. According to the *News,* by 1926 the party had reduced tax rates and debt, policed the county effectively, and had "stood by the interests of the workers and producers faithfully all of the time, against the exploiters and usurers and crop grabbers." Furthermore, the paper proclaimed, the party had "protected the interest of the most humble and the unfortunate as impartially and as fairly as it has the most powerful citizen in the county."[30]

Taylor found much about which to boast during the movement's early years. In less than four years, the Nonpartisan League had organized a broad slate of candidates for the August primary elections of 1922 in Sheridan County. Included on the ballot were Charles Taylor for state senator and NPL organizer Clair Stoner for state representative. Taylor's friend Rodney Salisbury, then the undersheriff, ran for county sheriff, and farmers' organization members sought election to almost every available county office. Taylor, Stoner, Salisbury, and the entire NPL ticket were elected in November, by modest margins in some cases and landslides in others.[31]

In 1923 the trio of Taylor, Stoner, and Salisbury helped guide the transition from the NPL to the FLP, a move that did not diminish the group's popularity with voters. Taylor ran for United States representative in 1924 on the FLP ticket and received 53 percent of the vote in Sheridan County, but not enough votes statewide to be elected. He was reelected to the state senate in 1926 and completed a four-year term. In the 1926 county elections the Farmer-Laborers won all but two county positions (county superintendent and county commissioner).[32]

The NPL, and later, the FLP virtually ran Sheridan County during the early 1920s. By 1928, however, their good fortune began to change when, for example, local radical leaders openly aligned themselves, and thus county government, with communism. And while the *News* played a central role and indeed succeeded in politicizing and radicalizing farmers in Sheridan County in the 1920s, so, too, did the paper play a critical role in the movement's demise at the close of the decade.

By his own admission Charles Taylor had become a Communist by 1922, although during the early years of his editorship he underplayed his political orientation and commitments. But as the movement gained momentum in the county the rhetoric of the *Producers News* lurched to the left. By 1928 there could be little doubt that many of the county radicals were actually Communists. A few months before the election Taylor ran an editorial that was a call to class consciousness: "The American dukes and lords of industry teach that there are no classes—that all are equal, and that one citizen is just the same as another. The reason for this is obvious. As long as the general public is persuaded there are no classes there will be no class organizations. . . . The comprehension of the existence of classes, and the consequental [sic] understanding of the class struggle . . . is the beginning of politico-economic wisdom."[33] Taylor's class manifesto signaled a rhetorical change for the farmers' movement in northeastern Montana. As the radicals became increasingly vocal about their true convictions, another group coalesced and employed the conservative *Plentywood Herald* to attack the Farmer-Labor Party.

Founded in 1908 the *Plentywood Herald* was the oldest paper in the county. It began to emerge as the voice of anticommunism in the mid-1920s by tapping growing public awareness of, and skepticism about, the party's radical leaders. A focal point for public concern was the robbery of the county treasury in 1926. On November 26, the last day for one to pay taxes without penalty, two masked men entered the courthouse office of Treasurer Engebret Thorstenson and Deputy Treasurer Anna Hovet.

After commanding Thorstenson and Hovet to lie down in the vault, the thieves absconded with approximately $105,000 in cash and bonds. They were never apprehended.[34] The robbery created abundant grist for Sheridan County's rumor mill, and some locals claimed the heist was an inside job. When an investigation was launched by the county's insurance company and its bonding agency, which resulted in a three-year delay in paying the county's claim, many people were convinced of local government's involvement.[35]

Shortly after the robbery, the *News* noted that rumors were rampant. Editor Taylor defended county officers when they were charged with allowing crime to flourish. "There is as little of these activities here in Sheridan county or about Plentywood," Taylor noted, "as in any other county in this section of the state." He denied any involvement and attacked the publishers of stories implicating radical leaders for conjuring up tales from their own imaginations.[36]

The robbery issue came back to haunt the Farmer-Laborers after Harry Polk purchased the *Plentywood Herald* in 1928. Polk was an educated man, erstwhile school superintendent, and editor of the daily *Williston Herald* in North Dakota.[37] Polk's first editorial in mid-June did little to reveal the position he would soon adopt; in fact he announced that the paper would have little to say about county politics. In only a matter of weeks, however, Polk was stealing rhetoric from the Farmer-Labor Party, referring to them as the "old gang who have posed as the friend of the farmer." Polk further claimed that Taylor and Salisbury had "sold the party and cause which they claim to represent."[38] The *Herald* resurrected the courthouse robbery specter before the 1928 elections, insinuating that county radicals had made the crime possible by inducing the county treasurer to "keep over $100,000 on hand instead of depositing it in the banks as the law called for" and to remain open after regular closing hours.[39]

County officials also were suspected of either overseeing or overlooking rumrunners' activities. Local residents recall such activity, and FBI reports support their recollections. Taylor explained that, although he and Salisbury saw Prohibition as a failure, they recognized the public's expectation of enforcement. Thus bootleggers were arrested to pacify "the Prohibitionists . . . and the teetotallers." When the lockup was full the suspects were allowed to leave the jail quietly and go home. Then the judge, who had been reelected by the farmer's group, would fine the men and contribute the money to the school fund to satisfy the county's "church-going people." Naturally, Taylor later said, he "played that in big headlines in the papers."[40]

A few bootlegger arrests did not silence the *Herald*. Its editors accused the *News* of inconsistency: while the radical newspaper formerly denounced the "dives, gambling joints and hell-holes . . . the man [Taylor] who declares himself boss of the county today draws down the profits of all the honky-tonks in the county and is to Sheridan county and Plentywood no less than Al Capone is to Chicago." The *Herald* suggested that Taylor was one of the worst of the "coffer filchers."[41]

The *Herald* assailed not only Charles Taylor but also Sheriff Rodney Salisbury and other radical leaders. On the front page of a preelection issue in 1928, the *Herald* reported that Sheriff Salisbury selectively enforced the law by driving into the country to personally sell auto licenses to farmers and by writing letters for his unlicensed friends "stating that the driver must not be molested." The *Herald* concluded, "There is nothing wrong with Salisbury—that is if you look at him through the eyes of a bootlegger, divekeeper or *Producers News* candidate."[42]

In addition to hurling insults, the *Herald* backed a unified ticket of Republicans and Democrats who had banded together to defeat the county "reds." The *Producers News* fought back, reporting that the fusion ticket was sponsored by "mainstreeters and their lickspittles" and that its only purpose was to save the county from the "horrible reds." Furthermore, the radicals claimed that the new coalition was composed of "all the boys looking for fat contracts from the county." Later in the election season editor Taylor cried foul at the vilification of the radical candidates by the *Plentywood Herald,* and placed farmers at the center of the conflict, explaining that this election season was just another in a long line of abuses by the enemies of the movement. Counterattacks notwithstanding, the radicals took a beating in the 1928 election. Sheriff Rodney Salisbury lost reelection and the FLP captured only two county offices. After the general election the *Producers News* announced, "We eat crow."[43]

There are several reasons for the radicals' dramatic loss at the polls. First, crops had been fairly good during the mid-1920s. Wheat prices also improved, averaging $1.42 per bushel in 1925 (the average price in 1922 had been \$.89; in 1932 it would fall to \$.35). Added to the relative prosperity of these years was the increasing vociferousness of the *Plentywood Herald* beginning in 1926.[44]

Vowing to support the new county officers, the formerly boastful *Producers News* was quieted but hopefully predicted ultimate triumph. According to the paper, the party had not "lost faith in the people of Sheridan county. . . . We will still serve the farmers as faithfully as we can, and we . . . will always be found fighting for the economic and political interests of the farmers and the workers."[45]

Radicalism suffered major losses at the polls in 1928 but did not lose all momentum in Sheridan County. Material conditions in the region were about to get worse with a moderate harvest in 1929, a poorer crop in 1930, and a complete failure in 1931. The movement still had its supporters, but the *Producers News* had to overcome immense rhetorical challenges if the radicals were to survive into the 1930s.

As the new decade began the farmers' organization in Sheridan County was undergoing significant change. In 1931 local leaders orchestrated the

Crop failure and low commodity prices fueled rural radicalism. So desperate was the situation in Sheridan County in 1931 that the Farmers Union Terminal Association of St. Paul sent food and clothing (pictured here) to those hardest hit.

MONTANA HISTORICAL SOCIETY PHOTOGRAPH ARCHIVES, HELENA

transition of the Farmer-Labor group into the United Farmers League, an organization sponsored by the CPUSA. Taylor, Salisbury, and CPUSA organizer Ella Reeve "Mother" Bloor, who came to Sheridan County to give stump speeches for the league, guided the move to the UFL. In late 1931 Taylor became the state organizer for the UFL in South Dakota and took an extended leave of absence from his duties at the *Producers News*. He was succeeded by Erik Bert, a New York Communist who edited the paper from November 1931 to September 1933.[46]

As an editor Bert did not compare to Taylor. First, Taylor understood that the task of radicalizing Americans was unique. He explained in 1965 that the United States "wasn't Russia, to start with. We didn't have any religious problems over here. . . . We didn't have a lot of things that [the Russians] emphasized." Additionally, while Taylor claimed to have received no particular editorial orders from the executive committee in New York, he said that Bert did.[47]

It is apparent that directives from the Communist International (Comintern) influenced the *Producers News* during Bert's tenure. The 1928 Comintern program, written in Russia, issued marching orders for Communist organizations worldwide, even prescribing the types of slogans to be used. In a section on Communist Party tactics, the program insisted that the demands and slogans of the party "must be bent to the revolutionary aim of capturing power and of overthrowing bourgeois capitalist society." It added that, although slogan-writers should not "stand aloof from the daily needs and struggles of the working class," these needs and struggles should be used primarily to express the necessity of a "revolutionary struggle for power." Furthermore the program dictated that Communist organizations must shamelessly and openly profess their beliefs and goals to bring about the forcible overthrow of capitalism.[48]

Bert followed the course set by Comintern and the CPUSA, cleansing the *News* of much of its bourgeois, middle-class influence. "Struggle," a word that was used repeatedly in the Comintern's Program, became a recurring theme in the *Producers News,* as Bert's first editorial in the paper indicates: "In the struggles that the United Farmers League leads against the robbery of the farmers by the bankers and the capitalist class, the *Producers News* will be not only an agitator but one of the chief organizers in the fight. It will not only report the news of the struggles of the farmers thruout the Northwest, but will give as much guidance and leadership to these struggles as is possible."[49]

Although "struggle" had a rich heritage for the Communist Party in the works of Karl Marx, it was a new symbol for most readers of the *News*. The 1932 New Year's edition of the paper offered a pessimistic editorial titled "A New Year of Struggle." This proclamation was in sharp contrast to 1918's New Year greeting, which read, quoting Abraham Lincoln: "And, again, with charity for all, with malice towards none, the *Producers News* wishes its many readers, patrons, and friends, together with all mankind, a very prosperous and happy new year."[50]

The *Producers News* of the 1930s contrasted with its earlier incarnation in many ways. When it was launched in 1918 the paper's motto invoked a phrase from Lincoln's "Gettysburg Address" by proclaiming that the *News* was "a paper of the people, by the people, and for the people." But Bert sterilized the motto; it became "the official organ of the United Farmers League in the Northwest." Later the masthead stated that it was "the paper of the oppressed and exploited."[51]

In the 1920s the *Producers News* ran engagement announcements and gossip columns on the front page alongside reports on the local farmers' revolt. In the 1930s such reformist diversions were eliminated. This was due, in part, to the paper's amalgamation with the *United Farmer,* the former official newspaper of the UFL. Although the *News* was published in local and national editions, little differentiated them. Now the paper reported on the "bloody exploitation of negro workers on levees," "exploited Wisconsin dairy farmers," and police abuse of Ohio reds. These were topics of great importance to the CPUSA, but they held little interest for wheat farmers in Sheridan County, Montana.[52]

By stressing militancy and revolution across the nation and around the world, the Communists in northeastern Montana virtually stripped their newspaper of the entertainment value that helped make it popular during the 1920s. It became an instrument of gloom. The best indication of the negativity readers sensed in the *News* comes from the paper itself. An editorial titled "Communists Knocking Everybody" began by noting that the editors had overheard farmers remarking that the Reds were too negative. After explaining why Communists were dissatisfied with the status quo and that "they are really people you can talk to," the editorialist concluded, "Communists are the best comrades and friends of farmers and workers who are fighting for a better world for people to live in."[53]

The orthodox Communist rhetoric of the *Producers News* alienated some local readers and failed to keep the editor safe from reproach by CPUSA leadership. In 1932 Bert denounced the milk strikes being led in Iowa by the Farm Holiday Association. The Holiday Association was, at the time, trying to assist farmers and dairymen in several plains states and, as such, was in competition with the United Farmers League. The *News* condemned the strike for failing to address more important issues such as foreclosures, evictions, and taxes. A week later the paper reversed its stance on the strike. The reversal probably came at the behest of the national party, for in July 1933, at a CPUSA conference, Henry Puro described the *News's* denunciation of the strike as a "mistake" that the Central Committee had taken pains to explain and correct.[54]

While the paper's tone and strategies grew less effective as tools of persuasion, county radicals attempted to contend with an even more slippery issue: religion. From the beginning the farmers' movement had encountered probes and accusations about its stance on religion. In response to questions about the religiosity of some local radicals, the *Producers News* published an editorial titled "The Religious Issue" in 1918. The editorialist, probably Taylor, claimed that "political scoundrels" and "lackeys of big business" who were unable to confront issues honestly used the topic of religion "to get the people fighting about something that has no merit one way or the other, in the hopes of attracting attention away from the real issues to the bogus quarrel."[55]

Sheridan County radicals negotiated the religious straits effectively during the 1920s, convincingly enough to avoid major upheaval. As the years passed, however, the *Plentywood Herald* became a more vigilant watchdog for religion. In 1929 a *Herald* editorial exposed Communist belief that "Christmas is a pagan holiday, that Jesus Christ is only a myth and the Christian religion is but a superstition fostered by the Bourgois [sic] to overawe the masses and keep them in check." Later, the *Herald* asserted that Communists advocated absolute hatred of all religion.[56]

The *Producers News* confronted the religion issue before the 1932 election with a front-page editorial titled "God and This Election Campaign." The columnist accused the editor of the *Herald* of trying to drag God into the election by declaring that Communists were godless and that they endangered the social institution of the church. The writer called for leaving religion out of the campaign, emphasized that Communists were not fighting God, and maintained that the party left spiritual matters to those "who profess to be versed in such matters." Incongruously the *Producers News* columnist declared that if Christ were to return on election day the *Herald* editor would cry "Crucify him," and then referred to "crucifiction day" in what, if not a misspelling, was a pun.[57]

Although the league claimed not to be atheistic, its actions disturbed locals, particularly in the case of a 1932 funeral. The Bolshevik funeral for Rodney Salisbury's daughter, according to the *News*, was not held in a church but rather in the county's Farmer-Labor Temple. A report on the service, prominently featured in the *News*, said in part:

> Our dear young Pioneer, Janis Salisbury . . . was buried Saturday afternoon. The funeral services were those for a Bolshevik . . . the coffin was accompanied from the entrance to the front of the hall by the Young Pioneers, led by two Pioneers bearing a Red Flag. When the coffin had been placed in the front of the hall, the Pioneers arranged the flowers which had been sent by the Young Pioneers, her school mates, the United Farmers League, the *Producers News* and the Communist party, and others.[58]

The article described the Farmer-Labor Temple, its windows and stage draped in red and black with hammer and sickle emblems. "The Internationale" was the musical selection, and members of the Young Pioneers sang "Red Flag," dubbed "Janis' song" by the article's author. After burial of the child's body the Young Pioneers recited their pledge: "Stand ready for the cause of the working class. Are you ready? Always ready! I pledge allegiance to the workers Red Flag and to the cause for which it stands. One aim thruout our lives—Freedom for the working class."[59]

A *Plentywood Herald* editorialist was livid at the heresy. If Communism were adopted, he wrote, "For the hope of a Hereafter, which in deepest sorrow has been the only source of comfort for those we loved . . . would be substituted a circus ritual at the tomb and an empty 'goodbye'." The funeral was the talk of the town, and writers for the *Producers News* became defensive.[60]

Some Sheridan County historians credit the Bolshevik funeral for Janis Salisbury with undermining the Communist cause more than any other event. But the funeral represented only part of the radicals' growing rhetorical insensitivity to the farmers' values and attitudes. In a 1965 interview Taylor noted that the paper had "not only lost kick and zest but had lost local interest." He faulted radicals, particularly Bert, for making the newspaper "the mouthpiece of the Communist Party" and for failing to recognize that the *News* had been founded as "the official paper for Sheridan County."[61]

By losing sight of the *Producers News*'s role as the "official" county paper, radical leaders failed to stem the tide of criticism or to recoup their electoral losses. In school board, county, and state elections in the early 1930s, Farmer-Labor and, later, United Farmers League candidates were beaten time and again. In the 1932 general elections, Rodney Salisbury was the Communist candidate for governor, Taylor ran for state representative, and ten other men and one woman ran for elective office. They were opposed by candidates running on the ticket of the Taxpayers Economy League, a bipartisan group with the stated purpose of encouraging more economical practices in local government and fighting Communism. In November all of the Economy League candidates won their respective offices. The Communist candidates received only 32 percent of the vote, down nearly 12 percent since 1930. The *Herald* announced that Communism had been dealt a "crushing . . . death blow."[62]

The *Producers News* seemed to suffer an identity crisis after the 1932 election. In early 1933 the staff box, which had previously declared that the paper was the official organ of the United Farmers League, now added, "Official paper of the City of Plentywood, Montana." Leadership at the paper was particularly unstable. The year began with Bert as editor and Taylor as managing editor, although Taylor's duties as a UFL organizer kept him out of the state most of time between 1931 and 1934. By September 1933 Bert was replaced by L. M. Lerner, formerly with the *Farmers National Weekly*. In February 1934 Rob F. Hall was listed as acting editor; two weeks later, with no published introduction, Alfred Miller assumed editorial duties.[63]

Under Miller, the *News* appeared to recapture the local focus that had characterized it in the 1920s. But such rhetorical efforts were not sufficient to undo years of neglect and abuse. The 1934 election season was the most disappointing yet: the *News* reported that the Communist Party was unable to overcome the "reactionary politicians" and garnered 450 votes or approximately 19 percent of the total cast.[64]

The following year, 1935, brought renewed attacks from the *Herald,* as well as the arrest and interrogation of *News* editor Miller, a German expatriate.[65] After several years of doing UFL work in South Dakota, Nebraska, and elsewhere, and at about the time he quit the Communist Party, Taylor returned to Plentywood. In July 1935 he engaged in a brief and successful fight for leadership of the *Producers News* at the annual stockholders' meeting. Alfred Miller and his business manager walked out of the meeting. With their departure a new board of directors wasted no time in appointing Taylor to his former position.[66]

Taylor's first editorial after his return was titled "Again, the Farmers' Paper." Although he left the Communist Party in 1935, he announced that the paper still would support a "mass labor party built upon the immediate needs of the farmers and workers," but that it would serve the farmers "in a better and more realistic way, in a more tolerant and less sectarian way." Furthermore the editor pledged to "let by gones be by gones" and nostalgically invited readers to make "the paper your headquarters as you did in the days gone by."[67]

Taylor did not receive the response he sought. Perhaps trying to make sense out of it all thirty years later, Taylor talked of the damage that had been done to the *News* during his absence, saying the paper "had gone downhill . . . after the Commies [Bert and other sectarian editors who followed him] took it over." Taylor himself had been a Communist from 1922 until 1931, but by referring to the "Commies" as he did, he implied that he was a different kind of Communist who knew how to include "kick and zest . . . and local interest" to create and maintain a following.[68]

Whatever the reasons Taylor's paper began a downward spiral into financial ruin despite his best efforts. Advertisers had all but abandoned the *Producers News* in favor of the *Plentywood Herald.* Without advertising revenue Taylor was unable to pay his employees. In 1936 the *News* halved its size and began to miss publication deadlines. The fall election made it clear: only 1 percent of the total county voted for the Communist candidate for president. Taylor managed to put out only three editions in 1937, and on March 5 the *Producers News* published its final edition.[69]

After the *Producers News* folded, Taylor packed up his printing press and moved to Seattle where he opened the Rainier Press and produced a variety of publications, including an Italian-language newspaper and weekly radio programming guides. As World War II approached, Taylor sold his printing business and took employment in the shipyards as a mechanic's assistant. He eventually returned to the newspaper business, working at a telephone book printing establishment and later, as a proofreader for the *Seattle Post Intelligencer.*

Taylor's life as a political activist did not cease when he left Montana. In Seattle he was active in the Socialist Workers Party and the Independent Socialist League. The FBI had been monitoring his activities for several years and, because of his association with subversive organizations, continued to do so until his death in 1967.[70]

With Taylor's departure from Plentywood, Sheridan County's status as a hotbed of farmer radicalism faded, and the paper of, by, and for the people was relegated to the shelves of the county library. Charles Taylor's *Producers News* grew up with the farmers' movement and helped the movement grow. During the teens and early 1920s the *News* instilled in farmers a sense of identification with the radicals and their program. When the paper evolved into a doctrinaire organ of the Communist Party, it lost its persuasive power and ultimately damaged the credibility of the farmers' organization. Over the years, however, the paper had been consistent in one particular: it had been at the center of radical activity in northeastern Montana. For better or worse, the *Producers News* had moved the farmers' movement.

NOTES

1. *The Communist Position on the Farmers' Movement* (New York, 1933), back cover.
2. Ellis Waldron, *An Atlas of Montana Politics since 1864* (Missoula, Mont., 1958), 355.
3. The phrase "red corner" is from Ivan Doig, *Bucking the Sun* (New York, 1996), 174.
4. Lowell Dyson, *Red Harvest: The Communist Party and American Farmers* (Lincoln, Neb., 1982); William C. Pratt, "Rural Radicalism on the Northern Plains, 1912–1950," *Montana The Magazine of Western History,* 41 (Winter 1992), 42–55; Charles Vindex, "Radical Rule in the State of Montana," *Montana The Magazine of Western History,* 18 (January 1968), 1–18; Gerald Zahavi, "'Who's Going to Dance with Somebody Who Calls You a Mainstreeter': Communism, Culture, and Community in Sheridan County, Montana, 1918–1934" (paper presented at the Organization of American

Historians and National Council on Public History annual meeting, Washington, D.C., March 31, 1995). "Rhetoric" as used here refers to the process by which people use symbols to create an impact on others. Contrary to the way in which the media commonly use the word, rhetoric is not necessarily opposed to reality and is not necessarily bombastic or misleading (although it certainly can be). The phrase "to move movements" is from Stephen E. Lucas, "Coming to Terms with Movement Studies," *Central States Speech Journal,* 31 (Winter 1980), 255–66.

5. Magnus Aasheim, ed., *Sheridan's Daybreak* (Great Falls, Mont., 1970), 2.

6. Robert L. Morlan, *Political Prairie Fire: The Nonpartisan League, 1915–1922* (St. Paul, Minn., 1985), viii.

7. Charles Taylor, interview by Lowell K. Dyson, August 2–3, 1965, p. 33, microfiche, Oral History Research Office, Columbia University, New York (hereafter Charles Taylor, interview); Aasheim, *Sheridan's Daybreak,* 10; Dyson, *Red Harvest,* 32.

8. Charles Taylor, interview, 1; Vindex, "Radical Rule," 6; *Plentywood (Mont.) Producers News,* August 18, 1922.

9. In 1916 the majority of the county's voters chose Woodrow Wilson and elected two Republican state legislators. Republican legislators were elected again in 1918. County voters chose Republican Warren Harding for president in 1920. Waldron, *Atlas of Montana Politics,* 151, 156, 160, 172, 176.

10. Charles Taylor, interview, 13, 15, 17, 22.

11. Various sources dispute the age at which Taylor entered the print trade. In his interview with Lowell Dyson, Taylor indicated that he first worked for an Aitkin, Minnesota, newspaper from approximately 1898 until 1900. Taylor's son, Carl, claims that his father worked for the *Aitkin Republican.* Carl Taylor, interview by author, September 3, 1993, Spanaway, Wash. If Taylor did work for an Aitkin paper before 1901, he probably did so at the *Age* or the *Independent,* as the *Republican* was founded in 1901. A biographical article notes that Taylor "edited a paper at Vesta, Minnesota," sometime after fall 1900. *Plentywood (Mont.) Producers News,* August 18, 1922. See also Charles Taylor, interview, 25.

12. Taylor claimed that the paper's circulation reached 3,500 in Sheridan County. Charles Taylor, interview, 100. A national newspaper directory indicates that average circulation during the *Producers News*'s "boom years" in the early 1920s did not exceed 2,500 in a county of approximately 12,000 to 14,000 people. *N. W. Ayer and Son's American Newspaper Annual and Directory* (Philadelphia, 1923); *N. W. Ayer and Son's American Newspaper Annual and Directory* (Philadelphia, 1924). In 1931 the *Producers News* became the official paper of the United Farmers League and began publishing both local and national editions. The *Producers News* reported that 5,000 copies were being printed shortly after the paper went national. *Plentywood (Mont.) Producers News,* December 4, 1931. The Ayer Directory indicates that approximately 3,000 copies were distributed per week in 1931 and only 2,400 were circulated in 1934. Dyson, *Red Harvest,* 32.

13. Vindex, "Radical Rule," 8; Charles Taylor, interview, 39. The competing *Plentywood Herald* reveled in reporting that, in 1929, there were only 377 stockholders and that only 192 of those individuals were Sheridan County residents. *Plentywood*

(Mont.) Herald, February 7, 1929. See also Charles Taylor, interview, 94; and *Plentywood (Mont.) Producers News*, April 19, 1918.

14. *Plentywood (Mont.) Producers News*, May 10, 1918, August 18, 1922.

15. Ibid., September 7, 1928. Editorials and articles in the *Producers News* were rarely signed during the 1920s. Carl Taylor said that other people wrote some articles but that his father dictated editorial policy. Carl Taylor, interview by author, August 7, 1996, Spanaway, Wash.

16. *Plentywood (Mont.) Producers News*, May 17, 1918.

17. Ibid., August 18, 1922, May 10, 1918, January 8, 15, 1926. The *News* had questioned capitalism earlier, but its indictments of the economic and political system became more strident in 1926 when it endorsed the diplomatic recognition of Russia.

18. Ibid., October 5, 1923, December 5, 1930.

19. Ibid., January 13, 1922, January 8, 1926.

20. Daniel Vichorek, *The Hi-Line Profiles of a Montana Land* (Helena, Mont., 1993), 41. The *Producers News* was more professional because it imitated the layout style of metropolitan papers in appearance and because it reprinted editorials and columns from the *Daily Worker* and other sources.

21. *Plentywood (Mont.) Producers News*, November 17, 1923, December 5, 1930, October 25, 1918.

22. Vindex, "Radical Rule," 8; Aasheim, *Sheridan's Daybreak*, 1.

23. *Plentywood (Mont.) Producers News*, November 2, 1932.

24. Ray Stoner, correspondence with author, March 1993 (hereafter Stoner correspondence).

25. See David H. Bennett, *Demagogues in the Depression: American Radicals and the Union Party, 1932–1936* (New Brunswick, N.J., 1969), 22; Aasheim, *Sheridan's Daybreak*, 561; Stoner correspondence.

26. Irwin "Shorty" Timmerman and Clifford Peterson, interviews by Jackie Day, May 13–17, 1985, Small Town Montana Oral History Project, Sheridan County Library, Plentywood, Montana (hereafter Small Town OH, SCL); Stoner correspondence.

27. Vindex, "Radical Rule," 6; *New York Times*, June 18, 1924; *Plentywood (Mont.) Producers News*, June 10, 1927.

28. *Plentywood (Mont.) Producers News*, December 6, 1918.

29. Ibid., October 20, 1922, January 8, 1926.

30. Ibid., October 22, 1926.

31. Aasheim, *Sheridan's Daybreak*, 11. Taylor, running on the Nonpartisan League ticket as a Republican, defeated his Democratic opponent by 124 votes, or 6 percent of the total. Others, such as Charles Lundeen, the Nonpartisan League county commission candidate, outpaced their opponents by up to 30 percent. *Plentywood (Mont.) Producers News*, November 10, 1922.

32. Waldron, *Atlas of Montana Politics*, 355; Aasheim, *Sheridan's Daybreak*, 11.

33. *Plentywood (Mont.) Producers News*, January 20, 1928.

34. Aasheim, *Sheridan's Daybreak*, 11.

35. See Nancy Marron, interview by Jackie Day, Small Town OH, SCL; Aasheim, *Sheridan's Daybreak*, 11.

36. *Plentywood (Mont.) Producers News*, December 10, 1926.

37. Polk continued as owner-publisher of the *Williston Herald* after he purchased the *Plentywood Herald,* spending one or two days in Plentywood each week. Joe Nistler, editor of the *Plentywood Herald* from 1982 to 1995, said Polk shaped editorial policy at the *Plentywood Herald.* Joe Nistler, interview by author, August 7, 1996, Plentywood, Mont. Despite his opposition to Sheridan County's farmer radicals, Polk had once edited a Nonpartisan League paper in Minnewaukan, North Dakota. *Plentywood (Mont.) Herald,* November 10, 1971.

38. *Plentywood (Mont.) Herald,* June 21, August 23, 1928.

39. Ibid., September 20, 1928.

40. "Communist Activities in the State of Montana," June 16, 1941, p. 82, report 100-3-51-16, in *Summary of CP Activities,* United States Department of Justice, Federal Bureau of Investigations (FBI), Washington, D.C.; Charles Taylor, interview, 54–55.

41. *Plentywood (Mont.) Herald,* September 20, 1928.

42. Ibid., October 25, 1928.

43. *Plentywood (Mont.) Producers News*, May 11, 1918, August 31, November 11, 1928.

44. Montana Department of Agriculture, *Montana Agricultural Statistics: State Series, 1867–1976* (Bozeman, Mont., 1978), 3–4.

45. *Plentywood (Mont.) Producers News,* November 11, 30, 1928.

46. Ibid., November 27, 1931, September 29, 1933.

47. Charles Taylor, interview, 95, 100.

48. *Program of the Communist International* (New York, 1928), 82, 87.

49. *Plentywood (Mont.) Producers News,* November 27, 1931.

50. Ibid., January 1, 1932, December 27, 1918.

51. Ibid., May 11, 1918, October 28, 1932, July 26, 1934.

52. Ibid., December 11, 1931, January 1, August 19, 1932.

53. Ibid., May 4, 1934.

54. Dyson, *Red Harvest,* 74, 75; *Plentywood (Mont.) Producers News,* August 12, 1932; *Communist Position on the Farmers' Movement,* 29, 32.

55. *Plentywood (Mont.) Producers News,* October 25, 1918.

56. *Plentywood (Mont.) Herald,* December 12, 1929, March 10, 1932.

57. It is possible that "crucifiction" was simply a misspelling. *Plentywood (Mont.) Producers News,* November 2, 1932.

58. Ibid., March 11, 1932.

59. Ibid.

60. *Plentywood (Mont.) Herald,* November 3, 1932; *Plentywood (Mont.) Producers News,* April 15, 1932.

61. *Plentywood Portrait: Toil, Soil, Oil* (Aberdeen, S.Dak., 1987), 35; Charles Taylor, interview, 234.

62. *Plentywood (Mont.) Herald,* July 14, November 10, 1932; *Plentywood (Mont.) Producers News,* November 4, 1932.

63. *Plentywood (Mont.) Producers News,* January 6, September 29, 1933, February 9, 23, 1934.

64. Ibid., November 9, 1934; *Plentywood (Mont.) Herald,* November 15, 1934.

65. Alfred Miller was charged under the Immigration Act of 1918 as "an alien who believes in, advises, advocates, and teaches the overthrow by force and violence of the government of the United States." *Producers News* reference file, excerpted from "*Producers News* References," March 3, 1943, p. 4, Philadelphia file 100-18264, FBI.

66. Taylor had a long history of deviating from the Communist Party line. He claimed to have left the party for one year, probably 1929. He reentered party life, occasionally fell out of favor with the leadership over various issues such as his sympathy for Leon Trotsky, and finally quit paying dues in 1935. Charles Taylor, interview, 138, 232.

67. *Plentywood (Mont.) Producers News,* July 26, 1935.

68. Charles Taylor, interview, 234.

69. Waldron, *Atlas of Montana Politics,* 355.

70. Carl Taylor, interview, September 3, 1993; "Personal History Form and Report," May 1, 1944, report 100-55987, Charles Taylor main file, FBI.

Bootlegging Mothers and Drinking Daughters

Gender and Prohibition in Butte, Montana

Mary Murphy

In 1919 America adopted the Eighteenth Amendment to the United States Constitution, a social experiment that banned the manufacture, sale, and transportation of intoxicating liquors. Women, who had seen families ravaged by alcohol abuse, had been some of the strongest supporters of Prohibition, working through such organizations as the Woman's Christian Temperance Union and the Anti-Saloon League. A dozen years later some of those same women organized to repeal Prohibition because they believed lax enforcement had bred moral anarchy.

Prohibition changed Americans' drinking habits in unforeseen ways. Mary Murphy, a professor of history at Montana State University, Bozeman, examines the history of drinking in Butte, Montana, a city in which the workforce of male copper miners dominated public entertainments and social spaces. Drinking was an integral part of male culture, and Prohibition did not change that. However, the restructuring of the illegal liquor trade unexpectedly created opportunities for women to enter the liquor business and to join men in new speakeasies and nightclubs that catered to both sexes. The dynamics of Prohibition proved to be an arena in which men and women negotiated new gender roles. Murphy's essay illustrates the concept of gender as a social category and the fact that appropriate behavior for men and women is not shaped by biology, but by social choices made in particular historical times and places.

LATE ONE EVENING IN 1922, AS FEDERAL PROHIBITION OFFICER BEN HOLTER DROVE along Nettie Street in Butte, Montana, his car broke down. He asked to use a phone at a nearby house, but his attention quickly shifted from the stranded car to "demon rum." The woman who answered his knock, Mrs. Maud Vogen, aroused Holter's suspicions when she denied having a phone, although one sat in plain view. Holter returned a short time later with two police officers, and his hunch paid off—they found Mrs. Vogen and another woman tending a twenty-gallon still and a quantity of whiskey and mash. A few days after Vogen's arrest, police apprehended her husband Andrew, who was living at another address, on the assumption that he had been in charge of the bootleg operation. Subsequent investigation, however, revealed that Maud and Andrew Vogen had not been living together as husband and wife for some time. Maud Vogen was "in sole charge" of the still, and the woman with her at the time of her arrest was her mother.[1]

In the 1920s Butte women made, sold, and drank liquor in unprecedented fashion. Decades later a Butte woman recalled the many evenings she donned her flapper finery and headed to the dance halls where she and her friends shimmied to jazz tunes and slipped outside to share a pint of moonshine. In 1929 a Butte judge, Dan Shea, proposed a city ordinance calling for police matrons in all the city's dance halls; his action was prompted by the number of women carrying whiskey flasks into the popular nightspots.[2]

Until the advent of Prohibition, drinking in Butte was governed by clearly defined and understood social rules. Saloons were male preserves and reflected the ethnic and occupational strata of the community. Any woman who drank in a saloon was assumed to be a prostitute at worst, "loose" at best. When reputable women drank, they did so at home. Prohibition rattled these traditional patterns. It curbed some drinking, but more significantly, it changed the drinking habits of youth and women. Blatant flouting of the law during Prohibition created new social spaces for drinking, and women began stepping up to the bar along with men, albeit in speakeasies and nightclubs rather than in the old corner saloons. Prohibition accelerated the advent of heterosocial night life as new watering holes welcomed young couples and groups of women as well as men.

Prohibition also allowed ethnic groups and women to capitalize on the underground economy by launching new businesses in the manufacturing and sale of liquor. Women cooked liquor on the kitchen stove to supplement the family income. Husbands and wives running "blind pigs," "moonshine joints," and "home speaks" competed with saloons hastily converted into soft drink parlors. A few women operated bustling roadhouses. In the 1920s judges and juries, whose previous contact with female criminals had been almost exclusively with prostitutes, were confounded by grey-haired mothers appearing in their courts on bootlegging charges. In all aspects of the liquor business, women moved into spaces that had once been reserved exclusively for men. Prohibition allowed women to rewrite the script of acceptable public behavior and to transform one arena of commercial leisure bounded by rigid gender roles.[3]

Drinking in the late nineteenth and early twentieth centuries was one of the most gender-segregated activities in the United States. No one denied that women drank. Some researchers estimated that women comprised between one-tenth and one-third of the problem drinkers during this period. However, with the rise of the saloon, men had begun drinking in public, commercial arenas while women were relegated to drinking at home. Changes in industrial capitalism doomed the "kitchen grog shops" traditionally operated by women. Increases in working-class income and free time, coupled with a search for relief from the monotony of more regimented work, led to the growth of public saloons for male workers. Women, meanwhile, stayed at home, losing both the income from their small businesses and the companionship of husbands and male neighbors.[4]

Recent studies exploring the "cheap amusements" of young, working-class women have uncovered evidence of some public drinking in the early twentieth century. But these youthful pleasure-seekers were not drinking in traditional corner saloons. They strutted into new institutions such as dance halls, beer gardens, amusements parks, and cabarets. Significantly, these entertainments were phenomena of very large cities, cities that had jobs that attracted girls from surrounding farms and small towns. These urban migrants lived in furnished-room districts on their own. Or, if they lived at home, they sought their pleasures in places that were perhaps a trolley-ride away from their own neighborhood and the judgmental gazes of parents and neighbors. Most of America, however, was not like Chicago or New York. In small and middling cities there were fewer of the new commercial amusements and few places women could go where someone would not know them or their families. Quite simply, most women lacked the anonymity that emboldened their urban sisters. Changes in traditional gender roles thus took place more slowly in the hinterlands. Not until Prohibition altered the institutional basis of nightlife and public drinking were women able to expand the boundaries of recreational behavior and still retain respectability. Even in Butte, Montana, the "wide open town" of the northern Rockies, change awaited Prohibition. In order to understand the magnitude of that change, it is necessary to understand just what a "man's town" Butte was.[5]

Butte, Montana, bore three monikers in the early twentieth century. To capitalists, it was "the richest hill on earth," a treasure trove of copper ore, control of which made the Anaconda Copper Mining Company one of the most powerful corporations in the country. Workers knew it as "the Gibraltar of Unionism," where nearly every working person from

Saloons were an important part of Butte's hard-rock mining culture. The bar in the basement of Hennessey's, pictured here, was one of many saloons that thrived in the days before Prohibition.

BASEMENT OF HENNESSEY'S, WORLD MUSEUM OF MINING, BUTTE, MONTANA theater usher to hoist engineer belonged to a labor union. And everyone recognized it as a "wide open town," meaning that a man could buy a drink, place a bet, or visit a prostitute at any hour of the day or night without worrying about being arrested. On the eve of World War I Butte, Montana—seat of Silver Bow County—was the largest metropolis between Spokane and Minneapolis–St. Paul: a hard-rock mining city, home to nearly ninety-five thousand residents, the majority of them men. In 1910 the population was 57 percent male; in 1920 it was still 54 percent male. Butte was rollicking, gritty, and famous for its nightlife, which was by no means confined to the hours of darkness. The city's main crossroads at Park and Main streets anchored a commercial district bustling with department stores, groceries, hotels, banks, cafes, saloons, pool rooms, and gambling halls. The red-light district, where prostitutes charged a dollar for a bottle of beer and a dollar for a trick, was just two blocks south. Everyone from newly arrived Finnish muckers living in boarding houses on the East Side to Irish-American girls housekeeping for West Side families came through uptown Butte and witnessed its pleasures and vices. The majority of the population probably never approved of prostitution, and many had reservations about gambling. Drinking, however, was such an accepted habit that it took a national movement to present any challenge to its dominion.[6]

In November 1916 Montanans voted on statewide Prohibition. The measure passed with a comfortable margin of 58 percent of the vote, only three urban counties dissenting: Deer Lodge, the site of the smelter city Anaconda; Lewis and Clark, home of Helena, the state capital; and Silver Bow. In fact Silver Bow County neatly reversed the statewide referendum with 58 percent of its voters opposing the measure, registering the largest vote against Prohibition in the state. The real strength of the Prohibition movement rested in the rural counties, several of which passed the referendum by 60 to 70 percent. Silver Bow County's vote against Prohibition was hardly surprising. Butte was the largest city in the state; drinking was an integral part of its male-dominated, urban culture. At the time of the referendum Silver Bow County had three breweries and 250 saloons.[7]

Saloons were endemic to the urban culture of the nineteenth century as centers of male conviviality; on the mining frontier they were multifunctional institutions. Often the first non-residential buildings constructed, saloons predated fraternal lodge halls, hotels, churches, schools, and city halls. Men used them as banks, employment agencies, and post offices.

As urban institutions developed, most saloons shed their many skins and returned to their original form as places where men drank, talked, and argued. However, in newly minted western cities, saloons were more likely to accommodate billiards, gambling, and prostitution than were more strictly regulated eastern taverns. In poor and immigrant neighborhoods saloons often continued to hold workers' savings in their safes, to distribute foreign language newspapers, and to let people from the neighborhood use their toilets. One saloon in Butte—known as a hobo retreat—served only beer and whiskey, always had a pot of stew on the stove, was festooned with clothes drying after a wash in back-room tubs, and served at night as a flophouse.[8]

Despite their many community functions, western saloons were first and foremost places for men to drink and socialize. A cross-cultural study of North American and Argentine frontier saloons refers to both as "theaters of excessive machismo." On their stages men played out ritualized roles of masculine culture: camaraderie and conflict, communality and competition. The denouement was often violence. Strong cultural links between manliness and drinking existed in both societies, as evidenced in nineteenth-century Idaho, where a man was scarcely able to do business if he was "a lemonade son of a bitch."[9]

Taking a drink was also a public proclamation of a boy's entry to manhood. In his autobiographical novel *Singermann,* set in early twentieth-century Butte, Myron Brinig charted young Michael Singermann's journey to adulthood. On the day he first donned long pants at age thirteen, he marched into the corner saloon, went straight up to the bar, and ordered a beer. Chastened because the bartender refused to serve him, he was about to retreat in humiliation when a man at the bar bought him a schooner. As Michael took his first sip, "The beer ran down his throat, into his stomach, down his thighs and seemed to love the feel of his long pants. Beer was good now that he was drinking it in his long pants. It was a man's drink, filling a man with a golden glow, lighting little torches all over his body until he was aflame for life." Drinking became Michael's rite of passage, and he soon adopted his companion's stance: "with one foot on the brass rail, his left elbow propped up on the bar, his right hand holding the schooner of beer."[10]

Although the law forbade the presence of minors in saloons, parents often sent their children to the bar with a pail, smeared inside with lard to keep down the foam, to be filled with beer and brought home. Pat O'Leary stopped at the back door of Stripey's saloon every night, handed over his money, and got a bucket of beer for his father and a Hershey bar for himself. Newsboys and messengers, hoping to earn a few cents running errands, plied their trade in saloons. Frank Carden remembered accompanying his father on rounds of Saturday chores and persuading him to take him to the Atlantic Bar for a liverwurst sandwich, a glass of milk, and a chance to watch the goings-on. These childhood forays contributed to young boys' socialization into the masculine club of the saloon. Mike McNelis early on realized that the measure of man, at least by a saloon's standards, had more to do with size than age. A boy was old enough to drink "if you were tall enough to put the money up on the bar."[11]

In Butte the masculine nature of the saloon grew not only from a long tradition of American drinking habits and the frontier experience, but also from patterns brought over from Europe—especially from Ireland, the country that provided the single largest group of immigrants to Butte. Historians and other investigators have observed that Irishmen traditionally used drinking as a safety valve for sexual tensions, the depressions of poverty, the frustrations of parental authority, and their hatred of the English. As long as he did not threaten his family's income, a hard-drinking man was admired by his peers or treated with maternal affection as "the poor boy." In the local tavern or shebeen a man's status was secure, unchallenged by his father, unthreatened by women. Both married and single men belonged to a "bachelor group," who spent their evenings in the shebeen, demonstrating that sexual divisions were far more significant than those between old and young or married and single. One historian has observed that when the Irish-American Catholic Church attacked whiskey and took up the temperance cause, it pulled "the keystone from the arch which was traditional male culture."[12]

Naturally the Irish were not the only ethnic group with established drinking patterns transplanted to Butte. Far fewer Italians were saloonkeepers, but the community was well known for its homemade wines and grappa, a potent brandy. Slavs, Germans, Finns, Greeks, English, and French all kept and patronized saloons. Unlike Irish women, who did not socialize in Irish shebeens or American saloons, Slavic women occasionally patronized ethnic saloons in America, which resembled the eastern European inns that had doubled as shops and served both sexes. Accustomed to light wines and liquors, and having taken to beer "like ducks to water," many Slavic immigrants, especially industrial workers, drank daily.[13]

While Old World customs influenced New World drinking, living and working conditions in Butte also drove men to saloons. Myron Brinig captured the feelings that many miners probably shared when he described the appeal of the saloon: "when you dig for copper all day in the moist drifts underground, and you come up, and there is no sunlight, no waves beating against a rocky shore, why, a saloon, is a heaven then." When miners finished work and headed home, they frequently traded one unpleasant environment for another. Miners' families created cozy homes where they could, but the lack of sanitation in the densely packed neighborhoods was a serious problem. Throughout the early 1910s the county and city health departments reported filthy alleys full of refuse and rotting food, unkempt animals, and privies dangerously close to houses. Garbage, standing water, and dead animals had grown to such a heap in one vacant East Side lot that nearby residents kept their windows closed to minimize the stench. The majority of miners returned not to family homes, but to cabins where they "batched" with a few other men, to furnished rooms in the upper stories of commercial buildings, or to boarding houses. Men who worked all day in the dark underground were reluctant to retire to small, inhospitable sleeping rooms. In fact a County Board of Health study demonstrated that the physical environment of some working-class saloons was far healthier than that of the men's boarding houses. It was not surprising that men sought the warmth, lights, and company of saloons, cigar stores, or fraternal lodges in uptown Butte.[14]

East Park Street was "a beehive" of working-class social life. Miners shopped for boots and overalls in Jewish dry goods stores, ate at Greek restaurants, and drank in Irish saloons. Butte's drinking establishments ran the gamut from "saw-dust joints" to places such as the Atlantic, which had a bar a block long and fifteen bartenders working each shift. Saloons were working-class institutions, but, within their ranks, hierarchies, and divisions based on ethnicity, occupation, and income prevailed. Electrical workers congregated at the Park Saloon; smeltermen favored the Atlantic. Pedestrians passing Tickell and Spargo's on West Broadway delighted in the harmonizing of Cornish and Welsh singers. The *Anaconda Standard*, reviewing Butte's saloon business on the eve of Prohibition, revealed its prejudice when it compared uptown, established saloons where "the talk is never loud and where order always maintains itself" to the rougher places owned by "Finlanders and other foreigners" on the East Side who served poor liquor and scarcely noticed fights. Journalist Byron E. Cooney, in an homage to Butte saloons, observed, "everyone who drank at all had their own pet saloon. Personally I felt very much at home in all of them."[15]

On the other end of the scale from even the plushest workingman's saloon was Butte's Silver Bow Club, organized by copper magnate William A. Clark and several colleagues in 1882, and incorporated in 1891. In 1905 the club bought a lot adjacent to the courthouse, hired Montana's most prominent architects, and built a four-story edifice replete with massive fireplaces, murals of English country life, copper and leaded glass chandeliers, and a bar decorated with stained glass panels of lush grapes and sinuous vines.[16]

The Silver Bow Club admitted women for special events, and they no doubt sampled its wine cellar, but for the most part, public drinking remained a male privilege until Prohibition. Even in freewheeling Butte, as Aili Goldberg declared, "you just didn't see a woman in a saloon." Alma and Lillie Muentzer were born above their father's brewery and saloon. Alma recalled that the Butte Brewery and Saloon had "a little room in case the ladies wanted anything . . . [but] it was never used much because women at that time didn't go to bars." Lillie remembered that the California Bar featured "booths for ladies," but she also noted, "you weren't a lady if you went in." Throughout the West the only women to frequent saloons openly were prostitutes. As custom became entrenched, any woman who entered a saloon was assumed to be of dubious character. Men in Denver capitalized on the universality of that assumption to taunt female reformers. When members of the Woman's Christian Temperance Union (WCTU) tried to enter saloons to record the conditions of drinkers, they were met by guards who shouted "Whore!"[17]

In 1907 Montana institutionalized the taboo against women drinking in saloons. That year the Republican-dominated state assembly enacted a program of progressive legislation designed to protect the physical and moral health of Montanans. Abolishing the "wineroom evil" targeted prostitution and garnered nearly unanimous legislative support. Winerooms—the partitioned areas in which some saloon owners permitted women to drink—were considered incubators of prostitution. The new law banned women from saloons and compelled saloon owners to dismantle any accommodations designed to provide space for female drinkers. Proprietors were instructed to remove signs that advertised a ladies' entrance or a private entrance and to demolish winerooms, private apartments, or screened areas. Butte complied with the state legislature and passed a complementary city ordinance the same year.[18]

Nevertheless, while the law barred women from saloons, it was not designed to stop them from purchasing alcohol. Women who never drank in saloons commonly bought liquor there. Catherine Hoy recalled neighborhood women in Dublin Gulch going themselves or sending their children to the back door of saloons for their buckets of beer. Many Slavic women, who apparently preferred wine, would also have a little glass at home. Women's drinking habits, barely recorded by historians, were widely recognized by contemporaries. Indeed, during the campaign for Prohibition in Montana, at least one dry advocate chastised "mothers in Butte who won't vote for Prohibition because you want to have beer on your own tables in your own homes." Until the reconstruction of social drinking during Prohibition, reputable women, with few exceptions, continued to drink at home while men drank in public.[19]

Factions for and against Prohibition in Montana paralleled divisions in other states. The dry forces were led by the WCTU and the Anti-Saloon League. Enrollment in Montana's WCTU, founded in 1883, peaked during the Prohibition campaign of 1916. Nevertheless, the WCTU's stalwart campaigners waged a losing battle in the mining city. On their program in 1920 was the question, "Does Prohibition Prohibit in Butte?" Reluctantly, they had to answer "no." By 1923, 156 of the 250 saloons that had operated in Butte in 1916 and 1917 were in the same locations, under the same proprietorships, thinly disguised as soft drink parlors. The city directory advertised another forty-four new soft drink parlors, and it is impossible to estimate the number of clandestine speakeasies. Frank Carden observed that "the saloons all stayed open and dispensed 'bootleg' whiskey, homemade wine and homemade beer, brandy, gin. . . . If they were raided by Federal officers they would just pause long enough to get in another stock of liquor and start over again." As federal judge George M. Bourquin proclaimed, "shabby, dingy holes in the wall, labeled 'soft drink parlors' do not fool anybody, least of all the court," especially when they were in the same location as former saloons. Clearly such parlors neither operated for the sale of ice cream and pop nor catered to women and children. Nevertheless, community-wide acceptance of illegal activity was a major factor encouraging women to get into the liquor business.[20]

To be sure, during the first few years of Prohibition, Montana authorities made some attempt to enforce the law. Statements from county attorneys across the state showed varying rates of success in prosecuting violators. In Butte, however, cooperation between the local authorities and state and federal officers was notoriously lacking. Affidavits by state enforcement agents attested to the fact that the Cyrus Noble Saloon was run by a former police chief and patronized by uniform and plainclothes detectives. During a two-year period from November 1920 to November 1922, Silver Bow County's attorney won convictions in 59 percent of its liquor cases. But, during that time, only 105 cases were prosecuted—compared to 271 in Cascade County, site of Great Falls, and 168 in Lewis and Clark County, both with smaller populations. Despite almost daily newspaper accounts of confiscation of stills and illegal liquor, law enforcement officials were not collecting sufficient evidence to convict. Even when they did Butte juries remained unsympathetic to the law. In 1928 Judge Bourquin replaced a jury which had been hearing Prohibition cases and admonished the twelve new men to bring in verdicts in accordance with the evidence: "I don't want men sitting in the jury box who have no regard for their oaths. We have had two such juries and I don't want anymore if we can escape it."[21]

By 1926 a majority of Montanans agreed with Helen Raymond, who thought "it was a shame they ever had [Prohibition] because I think it broke down a morale of the people. . . . Cause once you think you can break a law, you're in worse shape than if you'd never done it." Montanans judged the noble experiment a failure and that year voters repealed their state prohibition law with 53 percent of the vote. (Silver Bow County tallied 73 percent in favor of repeal.) Federal agents became entirely responsible for enforcement, and their efforts at times seemed farcical. In 1928 the newspaper reported a "dry sleuth" who had adopted a disguise designed to entrap young Butte fraternity men from the School of Mines. Bartenders noted that raids often followed the appearance of a hatless young man "flaunting white flannel trousers and black coat or corduroy pants and skin-tight sweater [with] hair . . . greased back from forehead and smile of sophistication . . . spread on his face." The alleged agent would gain the confidence of Butte youths "whose entry to the drink parlors is never questioned," buy them drinks, and leave. Shortly afterward a raid commenced.[22]

Prohibition did not appear to change the habits and economy of uptown drinking. And, contrary to its intent, it created economic opportunities for people who had never been involved in the liquor business. At one end of the bootlegging chain were children who collected empty bottles outside dance halls and sold them back to moonshiners or who discovered bootleggers' stores and pilfered a few bottles of liquor to sell on their own. Italians, who had traditionally made wine for their own families, expanded production for commerce. The commission houses ordered freight-car loads of grapes—the largest anyone remembered was thirty-four cars—and had them brought directly to a siding near the Italian suburb of Meaderville. Italians who lived in Brown's Gulch, northwest of the city, also made wine and grappa. Dorothy Martin, who taught school in the Gulch, recalled that a sudden cloudburst would sometimes flood a bootlegger's cache and barrels of wine and grappa would come rolling down by the schoolhouse.[23]

It may well have been profits from bootlegging that led to the creation of a zone of restaurant-nightclubs in Meaderville in the late 1920s and early 1930s. These nightclubs bore little relation to pre-Prohibition saloons, and it was within their walls that a new heterosocial nightlife emerged. The first clubs opened during the last years of Prohibition, and, by the time liquor again became legal, they were Butte institutions. The Rocky Mountain Cafe, Aro, Golden Fan, Copper Club, and Pera Cafe, among others, attracted all classes of men and women for drinking, dancing, gambling, and one- or two-dollar multicourse dinners. As in New York City's cabarets, the design of Butte clubs gave women social and physical protection. They offered privacy and distance not provided in open barrooms, where there were few tables or chairs, and where patrons freely mingled and jostled one another. In the Rocky Mountain Cafe, for example, booths lined the walls around a central dance floor and the gambling operation was in a back room. Many people patronized the clubs exclusively as restaurants and did not sample their other attractions. But Meaderville's nightclubs also created an atmosphere in which women felt comfortable drinking and gambling, if they so chose. As one customer observed, "Meaderville's night clubs lack the vigor, the hairy chests and the call of the wild that you'll find in the city. Women may gamble side by side with their men and loll at the bars with them." Unlike saloons, where women were welcome only at the back door, nightclubs encouraged women's attendance and trade.[24]

While the Meaderville clubs provided a spectrum of entertainment, more common throughout the city were "home speaks," which marked a return of kitchen grog shops, run by women or families. Mike Erick and his wife, for instance, owned a small dance hall and soft drink parlor that catered to fellow Slavic immigrants. Mr. and Mrs. Charles Martin, African Americans, ran a home speak on New Street. Pat O'Hara sold beer and moonshine in his cabin and denied that it was a dance hall, although he did admit that his customers sometimes danced to the music of a phonograph.[25]

Bootlegging, in fact, provided a new vehicle for women, especially widows and wives, to supplement their income. Slavic women began making wine and selling it to boarders with their dinners. Many working-class women in Dublin Gulch, on the East Side, and in gulches outside the city had their own stills or cared for family stills while their husbands were at work. One of the most elaborate outfits confiscated, a three-hundred-gallon capacity still, was operated by eighty-year-old Mrs. Lavinia Gilman. The court gave Mrs. Kate Farlan, "a gray-haired mother" convicted of manufacturing liquor in her home, a suspended sentence on condition she obey the law for one year. Shortly after sentencing agents found another still in her house. Mrs. Michael Murray, who had two children and claimed she could not work outside the home, confessed to being the "cook" in an operation in which her husband and a friend marketed her liquor. Widow Nora Gallagher told police she set up a still on her kitchen stove in order to outfit her five children for Easter. Police arrested women selling liquor and beer in grocery stores and boarding houses and others attempting to destroy incriminating evidence by dumping liquor and mash into cellars.[26]

Home bootlegging was, for the most part, a working-class practice, but at least a few middle-class women set up their own stills, presumably more for the thrill than from any economic need. Arriving home one day to find a peculiar odor in the house, Dr. Carl Horst traced it to the basement where he discovered his wife had assembled a still. He demolished it over her protests, allowing her to keep one gallon for her ladies club. The public did not expect the middle class to manufacture their own liquor. When police found a still "within a stone's throw of the classic halls of the School of Mines and surrounded by residences of men of high standing in the community," it was "an astounding revelation."[27]

The independence of female bootleggers also challenged male notions of women's place. While police and judges had long experience with prostitutes and woman drunkards, bootlegging women were beyond their ken. When police arrested Susie Gallagher Kerr along with two men, Kerr admitted that the seized still was her operation, but the police preferred to believe that the men were in charge. The judge who tried eighty-year-old Lavinia Gilman felt her son was the "real culprit" and hoped that he would come forward to save his mother. The younger Gilman apparently did not share the court's chivalrous attitude and never appeared. Judge Bourquin, a staunch upholder of the law, did not like to commit women to jail, but, in the case of twice-caught Kate Farlan, he felt compelled to carry out the court's order and reluctantly locked her up for six months.[28]

Many writers in the 1920s and early 1930s commented on the appearance of women in speakeasies, most portraying their actions as silly or comic. But caricatures of well-to-do young flappers or matrons, with their high heels hooked over the brass rail of a smoky speakeasy, trivialized an important and, certainly for some, disturbing change in women's behavior and values. Butte author Reuben Maury, writing in *Scribner's Magazine* in 1926, captured the anxiety of a mining city mother, whose daughter seemed to care more for "comfort and an automobile and an able bootlegger" than for the prospect of marriage and children. Mothers feared that their daughters were eschewing domesticity for frivolity.[29]

Men shared an uneasy feeling that more was at stake than a woman having a drink. Indeed male writers' caustic remarks about ladies lunching in speakeasies were a defensive response to women's invasion of traditional male territory. As one scholar of drinking habits noted, men defined the use and abuse of alcohol as a male privilege, a symbol of power and prestige. What bothered men was not that women drank, but that they drank in public commercial institutions. It was not only the anti-saloon thrust of the Prohibition movement, but the heterosociability of new watering holes that seemed to spell doom for that long-cherished male bastion, the saloon.[30]

Women who made whiskey and those who patronized speakeasies were breaking both custom and the law. Their actions were deliberate and self-conscious. For working-class women bootlegging was a logical extension of the many kinds of home work they had traditionally undertaken to supplement family income; admittedly it carried some risks but presumably offered greater rewards. For unmarried women—both working and middle-class—drinking and visiting speakeasies were open acts of rebellion since "nice girls" did not do such things.

The speakeasy culture that gave more freedom to young women also became associated with other symbols of independence not necessarily connected to drinking such as cigarette-smoking and bobbed hair. Embracing these fads became rites of passage for young women in the 1920s. Peer pressure, as well as the lure of the forbidden, was clearly at work. Alma Muentzer Hileman recalled that none of her girlfriends drank until Prohibition, "then everybody ha[d] to taste and see what it [was]. . . . That's the first that any of us ever knew what a highball and all that stuff was. And we were born in a brewery."[31]

Many daughters deliberately violated long-held conventions defining respectability and tested the strength of familial bonds. Both Helen Harrington and Dorothy Martin spent a considerable amount of time preparing their parents for the day they came home with bobbed hair. Dorothy's father had initially dissuaded her from having her hair cut when he told her that only prostitutes wore bobbed hair. She persisted, but it was only after her mother saw that nearly all Dorothy's friends were having their hair cut that she succeeded in getting a bob. For several weeks as she came home from work each day Helen Harrington told her mother

With the girls displaying their popular bobbed hairstyles,
two courting couples pose in front of an automobile dealership.

BUTTE–SILVER BOW COUNTY ARCHIVES

that she was going to get her hair bobbed. Her sister remembered the day she finally did: Helen came home and said, "'Ma, I got my hair bobbed,' and Ma never looked at her. Finally after a while, she peeked over her 15-cent-store glasses and all she said was, 'I guess you'll be going to the roadhouses next.'"[32]

Josephine Weiss Casey did go to the roadhouses. Wearing her "pretty dress," she and her boyfriend and two or three other couples would drive over from Anaconda to eat, drink, and dance in the Meaderville clubs. For a dollar they could get a chicken dinner and two highballs; the third was, by custom, on the house. Other nights after a movie they would go to a speakeasy that served "the best gin fizzes in the world." It was not just the quality of the liquor, but the fact that they were "swanky drinks," served in "tall nice glasses," in a place that was "packed, packed and not all [with] kids like us," that made the evening so tantalizing.[33]

For young women the speakeasies often seemed mysterious and thrilling. Dorothy Martin recalled that going to the clubs "was probably the most daring and frightening thing that I did." She remembered climbing down a ladder to get in one place. "You couldn't see through the smoke because everybody smoked. And I thought, 'Oh, boy, what a wonderful place for tragedy.'" But Dorothy didn't like liquor, and she ended up dumping her drinks in the spittoon when no one was looking. Clearly, it was not alcohol but adventure that drew her and perhaps many of her peers to the "downright honest-to-God bootleg joints."[34]

The Meaderville nightclubs eventually posed a challenge to women's traditional forms of leisure. In the late 1930s the Daughters of Norway engaged in a considerable discussion over the relative merits of having their annual picnic or going to a Meaderville cafe for a ravioli dinner. Ravioli triumphed over tradition, and the women had such a good time that they made it an annual event. Club minutes recorded their pleasure: "We all had a glorious evening, an evening that will live in our memory for a long, long time; after a hi-ball or two, Mrs. Sontum got hot clear down to her feet, & [if] that wasn't enough, she also emptied their slot machines." In an addendum to the minutes, the secretary noted, "It was moved and seconded that we should take the dollar Mrs. Larsen & Mrs. Langstadt gave us to treat ourselfs [sic] to some wine, which we did."[35]

Prohibition's new speakeasies, nightclubs, and roadhouses catered to couples and sanctioned and encouraged drinking for women. Young women who ventured into these new institutions knew they were crossing a divide between an old set of assumptions about behavior and morality, and a new code they were creating. Some faced the divide with a bittersweet knowledge of the price of innovation. As Dorothy Martin recalled, when she finally got her hair cut, "I kind of cried myself when I looked at me with my short hair. But, it was done." The actions of Dorothy Martin, a schoolteacher, Helen Harrington, a shop clerk, and hundreds of other young women forced changes in the public perception of female drinking. Female patrons of speakeasies were neither "loose women" nor "floozies." They were "good" women and they compelled people to acknowledge that they could retain their respectability while taking a drink in public.[36]

There is great irony in Prohibition. The law had, in effect, created a vacuum of rules, and women exploited the opportunity to slip into niches in the economy of liquor production, distribution, and consumption.

Women had been in the vanguard of the Prohibition movement, a movement designed to restrict male behavior by abolishing the vice-ridden retreat of the saloon and curbing male drinking. Yet a decade after legislative success, some of the very same women led the campaign for repeal of the Eighteenth Amendment, having concluded that some kind of regulated liquor trade was preferable to moral anarchy. Much to their dismay, during Prohibition, drinking had become an equal opportunity vice. True, many saloons closed their doors forever and the consumption of alcohol did decrease. But during Prohibition men and women reconstructed social drinking habits and the greatest change was women's new-found penchant to belly up to the bar. Unforeseen by proponents and opponents, Prohibition effectively created new social spaces in speakeasies and nightclubs, sparking redefinition of sex roles in one of the most gender-segregated arenas of leisure—getting together for a drink. Behavior followed structural change. Public drinking was not on the list of rights demanded by twentieth-century feminists. Indeed the seemingly frivolous activities of young women in the 1920s dismayed feminists who saw them diverting energy from politics. Nevertheless, the reorganization of drinking did increase women's autonomy. Whether they spent an evening drinking and dancing with their boyfriends, husbands, or members of their ladies club, doors that had been closed to them now opened in welcome. Prohibition provided women with new economic opportunities, greater choices of public leisure, and a chance to broaden the definition of reputable female behavior.[37]

NOTES

My thanks to David Emmons, Jacquelyn Dowd Hall, Dale Martin, Laurie Mercier, Susan Rhoades Neel, and Anastatia Sims for their generous and incisive reading of this essay. Special thanks to Alice Finnegan for sharing her Anaconda interviews and to Joyce Justice for assistance with the District Court records.

1. *United States v. Maud Vogen,* November 11, 1922, judgment roll 928, United States District Court, Montana, Record Group 21, District of Montana Criminal Register and Dockets, National Archives, Pacific Northwest Region, Seattle, Washington. Between 1920 and 1934, 134 Butte women were prosecuted in the court for violations of the Volstead Act.

2. Anonymous letter to John Hughes, Butte–Silver Bow archivist, September 27, 1982; *Butte Montana Standard,* April 11, 1929.

3. On changing gender roles in the 1920s, see Loren Baritz, "The Culture of the Twenties," in *The Development of an American Culture,* ed. Stanley Coben and Lorman Ratner (New York, 1983); Gerald E. Critoph, "The Flapper and Her Critics," in *"Remember the Ladies": New Perspectives on Women in American History,* ed. Carol V. R. George (New York, 1975); Peter G. Filene, *Him/Her/Self: Sex Roles in Modern America* (Baltimore, 1986); Estelle B. Freedman, "The New Woman: Changing Views of Women in the 1920s," *Journal of American History,* 61 (September 1974), 372–93; Ruth Freeman and Patricia Klaus, "Blessed or Not? The New Spinster in England and the United States in the Late Nineteenth and Early Twentieth Centuries," *Journal of Family History,* 9 (Winter 1984), 394–414; John D. Hewitt, "Patterns of Female Criminality in Middletown: 1900 to 1920," *Indiana Social Studies Quarterly,* 38 (Autumn 1986), 49–59; J. Stanley Lemons, *The Woman Citizen: Social Feminism in the 1920s* (Urbana, Ill., 1973); James R. McGovern, "The American Woman's Pre–World War I Freedom in Manners and Morals," *Journal of American History,* 55 (September 1968), 315–33; Carroll Smith-Rosenberg, "The New Woman as Androgyne: Social Disorder and Gender Crisis, 1870–1936," in *Disorderly Conduct: Visions of Gender in Victorian America* (New York, 1985); June Sochen, *The New Woman: Feminism in Greenwich Village, 1910–1920* (New York, 1972); and Kenneth A. Yellis, "Prosperity's Child: Some Thoughts on the Flapper," *American Quarterly,* 21 (Spring 1969), 49–64.

4. Mark Edward Lender and James Kirby Martin, *Drinking in America: A History* (New York, 1982), 117; Albert J. Kennedy, "The Saloon in Retrospect and Prospect," *Survey Graphic,* 22 (April 1933), 206. Thomas Brennan discusses the growth in the diversity of public drinking places in *Public Drinking and Popular Culture in Eighteenth-Century Paris* (Princeton, N.J., 1988), 14–19. Perry R. Duis discusses gender-segregated drinking along public-private lines in *The Saloon: Public Drinking in Chicago and Boston, 1880–1920* (Urbana, Ill., 1983), 105–7. Roy Rosenzweig describes the demise of kitchen grog shops in *Eight Hours for What We Will: Workers and Leisure in an Industrial City, 1870–1920* (New York, 1983), 41–49, 63.

5. For working women's commercial amusements and the changing gender use of public spaces, see Kathy Peiss, *Cheap Amusements: Working Women and Leisure in Turn-of-the-Century New York* (Philadelphia, 1986); Joanne J. Meyerowitz, *Women Adrift: Independent Wage Earners in Chicago, 1880–1930* (Chicago, 1988); Elizabeth Ewen, *Immigrant Women in the Land of Dollars: Life and Culture on the Lower East Side, 1890–1925* (New York, 1985); Christine Stansell, *City of Women: Sex and Class in New York, 1789–1860* (Urbana, Ill., 1986); and Michael Schudson, "Women, Cigarettes and Advertising in the 1920s: A Study in the Sociology of Consumption," in *Mass Media between the Wars: Perceptions of Cultural Tension, 1918–1941,* ed. Catherine L. Covert and John D. Stevens (Syracuse, N.Y., 1984), 71–83.

Peiss specifically notes the absence of reputable women from saloons, 20–28. On this topic, see also Madelon Powers, "Decay from Within: The Inevitable Doom of the American Saloon," in *Drinking: Behavior and Belief in Modern History,* ed. Susanna Barrows and Robin Room (Berkeley, Calif., 1991), 115; Hutchins Hapgood, "McSorley's

Saloon," *Harper's Weekly*, 58 (October 25, 1913), 15; Royal L. Melendy, "The Saloon in Chicago," *American Journal of Sociology*, 6 (November 1900), 300; and Travis Hoke, "Corner Saloon," *American Mercury*, 22 (March 1931), 313–15.

Lewis A. Erenberg, in *Steppin' Out: New York Nightlife and the Transformation of American Culture, 1890–1930* (Chicago, 1981), discusses the rise of New York cabarets at the turn of the century as a place where reputable, well-to-do women could drink in public. Cabarets were not, of course, common outside the largest of American cities.

6. In 1900 the sex ratio between men and women was 147.7 to 100; in 1910 it was 132.4 to 100; and in 1920 it was 119.6 to 100. Bureau of the Census, *Thirteenth Census of the United States, 1910*, vol. 2 (Washington, D.C., 1910), 1147; Bureau of the Census, *Abstract of the Fourteenth Census of the United States* (Washington, D.C., 1920), 131.

For general works on Butte, see Ray Calkins, comp., *Looking Back from the Hill: Recollections of Butte People* (Butte, Mont., 1982); Jerry W. Calvert, *The Gibraltar: Socialism and Labor in Butte, Montana, 1885–1920* (Helena, Mont., 1988); David M. Emmons, *The Butte Irish: Class and Ethnicity in an American Mining Town, 1875–1925* (Urbana, Ill., 1989); Michael P. Malone, *The Battle for Butte: Mining and Politics on the Northern Frontier, 1864–1906* (Seattle, 1981); and Work Projects Administration (WPA), *Copper Camp: Stories of the World's Greatest Mining Town, Butte, Montana* (New York, 1943). On the red-light district, see Mary Murphy, "Women on the Line: Prostitution in Butte, Montana, 1878–1917" (master's thesis, University of North Carolina, 1983).

7. Louis J. Bahin, "The Campaign for Prohibition in Montana: Agrarian Radicalism and Liquor Reform, 1883–1926" (master's thesis, University of Montana, 1984), 94–96; *Butte City Directory, 1916.*

8. On the multifunctional nature of western saloons, see Edison K. Putnam, "The Prohibition Movement in Idaho, 1863–1934" (Ph.D. diss., University of Idaho, 1979), 54, 403; Elliott West, *The Saloon on the Rocky Mountain Mining Frontier* (Lincoln, Neb., 1979), 131–32; Thomas J. Noel, *The City and the Saloon: Denver, 1858–1916* (Lincoln, Neb., 1982), 13, 65; David Brundage, "The Producing Classes and the Saloon: Denver in the 1880s," *Labor History*, 26 (Winter 1985), 30–32; Ann Burk, "The Mining Camp Saloon as a Social Center," *Red River Valley Historical Review*, 2 (Fall 1975), 385; Jon M. Kingsdale, "The 'Poor Man's Club': Social Functions of the Urban Working-Class Saloon," in *The American Man*, ed. Joseph H. Pleck and Elizabeth H. Pleck (Englewood Cliffs, N.J., 1980), 265, 267; and WPA, *Copper Camp*, 83.

9. Richard W. Slatta, "Comparative Frontier Social Life: Western Saloons and Argentine Pulperias," *Great Plains Quarterly*, 7 (Summer 1987), 158–59; West, *Saloon*, 19–21; Putnam, "Prohibition Movement," 10.

10. Myron Brinig, *Singermann* (New York, 1929), 292–93.

11. On children in saloons, see Noel, *City and the Saloon*, 89; Robert Alston Stevenson, "Saloons," *Scribner's Magazine*, 29 (May 1901), 571, 577; and "The Experience and Observation of a New York Saloon-Keeper," *McClure's Magazine*, 32 (January 1909), 311. Pat O'Leary, interview by Ray Calkins, July 22, 1980, transcript, p. 17–18, Butte–Silver Bow Public Archives, Butte, Montana (hereafter BSBA); Frank Carden, "A Walk from 228 S. Gaylord Street to Park and Main Streets and Beyond in Butte, Montana, in

the 1920's and 1930's," TS, ca. 1987, p. 6–7, BSBA; Mike McNelis, interview by Alice Finnegan, October 18, 1985, transcript, p. 8.

12. On Irish culture and drinking, see Robert F. Bales, "Attitudes toward Drinking in the Irish Culture" in *Society, Culture, and Drinking Patterns,* ed. David J. Pittman and Charles R. Snyder (New York, 1962), 157–87; James R. Barrett, "Why Paddy Drank: The Social Importance of Whiskey in Pre-Famine Ireland," *Journal of Popular Culture,* 11 (Summer 1977), 155/17–166/28; and Dennis Clark, *The Irish Relations: Trials of an Immigrant Tradition* (East Brunswick, N.J., 1982), chap. 4. Richard Stivers discusses Irish bachelor culture in *A Hair of the Dog: Irish Drinking and American Stereotype* (University Park, Pa., 1976), 76–97. Colleen McDannell, "'True Men as We Need Them': Catholicism and the Irish-American Male," *American Studies,* 27 (Fall 1986), 24.

13. On Slavic drinking habits see Emily Greene Balch, *Our Slavic Fellow Citizens* (New York, 1910), 95, 365–69, quote on 365. On Slavic drinking habits in Montana see Anna Zellick, "Fire in the Hole: Slovenians, Croatians, and Coal Mining on the Musselshell," *Montana The Magazine of Western History,* 40 (Spring 1990), 24–26.

14. Myron Brinig, *Wide Open Town* (New York, 1931), 15–16; Silver Bow County Board of Health, "Report on Sanitary Conditions in the Mines and Community, Silver Bow County, December 1908–April 1912," TS, Small Collection 89, Silver Bow County Sanitary Conditions Report, Montana Historical Society Archives, Helena (hereafter MHS); Silver Bow County Board of Health, "Report Showing Results of Inspection of Dwellings, Hotels, Rooming Houses, and Boarding Houses and Their Surroundings, 1912," TS, MHS; Annual Reports of the City Officers, City of Butte for the Fiscal Years Ending April 30, 1908–09 (n.p., n.d.), 175–76; *Annual Reports of the City Officers, City of Butte for the Fiscal Years Ending April 30, 1910–11* (Butte, Mont., n.d.), 163; *Annual Reports of the City Officers of the City of Butte, Montana, Fiscal Year Ending April 30, 1912* (Butte, Mont., n.d.), 80; and Emmons, *Butte Irish,* 152. For a comparable situation regarding boardinghouse life and patronage of saloons, see Rosenzweig, *Eight Hours for What We Will,* 56.

15. Brinig, *Singermann,* 34; Joe H. Duffy, *Butte Was Like That* (Butte, Mont., 1941), 41, 47; WPA, *Copper Camp,* 74; George Butler, "Impressions of a Hobo," *Pacific Review,* 11 (September 1921), 205; *Butte Montana Standard,* October 25, 1959; *Anaconda (Mont.) Standard,* January 14, 1917; Byron E. Cooney, "The Saloons of Yester-Year," *Montana American,* July 18, 1919, 64.

Several Butte saloons are described in *North American Industrial Review, Montana* (Butte, Mont., n.d.), 16, 24, 25, 40, 78; and Bill Burke depicted the flavor of Butte saloons in 106 verses in "The Saloons of Old Time Butte," in *Rhymes of the Mines* (Vancouver, Wash., 1964), 65–75.

16. Jon Hopwood, "History of the Silver Bow Club," 1980, Merrill G. Burlingame Special Collections, Montana State University Libraries, Bozeman, Montana.

17. Aili Goldberg, interview by author, February 29, 1980, transcript, p. 18, BSBA; Alma E. Hileman, interview by Ray Calkins, June 27, 1980, transcript, p. 7, BSBA; Noel, *City and the Saloon,* 112.

18. *Laws, Resolutions and Memorials of the State of Montana Passed at the Tenth Regular Session of the Legislative Assembly* (Helena, Mont., 1907), 434–37; William E.

Carroll, comp., *The Revised Ordinances of the City of Butte, 1914* (Butte, Mont., 1914), 463–64. Richard B. Roeder discusses the Progressives' thinking in "Montana in the Early Years of the Progressive Period" (Ph.D. diss., University of Pennsylvania, 1971), 202–5. Other cities and states passed or attempted to pass similar laws. See Edison K. Putnam, "Travail at the Turn of the Century: Efforts at Liquor Control in Idaho," *Idaho Yesterdays,* 33 (Spring 1989), 15–16; Duis, *Saloon,* 254.

In at least two cases, Butte tried to enforce the law. In 1912 the city revoked the liquor license of the Canteen Saloon for violating the city ordinance, and in 1917 sheriffs arrested the owners of a roadhouse for permitting females to frequent the establishment. Petition of Centennial Brewing Company, Revocation of Liquor license at 27 1/2 West Granite St., January 17, 1912, City Council Petitions, BSBA; *Butte (Mont.) Miner,* April 6, 1917.

19. Catherine Hoy, interview by Ray Calkins and Caroline Smithson, May 11, 1979, transcript, p. 10–11, BSBA; Ann Pentilla, interview by Ray Calkins and Caroline Smithson, April 27, 1979, transcript, 53, BSBA; *Butte (Mont.) Miner,* April 10, 1916.

20. Mary Long Alderson, *Thirty-Four Years in the Montana Woman's Christian Temperance Union, 1896–1930* (Helena, Mont., 1932), 14; Bahin discusses the role of the Anti-Saloon League in *Butte (Mont.) Daily Bulletin,* January 10, 1920; *Butte City Directory, 1916; Butte City Directory, 1917; Butte City Directory, 1923;* Carden, "A Walk . . . in Butte, Montana," 9; *Butte (Mont.) Miner,* May 3, 1923.

For works on Prohibition in western states, see Official Records of the National Commission on Law Observance and Enforcement, *Enforcement of the Prohibition Laws,* vol. 4 of *Prohibition Surveys of the States,* 71st Cong., 3d sess., 1931, S. Doc. 307. Studies of Prohibition enforcement were conducted in several northern Rockies states, including Colorado, Wyoming, and Idaho. Unfortunately no study was conducted in Montana; however, reports of these states provide valuable insights into the problems of enforcement in the West. Also see Jody Bailey and Robert S. McPherson, "'Practically Free from the Taint of the Bootlegger': A Closer Look at Prohibition in Southeastern Utah," *Utah Historical Quarterly,* 57 (Spring 1989), 150–64; Helena Z. Papanikolas, "Bootlegging in Zion: Making and Selling the 'Good Stuff'," *Utah Historical Quarterly,* 53 (Summer 1985), 268–91; Norman Clark, *The Dry Years: Prohibition and Social Change in Washington,* 2d ed. (Seattle, 1988); Edmund Fahey, *Rum Road to Spokane: A Story of Prohibition* (Missoula, Mont., 1972); David J. McCullough, "Bone Dry?: Prohibition New Mexico Style, 1918–1933," *New Mexico Historical Review,* 63 (January 1988), 25–42; Walter R. Jones, "Casper's Prohibition Years," *Annals of Wyoming,* 48 (Fall 1976), 264–73; Gary A. Wilson, *Honky-Tonk Town: Havre's Bootlegging Days* (Helena, Mont., 1985); Patrick G. O'Brien, "Prohibition and the Kansas Progressive Example," *Great Plains Quarterly,* 7 (Fall 1987), 219–31; Gilman M. Ostrander, *The Prohibition Movement in California, 1848–1933* (Berkeley, Calif., 1957); and four studies by Kenneth D. Rose, "Booze and News in 1924: Prohibition in Seattle," *Portage,* 5 (Winter 1984), 16–22; "The Labbe Affair and Prohibition Enforcement in Portland," *Pacific Northwest Quarterly,* 77 (April 1986), 42–51; "'Dry' Los Angeles and Its Liquor Problems in 1924," *Southern California Quarterly,* 69 (Spring

1987), 51–74; and "Wettest in the West: San Francisco and Prohibition in 1924," *California History*, 65 (December 1986), 284–95, 314–15.

21. *Report of County Attorneys for 2 years from November 30, 1920, to November 30, 1922, on Liquor Cases,* copy in folder 16, box 15, Record Series 76, Montana Attorney General Records, 1893–1969, MHS (hereafter RS 76); "Agents' Reports," folder 11, box 7, RS 76, MHS; *Butte Montana Standard*, December 20, 1928.

22. Helena Shute Raymond, interview by Laurie Mercier, October 9, 1981, Butte, Montana, Oral History 196, MHS; Bahin, "Campaign for Prohibition," 133; *Butte Montana Standard*, September 12, 1928.

23. Calkins, *Looking Back*, 15–17; James Blakely, interview by Ray Calkins, November 15, 1979, transcript, p. 4, BSBA; Camille Maffei, interview by Russ Magnaghi, May 4, 1983, Oral History 583, MHS; *Butte Montana Standard*, November 4, 1962; Dorothy A. Martin, interview by author, May 23, 1988, transcript, pp. 29–30, MHS.

24. Teddy Traparish scrapbook, Teddy Traparish Papers, BSBA; *Butte Montana Standard*, November 4, 1962; Calkins, *Looking Back*, 71. Quotation is from Walter Davenport, "The Richest Hill on Earth," *Collier's*, February 6, 1937, 53.

On the rise of restaurant-nightclubs after the repeal of Prohibition, see Lewis A. Erenberg, "From New York to Middletown: Repeal and the Legitimization of Night-life in the Great Depression," *American Quarterly*, 38 (Winter 1986), 761–78. On economic gains made by Italians during Prohibition, see Gary Ross Mormino, *Immigrants on the Hill: Italian-Americans in St. Louis, 1882–1982* (Urbana, Ill., 1986), chap. 5. On business aspects of bootlegging, see Mark H. Haller, "Philadelphia Bootlegging and the Report of the Special August Grand Jury," *Pennsylvania Magazine of History and Biography*, 109 (April 1985), 215–33.

25. *Butte (Mont.) Miner*, July 31, 1922; *Butte (Mont.) Miner*, August 27, 1922; *Butte Montana Free Press*, January 21, 1929. John Chapman Hilder notes "home speaks" as a phenomenon of the West in "New York Speakeasy, A Study of a Social Institution," *Harper's Monthly*, 164 (April 1932), 591.

26. Pentilla, interview, 54; *Butte (Mont.) Miner*, November 23, 1924; *Butte Montana Standard*, December 28, 1928; *Butte (Mont.) Daily Post*, March 14, 1921; *Anaconda (Mont.) Standard*, March 26, 1921; *Butte Montana Standard*, December 23, 1928; *Butte (Mont.) Miner*, December 4, 1920, September 5, 1928.

John Kobler, in *Ardent Spirits: The Rise and Fall of Prohibition* (New York, 1973), 252, relates the concern of a priest in Pennsylvania who attributed women's unfaithfulness and penchant to run off with star boarders to tending home stills.

27. Betty Horst, unrecorded interview by author, May 23, 1988; *Butte (Mont.) Miner*, July 3, 1924.

28. *Butte (Mont.) Daily Post*, April 9, 1927; *Butte (Mont.) Miner*, November 23, 1924; *Butte Montana Standard*, December 28, 1928. Bourquin usually placed female first offenders who pleaded guilty on probation. *Butte Montana Standard*, May 18, 1929.

29. Reuben Maury, "Home," *Scribner's*, 79 (June 1926), 640. According to the New York City Investigating Committee of Fourteen, in 1925 the number of women seen in places illegally selling liquor was "astounding." George E. Mowry and Blaine A. Brownell, *The Urban Nation, 1920–1980*, rev. ed. (New York, 1981), 25. On women in

speakeasies, see Frederick Lewis Allen, *Only Yesterday: An Informal History of the 1920s* (New York, 1931), 211; Hilder, "New York Speakeasy," 591–601; Margaret Culkin Banning, "On the Wagon," *Harper's Monthly*, 163 (June 1931), 11–21; and Ida M. Tarbell, "Ladies at the Bar," *Liberty*, July 26, 1930, 6–10.

30. Joseph R. Gusfield, "Status Conflicts and the Changing Ideologies of the American Temperance Movement" in *Society, Culture and Drinking Patterns*, ed. David J. Pittman and Charles R. Snyder (New York, 1962), 102.

31. Hileman, interview, 32.

32. Martin, interview, 8–9; Julia McHugh, "The Gulch and I," TS, ca. 1986, p. 20–21, BSBA. The press contributed to the notion that the fashions of the 1920s were linked to prostitution. For example, a prostitute, who charged her husband with assault after he broke her jaw for not earning enough money on the street, was described as "a pretty girl with bobbed hair and dressed in the style of a flapper." *Butte (Mont.) Miner*, August 29, 1922.

33. Josephine Weiss Casey, interview by Alice Finnegan, May 18, 1989, transcript, p. 17.

34. Martin, interview, 30–31; Casey, interview, 17.

35. Minutes of January 3, 1939, meeting, Daughters of Norway, Solheim Lodge No. 20 Records, BSBA.

36. Martin, interview, 9.

37. Women's attempts to repeal the Eighteenth Amendment were coordinated by the Women's Organization for National Prohibition Repeal (WONPR). On the WONPR, see David E. Kyvig, *Repealing National Prohibition* (Chicago, 1979); Kyvig, "Women against Prohibition," *American Quarterly*, 28 (Fall 1976), 564–82; Grace C. Root, *Women and Repeal: The Story of the Women's Organization for National Prohibition Reform* (New York, 1934); and the Papers of the Association Against the Prohibition Amendment and the Women's Organization for National Prohibition Reform, Eleutherian Mills Historical Library, Wilmington, Delaware.

The Great Falls Home Front during World War II

WILLIAM J. FURDELL

The Second World War remains, for the most part, uncharted territory in Montana history. Did not the great turning point of the twentieth century affect the Treasure State? William Furdell, a professor of history at the University of Great Falls, argues that at least for his town it did.

Founded in 1883 by entrepreneur Paris Gibson and railroad magnate Jim Hill, Great Falls began as a planned power city, situated to take advantage of the hydroelectric power potential of the Great Falls of the Missouri River. It quickly became a thriving industrial center boasting a copper smelter, a rich ethnic mix of workers, and the studio of cowboy artist Charlie Russell. But the Great Depression brought economic decline and demographic stagnation. The war itself meant shortages and sacrifice. Nevertheless, the impact of the war on Great Falls offered the community a new lease on life and a turning point in the history of the city. The question still remains: are Furdell's conclusions applicable to other parts of the state?

WITH THE BOMBING OF PEARL HARBOR ON DECEMBER 7, 1941, AND THE NATION'S entry into World War II, Great Falls residents, like Americans everywhere, readily embraced the need for sacrifice to support the war effort. Among the Montanans to die in combat during the war were 129 servicemen from Great Falls and surrounding Cascade County. Their deaths visited untold grief on their Montana families and friends, and their loss undoubtedly caused the single greatest source of suffering for those on the home front.[1] With that notable and most significant exception, however, the sacrifices the people of Great Falls made in support of the war consisted more of minor inconveniences relating to wartime shortages than anything else. Indeed the most significant, long-term impact from the war came with the establishment of East Base, a major military installation just outside of town, giving rise to growth and change.

As was true elsewhere, the people of Great Falls were not only dismayed at the news of the Japanese attack on Pearl Harbor but fearful of imminent air attacks or sabotage in the United States itself. Such anxieties soon receded, however, and Great Falls citizens, confident of the nation's ability to secure ultimate victory, adjusted to wartime needs and routines. They not only tolerated shortages and endured the rationing of gasoline, tires, shoes, butter, meat, and a myriad of other products, but they also embraced the war effort enthusiastically, volunteering their help for everything from blackout enforcement to scrap drives and bond sales. Women went to work at the new air base and, for the first time ever, took jobs in production and industrial maintenance at the Anaconda Company smelter in Great Falls.

For most people in the greater Great Falls community, the war was a positive experience. It constituted a unifying cause around which local citizens could rally and within which individuals could find meaning and purpose. Even as they accepted necessary sacrifices, they enjoyed the psychic benefits that came with being part of a community practically unanimous in its support of the war. The Great Falls community embraced the economic benefits brought by wartime demands for what local farms and factories could produce and by the employment and contracting opportunities generated by the location of East Base, with its rapid addition of some four thousand personnel to Great Falls's population.[2]

Indeed East Base, as it was called initially, would have the greatest impact on Great Falls. In addition to its tremendous economic influence on the community during the war and after, it reshaped the social and cultural character of Great Falls for decades. East Base, so named because it was east of Great Falls, but renamed Malmstrom Air Force Base in 1954 in honor of Colonel Einer Axel Malmstrom, who died when his T-33 trainer jet crashed in the vacant countryside eleven miles southwest of the base, brought military personnel of diverse origins from throughout the United States to the community.[3] Many came after tours of duty in England,

Germany, Korea, Japan, and the Philippines, where some had found spouses. Others married into Great Falls families. During the war and for years afterward, many of the military personnel who experienced Great Falls during the war chose to make the city their permanent home. Active and retired military personnel and their families both increased and diversified the city's population.

On the eve of the nation's entry into World War II, Great Falls struggled to overcome the effects of the Great Depression. Hard times had slowed the city's growth to a virtual halt, and the city's population, which had stagnated at about thirty thousand people throughout the 1930s, went unchanged through late 1941.

Such conditions did not reflect the ambitions of the city's founders. Unlike the lawless mining camps and roaring cattle towns so much a part of the lore of Montana and the Old West, Great Falls began as a businessman's town. It was said that the city "couldn't point to a boot hill or a hangin' tree." Great Falls had its origins in the dreams of Paris Gibson. After the Panic of 1873 Gibson, a Minneapolis entrepreneur, abandoned failed business interests in Minnesota and traveled west to Fort Benton, Montana, the head of upper Missouri River navigation. There he raised sheep and engaged in the wool trade. Gibson first saw the nearby falls of the Missouri in 1880 and with a businessman's eye quickly recognized their potential for the production of power. Gibson convinced his friend, railroad magnate James J. Hill, to invest in a townsite at the falls and urged that Hill extend his railroad through the new city on its way to the Pacific Ocean. By 1887 Hill had completed rail lines linking Great Falls to Butte and Helena, and over these lines copper ore soon arrived for processing in Great Falls plants. To Gibson's chagrin, however, Hill took advantage of the rediscovered "Lost" Marias Pass and built a more direct transcontinental route through the Rocky Mountains on its way from St. Paul to Tacoma, Washington. The main line of his Great Northern Railway thus bypassed Great Falls to the north.[4]

Despite this setback Great Falls, located on a plain just forty miles east of the foothills of the Rocky Mountain front, became a major center of trade for area farmers and ranchers, and its dams on the Missouri River contributed power for ore processing and grain milling industries. Through the end of the nineteenth century and the early years of the twentieth,

Great Falls prospered or suffered in response to fluctuating markets for copper and grain. The World War I years were prosperous for the city, but in the years that followed drought and declining wheat prices crippled Montana's farm economy and undermined the Great Falls economy as well. Then came the Great Depression of the 1930s, which wrought additional cutbacks in the mining and smelting industries. Hard times kept the city's growth in check until events at Pearl Harbor put the city on an entirely new course.

At first the community's response to war was precautionary. To prevent sabotage guards were posted at city reservoirs, at the water intake at the river, and at the airport. Off-duty firemen and policemen were ordered to remain available and be on alert in case of emergency. The Great Falls city council passed a defense ordinance and immediately after the declaration of war prepared the city for potential air raids. Issuing the first blackout

With the stack of the Anaconda Company's smelter in the background at upper left, a single-engine 7th Ferrying Group P-39 makes its way over Great Falls during World War II.

CASCADE COUNTY HISTORICAL SOCIETY, GREAT FALLS, MONTANA

proclamation on December 21, 1941, Mayor Edward L. Shields spelled out procedures to be followed. Three long blasts of whistles or sirens accompanied by the blinking of streetlights signaled an impending air raid. Citizens, who were enjoined to "Turn out all outside lights and inside lights that can be seen from the outside," were also told: "Don't forget your skylight!" For safety's sake everyone was to remain where they were when the signal was given, "inside or outside, at home, in theaters or any other place, stay there while the blackout is on. This means everybody—men, women, and children." The proclamation prohibited driving without lights, so anyone driving, whether in a motorized vehicle or on a bicycle, was to pull to the curb immediately and turn off their lights. People were reminded to turn off their lights at home any time they planned to be away at night in case of a blackout. Three short and one long siren blast with the street lights back on meant "all clear."[5]

As was typical of community groups' involvement on the home front, the Great Falls Boy Scouts responsibly distributed 7,500 blackout regulation sheets. Three hundred adult volunteers formed twenty divisions under subwardens or captains to oversee the blackouts. Failure to comply with blackout rules could mean a fine of up to three hundred dollars and up to ninety days in jail, but according to one account, "almost everyone responded loyally and heartily." The *Great Falls Tribune* urged "nervous people" not to be frightened by the necessary precautionary measures and assured its readers that the danger of air raids would remain negligible unless the Japanese secured bases in Alaska.[6]

Great Falls residents showed no signs of panic and seemed to take the war in stride, although they expressed anger toward the Japanese in the aftermath of Pearl Harbor and the Bataan death march. In the Great Falls High School 1942 yearbook, seniors proclaimed their ambitions "to fight the Japs; to shoot Japs; to bomb Tokyo." Some students looked forward to joining the United States Army, Army Air Corps, or Navy. One senior high school girl said she aspired to be "a war nurse." Most students, however, listed conventional career ambitions or simply evinced desires "to be married" or "gay." Patriotism and war-related themes permeated the Great Falls High School yearbooks, but by 1945 "Japs" were not mentioned in text. Rather, the message from Principal Armin G. Jahr was more conciliatory, sounding a theme of how "Real life knows no differences in class, race, and religion." Students took pride in a B-29 bomber being christened "Bisons" in honor of their record-breaking per capita purchases of stamps and bonds, and their yearbook included photos of several patriotic young men who had joined the service before graduating.[7]

Nonetheless, Great Falls High School students, like everyone else, were affected by the ever-present fact of war. Paper and supply shortages, as well as teacher shortages, were all noted in their 1945 yearbook. A photograph that showed a football program cover announcing one of the previous fall's football games also revealed how drawings of fighter planes, warships, and army tanks festooned the poster. Still, there was plenty of ordinary content relating to social and athletic events and little overt militaristic chauvinism. Agora Club members, for example, were pleased that despite the shortage of paper they had successfully sponsored their traditional confetti booth at the Booster Carnival. Boys' athletics received emphasis, but girls' activities were not ignored. Some two hundred to three hundred girls were reported active in school sports during the 1944–45 school year, most in volleyball, basketball, and tennis. Bowling, also a popular choice, had been added during the last year of the war. "Although they do not assume the highly competitive aspect which colors boys' sports," one yearbook writer observed, "girls' athletic activities continue to interest a large proportion of the female population." Such remarks, by today's standards, reflect primitive attitudes toward women's athletics, but it was a positive recognition that participation and interest were on the rise, perhaps in turn reflecting the increasingly visible role women were taking in many endeavors during the war.[8]

As in peacetime, students focused on social activities, athletic events, and academic studies. And while day-to-day activities continued as before, concerns related to the war were ever-present. Few people, children or adults, were unaffected, and on the heels of Pearl Harbor and the horrors associated with Bataan, xenophobic reactions against Japanese Americans were manifest. Racism, a recurrent flaw seemingly in all cultures, was present even in peacetime, and anti-Japanese sentiments intensified as military casualties and reports of atrocities mounted. Cartoon portrayals and newspaper drawings perpetuated and enlarged racist stereotypes. One advertisement in the *Great Falls Tribune* gave Japanese soldiers a particularly sinister, animal-like appearance, portraying them with arched eyebrows, opened mouths, and jagged teeth. Another depiction, an attempt at humor but still racist, portrayed a Japanese man sporting huge canines and pointy ears and exhorting Americans, "Please Not To Buy U.S. War Bonds And Thank You So Much."[9]

Although racist portrayals and stereotypes persisted, the Great Falls press actually cautioned against inappropriate anti-Japanese attitudes and actions. Two weeks after Pearl Harbor, a *Tribune* editorial sympathized with the plight of Japanese Americans living in Montana and called upon readers to recognize that these people were "good Americans" who deserved fair and decent treatment. Noting that a number of Japanese families resided in the High Line area, one writer observed: "These are families that have accepted American [sic] completely and their children know no other country or patriotism." Another editorial reported private citizens "taking severe measures" against "dangerous and subversive aliens" elsewhere in the country, but urged Great Falls readers not to act individually. Instead, they should leave matters relating to subversive aliens to the government.[10] Great Falls residents seemed to agree with such an approach. There were no accounts of actions taken locally by private citizens—nor by government authorities, for that matter.

By late March 1942 federal authorities had relocated approximately one thousand West Coast Japanese to Fort Missoula. In Great Falls the matter was reported briefly but without extended discussion or opinion on internment practices. When the state of Montana put in a request for forty-five hundred "Jap workers" for the sugar beet fields, Helena authorities insisted they labor under federal supervision and not be allowed to remain in Montana after the war. Such provisions no doubt mirrored the prevailing viewpoint throughout the state and region—Great Falls included—but nothing indicated discussion about or interest in the matter locally. Local theatergoers might have needed the *Great Falls Leader's* assurance that they should not stay away from a touring performance of Gilbert and Sullivan's Mikado "simply because it is a story of the Japs," but even in peacetime Great Falls audiences would likely have turned out for this operetta in only modest numbers.[11]

The people of Great Falls, energized by the war, may have shared widely held racist attitudes toward the Japanese, but their enthusiasm did not translate into anything approaching wartime hysteria. Instead residents focused their attention on home-front projects that supported the war effort. Camp Fire Girls, for example, figured prominently in the collection of scrap grease to preserve the glycerin that could be salvaged from fats for use in explosives. The girls had collected more than six tons—12,700 pounds—of grease by November 1942 and were reported to have obtained some ten tons of it by March 1943.[12] Neighborhood signs appeared on homes throughout the city to designate collection depots where donors, who received three cents per pound, were encouraged to deliver their waste fats. Or they could call for someone to pick it up.

The 625 Great Falls girls in Camp Fire, assisted by as many as 275 adult volunteers, including Camp Fire board members, Camp Fire leaders, and parents, were commended roundly by the *Great Falls Leader*. In a front-page headline, the paper reported: "Falls Girls Doing Major War Job" and went on to note that local Camp Fire Girls had received special recognition on a "nationwide Columbia broadcast" that morning for their grease collection work. The same article, which appeared on a July Saturday, announced an intensified grease drive for the following Tuesday, Wednesday, and Thursday. The *Leader* said adults would drive cars throughout the city during the three-day campaign and Camp Fire Girls would call at individual homes.[13]

In addition to grease the Great Falls community supported scrap metal, rubber, and paper drives. The Cascade County Salvage Committee was reported to have obtained 2,240,498 pounds of such materials by October 22, 1942. One story related that in a gesture of patriotic enthusiasm an eleven-year-old boy had thrown his dad's fishing boots into the scrap pile. Repenting his rash act the youth attempted to obtain a certificate of authorization to purchase replacements, but rubber boots could not be had without demonstration of need. Recreational fishing apparently was insufficient justification.[14]

To assist the scrap efforts 250 Teamsters volunteered to drive trucks provided by the county, city, and the local headquarters of the WPA. Scrap yards in Great Falls were piled so high that some voiced doubts there was any need for it all, but the doubters were assured that shipments from the Great Falls yard had already begun and that the scrap would indeed go into the war effort.[15]

Area farms also yielded massive amounts of scrap metal. Abandoned mining camps, with their ghostly "old hoists, or crushers, tramways and mills," proved rich in scrap metal. Even the artillery on the courthouse grounds went into the collection heap. The Civil War–era cannons, weighing 5,385 pounds each, were "Destined to 'fire' again . . . at a more ruthless enemy," the *Tribune* observed. The empty granite gun mounts, left as they were, remained vacant for two decades after the war. Not until 1965 were two other Civil War cannons obtained and set in place.[16]

Support for the war effort was practically universal throughout the war. David Davidson, a longtime resident and prominent Great Falls businessman, remembered his mother's work with the local Greek War Relief Agency. Recalling the era's numerous volunteer organizations and prevailing enthusiasm and military support activities, he likely was correct in judging the community to have been "pretty close to 100% behind the war effort." Men and women of all ages were actively involved on the home front. In addition to helping distribute blackout rules, local Boy Scouts regularly participated in waste paper, scrap metals, and scrap rubber collections, and were often called upon to distribute posters and leaflets advertising defense bond drives and savings stamp sales. In addition to their grease collections, Camp Fire Girls supported the war with other activities such as cutting cloth squares for a wool blanket destined for the Red Cross. Blue Bird girls made a box of cookies "for a young soldier," and Girl Scouts attended an "institute on civil defense" where, among other things, they learned how to extinguish fires properly. As their "service to others" Great Falls Brownie troops spent two weeks collecting coat hangers for use in the dayroom at the army air base.[17]

Voluntarism abounded. By late February 1942 no fewer than four hundred women had signed up for civil defense work, and one women's group—the Athena Sorosis—proudly proclaimed that all of its members were involved. Besides the standard eighty hours of required classroom preparation, women in civil defense could take condensed, twenty-hour classes in mechanics, nutrition, or telegraphy. A special "Canteen Corps" prepared meal trays to alleviate staff shortages in the local hospitals, and the American Association of University Women and a men's organization helped furnish the Officers' Club at the local air base.[18]

As plentiful as were volunteers, labor was in short supply. Female as well as male workers were in great demand. While Great Falls lacked the aircraft plants and shipyards often associated with the image of "Rosie the Riveter," women workers entered an even more intensely male occupational bastion—the Great Falls smelter. Work there was heavy, dirty, and dangerous, and women had not been employed in the copper and zinc plants prior to the war. Anaconda Company records for the Great Falls operations indicate that relatively few women found work at the smelter, even during the war years. Employment statistics were recorded by gender on a monthly basis beginning in July 1944. Of a total 1,605 workers employed at that time, 45 were women. At war's end that number fell off abruptly. Only 27 women were counted among the 1,394-member work force on October 1, 1945.[19] Women smelter workers were a curiosity at first. Smeltermen's wives worried about the possibility of illicit affairs, and one woman later recalled, "We began to wonder about the respectability of these women." She added that such attitudes did not persist, however, because those employed were local women. "We knew them," she said, and "thought it was alright [sic]."[20]

The record is vague on precisely what kind of work women did in the Great Falls smelter. One veteran smelterman remembered that the women were good workers and were paid union wages. He believed they "got the easiest jobs," however. Another man recalled that women mostly "did cleaning." Still another said they performed tasks "that to me would have been godawful heavy for women," and that "they actually, all told, did a damn good job."[21]

"Who Says It's a Man's War?" read the title to an article appearing in the *Copper Commando,* the Anaconda Company's wartime "official newspaper of the Victory Labor-Management Production Committee of Butte, Anaconda, and Great Falls." The "two gals" featured in the July 1943 article had replaced two male messenger boys from the Great Falls plant who had gone to war. The caption to an accompanying photograph said the women workers demonstrated that "it's everybody's war." On the same date the "Smelter News and Notes" column in the *Great Falls Leader* reported "a rumor that there is to be a girl in the drafting room." Sexual harassment in the workplace was not a public concern in those days, but the columnist speculated that "Now the boys will have to buy an Emily

Women participated in many, often less visible ways to support the war effort.
Here they assist LeRoy Stahl of Great Falls KFBB radio to urge
purchase of war bonds at a downtown broadcast booth.

CASCADE COUNTY HISTORICAL SOCIETY, GREAT FALLS, MONTANA

Post on 'office conduct,' and those stories that originated in the engineering department will be a thing of the past."[22]

Male and female workers alike were in great demand in defense production, and thousands may have abandoned Montana's mining and metals industries to seek higher wages on the West Coast and elsewhere.[23] Long before America entered the war, Great Falls community and business leaders, like their counterparts across the nation, had sought location of a government-sponsored airplane factory or other military production facility for their city. They learned that, despite certain attributes, the prospect was slight. Level ground and abundant electric power were prerequisites. Neither was a problem for Great Falls, situated as it is on a flat plain and in close proximity to hydroelectric dams at the nearby falls on the Missouri. Other requirements, however, such as the availability of manpower, raw materials, machine tool factories and forge shops, and the further stipulation that none of these be any closer than two hundred miles to the Canadian border, posed significant difficulties for the community. As a result, neither Great Falls nor any other Montana community secured manufacturing facilities of the sort that sprang up along the West Coast, where conditions were more favorable.[24]

In summer 1941, however, community leaders learned that the Army Air Corps was considering locating a base in Great Falls with a potential personnel force of four thousand airmen and a $1 million-per-year impact on the city's economy. Interest focused on a large tract east of town. The "Green Mill," a notorious Depression-era nightspot, was the only facility located there and city business interests took steps to secure the property.[25] On the opposite side of town the Seventh Ferrying group operated from Gore Hill, and the Thirty-fourth Sub-Depot, a supply and equipment center, was situated at the fairgrounds. The sub-depot and some of the Gore Hill operations were ultimately relocated to what came to be called East Base.[26]

If World War II "transformed" the West, as one historian has claimed, East Base did just that for Great Falls. The transformation was greatest on the West Coast, where wartime production plants and military facilities worked immense socioeconomic change in Washington, Oregon, and California. War industries stimulated new migrations, greater ethnic diversity, and, for the West, cultural autonomy and a sense of liberation from "colonial" dependence on the East.[27]

By contrast Montana and other states of the western interior did not experience the same degree of transformation. Few production facilities or military bases of any size were established in the interior West during the war. Billings received a temporary boost when the Pacific Car and Foundry Company leased the fairgrounds facilities there to assemble "tank recovery" vehicles, but the work, prompted by an overload situation at the company's Renton, Washington, plant, proved temporary. Companies in Billings and Butte received defense contracts, but little direct military production centered in Montana. With the exception of East Base at Great Falls, there were no sizable military bases sited in Montana. As a result, of all of Montana's communities, Great Falls experienced the greatest wartime social and economic transformation, and the subsequent emergence of the Cold War insured that a Great Falls economy tied closely to the military would continue well into the future.[28]

Great Falls warmly welcomed East Base and its military personnel. People donated everything from books and athletic equipment to clothes hangers and furniture. Nor were the social needs of the new airmen neglected. Chamber of Commerce members were advised that the army "will have to depend upon the people and agencies of Great Falls to supply the social life and recreation for its men with passes."[29] The Army Air Corps was not disappointed. Social opportunities abounded. Nurses from Deaconess Hospital hosted weekly "socials" for the servicemen. The YWCA sponsored weekly dance lessons for military men, so that they might better enjoy the USO dances. When the call went out, no fewer than eight hundred Great Falls women registered as "victory belles" to act as female partners at USO dances, and hundreds more would volunteer in the months to follow. The local musicians' union, which supplied a four-piece band for the weekly dances, advertised for a volunteer "songbird" with the promise of "a good time guaranteed."[30]

Servicemen and civilian workers attached to East Base came from all over the country, adding a new dimension to the community's social life and cultural diversity. A newspaper column reporting on East Base matters included the following item: "From the Q.M. comes the word that the woe-begotten look on Corporal (Tex) Stewart's face is caused by the fact that his bride-to-be is a resident of Great Falls and therefore a Yankee. (P.S. His dad said 'no,' but love will conquer all.)" No doubt Corporal Stewart's dilemma was not unique. Many a match united Great Falls women with servicemen of diverse regional and cultural backgrounds, and some chose to make Great Falls their permanent home. As longtime resident Robert Allen observed, "a lot of them settled down and filtered into our own population now. So they're natives."[31]

With the coming of East Base, the city's population increased dramatically, from 29,990 in 1940 to an estimated 35,000 by the end of 1943, which in turn promoted a serious housing shortage. A war housing grant produced a hundred new units, bringing the total of new units to three hundred, but it was not enough to accommodate the 5,000 new people. Savings and loan advertisements assured residents that the federal government was aware that war workers were short of housing and employed a variety of programs to assist with financing expansions and new construction.[32] Government-insured mortgage loans were not readily available during the war, however, and home building, with labor and materials diverted to other uses, was generally curtailed. The War Housing Administration did authorize an additional one hundred units, but delays postponed final approval for construction. In May 1945 the city's chamber of commerce held discussions "concerning the acute housing situation," but with increasing numbers of military personnel and East Base–associated civilian workers, housing remained in short supply throughout the war years.[33]

Like people all across the nation, Great Falls residents faced other shortages as well. Montanans especially bristled at tight gasoline rationing, which began on December 1, 1942. Longer traveling distances than in other parts of the country and visibly plentiful supplies of petroleum locally made restrictions seem extreme. Drivers, allotted only four gallons of gasoline per week, could drive first no more than forty and then only thirty-five miles per hour.[34] The *Great Falls Tribune* reported that all the city's car owners had filled their tanks in anticipation of rationing. Nine thousand "A" books, indicating "no occupational need" and entitling holders to only four gallons per week, were issued in Cascade County. Two thousand other people received "B" or "C" books, depending upon demonstrated need for greater amounts. Those who drove more than six miles per day to and from work qualified for "B" books, while truckers, ambulance drivers, doctors, veterinarians, government officials, and others in occupations deemed "essential" qualified for "C" books. Farmers and ranchers were allowed unlimited bulk purchases of gasoline for use in agricultural production.[35]

Gasoline rationing was intended mainly to save rubber. The anticipated takeover of rubber plantations in Southeast Asia and the Dutch East Indies by the Japanese prompted fear of an immediate wartime shortage. From the start it was evident that new tires would soon be unavailable. As one reporter put it a few days after Pearl Harbor, the use of synthetic rubber in tires was still in the "magazine article stage." As of January 5, 1942, new tires were officially no longer available to the general public. "Recaps" were also scarce, and prices were frozen. Tire thefts soon became common, and the Great Falls police department advised residents to take

POWER

BEHIND THE GUNS

OUR FIGHTING MEN at the front *have* plenty of courage, but courage alone will not win battles in this day of machine warfare.

IT IS UP TO US who are behind the lines to provide them with machines and other munitions.

Every real Montanan is helping in some way.

Your Power Company's job is to supply electrical energy.

We are constantly delivering to the Anaconda Copper Mining Company alone, over 200,000 electrical horsepower for the production of Montana metals vital to Victory.

The Montana Power Company

The Montana Power Company offered a heroic advertisement for the January 3, 1942, edition of the Great Falls Leader *to publicize its efforts in producing electric power on behalf of war production.*

precautions. Cars should not be parked outside all night; trunks should be locked; and serial numbers on tires should be recorded to assist recovery in the event of theft. Gasoline stations and tire dealers advertised registration services. They would record a proof of ownership and then provide a warning sticker to discourage thieves.[36]

Other rubber products were soon in short supply. Everything from erasers and sink stoppers to women's foundation garments became scarce. A nationally syndicated newspaper article warned women that hoarding was futile because elastic would deteriorate. Women were advised to make foundation garments "after the English example," that is, without the use of rubberized fabric.[37]

Wartime material needs and shortages affected styles. Fabric was in generally short supply, and the scarcity of dyes for civilian cloth meant fewer bright colors. Photographs of "starlets," common in newspapers, were often associated with bond drives or other activities supporting the war effort. One such photograph posed a young woman with clothing and accessories appropriate to the stringent demands of the time. She had very little make-up, used no hair pins, bobby pins, hair dye, or bleach, wore no metal jewelry, and used finger nail "polishes" rather than enamel. Her skirt was shorter to conserve material, and her shoes were said to be comfortable and practical for all occasions. She wore no silk stockings. The latter, a prized luxury, could seldom be had. Nylon stockings, an acceptable substitute, also became scarce. A survey of local retail stores in late 1942 revealed that virtually no nylon stockings would be available for the Christmas season.[38]

Food items of various kinds were also in short supply. Government guidelines discouraged hoarding by stipulating that families should keep no more than a four days' supply of food on hand. Judging the requirement extreme, a *Great Falls Tribune* editorial exclaimed: "We don't want hoarding, but Washington should not talk scary stuff to the housewife."[39] Meat was rationed. So were sugar, canned goods, butter, and shortening. Ice cream became scarce. One woman recalled that her husband had particularly missed real mayonnaise, which disappeared from market shelves.[40] "Victory food specials" featured dried beans. Fresh fruits and vegetables escaped rationing and were encouraged. Before the war customers routinely called in orders and had their groceries delivered. During the war the practice was restricted to cases of real need.[41]

As with the rest of the nation, food shortages in Great Falls were real but not severe, and there were reasonable alternatives for items in short supply. A nationally distributed cookbook found in a Great Falls kitchen featured a wide variety of cakes, cookies, and pastries which could be prepared "by the Ration Book." It suggested cooking with "unrationed fats" such as chicken fat or home rendered lard.[42] The scarcity of meat prompted fears that a multitude of inexperienced hunters might try to supplement their supplies with local hunting. Ordinary hunters found ammunition in short supply, however, although area ranchers and farmers were allocated ammunition to control predators.[43]

In addition to fresh fruits and vegetables, fish were generally plentiful, and coffee, sugar, butter, and meat were available on a limited basis. Shortages of food, as with gasoline, tires, rubber products, small and large appliances, automobiles, and a host of other products, were more an inconvenience than a real privation. As one observer noted, people in Great Falls and elsewhere would "need to learn to live more simply." They may have to walk more and stay home more, but they would "have enough of the really essential things."[44]

In many ways life in Great Falls seemed only peripherally affected by the war. A candidate for the Montana State Legislature could list "more war effort" as part of his platform, but he gave equal weight to "fewer new laws," and "no Montana Sales Tax." Such positions were popular before, during, and after the war. Never really doubting the outcome of the war, people in Great Falls held postwar planning discussions within city government and in other public forums as early as April 1943.[45] Like other Montana communities, Great Falls did not experience the influx of major new war industries. But unlike other Montana cities, it did get the air base, which in turn brought significant new population—an increase of 15 percent or more—and with it economic development and social change that has continued down to the present time.[46]

NOTES

1. Bill Sharp, *Montana G.I.s Lost in World War II* (Helena, Mont., 1994), appendix 2. In Cascade County 129 were counted dead or missing and in the state of Montana, 1,553. As percentages of the total 1940 population, these numbers represent 0.31 percent and 0.28 percent, respectively. The figure for the United States and its possessions was 0.42 percent, indicating that Montana and Cascade County's casualty figures were somewhat below the national average.

2. *Great Falls (Mont.) Tribune,* November 7, 1943. The war brought a significant increase in the city's population. Official off-year census figures are not available, but the *Tribune* reported that the population had grown from 29,990 in 1940 to 35,500 by the end of 1943. Mayor E. L. Shields, perhaps overenthusiastically, estimated the city's population to be 50,000 in May 1943. *Journal of the Proceedings of the Council: City of Great Falls, State of Montana,* May 3, 1943, vol. 17, p. 65, City Attorney's Office, Civic Center, Great Falls, Montana (hereafter *Proceedings of the Council . . . Great Falls*).

3. Malmstrom Air Force Base, *Environmental Narrative* (n.p., 1975), sec. 2, p. 1. The base was renamed in Colonel Einer Axel Malmstrom's honor in 1955.

4. William J. and Elizabeth Lane Furdell, *Great Falls: A Pictorial History* (Norfolk, Va., 1984), 24–25; Michael P. Malone, *Jim Hill: Empire Builder of the Northwest* (Norman, Okla., 1996), 132–33.

5. *Proceedings of the Council . . . Great Falls,* December 8, 15, 18, 1941, vol. 16, pp. 413–14, 418, 423–24. See also the *Great Falls (Mont.) Tribune,* December 23, 1941.

6. *Great Falls (Mont.) Tribune,* December 27, 1941, January 2, 1942.

7. Great Falls High School, *1942 Roundup,* vol. 35 (Great Falls, Mont., 1942), 25–26, 34, 39, 50–51; Great Falls High School, *1945 Roundup,* vol. 38 (Great Falls, Mont., 1945), 15, 83–85.

8. *1945 Roundup,* 38:14, 86–87, 105, 107.

9. *Great Falls (Mont.) Tribune,* July 4, 1943; *Great Falls (Mont.) Leader,* June 23, 1942, July 5, 1943.

10. *Great Falls (Mont.) Tribune,* December 22, 1941, January 26, 1942.

11. *Great Falls (Mont.) Leader,* March 27, 1942. The *Leader* reported that 1,859 Japanese were located at Fort Missoula. Figures are uncertain, but there were probably about two thousand detainees, approximately one-half of whom were Japanese and the others Italian seamen. Steve Braun, "Japanese Prisoners at Fort Missoula, Montana" (paper presented at the Montana at War Conference, Montana State University, Bozeman, September 16, 1995); *Great Falls (Mont.) Leader,* April 28, 1943.

12. *Great Falls (Mont.) Leader,* November 17, 1942, March 6, 1943.

13. Figures provided by the Camp Fire Girls office, Great Falls, Montana, June 28, 1996; *Great Falls (Mont.) Leader,* July 11, 1942.

14. *Great Falls (Mont.) Leader,* October 22, 1942.

15. *Great Falls (Mont.) Tribune,* October 16, 1942.

16. Ibid., October 4, 15, 1942; Charles B. Snyder to Senator Mike Mansfield, June 17, 1965, Civil War Cannons Memorial Scrapbook, Cascade County Historical Society Archives, Great Falls Public Library, Great Falls, Montana (hereafter CCHS).

17. David Davidson interview, p. 4, Oral History 15, CCHS; "Boy Scouts at War," *Time,* June 15, 1942, 14–15; Edabelle Hall to Mrs. Williams, February 10, 1942, Montana Federation of Women's Clubs file, CCHS; *Great Falls (Mont.) Leader,* February 3, 1942, January 8, 1943.

18. *Great Falls (Mont.) Leader,* November 3, February 26, 1942; *Great Falls (Mont.) Tribune,* November 24, 1942; *Great Falls (Mont.) Leader,* November 3, December 9, 1942.

19. Box 229, Manuscript Collection 169, Anaconda Copper Mining Company Records, Montana Historical Society Archives, Helena.

20. Lois Nicholls, interview by Lana N. Furdell, July 1995, in collection of author; Claire Vangelista Del Guerra, interview by Laurie Mercier, p. 935, Oral History 120, CCHS.

21. Eugene Cox, interview by Laurie Mercier, p. 934, Oral History 107, CCHS; Fred Nicholls, interview by Lana N. Furdell, July 1995, in collection of author; Lorado Maffit, interview by Laurie Mercier, p. 916, Oral History 109, CCHS.

22. "Who Says It's a Man's War?" *Copper Commando,* Anaconda Copper Mining Company–Labor newspaper, July 16, 1943; *Great Falls (Mont.) Leader,* July 16, 1943.

23. Scott C. Loken, "Montana during World War II" (master's thesis, University of Montana, 1993), 33. Montana's population numbered 463,000 in 1945, 93,000 fewer than the 556,000 listed in the 1940 census. By 1949 the state's population increased to 562,000, surpassing the prewar figure, and grew to 591,000 by 1950. Harold J. Hoflich, *The Economy of Montana* (Bozeman, Mont., 1951), 16.

24. Chamber of Commerce file, July 25, 1940, CCHS (hereafter Chamber file); Loken, "Montana during World War II," 25–33.

25. Chamber file, August 27, November 5, 1941, CCHS.

26. Jane Willits Stuwe, *East Base, 1940–1946* (n.p., 1974), 33.

27. Gerald D. Nash, *The American West Transformed: The Impact of the Second World War* (Lincoln, Neb., 1985).

28. Gary Glynn, *Montana's Home Front during World War II* (Missoula, Mont., 1994), 116. One firm, A. N. Metal Products of Billings, reportedly turned out fifteen pontoons per day for the United States Navy, and Sullivan Valve and Engineering of Butte also had a government contract during the war. There was a military buildup in Helena, Montana, in 1942, where a commando force of approximately nineteen hundred men intended for operations in occupied Norway underwent training. Ultimately, the Devil's Brigade did not deploy to Norway but instead distinguished itself fighting in the Italian campaign. Glynn, *Montana's Home Front,* 31–42, 111.

29. Captain Charles M. Derry to A. J. Breitenstein, September 1, 1942, Chamber file, CCHS.

30. *Great Falls (Mont.) Tribune,* October 23, 1942; Great Falls (Mont.) Leader, December 30, 1942, January 28, 1943.

31. *Great Falls (Mont.) Tribune,* October 4, 1942; Stuwe, *East Base, 1940–1946,* 3; Robert E. Allen interview, p. 3, Oral History 1, CCHS.

32. *Great Falls (Mont.) Tribune,* May 15, November 7, 1943.

33. Minutes of Chamber of Commerce meeting, May 17, 1945, Chamber file, CCHS.

34. Loken, "Montana during World War II," 41–42; *Great Falls (Mont.) Leader,* October 10, 1942, July 15, 1943.

35. *Great Falls (Mont.) Tribune,* December 1, 1942; "A Rationed Nation," *Business Week,* October 3, 1942, 14; "War Loads Come First," *Business Week,* May 16, 1942, 16.

36. *Great Falls (Mont.) Tribune,* December 13, 1941; *Great Falls (Mont.) Leader,* January 16, June 13, 1942.

37. *Great Falls (Mont.) Leader,* January 28, 1942.

38. Ibid., February 17, November 18, 1942, February 3, 1943.

39. *Great Falls (Mont.) Tribune,* January 3, 1942.

40. Donna Wahlberg, interview by author, June 6, 1995, Great Falls, Mont.

41. *Great Falls (Mont.) Leader,* January 14, 1943; *Great Falls (Mont.) Tribune,* December 8, 1943.

42. *Great Falls (Mont.) Tribune,* October 30, December 17, 1943.

43. Swans Down, *How to Bake by the Ration Book: Swans Down Wartime Recipes* (n.p., 1944).

44. *Great Falls (Mont.) Leader,* February 13, 1942.

45. Ibid., November 2, 1942, April 27, August 27, 1943; *Great Falls (Mont.) Tribune,* November 8, 1943.

46. Montana's population dropped from 556,000 in 1940 to 463,000 in 1945. By contrast Great Falls's population increased from 29,990 in 1940 to an estimated 35,000 during the war. *Great Falls (Mont.) Tribune,* November 7, 1943. Coastal states attracted thousands of new residents. Washington state's population, for example, went from 1,741,000 to 2,274,000 during the same period. Nash, *American West Transformed,* 22.

Creating a New Community in the North

Mexican Americans of the Yellowstone Valley

Laurie Mercier

As already suggested by various essays in this volume, ethnic diversity has been an important feature of Montana society throughout its history. While this diversity is often associated with certain social groups arriving in the nineteenth century— such as the Chinese and the Irish—other groups would not make their appearance, at least in a major fashion, until the twentieth century. The following essay by Laurie Mercier, a professor of history at Washington State University, Vancouver, traces the evolution of the Mexican-American community in the Yellowstone valley from the 1920s to the 1990s.

This essay effectively demonstrates the value of using personal interviews to preserve history—in this case of a largely working-class community—that might otherwise be lost through the passage of time. The story of this particular community also reminds us of the dilemma that almost all ethnic groups in Montana, and in America, have faced over the past three centuries: that is, how to preserve social and cultural traditions within one's ethnic group while also attempting to become a part of the larger society.

THE YELLOWSTONE RIVER WETS THE RICHEST AGRICULTURAL LANDS IN EASTERN Montana. Since the early twentieth century, irrigation projects and the nation's sweet tooth have made sugar beets the most profitable and enduring crop grown. Unlike agricultural products such as grain and livestock, which demand little more than the labors of a single family, sugar beets have required an army of temporary workers to thin, cultivate, and harvest the persnickety roots. Mexican Americans have provided much of this essential labor, yet their contributions have gone unheralded. This essay traces the history of the Mexican Americans who came to the Yellowstone as seasonal workers and created a vital ethnic community, which has persisted despite years of economic hardship, discrimination, and cultural and social change.

Long before Montana became a state, Hispanic explores, trappers, miners, and *vaqueros* were among the first non-natives to visit the region. After the United States annexed the northern half of Mexico in 1848, many Latin Americans continued to migrate to the north, but it was not until the 1920s that Mexico's dramatically increasing population and an expanding western United States economy combined to persuade millions of residents to seek work across the border. By 1930 more than one thousand Mexicans and Mexican Americans had come to the Yellowstone valley.

Federally financed reclamation projects transformed the arid West in the early 1900s, including the Yellowstone valley, where Billings capitalist I. D. O'Donnell and other local businessmen invested in growing sugar beets, an expensive and labor-intensive crop. They incorporated the Billings Sugar Company in 1905 and built one of the largest sugar beet factories in the world the following year. A dozen years later, during the height of wartime agricultural demand, the Great Western Sugar Company bought the factory and encouraged area farmers to plant beets instead of wheat. Beets became a profitable investment up and down the Yellowstone, and Great Western became Montana's (and the nation's) largest sugar producer. Holly Sugar Company also built factories in the region at Sidney in 1925 and at Hardin in 1937.

Profitable sugar beet production required a reliable supply of low-cost labor, which the Montana labor market could not supply. Sugar companies began to recruit from areas where labor was more abundant and from groups of people who had been denied access to other kinds of employment. In 1921 Great Western's Labor Bureau in Denver recruited 385 beet laborers from "southern points" in Texas, California, Colorado, and Mexico for Montana farms. Two years later the company reported that most of the 500 workers they imported were "of the Mexican type," the beginning of a seven-decade reliance by the beet industry on cheap labor from the American Southwest and Mexico. Government and industry worked together to maintain this employment niche for Latinos. Even when many Americans clamored for immigration restrictions in 1924, for example, growers lobbied for unrestricted movement of Mexican labor and Congress exempted Mexicans from new immigration quotas.

The Great Western Company cultivated its dependence on two ethnic groups to tend valley beets. In 1924 it brought to Montana 3,604 Mexicans and 1,231 German Russians to harvest a record 31,000 acres that year. But the company had different long-range plans for each ethnic group. Great Western loaned money to its German Russian growers, hoping to attract their peasant relatives, who could provide temporary labor for thinning and harvests and eventually become tenants and even landowners. This Company encouragement, along with kinship ties, community acceptance, and ready adjustment to Montana's climate probably explains why 77 percent of the German work force remained in the Billings district that winter, a sharp contrast to just 25 percent of the Mexicans. Company actions reflected American racial assumptions that European immigrants made more capable landowners then Mexicans, who many insisted were more suited to agricultural labor than farming.

The racist underpinnings of American culture, together with restrictive legislation and hiring practices, hindered Latino economic mobility, and the low wages made agricultural labor a family endeavor. Families migrated and worked together as a unit and sold their collective labor to farmers. This pattern of family migration and family wage work shaped the character of the Yellowstone's Latino community and helped maintain fairly equal male to female ratios. It also stimulated the growth of a settled community. Sugar companies, which sought to maintain a stable work force, promoted family settlement by providing transportation, labor contracts, and housing for families.

The Great Western and Holly Sugar companies created colonias near their factories to encourage Mexican workers to "winter over" in Montana. In 1924 the Great Western Company invested improvements in the Billings colonia, which housed forty-two families. Mexican laborers built ten new adobe apartments, cindered streets, extended the water line, constructed a drainage ditch, and leveled and planted grass on the compound grounds.

*Mexican-American sugar beet workers pose with their families
outside a Billings-area colonia in this circa 1938 photograph.*

MERRILL G. BURLINGAME SPECIAL COLLECTIONS, MONTANA STATE UNIVERSITY, BOZEMAN

Severo "Sal" Briceno came with his family to Billings in 1928, and he recalled that the forty-odd adobe homes of the colonia each had one bedroom, a woodstove, and an outhouse. Briceno's family of nine spread into two of the small homes. Residents were responsible for upkeep, and the factory donated tar to patch pervasive leaks in the flat roofs. An outdoor water faucet served every five houses, and when temperatures dipped, Briceno remembered, "we'd have to go out there and make fires around it to unfreeze it."

As in other industrial labor arrangements, settled families fostered a stable workforce, and the colonias helped families remain and survive on their meager wages. Colonia residents could raise chickens, pigs, and gardens to supplement their diets. The company also created a winter jobs program on the factory grounds, believing that in the spring "there would not be a big debt hanging over [farmworkers'] heads, making them more willing to work in the territory rather than to leave . . . in order to get away from their debts." The colonia provided a clinic and school for migrant children and unified the Latino community. Esther Rivera' recalled that her father, Fred Duran, "used to talk about the colonia all the time. Everybody knew everybody. The people really hung together."

As the colonia provided the immigrants with a sense of community, it also isolated them from other residents, while their growing numbers also aroused prejudice. The Great Western Company campaigned against the baseless fears directed at its Latino labor pool. During the 1920s the company's annual reports emphasized that Mexican laborers had "solved the farm labor problem," that many were United States citizens, and that they were skilled workers. These reports concealed the racial tensions that predominated in white Billings.

During the first half of the century, people who spoke Spanish and/or were perceived of as "Mexicans" faced great discrimination in Billings. Sal Briceno recalled that Latino children could not participate in the annual Kiwanis Easter egg hunt in South Park: "They had men on horses riding around that South Park kicking us out. There were a lot of kids that wanted candy, but they'd kick us out." Latinos were banned from the public swimming pool, segregated in theaters, and not allowed in restaurants. Signs above some Billings business doors read, "No Mexicans or dogs allowed." Mexican Americans knew racism's unwritten rules and the boundaries of acceptable behavior. Robert Federico's four aunts and mother told vivid stories of "where they could go and could not go." If they could endure stares and taunts, for example, they could venture into the local skating rink. But most places, such as bowling alleys, were off limits. Sal Briceno noted: "they [whites] would have kicked me in the head with a bowling ball" if he had ventured there. Barred from most stores, Mexican Americans were dependent on their farm employers to do their shopping.

Farmworker families usually came as part of a crew or group of families recruited. Robert Rivera's family was part of a trainload of Californians who were recruited and promised "opportunities" in Montana during the 1920s. Once in Billings farmworker families often stayed at the St. Louis Hotel on Montana Avenue across from the depot while they waited for the Great Western Sugar Company to match them with farmers and take them to the farms. The Riveras and other families, who wintered over for beet planting in the spring, stayed in the colonia until the company transported them once again to Custer, Hysham, Belfry, Joliet, and other places where farmers needed labor. The company also arranged credit at the local grocery until workers were paid and brought farmworkers back to the colonia at the end of the beet season. But with limited earnings families faced many a grim winter. Rivera recalled that his family and most others took their beet earnings to Sawyer's on Twenty-ninth Street and invested in bulk groceries: "That's where most of the people traded, and if they had 3-400 dollars to spend on groceries for the winter, they would buy in big lots, flour by the 100-pound, coffee by the 25-pounds, lard by the 50-pounds, and as much groceries as they could afford they'd take in provisions for the winter. Of course when that was gone, that was it."

Some migrant workers developed lasting relationships with farmers and sought to renew their associations each spring, while some other families remained with farmers throughout the year and helped in feeding cattle and mending fences during the winter while they waited for the beet season to begin. As Robert Rivera noted, these arrangements helped sustain farmworker families and also initiate permanent resident status: "If they wanted you to stay, a lot of times they would offer you the place to stay for the winter if you wanted to. Then the men would work for them . . . which was better than moving back to the colony, because once you moved back there was nothing to carry you through the winter."

Mutual friendships often developed between female farmworkers and owners because of shared concerns about children's welfare or for female companionship on isolated farms. Farm women frequently helped with childcare, dispensed advice, and supplied eggs and other farm products to supplement their workers' earnings. Maria Cantu usually took her children with her to the fields, but when it was cold, she often left them with the female farm owner, whom she fondly remembered: "This lady was just like my mother. She was nice and so sweet." Esther Rivera recalled that a farm woman taught her mother "how to cook American food, she learned how to do everything there. She let her have her own garden spot to raise a garden, so we were very fortunate there."

The beet cultivation cycle changed little over time. In mid-April farmers began planting; workers hoed and thinned from late May to mid-July. Until farmers began mechanizing and applying herbicides in the 1950s, many migrant families remained over the summer to weed and through the fall to harvest and top the beets. The stoop labor and distinctive tools—a short-handled hoe for thinning and curved knife for topping—also remained the same. "You worked backbreaking long hours," Esther Rivera recalled: "everything was done by hand." It was arduous work, as Sal Briceno remembered, but there were few choices. "The work was hard, [but] you had to do it, you had no alternative." As Esther Rivera remembered it, "both parents really worked day and night to keep eight of us children going. You didn't think anything of the work because it was your way of life."

Latino parents often had to care for young children while they worked, and children assisted as soon as they were old enough. Dora Cantu recalled that her father always carried an extra hoe in the car; when one of his children reached eight or nine years, he enticed them to "help mom out" so they could go home early. Her mother distracted her children from the drudgery by telling folktales, which often featured children and animals and emphasized cooperation and sharing, crucial themes in the lives of families dependent on the contributions of all their members to survive.

Economic realities also forced many married women to do fieldwork, sometimes on the days when they went into labor and gave birth. As in most American families, the "double day" prevailed for female farmworkers, extending work into the evening: "Father would sit down, mother would cook, she would wash clothes . . . no one questioned it, all the women were in the kitchen, all the men ate."

When possible families sacrificed women's critical field labor to manage the household, cook, and care for young children and boarders. Ruth Contreraz remembered her mother "practically cooking all day long" to feed her family and ten male boarders who helped her husband work beets. Women often raised gardens and chickens for food and created clothing and household goods from available materials, such as feed sacks. Many woman found time also to make functional products more attractive. "I don't know how she found the time," Esther Rivera recalled of her mother's determination to create beauty in her family's home: "She made the quilts, she made our clothes, she made homemade cheese, she made everything from scratch, plus she always had time to embroider every pillowcase . . . and had everything fancy. I guess that was their way of expressing . . . having something beautiful for themselves."

The 1930s Depression halted recruitment of Latino laborers, and the government even deported many to Mexico, including United States citizens. In the Yellowstone opposition to the employment of migrant workers compelled the Great Western Company to hire local workers before hiring outsiders. The company also agreed to employ "solos" from outside the district to discourage families from "remaining and becoming a charge on relief." This reversal of the company's earlier promotion of family settlement resulted in a reduction of wintering employees from 221 in 1935 to 173 in 1937.

Spurred by labor demonstrations across the nation during the 1930s, many farmworkers protested poor wages and working conditions. Yellowstone farmworkers, like other agricultural workers, faced numerous obstacles in labor organizing. Often without supportive communities and dependent on individual growers for jobs, farmworkers were vulnerable to companies and growers, who could retaliate by ejecting rebellious families from housing, refusing to pay back wages and transportation, and importing replacement workers. Nonetheless, from 1934 through 1937, Beet Workers Union strikes and threats of strikes periodically interrupted thinning and harvests, reminding sugar producers of the workers' importance. In 1937 the Yellowstone Growers' Association and beet laborer representatives settled on a piecerate of $21.50 per acre, or $9.50 for thinning, $2.25 for hoeing, $1.35 for weeding, and $.70 per ton for topping.

Second World War production demands and labor shortages generated new calls for Mexican and Mexican-American agricultural workers, but new opportunities in defense work on the West Coast, armed services recruitment, and other industry jobs beckoned the nation's Latinos. In the Yellowstone valley, the percent of acres thinned by local Mexican-American farmworkers steadily declined during the war years, from 44 percent in 1941 to just 9 percent in 1946. Sugar companies and growers frantically pursued workers from the Southwest and increasingly from Indian reservations, local high schools, German prisoner-of-war camps, and the Japanese-American internment camp at Heart Mountain. With fewer resident Latino families interested in farm labor, Great Western resumed its recruitment efforts, soliciting by mail and by personal visits to Mexican-American prospects in California and Texas.

Wartime demand was so great that western growers and agricultural industries in 1943 pressured Congress to create the "bracero" program, Public Law 78, which allowed farmers to employ Mexican nationals to harvest crops. Under the program's agreement with the Mexican government, employers paid transportation and living expenses, provided individual contracts, and promised not to undercut existing wages. From

1943 through 1946 the Great Western's Billings district relied on Mexicans to thin up to 30 percent of its beet fields, and top up to half its crop in the fall when labor was even more difficult to procure.

After the war farmers accelerated their demand for beet labor and the sugar companies assisted. Santos Carranza began his thirty-three-year career as a labor recruiter for Holly Sugar Company in Sidney during the war. As field office supervisor Carranza traveled to Texas each spring and distributed cards announcing Montana employment needs, located workers, and advanced money for the trip north, where he linked families with lower Yellowstone farmers. After 1963, when Congress terminated the bracero program, companies continued recruiting workers to assure contract farmers of sufficient labor.

Many migrant workers in the Yellowstone valley sought permanent jobs and better livelihoods, and some actually purchased farms. Anastacio and Brigida Carranza brought their family to the lower Yellowstone from Colorado in 1925 to work beets, and ten years later they managed to buy their first beet farm near Sidney. Maria Cantu and her husband came to the Yellowstone valley in 1951 with a south Texas contractor's team that worked Great Western's fields in Colorado and Montana. Maria wanted to keep her children from a life on the road, so despite the hardships she insisted that her family find a way to stay in Montana. The Cantus felt lucky to find year-round employment with the same Worden-area farmer for eleven years. They saved and purchased a small farm in 1962, while they continued to thin and harvest beets for area farmers. To supplement the family income, Mr. Cantu periodically worked during harvest loading beets on trains at Pompey's Pillar, Worden, Huntley, Shepherd, and Park City and also during the winter at the sugar factory.

Farmworker families generally left agricultural work for better paying, steady jobs as soon as they could. As Robert Rivera explained: "The Spanish people would work the fields and work their hearts out trying to make a living, but there was nothing in return, nothing like social security or retirement." But it was not easy to find alternative work. Workers occasionally were hired to "work the beet cars" in the wintertime unloading beets for factory processing. "It was hard work, cold, working through the night," as Robert Rivera reported, "but then it meant that you had a better chance to go through the winter." Still, widespread discrimination limited opportunities for Mexican Americans, as Sal Briceno remembered, because "they'd get white people for the better jobs." Race was a factor in finding any kind of employment: "There was a lot of discrimination in those days. If you were of Mexican descent, you couldn't do nothing."

Mexican-American women often took wage jobs to ensure their families' survival. Esther Rivera believed that Mexican-American men—not unlike men in the larger society—felt "embarrassment if your wife worked" outside the home before social mores began to change in the 1970s. But economic realities often defy popular ideals. Robert Rivera remembered that his mother had to work "out of the home" cleaning hotels to provide for the family. And Mexican-American women also faced discrimination. Esther Rivera recalled that there was considerable employment discrimination during the 1940s and 1950s. She had taken a business course in high school in 1949, for example, but when she sought advertised jobs the doors were often closed. "I applied for jobs all over town, and I couldn't get anything, so I had to take a dishwashing job."

Landing a job with the Northern Pacific Railroad or a Billings factory was often Mexican Americans' first real break. "Most of your Spanish people here in Billings," Robert Rivera believed: "since they started working for the railroads, that's what really made a better life for them, because they got steady work, and they got pretty good pay, and the majority bought their little house and moved up, educated their children, and they got retirement from the railroad." Ralph "Chino" Armendariz was one such success story. He came with his father to the Yellowstone in 1936 to work beets, and in 1939 he was hired as a section laborer for the Northern Pacific where he worked until he retired in 1964.

The Second World War was a watershed period for the nation's Latinos. When veterans returned to their communities and sought nonagricultural jobs, many insisted on equal treatment. Robert Rivera and his five brothers, who served in the military while many of the area's Euro-American residents received deferments to work in agriculture, felt strongly: "I've fought for this country, and my brothers have fought for this country, and we feel like we belong here just like anybody else." Rivera became an ironworker and welder while his brothers became carpenters. Sal Briceno chose to drive a Yellow Cab after his release from service, and Ynes Contreraz worked at Pierce Packing Company from 1948 to 1982, where she received several promotions and felt no discrimination. Contreraz believed that discriminatory practices at local businesses discouraged Mexican applicants, but "when younger people saw Pierce hiring Mexicans, they knew they had an alternative to working beets."

Mexican-American young people eagerly sought nonagricultural work. Robert Rivera remembered as a teenager longing for a different life: "I would just say to myself when I was in those fields, 'I hope to God I never have to do this again, and as soon as I'm able I'm gonna get out of here and never do this again.' And I did." Esther Rivera claimed that "all" Mexican-American youth were determined not to live farmworker lives: "We just got out the minute we were fifteen or sixteen and didn't have to work in those fields, then you'd do anything else. When I turned sixteen I applied for my first job at a Billings laundry."

Yellowstone valley Latinos believed that education was key to attaining the American dream. Beginning in the 1940s, when many farmworkers acquired their own transportation to "come and go everyday to the beet fields," many families moved to Billings and other towns to secure year-round schooling for their children. "My dad felt that we were not getting enough education," Ruth Contreraz remembered. "They would always tell us, you kids have to continue going to school no matter what, so you guys can end up with better jobs." Esther Peralez's parents also remained in the Yellowstone valley so their children could attend school. She recalled a phrase repeated by "everybody's Mexican parent," including her father: "to study so you learn so you're not ignorant like we are." Her father emphasized the importance of education as "what you have to do to get out of [beet work] because I don't have a choice." Parents repeatedly sacrificed and labored long hours hoping that their children would prosper. Dora Cantu remembered that her mother had been educated in Mexico and had hoped to be a teacher: "That was her dream to be a schoolteacher, and she was denied this. She always dreamed that one of us would be a schoolteacher. From the time that we were little, 'you've got to learn, you've got to learn to read, you've got to learn to do this. You don't always want to be out here working beets. . . . Go to school and learn. If you don't, this is the kind of life that you'll have'."

Two realities hindered children's education: family economic needs and discrimination. Spring thinning and fall harvesting schedules, for example, placed difficult demands on schoolchildren. Dora Cantu and her sister missed school on alternate days to watch younger siblings while their parents worked beets, and they also adapted work schedules to accommodate school:

> We would get up at four o'clock in the morning, we would work until an hour before the bus would come and pick us up. We would be out until six or seven. We would go down to the house, or we would take our clothes to the field with us, change from our work clothes into our school clothes, run and catch the bus, go to school, come home, and then work again until sundown. This was from early spring when they started thinning beets until we got out of school in June. Then in the fall, when they were topping beets, we would get up again in the frost, and we would go out and pile beets. . . . We'd stack them in the evenings, we'd do at least two or three of those rows, enough so Mom and Dad would have enough beets the next day to top. . . . Sometimes it'd be dark when we went home.

Cantu remembered that Mexican-American children whose parents had a small farm or worked for the railroad were able to attend school regularly; those who did farm labor often had to drop out. Her parents emphasized the importance of school, so despite the interference of farm labor, she struggled to learn, even though she missed out on important instruction—such as how to calculate percentages—that hindered her.

Although parents supported them, many children encountered prejudice from students and teachers. Ruth Contreraz remembered her experience at Garfield School, where the city's Mexican-American students attended classes: "We were a minority, and we never felt that the teachers defended us in any way. When we got accused of anything, they would go as far as saying well don't even come back to school if you don't want to. They just did not accept us." Fights erupted when Mexican-American youth refused to ignore racial slurs, such as "dirty Mexican," "greaser," and "bean eater." Ruth Contreraz's mother told her to disregard taunts, but she beat up kids who called her names and then feared her mother would discover that she had been fighting: "We were already thinking why don't Mom and Dad stand up a little bit for our rights. . . . [When] the ones with authority, the teacher and principal, don't defend you in any way or form, even I started hating school." Contreraz "begged" her father to let her drop out of school and go to work. He agreed to allow her to stay out for one year; she never returned. Nonetheless, she insisted that her own children remain in school, so they would not "have to work as maids or go through what I had to."

Education provided many Mexican-American parents and youth with a greater awareness of their stake in American society. Ruth Contreraz believed that "with education you start recognizing your rights. . . . The younger parents felt they were going to get their kids educated and they can live where they want, we don't have to hold back anymore." But racism and their children's poor performance in the schools convinced many parents that mere access to education was insufficient. Contreraz noted, "That's when I feel that our parents started thinking, no, this is not right, our kids are not getting the education they need. First it was because we lived in farms, and a lot of the kids had to work, so they would always kind of lag behind." Mexican-American parents began joining PTAs and voicing their complaints.

During the 1960s many of the Yellowstone's Mexican-American youth, influenced by the Chicano civil rights movements, worked to change social attitudes and increase educational and employment opportunities. Robert Federico, who was inspired by VISTA antipoverty volunteers while still a student at Rocky Mountain College, began organizing the Latino community to combat discrimination, improve housing, increase voter registration, and promote affirmative action hiring. Esther Peralez, who had worked in Oregon and observed many militant Chicano students demanding equal rights, returned to Billings in the early 1970s and joined Federico and others in mobilizing the Mexican-American community to pressure the city to hire a Chicano school counselor and help more young people enter college. At that time, she recalled, there were many Latino social activities—dances and picnics and cultural events, such as *Cinco de Mayo* celebrations—but few organized attempts to challenge the Billings city government and implement reforms.

Latino youth often clashed with their elders over their reform goals and their militancy. Older residents wanted to preserve cultural traditions and promote community events while younger people wanted social change. "We just did not click," Robert Federico recalled, between "those who wanted to go slower, and those who wanted to move faster." Another activist explained that many preferred working quietly behind the scenes to effect change: "When we have wanted something, we have never done it like they do in the big cities. Hispanics there will raise their fists and are very demanding." Jim Gonzalez, a Mexican-American leader and respected Billings city council member from 1977 to 1985, represented the "old school" belief in working slowly through the system. Federico represented the younger generation's more aggressive assertion of reformist demands and opposition to discrimination. Esther Peralez saw the differences as generational. She remembered her mother's complaints about one young activist: "'What is his problem? Things are good now. He should have been here when we were younger, because they wouldn't allow Mexicans in school, they would beat them up. Things are good now.'" But, as Peralez recalled, her generation's thinking was different: "We were saying, 'no that's not good enough. We shouldn't be thankful. . . . There should be rights that everybody has.'" Still, Peralez and other youth felt "cultural frustration" because "in our culture you respect your elders, and I was taught that way," even though she disagreed with their tactics.

By the mid-1970s second- and third-generation Mexican Americans had established several political and cultural associations to improve the welfare of Billings-area Latinos. Since the 1920s Yellowstone Latinos had organized dances to raise money to help families burdened by hospital debts or victimized by the legal system. Beginning in the 1960s community members chartered more formal groups. The Latino Club sponsored cultural events and sought to preserve Mexican history and culture. *Concilio Mexicano*, composed of educated, middle-class Hispanics, advocated jobs and education programs for their community. The Mexican American Community Organization (MACO) tried to coordinate Mexican-American organizations' activities and responses to crises that affected the larger Latino community. Nevertheless, young and old frequently united on major issues, such as successfully lobbying the city government to take action on an incidence of police brutality and persuading the *Billings Gazette* to curb stereotypical coverage of area Latinos.

The Billings South Side neighborhood had long been the heart of the Yellowstone's Latino community. As the traditional home for many of Billings's immigrants and industrial workers, the South Side accepted the new migrants while other neighborhoods did not. They continued to

1810   1936

LOOR A LOS HEROES   QUE NOS DIERON LIBERTAD

COMPATRIOTAS: Lejos del territorio de la Patria los mexicanos sentimos la ineludible obligación de conmemorar sus fechas gloriosas, de celebrarlas dignamente, y dedicar un recuerdo de gratitud a los esforzados varones que sacrificaron sus vidas por legarnos el preciado tesoro de la libertad.

A medida que transcurre el tiempo, se aviva en el corazón de los verdaderos patriotas el amor y gratitud por sus libertadores. El COMITE PATRIOTICO MEXICANO, de BILLINGS, MONTANA, invita cordialmente a todos los mexicanos residentes en este lugar para que concurran a la celebración patriótica, que se desarrollará conforme al siguiente

P R O G R A M A

– DIA 15 –

A las 7.30 p. reunidos en el lugar de la fiesta el Comité Patriótico y pueblo en general, se desarrollará el acto oficial siguiente:

1. —Himnos nacionales Mexicano y Americano, cantados por un grupo de niños y señoritas, acompañados por la Orquesta.
2. —Obertura por la Orquesta.
3. —Discurso del Sr. J. J. González.
4. —Recitación por el joven Marcelino Pérez.
5. —Recitación por la señora María H. Herrera.
6. —Discurso por el joven Alfonso Galván.
7. —Recitación por el joven Vicente Pérez.
8. —Poesía por la niña Rosa Díaz.
9. —Discurso por la señora Natalia B. Núñez.
10. —Recitación por el niño Pablo Pérez.
11. —Recitación por el joven Andrés Duarte.
12. —Recitación por el joven Salvador Hinojos.

13. —
"HIDALGO O EL GLORIOSO GRITO DE INDEPENDENCIA"

Drama en cuatro cuadros.

REPARTO:

Hidalgo .... Sr. Emeterio Pérez
Mercedes .... Srita. Sofía Ronquillo
Aldana .... Joven Francisco Duarte
Allende .... Joven Severo Briceño
Abasolo .... Joven Juan Hernández
Alcalde .... Joven Juan Acosta
Pérez .... Sr. Roberto Hernández

Presos 1o., 2o. y 3o., serán improvisados

14. —Himnos nacionales Mexicano y Americano, cantados por el grupo de niños y señoritas, acompañados por la Orquesta.
15. —Tribuna libre.

– DIA 16 –

A las 4.30 p. m. reunidos el Comité Patriótico y pueblo en general, se desarrollará el siguiente programa:

1. —Himnos nacionales Mexicano y Americano, cantados por un grupo de niños y señoritas, acompañados por la Orquesta.
2. —Obertura por la Orquesta.
3. —Discurso por el Sr. Manuel Hinojos.

4. —Recitación por la niña Eustacia Pérez.
5. —"Muerte de Hidalgo", por la señora Alfonsa G. Vargas.
6. —Recitación por el joven Juan Hernández.
7. —Recitación por la señorita Belén Beltrán.
8. —Recitación por la Srita. María de la Luz Pérez.
9. —Recitación por el niño Julio Hinojos.
10. —Discurso por el Sr. Ramón Mascareñas.

11. —
"CORTES Y CUAUHTEMOC"

Drama en dos cuadros.

REPARTO:

Cortés .... Sr. Fernando Núñez
Cuauhtémoc .... Sr. Juan Sánchez
Alvarado .... Joven Guadalupe Hinojos
García de Holguín .... Joven Severo Briceño
Bernal Díaz del Castillo . Sr. Roberto Hernández
Tetlepanquetsalt .... Joven Marcelino Pérez

12. —Himnos nacionales Mexicano y Americano, cantados por el grupo de niñas y señoritas, acompañados por la Orquesta.
13. —Tribuna libre.

Los intermedios serán cubiertos por la Orquesta.

BILLINGS, MONT., SEPTIEMBRE DE 1936

EL COMITE PATRIOTICO MEXICANO – Presidente, Sr. José Silva; Secretario, Sr. Luis Díaz; Tesorero, Sr. Emeterio Pérez; 1er. Vocal, Sr. José Hilario; 2o. Vocal, Sr. Antonio Montes; Abanderados: los Sres.

Angel Magallanes y Roberto Hernández. - Director de Fiestas Patrias, Sr. Julio Lemus.
Habrá orden y respeto para todas las familias.
Las fiestas se efectuarán en el Salón COLISEUM.

(J)

Celebrating traditional holidays became an important way for Yellowstone Latinos to preserve their Mexican heritage. This poster invited community members to a commemoration of Mexican Independence Day (September 16) in 1936.

establish permanent homes there, Robert Rivera believed, because they felt "more like being around your own people." Some Mexican Americans who joined the middle class later chose to move away from their South Side roots to other parts of the city. Esther Peralez moved to the Heights, she explained, as part of living out "the American Dream." As someone who grew up in poverty, she wanted "a piece of that pie," "to have a brand new home made from scratch" instead of the older housing available on the South Side. Esther Rivera's family also moved from the South Side to the Heights, but they missed their former neighborhood and ties they had kept since moving to the valley: "The minute I could drive I was back down there. We attended all the social functions, we went to the same church. . . . [My dad] used to like to go to the Mexican dances. If there wasn't a dance, he'd make one, he'd sponsor one. We never lost contact with our [South Side] friends. . . . My parents were very social. They met all these people at the colonia, and they never forgot them."

The South Side's major landmark, Our Lady of Guadalupe Catholic Church, has played an important role in solidifying the Yellowstone's Latino community during the last forty years. Most farmworkers were devout Catholics, but poor transportation and Sunday work demands often prevented them from attending church. Nonetheless, families made special efforts to give their children proper religious instruction. Dora Cantu remembered her father working in fields close to the Ballantine Catholic Church when his children needed to take first communion lessons. Yellowstone Latino families attended a variety of Catholic churches but they desired a setting that nourished their culture. To that end Sal Briceno helped build the Little Flower Catholic Church on the South Side in the early 1930s. But an increasing white membership in the new church, Briceno felt, soon began "pushing the Mexicans away." Esther Rivera also "never felt like Little Flower was our special church. We always felt like we might be a little in the way." In the early 1950s, as Ruth Contreraz recalled, residents began planning a special ethnic church:

> I think what helped a lot was when a lot of the older Mexican people started talking about how we should have our own church and how we should better our own community. . . . I think all the different circles at St. Ann's and other churches started talking about developing this and

that. They would hold meetings and then everyone had their say on what they felt, what they wanted . . . That's how it started changing.

After its construction in 1952 Our Lady of Guadalupe Church attracted Latinos from Ballantine, Huntley, and other Yellowstone communities as well the sizable South Side Mexican-American community. "We could attend mass anywhere," Esther Rivera explained, "but there we congregated because we needed to keep continuity in the community. You're at home." Other residents, such as Liz Castro, agreed that the church attracted people with ethnic, kin, and neighborhood ties: "Everybody knows everybody, it's just a neat place to be." Esther Peralez tried attending other churches in her Heights neighborhood, but she was drawn back to Guadalupe: "It was like old home week. You fit right in, you know people, it's just a comfortable place. . . . So many places, I'm always the only minority, and I think when is this ever going to end . . . you can always pick up subtle discrimination. . . . But going to Guadalupe I always feel comfortable."

In addition to providing for the spiritual needs of the Latino community, the church strengthened ethnic identity. Esther Rivera explained: "Before that we were unified, but yet kind of distant, each to his own. But when the church started out, that's when all the people started thinking more or less alike." The church enhanced ethnic pride by providing a gathering place for people to organize cultural events such as Cinco de Mayo and September 16 (*die Ciseis*) celebrations. "They used to celebrate . . . in little surrounding towns like Huntley, Worden, Ballantine," Ruth Contreraz remembered, "but here in Billings, nothing . . . because there was no place to get started with it." Since Our Lady of Guadalupe's inauguration in 1952, Contreraz believed that Yellowstone Hispanics "have really come a long ways. . . . Now our culture is being recognized, we have identity, and it's being shared by many other nationalities besides us."

The annual December 12 celebration commemorates the day when the Virgen de Guadalupe appeared before Mexico's Juan Diego. After a special mass the congregation sings to the Virgin and girls present flowers to the church alter. Celebrants then adjourn to the church hall for more singing, refreshments, and piñatas. Before Christmas parishioners celebrate another Mexican tradition in the processions of Las Posadas. Participants reenact Mary and Joseph's search for lodging and share Christmas greetings, refreshments, and songs.

Before building Our Lady of Guadalupe Yellowstone Latinos made both formal and informal attempts to preserve their Mexican heritage. In 1929 Mexican Americans in Billings formed La Honorifica Mexicana to celebrate fiestas on the important Mexican holidays, Cinco de Mayo, which commemorates the courageous Mexican defeat of an invading French army in 1862, and September 16, Mexican Independence Day. At these fiestas, Robert Rivera recalled, older men in the community would often discuss the history of Mexico. "They were the ones that really carried the tradition and remembered the customs and everything from the old country. They tried to teach that to the younger people." Adapting traditions to Montana's harvest schedule and unpredictable weather, Billings organizers in recent years have combined the May and September commemorations in one August celebration.

Cultural activities, especially with music, took place on a more informal basis among extended families and groups of friends. Sal Briceno recalled: "Everybody used to get together to sing. I don't think there was a Mexican man who didn't know how to sing and play guitar and dance the juarabe tapatilla." People frequently organized dances, which engaged many area Mexican-American bands, such as Little Joe and the Alegres, Harold Garza and the Rebeldes, and Andy Martinez and the Bandoleros. Other residents have periodically sought to preserve and perpetuate Latino culture. Ruth Contreraz, for example, organized a group of young women to learn and perform traditional Mexican dances.

Food arts are often the most persistent cultural activity among American ethnic groups. Yellowstone Latinos introduced the region to a cuisine that has become a standard feature in many restaurants and households. Many women still proudly prepare dishes and employ methods learned from their Mexican mothers and grandmothers. Maria Cantu described how she makes tortillas from scratch, shunning packaged varieties: "I don't even use corn meal or masa harina. I plant my own corn, I cook my own corn, I grind my own corn, and I use my own corn. I let the corn dry, and shell it and put it away in a barrel. Anytime I need it . . . I have a machine to grind it. I cook the corn with lime, and it takes the shell off, and I have to watch it until it turns completely white." For holidays and special occasions women sometimes joined other female kin and friends to prepare traditional foods. Sal Briceno remembered his mother often joined with three or four families to buy and roast a pig and then make tamales with pork or turkey and spices for holidays. "All the women would get together" to scrape the meat off the skull, and make chicharrones and flour tortillas.

A few women combined their culinary expertise with business acumen and opened restaurants in Billings. Hermina Torres, who came to the Yellowstone valley with her husband in 1940 as a migrant farmworker, opened Torres Cafe in 1963; her daughter Josie Torres Quarnberg took over the operation in 1977. Liz Castro and her family operated the El Paso Cafe during the 1980s. The restaurant opened on South Twenty-ninth Street, then moved to Montana Avenue to serve "the South Side people."

The Yellowstone's Latino community often faced difficult choices. Sometimes they had to sacrifice cultural identity to obtain greater respect and economic prosperity. Many second- and third-generation Mexican Americans hoped acculturation would engender tolerance. Sal Briceno, for example, recalled that his family was "more Americanized" and therefore "treated better" by the dominant society. But assimilation into the larger community often made economic class rather than "race" the significant factor in distinguishing Latinos. Esther Rivera thought that the larger community became more tolerant when "we became middle class" and that farmworker families became middle class because they "wanted something different for our children," and struggled to attain a more prosperous lifestyle. But the poorer migrant farmworkers were still viewed as the "other," in racial terms, by many non-Latinos in the Yellowstone. Gaining acceptance and opportunity in the larger community has sometimes been won at the expense of cultural cohesion, which has troubled many Yellowstone Latinos who regret the loss of the Spanish language and other aspects of cultural identity.

In this respect, the Yellowstone's Latino community has faced greater obstacles than Spanish-language communities in the Southwest and the nation's larger cities, where the density of ethnic populations has provided a measure of ethnic security and diminished the demand to assimilate. Sal Briceno noted that his children lost interest in traditional Mexican music because "there are so many things that they can do now." Traditional culture was no longer central to their lives. "Their culture doesn't mean anything, they're Americans. They consider themselves just as 'white' as anybody else." Intermarriage between the children of Euro-Americans

*Community activities were not limited to celebrations of Mexican tradition.
Participating in the quintessential American sport, the Mexican Aztecs
(pictured here in 1949) were an all-Latino baseball team in Billings.*

COURTESY MR. AND MRS. SEVERO BRICENO,
WESTERN HERITAGE CENTER PERMANENT COLLECTION, BILLINGS, MONTANA

and Mexican Americans, however, has provided a mixed blessing. "So
what's happening is our race is getting very diluted." Esther Rivera noted,
"You're losing your language, you're losing a lot there. I see it with every
generation it's more and more. . . . They don't have memories, they're
losing a lot of their culture."

The decline of Spanish as a second language for third- and fourth-
generation Mexican Americans alarms many, while some parents
remember problems they faced learning English and insist on speaking
English to their children. Ruth Contreraz remembered her frustrations as
a child trying to learn English in school: "I thought, darn it, when I get
married and have children I'm going to talk to them in English. I love my
culture, and I'll teach my kids anything to do with my Mexican culture,
but English is the important language now. I didn't want my kids to go
through that." Families were forced to choose between their language
and their children's success. When her older brother failed the first grade

because he could not speak English, Esther Peralez's parents resolved to do "whatever we have to do to get you through school," and they "spoke in Spanish, and we spoke in English." Peralez noted that Billings is unusual because so many Chicanos understand Spanish but cannot speak it: "It's sad, that that was the trade-off in order to survive in these schools." The Yellowstone Mexican-American experience illustrates the dilemma of cultural pluralism in the United States, where "either/or" demands to assimilate to avoid discrimination and enjoy equal opportunity often impede the formation of dynamic ethnic cultures that can play an equal and beneficial role in society.

Economic and educational success eluded many resident Latinos. Augie Lopez, who became Billings's first counselor for Latino students in 1973, found an "astronomical" dropout rate because of a hostile school environment and poverty. But increased bilingual instruction dramatically improved conditions and the retention rate. In 1980 concerned Latinos initiated the Eastern Montana College Hispanic Student Scholarship Fund Board to increase Chicano college enrollment. Esther Peralez, a counselor at Eastern Montana College, lamented that still too few Chicano youth were graduating to college, but since the 1980s area educators have begun to link educational progress to positive ethnic identity and have worked to improve cultural sensitivity. In 1990 Latinos comprised almost half of Garfield School's students, and their parents actively participated in school activities to foster cultural awareness. At an annual teacher-appreciation day, for example, they present homemade tortillas and Mexican paper flowers.

Mexican-American school populations increased in Billings because economic changes made the Latino community more urban rather than rural. Beginning in the 1950s, when agriculture became more mechanized and some discriminatory barriers in urban employment lifted, the state's Latinos began moving to Billings. In 1950, 31 percent of Montana's Mexican-born population resided in urban areas; by 1960, 60 percent lived in cities. By 1980 only 2 percent of Yellowstone County's Hispanic residents were involved in agriculture. This shift in employment patterns reflected general trends in the Northwest region as Latino immigrants "settled out" and moved to larger towns and cities for jobs and the comforts of established ethnic community.

The mechanization of the beet industry substantially reduced immigration to Montana. Sal Briceno noted, "We have very few people that come here now to work beets. Most of it's mechanical now." Merle Riggs, former labor recruiter and agricultural manager for the Billings plant, explained that herbicides greatly reduced the need for hand labor and allowed "workers that came up here to perform more acres per day." A severe wild oats infestation in the 1950s and 1960s prompted Billings-area growers to apply chemicals before other states because they did not have alternative crops to grow. In 1976 an era ended when the Great Western Company stopped furnishing transportation for migrant workers, transferring the burden to individual growers and migrant laborers.

In addition to the declining need for farmworkers, declining blue-collar work opportunities discouraged Latinos from settling in the valley. Railroad and packing plant jobs have disappeared, and as Robert Rivera noted, "There was just hundreds of Mexicans working at those [packing] plants, so when those plants shut down, by golly that put a hardship on this town." Esther Rivera agreed that a vital economy was essential to a flourishing Latino community: "A lot of your people have gone and settled elsewhere, and stayed away. Like my aunt and uncle left. We lost a lot of people in our Hispanic community because of the economy, because they will go where the work is."

Despite farm mechanization beet growers still depend on hand labor. Every spring about six thousand migrant farmworkers—mostly Mexican Americans from the Rio Grande valley of Texas—come to the Yellowstone to work, following a migrant route that takes them on to Oregon to top and bag onions, to Washington to pick apples, and to Minnesota to harvest beans before returning to Texas in late fall. Successful farmworker organizing during the 1960s and 1970s, however, provided families with benefits not available to their predecessors. In 1972, for example, the Montana Migrant Council was established to provide labor, health, housing, and educational assistance to migrant families. Many Yellowstone Mexican Americans, who retained ties with families from Texas, often worked with federal migrant programs. Parishioners at Our Lady of Guadalupe Church have also extended aid to farmworker families, helping newcomers find housing, farm employment, and food. Ruth Contreraz noted that, "The Mexicans that were settled already in the Hispanic community were helping the migrants that were coming in . . . because a lot of them knew what it was like to be a fieldworker."

Despite their importance to the area economy, many Montanans refuse to acknowledge that migrant farmworkers have permanent connections to this place, even though Mexican-American families return year after year to the same area farms. The term "migrant" is a misleading title for many Latino families who loyally return to the valley each spring. Just as many Montana "snowbirds" annually escape winter's icy grip for the warmer Southwest, many Texans routinely join the "migrant stream" to thin beets each cool Montana spring. Some, such as Juan Montes, have been migrant farmworkers for several decades and have not realized their dream for more settled employment or a "piece of land" to farm. Others, who consider Texas their home, continue to work beets during the summer to supplement family incomes. Mario Iracheta, a Texas construction worker, has come to the Yellowstone to work beets since 1952 and has children who were born here.

The persistence of the Yellowstone's Latino community is distinct in the Northwest and Rocky Mountain West. The Hispanic population in Colorado and Idaho, for example, has grown dramatically in the last few decades, but Montana's has remained relatively stable and constant with the rest of the state's population. Scant economic opportunities draw fewer working immigrants to the Big Sky Country, and declining infusions of Spanish-speaking immigrants challenge the established second-and third-generation Billings community to retain links with their ethnic heritage. Yet Latinos young and old in the Yellowstone continue to find meaning in family reunions, traditional celebrations, religious observances, and other social, cultural, and political activities. Like their predecessors, third- and fourth-generation Mexican Americans continue to honor their history and reshape their cultural identity.

The Latinos who moved north to the Yellowstone valley have left a vital legacy to the area's heritage. The region's agricultural prosperity, according to one former migrant, depended on the essential labor of Latino farmworkers: "If it hadn't been for the Mexicans, the farmers wouldn't have succeeded." Besides their crucial economic role, Mexican Americans have contributed an enduring ethnic community and enriched the Yellowstone's culture.

NOTE ON SOURCES

Resources on Montana's and the Yellowstone's Mexican-American community are few. This essay relies to a great extent on the reminiscences of Yellowstone valley Latino residents. In providing a sense of the past and information on elusive topics such as ethnic identity, oral history interviews are a crucial source of information about people in the twentieth century. Interviewers Linda Lee Hickey, Laurie Mercier, Lynda Moss, Nancy Olson, and Wanda Walker interviewed Sal Briceno, Maria Cantu, Liz Castro, Ruth Contreraz, Ynes Contreraz, Robert Federico, Dora Cantu Flannigan, Esther Peralez, Don Pippin, Merle Riggs, Esther Rivera, and Robert Rivera as part of the Yellowstone Sugar Beet Oral History Project. The project was funded by the American Association of State and Local History and Western Sugar Company, Tate & Lyle, Ltd. The tape-recorded interviews and transcripts are preserved in the Western Heritage Center's archives. An interview with Santos Carranza of Sidney, by Laurie Mercier, is deposited with the Montana Historical Society archives. Also critical to understanding the historical role of Latino beet workers, or betabeleros, were the annual reports of the Billings Sugar Factory and Great Western Sugar Company, produced by factory managers for the years 1917–1950. These records are also deposited with the Western Heritage Center (WHC). Clippings and pamphlets in the vertical files of the Billings Public Library, typescripts and reports in the vertical files of the Montana Historical Society library, articles on the Yellowstone Hispanic community in the *Billings Gazette* (appearing more frequently after 1976) also significantly aided research.

The researcher using census records to estimate Latino populations must use caution. Early classifiers branded Mexican people as a "race," ignoring the diversity found within Mexico and the United States origins of many Mexican Americans. Official definitions shifted over time, reflected in the confusing Bureau of Census demarcations that range from a racial category, "Mexicans," in 1930 to a more ambiguous language identity "Hispanic" in 1990. Since 1970 the census came closer to ethnic identity by classifying Spanish-language residents, which included second- and third-generation Mexican Americans, in addition to those born in Mexico. Only 7 percent of Montana Hispanic residents in 1970 and 1980 were foreign born, and close to half were born in Montana, indicating the stability and slow growth of the community. As late as 1990 Montana's 12,000 Hispanics accounted for just 2 percent of the entire state population. Census records, however, notoriously undercount Latinos and often do not include those who identify with the culture but do not consider Spanish their primary language. This particularly applies to Montana and the Yellowstone, where Spanish is more selectively spoken.

The following bibliography indicates the paucity of materials on Latino communities in Montana and the Yellowstone, but these sources will assist those interested in further research. The author extends special thanks to Emily Witcher, Lynda Moss, Wanda Walker, and Dave Walter for their assistance in locating materials, to Esther Rivera for reviewing the manuscript and offering her suggestions, and to the narrators who volunteered their recollections for the WHC oral history project.

SELECTED BIBLIOGRAPHY

Adams, Helen D. "History of the South Park Neighborhood." South Park Neighborhood Task Force and Billings–Yellowstone City-County Planning Board, 1978. Pamphlet file, Billings History, Billings Public Library, Billings, Montana.

Cardoso, Lawrence A. *Mexican Emigration to the U.S., 1897–1931.* Tucson, Ariz., 1980.

Devitt, Steve. "We Montanans: The Billings Hispanic Community." *Montana Magazine,* September 1987, 6-13.

Gamboa, Erasmo. *Mexican Labor and World War II: Braceros in the Pacific Northwest, 1942–1947.* Austin, Tex., 1990.

Gutierrez, Robert F. "The Montana Migrant Workers." TS, 1982. Vertical file, Montana Historical Society Library, Helena, Montana (hereafter MHS).

Hispanic Task Force. Hispanics in Montana: Report to the 47th Montana Legislative Assembly. Montana Department of Community Affairs, 1980. Vertical file, MHS.

Holterman, Jack. "Californios in Far Montana." MS, 1980. Small Collection 1653, Jack Holterman Papers, MHS.

Reisler, Mark. *By the Sweat of Their Brow: Mexican Immigrant Labor in the U.S. 1900–1940.* Westport, Conn., 1976.

Rural Employment Opportunities, Inc. Interviews by Patricia Nelson. Oral History 634, Migrant Farmworkers Oral History Project, MHS.

Slatta, Richard W. "Chicanos in the Pacific Northwest." *Pacific Northwest Quarterly,* 70 (October 1979), 155-62,

Spomer, Pete. "History of Sugar Beets." Big Horn County Historical Society Newsletter, n.d. Vertical file, Western Heritage Center, Billings, Montana.

*Warden Floyd Powell and others gaze up at the prison during the 1959 riot
and wonder what to do next. Prior to taking the warden's job in 1958,
Powell toured the facility and found conditions for the inmates "shocking."*

C. Owen Smithers, photographer
Courtesy Keith Edgerton

"A Tough Place to Live"

The 1959 Montana State Prison Riot

Keith Edgerton

Sometimes a single dramatic event opens a window into a larger story of longer historical duration. Such is the case with the Montana Prison Riot of 1959, which attracted national attention. The story is compelling enough. A handful of inmates in a desperate escape attempt killed the deputy warden and took control of the institution for some thirty-six hours. In a splashy display of pyrotechnics (including blasts from a bazooka), the Montana National Guard stormed the prison, freed over twenty hostages, and killed two ringleaders in a hail of gunfire.

According to Keith Edgerton, a professor of history at Montana State University-Billings, in the aftermath of the riot a less compelling but no less gruesome story emerged. Since its inception in 1871 Montana's prison system had been plagued with chronic underfunding, overcrowding, graft, and political indifference. On an even larger canvas the riot revealed the problems state government has faced when it cuts corners and neglects its social, educational, or correctional institutions. What was the immediate result of the 1959 Prison Riot? Is there a lesson here for current state leaders?

GUARD GUS BYERS, ON ROUTINE PATROL IN THE OLD MONTANA STATE PRISON IN Deer Lodge the afternoon of April 16, 1959, cracked open a window to freshen the stale air in cellblock #1. Behind him, about six and one-half feet from the window, four tiers of cell galleries rose along the opposite wall of the catwalk that encircled the interior of the building. Byers paused, then turned to resume his patrol. Without warning he "caught a bunch of gasoline and paint thinner in the face." Suddenly aware of flaming rag torches tied to mop handles blocking both ends of the walk, Byers stared through stinging, teary eyes into the face of an inmate who was waving a fiery torch. "Don't burn me, don't burn me," Byers pleaded. Nineteen-year-old murderer Lee Smart held him at bay.

Within seconds, forty-two-year-old, six-time loser Jerry Myles and twenty-five-year-old convicted burglar George Alton climbed across bars near the south end of the cellblock, scrambled onto the catwalk, and relieved Byers of his keys to the gun cage located at the catwalk's terminus. Simultaneously, knife-wielding inmates Jerry Walker and Mike Maciel subdued guards Marvin Wallace and Erwin Seiler sitting at a desk on the ground floor of cellblock #1 directly beneath the gun cage. The three guards were shoved into "the hole," dank isolation cells beneath the cellblock's lobby.[1]

After unlocking the cabinet in the gun cage and removing an empty .30-.30 Winchester lever-action rifle, the five conspirators raced to the basement kitchen connecting the two main cellblocks, overpowered the unarmed guard, and pilfered an assortment of butcher knives and cleavers. Hurrying back into the cellblock, they captured several unsuspecting staff members as they arrived for the four o'clock shift.[2]

With Lieutenant Charles Brown as a hostage, Myles, Smart, and Alton made their way back down through the kitchen then up to the old cellblock where ammunition was locked in the gun cage. Used as the maximum security unit, the old cellblock was patrolled by armed guards and was considered invulnerable. Myles planned to have Brown get the guard's gun, but James Hubbard, a burglar from Sweetgrass, saved him the trouble. Before Myles and his group reached the cellblock Hubbard had climbed across the bars separating the cell galleries from the catwalk and confronted Lawrence Backman, the catwalk guard. Hubbard demanded the gun. Backman cocked the trigger and aimed, but the wiry Hubbard pounced on him before he could fire.

In the ensuing scuffle Backman suddenly saw Myles, Smart, and Alton, with Brown in tow, holding knives on Vic Baldwin and Lawrence Cozzens, two guards on cellblock desk duty. "I could have killed Jimmy Hubbard," Backman recalled, "but when I . . . saw Myles down there with that knife in Cozzen's stomach, well, I thought, what the hell is the use." Backman handed over the rifle, which was loaded with four rounds, and an ammo pouch holding six more rounds. Hubbard snatched an additional seven rounds from a desk in the gun cage before tossing the rifle to Smart who quickly concealed it in a roll of canvas.[3]

Smart, Myles, and Donald Toms, another inmate who had joined the fray, nonchalantly strolled out of the old cellblock and down the sidewalk to the administration building. There they convinced Deforest Thompson, the guard at the grating door, to let Myles inside to talk with William Cox, a guard who was Deputy Warden Theodore (Ted) Rothe's assistant. Myles suffered from migraine headaches and routinely requested prescription medication, which the deputy warden locked in his office. Once inside Myles asked Cox for his pills. As Cox stepped into the office, Myles raced past him into the room brandishing a butcher knife at Rothe. Rothe instinctively picked up a wooden file box from his desk and fended off the blows of the smaller Myles. Cox grabbed a chair and raised it, but before he could bring it down on Myles, he was startled by the crack of a rifle. In the melee Smart had entered the office and shot Rothe through the heart. Myles wheeled around and stabbed Cox, ripping his arm from elbow to armpit. Smart, Myles, and Toms, now joined by several others, locked Cox and other staff members in an adjacent bathroom.

Within approximately seventeen minutes a handful of inmates had taken control of most of the interior of the Montana State Prison, killed the deputy warden, and captured nearly twenty hostages. No one on the outside or even in other parts of the prison was aware of anything out of the ordinary.[4]

"Shocking," had been Warden Floyd Powell's initial impression of prison conditions when he first toured the Deer Lodge facility in late summer of 1958. At the time Powell, who had more than two decades of professional experience in the Wisconsin penal system, was an applicant for the warden's job. He could not believe "that a place housing human beings could be so degenerate. I had twenty years experience in penology at the time," he recalled, but "I didn't need that experience to know that [it was] a hell-hole there . . . the worst I'd ever seen." Official studies, commissioned by the state at various times over nearly three decades, corroborated Powell's impression. Years of neglect exacerbated by decades of inadequate funding and a series of nonprofessional, inept wardens had brought the prison to the verge of chaos, which even the most far-reaching reforms could not stabilize immediately. In the late 1950s Montana's penitentiary was a disgrace to the state and undoubtedly was one of the worst prisons in the nation.[5]

The intolerable situation culminated finally in two riots, a minor rebellion in 1957 and the tragic 1959 riot, which was not a direct result of the antiquated prison system but was instead an escape attempt gone awry after reform had begun. Whatever the direct causes, the events that April weekend in 1959 dramatically and publicly underscored just how deeply rooted the myriad problems were. After decades of neglect and malaise, Montana, like many other states, was forced to modernize, albeit reluctantly, its aging penal institution. The calamitous situation at Deer Lodge was not unique to Montana, the region, or even the nation. From 1952 to 1959 riots of various proportions and intensities erupted in New Jersey, Michigan, Louisiana, North Carolina, Georgia, Kentucky, California, Massachusetts, Ohio, Illinois, Utah, Pennsylvania, Arizona, Oregon, and New Mexico.[6] Many state facilities had been built near the turn of the century and had either outlived their usefulness or were too overcrowded to accommodate their residents safely.

Montana's first prison was built in Deer Lodge in 1871 by the federal government as a territorial penitentiary. The fledgling state of Montana added to it in 1889 and, four years later, built an eighteen-foot wall, which still stands just off Main Street in Deer Lodge. In 1896 the first of two cellblocks was built. In 1912 Warden Frank Conley used convict labor to build a second cellblock just north of the first. These two structures accommodated about 550 inmates and formed the backbone of the physical plant for the next fifty-seven years. Conley ran the prison energetically from 1890 to 1921, using convicts as construction workers as well as strike breakers in the company town of Anaconda about twenty-six miles southwest of Deer Lodge. He also allegedly skimmed off thousands of state dollars for personal gain before Governor Joseph Dixon fired him in 1921.[7]

With the onset of the Great Depression, state appropriations for the prison shrank. In 1933 the legislature, bowing to pressure from organized labor, abolished another source of funds by prohibiting sale of many inmate-manufactured goods on the open market, setting a precedent that remained virtually intact for thirty years. At the same time that money sources were drying up, the physical plant was deteriorating, particularly the 1896 cellblock.[8]

The cellblock never had the luxury of interior plumbing. Two buckets sufficed in each cell; one for drinking and the other for human waste (still the case in 1959). A woefully inadequate electrical wiring system barely supported in each cell a single twenty-five watt bulb, too dim to read by. As early as 1931 a legislative committee touring the prison commented that the 1896 cellblock was "an eyesore to the state and is crying out in its filth and unsanitary condition." Inmates were "lying idle, rotting away in stink and stench. The place as it is, is lousy with bed bugs and the cells are dark and grimy." The committee described the isolation area beneath the ground floor of the new cellblock as "a hideous place to throw a man." Even in the austere days of 1931 the committee recommended appropriating $300,000 to remodel the structures using inmate labor. Its recommendation, however, never made it to the floor of the legislature.[9]

Few improvements occurred during the next two decades. After Conley's dismissal in 1921 Montana's governors used the prison's top position as a political plum to reward party loyalists, men who were often inexperienced in even rudimentary penological techniques. Between 1924 and 1958 governors appointed as wardens two rural county sheriffs, a state highway commissioner who was a road engineer, the postmaster from Baker, a cattle rancher, a former salesman with the Folger Coffee Company, a conductor for the Milwaukee Railroad, and a sergeant in the Montana Highway Patrol. None had any professional penological experience, and few had the necessary administrative acumen to run such a complex apparatus as a state prison, yet almost exclusive financial and administrative control of prison affairs gradually devolved to the warden. He implemented policy, lobbied for new building projects (unsuccessfully from 1931 to 1959), planned the budget, and hired and fired staff.

Faye O. Burrell, warden from 1953 until early 1958, whose previous penal experience had been as Ravalli county sheriff in charge of the two-cell county jail, was especially inept at managing both personnel and prison budget. In the early 1950s the legislature, aware of the advancing decay of the prison, appropriated money for physical plant maintenance.

Burrell, in a spirit of stifling frugality, simply did not spend his appropriations, allowing thousands of dollars to revert to the general fund. Between 1953 and 1955 Burrell allowed at least $18,529.41 to return to the state. In 1955, for example, the legislature appropriated $105,000 to build a desperately needed minimum security building on the prison ranch four miles outside of Deer Lodge. By late 1957 Warden Burrell had spent only $125 on the project while conditions worsened and the prison population swelled. Except for 1956 when the population averaged 566, the yearly prison population between 1952 and 1958 averaged six hundred, well above the 543 yearly average of the previous three decades.[10]

The staff, both guards and support personnel, were nonprofessional, poorly trained, and even more poorly paid. A visiting official commented in late 1957 that the Montana State Prison suffered from "the lowest employee morale" he had "ever encountered in a penal institution." According to a 1946 study the pay of a prison guard in Montana ranked 115 out of 120 state and local institutions surveyed, ahead of only five Arkansas and North Carolina facilities, where inmate trustees were used as guards. The national average starting salary that year for a prison guard was $2,000. In Montana it was $1,200. Although salaries increased to $2,400 by the 1950s, they remained far below the rate of inflation. Eighty percent of the guards at Deer Lodge were retirees over the age of fifty-five. Many were drifters who stayed in the position only temporarily. In 1957, for example, three out of every four guards were newly hired. The warden requested no background checks on applicants, and prospective employees took no written examination. Once hired prison guards received no formal training.[11]

For inmates there was hardly a less appealing prison in which to do time than the one provided by Montana. After the legislature effectively curtailed prison labor in 1933, only a few minimum security inmates and a handful of trustees were employed. Some worked at the ranch run by the penitentiary or in the prison's garment, shoe, and toy repair shops; laundry; license tag plant; or infirmary. Others were clerks in the office of the registrar of motor vehicles adjacent to the prison. At any given time approximately two hundred of an average of nearly 550 prisoners were employed. For those who were not employed, idleness and long stretches in the cell—often twenty-two hours a day—were commonplace.

This view of the prison's well-tended interior grounds in the 1940s shows guard tower number three in the foreground and a yard control station in the distance.

Montana Historical Society Photograph Archives, Helena

Inmate toughs, who controlled the few job opportunities, aggravated the employment predicament. The prison employed no professionally trained or experienced managers to oversee inmate labor. Instead convicts bullied, cajoled, or bribed their way into management positions. These con-bosses were free to hire inmates they wanted working in their shops. Inmates with jobs varied their monotonous routine and, even more important, received "good-time" credit to reduce their sentences. The con-boss system eventually led to flagrant abuses of power, rampant favoritism, inefficiency, and dangerously low prisoner morale.[12]

Until late 1958 the prison offered no recreational facilities and few organized athletic events. Recreation and exercise normally consisted of a daily fifteen-minute walk around the vegetable garden that filled the prison yard or an occasional, sanctioned boxing match. A modified Auburn system, a vestige from the nineteenth century that prohibited prisoners from speaking while eating or exercising, was enforced. There was no classification system, and the staff rarely separated inmates according to age, types of crime, or sexual proclivities. An overwhelming majority of the prison population were two-bit check chiselers, petty thieves, overgrown juvenile delinquents, or ranch hands who robbed the local grocery store, usually while drunk. Yet oftentimes they shared cells with older, hardened, sometimes homosexual cons. No parole system existed prior to 1955. Instead an ambiguous, inconsistently administered "good-time" policy often deprived an inmate, who had honestly served time, of a legitimate early release. Neither educational nor rehabilitative training was available, and the small, wholly inadequate library had last been updated in the 1920s. The prison had no full-time doctor or dentist.[13]

In the hot days of late July 1957 the years of simmering discontent finally boiled over when inmates, suffering oppression under Vern Lockwood, a particularly sadistic deputy warden, staged a bloodless insurrection, took hostages, and presented a list of grievances and demands including a federal investigation of the prison.[14] Governor J. Hugo Aronson, a staunchly conservative Republican, reluctantly promised changes, much to the chagrin of a public who viewed improved prison conditions as mere coddling of hoodlums.[15] In spring 1958 Aronson agreed to employ a professionally trained penologist to run the prison.[16]

That fall the state hired Floyd Powell as warden. Tough minded and honest, Powell had been an assistant warden in Wisconsin. He and his deputy warden, Theodore Rothe, also from Wisconsin, promised sweeping reform for the mess in Deer Lodge. Late in 1958, with lukewarm blessings from Aronson, Powell and Rothe began to clean up the prison. They were aided by Attorney General Forrest Anderson, Secretary of State Frank Murray, and several concerned citizens' groups. Anderson, the progressive Democrat who had negotiated with inmates during the two-day riot in 1957, and Murray sat on the Board of Prison Commissioners and the Board of Examiners with Governor Aronson.[17]

Powell and Rothe also tried, unsuccessfully, to institute professional training for the staff. Powell categorically opposed weapons inside the prison walls, considering they were under the control of ill-trained personnel, but when threatened with a walkout by guards, he grudgingly allowed a rifle in each cellblock. In the old wing—the maximum security section which housed the more violent and dangerous offenders—the guard on duty carried a loaded .30-.30 rifle. In the new cellblock a rifle was stowed inside a cabinet in the gun cage that opened onto the catwalk. Powell and Rothe had planned to remove the guns the week of the riot.[18] The two men initiated an educational program, classified and segregated some prisoners, standardized discipline, increased the quality and quantity of prison food, developed a meaningful recreation program, and removed the con-boss from prison industries.

Powell's actions were long overdue, yet as one inmate observed in an interview, "there is a definite pecking order in prison, in any prison, and when that pecking order is disturbed," he said, a storm is bound to follow.[19] In addition to prisoners, some conservatives in the state were not impressed with Powell's energetic changes. During the fall and winter 1958–59, J. O. Gehrett, editor of the *Silver State Post* in Deer Lodge, reflecting conservative sentiment, leveled a series of editorial broadsides against Powell and his reforms.[20]

When Jerry Myles came to the prison in June 1958, after being convicted of a burglary in Butte, he had been in Montana less than a week. Before that, not counting juvenile facilities or reform schools, he had spent twenty-four years in at least twenty-four different institutions, including three years in the federal penitentiary at Atlanta and seven in Alcatraz. Clearly Myles was a rough character, an incorrigible, career con. While in the Atlanta penitentiary he was convicted of conspiring to mutiny. At Alcatraz he had had a bird's-eye view of the genesis and evolution of a bloody prison riot in 1946, when inmates overpowered armed guards on the catwalks and caused the deaths of two guards and three inmates. Myles, from a broken home, had been abused as a youngster. A homosexual, he had no family or friends. In Deer Lodge he quickly bullied his way into becoming con-boss of the tailor shop. Taking advantage of the chaotic atmosphere inside the walls, Myles intimidated the compliant staff into allowing him late-night forays in the shop where he forced younger, more vulnerable inmates into homosexual acts. Soon after Powell and Rothe arrived they caught Myles in a lascivious act with teenager Lee Smart. Deputy Warden Rothe, who managed the daily internal affairs of the prison, stripped Myles of his position as con-boss and placed him in isolation for several weeks. Myles was enraged at his unceremonious dethronement. "Prison is my home," he snapped at a staff member a few months later, "and you're making it a tough place for me to live."[21]

Despite his youth and relative inexperience, the moody, ill-tempered Smart was considered more dangerous than Myles by most inmates. In 1956, at the age of sixteen, he bludgeoned to death a traveling salesman near Pendroy, Montana. He claimed he was resisting the man's homosexual advances, but the jury did not believe Smart and sentenced him to thirty years in Deer Lodge, where he met Myles and soon became his lover and loyal follower.[22] The younger Smart and his cell mate George Alton, a small-time burglar and prison boxing champ, were able to associate with Myles because the prison had no classification system. Although Montana law required prison officials to segregate inmates under the age of twenty-one, the reality of overcrowding prevented implementation of the law.[23]

In early spring 1959 Myles, still incensed by Rothe's actions six months earlier, planned his personal revenge against the assistant warden and sold his scheme to Smart and Alton as a plan of escape. The youthful Smart, facing most of his life in prison, had nothing to lose, and Alton already had one escape to his credit. Fleeing prison in June 1958 he had eluded capture until September. Indeed, escape was a popular pastime at the prison in the 1950s when seventy-two inmates escaped between 1953 and 1958. Myles assured his cronies that, similar to Alcatraz in 1946, the threesome could jump the guards on the catwalks, take hostages, and then either walk out of the prison in guards' uniforms or, if word leaked out, walk out behind the hostages. They spun their scheme into motion midafternoon on April 16.[24]

Shortly after four o'clock the rioters, by now perhaps six or eight men, forced John Simonsen, an administrative assistant, to call Warden Powell in his office across Main Street from the prison. With a rifle at his head Simonsen told Powell, "There's been a stabbing in the prison, Warden, you'd better get over here right away." At approximately the same moment guard Fred Dawson, who had entered the old cellblock from an outside tower entrance, saw that a scuffle had taken place on the catwalk and gun cage. Looking down he watched as several inmates smashed locks off the cells. He turned and ran just as Powell and two aides hurried across the street below. Dawson yelled a warning but the three men strode to the prison's main entrance. As Powell ran up the stairs James Randall, a twenty-three-year-old forger, yanked him into the building. The two assistants retreated and immediately alerted authorities.[25]

Inside the dim prison lobby Powell focused on Smart pointing a .30-.30 muzzle at him. "You know you are making a mistake," the warden reasoned with his captors. "You now that both Mr. Rothe and I are working toward improvements in here and that this is going to set us back." Powell implored them to release the hostages and keep him. Instead they marched him into Rothe's office, where he saw his longtime colleague and friend on the blood-soaked floor. Smart pointed the rifle at Powell, and Myles ordered him to call Governor Aronson. Myles and Smart wanted cars with full gas tanks and radios and a four-hour head start out of the prison or the hostages would burn.[26]

Aronson was out, so Powell told the secretary, "Have him call me at number eight," a prearranged code that meant Powell was calling under duress from inside the prison. Aronson never returned the call.[27] While awaiting the governor's call, Powell convinced Myles that Cox needed medical attention and that perhaps there was a slight chance Rothe could be saved. Myles summoned an ambulance, and attendants were allowed to carry Rothe's body out of the prison and to escort Cox, who survived his wound, to the waiting ambulance. Later the conspirators paraded a handcuffed Powell through the new cellblock and into the kitchen, where inmates politely served him cake and coffee.[28]

Around a quarter of seven, three hours after the disturbance began, off-duty guards and highway patrolmen armed with high-powered rifles manned the towers and surrounding walls. The rioters, concluding that Aronson was not going to call, became increasingly apprehensive and decided to act. They moved Powell into Rothe's office and then conferred in the lobby about the best method of executing him. Finally they agreed that one of them would slit Powell's throat while the others disappeared to avoid complicity. They would return later and hang his corpse upside down in a window to alert the world that they meant business. Walter Trotchie, a burglar from Black Eagle, was designated executioner. Trotchie, who by this time had imbibed a goodly amount of prison-brewed pruno—crudely concocted liquor—confronted Powell, then began telling him about his wife and children. In one of many odd twists, he broke down crying and handed the knife to Powell, who persuaded Trotchie to let him and several inmates escape through the front gate.

Once outside Powell called Aronson who had already alerted the Montana National Guard. By late evening guard units, comprising several hundred men, reinforced the highway patrolmen circling the prison. Local and national media converged on Deer Lodge, and curious townspeople flooded into the streets for a firsthand glimpse of the commotion. Deer Lodge residents had not witnessed anything similar at the prison in the town's ninety-year history, although Conley and an assistant warden had been stabbed in an unsuccessful escape attempt in 1908 and the near-disaster of 1957 was still fresh in many people's minds.[29]

At the outset of the escape attempt Myles had locked most of the inmates in their cells. The eighteen to twenty participants, many of whom were high on drugs pilfered from Rothe's office, roamed from building to building, smashing windows and doors and drinking pruno. They moved the hostages from area to area making detection difficult for rescuers. Finally the hostages were secured in two cells on the second tier closest to the northwest tower, which was Myles's center of operation. Eventually twenty-five hostages were captured. Two were released during the riot, one escaped, and two others were given sanctuary in the infirmary.

"There were a couple of guys who treated us real well while we were locked up," guard captain Everett Felix remembered. "They tried to feed us with what they had: scrambled eggs and green beans, spinach and fruit cocktail. And they kept us in cigarettes." Another hostage, Clyde Solars, remembered being "flooded with coffee" and that some of the inmates, at considerable personal risk, offered to smuggle notes to frantic family members on the outside.[30] In contrast to such hospitality, Myles ordered that naphtha be kept near cell doors to immolate hostages if the National Guard attempted rescue, and some inmates seized the opportunity to settle old scores. Earl Jackson punched Lawrence Backman, bloodying his nose and face. Myles hurled George Axtell, an elderly typist, down a flight of stairs injuring his back. Myles and James Randall, high on benzedrine and pruno, swaggered in front of the cells berating the hostages and threatening them with death.[31]

Thursday evening and Friday morning Myles used a bullhorn to bray rambling diatribes, irrational demands, and answers to reporters' shouted questions. "We're not fighting for today, but for the next guy who comes in here," Myles yelled. It was a ruse. This was an escape attempt gone sour not an uprising over conditions. Myles had no backing from the general inmate population, and he genuinely feared they would squelch his escape plans if given the chance, particularly after they learned of Rothe's murder.[32]

Only Smart and Alton were in on the escape; Myles duped the other rioters into believing that they could bring about change. Admittedly many inmates were miffed over the modification in routine triggered by Powell's reforms and by an inconsistently administered parole policy, but most had adopted a wait-and-see attitude. Conditions were better than in 1957, and Powell and Rothe had improved work conditions and opportunities, attempted to institute some type of classification system, lobbied for standardization of parole procedures, allowed more recreation time, and—perhaps most importantly—had improved the quality and quantity of food. Most of the prison population saw no pressing need to riot. Upon scrutiny the 1959 Montana prison uprising seems curiously out of sync with traditional prison disturbances. The spontaneous sit-down strike of 1957, though nonviolent, was in nearly all respects a classic riot—when hundreds of disgruntled inmates simply take over an institution and demand much-needed changes.

On numerous occasions Thursday evening and Friday, Warden Powell, accompanied by several of his assistants and a handful of reporters, entered the prison to negotiate with the ringleaders.[33] During one session Myles insisted that thirty out-of-state journalists tour the prison, take pictures, and interview inmates. Powell refused. Myles then demanded the dismissal of Benjamin Wright, director of the Board of Parole, because of his erratic actions and policies.[34] Throughout its four years of existence the board was severely underfunded, understaffed, and overworked. Wright did little to remedy the deficiencies. Instead he promulgated inconsistent policies and procedures. A few weeks prior to the uprising a legislative subcommittee conducted a secret investigation and recommended—among numerous modifications—that Wright be dismissed effective in June. Friday evening Wright tendered his resignation publicly to the relief of inmates and officials alike.[35] In yet another turn during the riot's strange odyssey, Myles released Walter Jones, the prison sociologist, twice on Friday—on his promise to return—to voice new demands. After the second release Powell refused to let Jones reenter the prison.

During a negotiating session Friday evening a concerned inmate secretly dropped Powell a note stating that the rioters had begun a tunnel and upon its imminent completion planned to burn the hostages alive. Myles had coerced a few inmates to dig a tunnel beginning at the base of the northwest tower and continuing under the wall into the middle of the outside street where it would hit the city's main sewer pipe, which, he thought, might lead to the nearby Clark Fork River. After several hours of digging at gunpoint the would-be escapists hit a concrete footing at the base of the tower and did not continue. The sewer pipe Myles sought never existed.

Friday evening, some thirty-three hours into the uprising, many of the participants, including Alton, had quit. Drugs and alcohol had run their course, and the men, tiring of Myles's braggadocio, returned quietly to their cells to wait out the looming National Guard attack. By early Saturday morning only five inmates remained holed up in the northwest tower.[36] Powell and the National Guard commanders decided they could risk no further waiting, and at three-thirty Saturday morning a bazooka blast from the outer northwest wall hit the second level of the northwest tower where the insurgents were thought to be. "The temperature was about 16," Powell recalled, "but I noticed I was sweating . . . profusely." While a highway patrolman sprayed the tower from the opposite side with a machine gun to pin down inmates and keep them away from cells holding the hostages, a contingent of National Guardsmen sprinted across the main yard while others took up strategic positions along the walls and lobbed tear gas into the tower. The guardsmen blew the jammed lock off the cell house door and scrambled up to the tier where hostages were holding blankets and mattresses, soaked in the toilets, against the bars to ward off an expected shower of naphtha. Within ninety seconds the guard team rescued all the hostages unharmed.[37]

Meanwhile Smart, Myles, and the three other inmates remained in the tower. Carl Frodsham remembers being "blown off the bed I was on" when the bazooka blast hit. "I could hear the machine gun and the national guardsmen yelling, but it was so dark I really couldn't see anything." The group had agreed that they would not be taken alive. After wounding Lieutenant Francis Pulliam of Missoula, who had entered the tower in an attempt to flush them out, Smart, sensing the end, turned his rifle on

Frodsham. But it was Smart who fell, shot in the head by Myles, who then turned the rifle on himself. Frodsham and the other two inmates surrendered quietly.[38]

Publicity about the 1959 insurrection focused public attention on the dangerous conditions that existed in the state's nineteenth-century prison despite positive changes since the 1957 disturbance. Significantly, the 1959 riot, though not directly related to prison conditions, forced the issue of prison reform onto the public's conscience and into the political arena. Mike Mansfield, Montana's United States senator, promised that federal money would be available for research and architectural plans for a new, safer prison.[39]

In 1960 Warden Powell barnstormed the state seeking support for a $5 million bond issue enabling the state to levy bonds financed by increased property taxes to construct a new facility at Deer Lodge. The only civic groups to publicly support the measure were the AFL-CIO, Montana's Farmers Union, and the Montana Council on Corrections. On election day 70 percent of the electorate opposed it. The hard reality that Montana property owners were the most heavily taxed of all those in the western states in 1959 and the lack of education about prison conditions foreordained the bond issue's failure. Despite the swirl of publicity surrounding the aging institution and its myriad ailments in the late 1950s, most Montanans were undoubtedly ill-versed in the problems at the prison while a good many believed that hoodlums in Deer Lodge did not deserve the comforts of a new facility.[40] Incredibly, Governor Aronson, too, reflected the lack of knowledge about prison affairs. Despite the extensive, written reports he received about the 1959 riot, he wrote of the riot in his memoirs several years later: "I'll never know just exactly what caused it. I think probably a lot of men wanted individual TVs in the cells and some other conveniences and comforts."[41]

Though voters did not approve a new prison in 1960, the 1959 riot did increase awareness of and galvanize support in the legislature for working on the prison's problems. Within a year of the riot several minor building projects were hastily completed on the prison ranch outside Deer Lodge to ease overcrowding at the main facility. University of Montana law professor William Crowley, who investigated the riot as assistant to the attorney general in 1959, believes that, "after 1957 a lot of people weren't convinced that anything was needed [to change the system]. I think that when this thing came along in 1959, it actively convinced everybody that something had to be done. It acted as a catalyst, that's its true historical importance."[42]

In the mid-1960s feasibility studies were done and architectural plans drawn for a new prison. In 1971, with strong support from Democratic Governor Forrest Anderson, veteran of the political struggles over the prison in the late 1950s, the state secured $3.8 million in federal revenue-sharing funds to build a new facility. Despite these efforts, the fact that it took more than twelve years to "find" funds to construct a new institution points sadly to the chronic fiscal problems plaguing Montana for most of its history.

Despite the good intentions of some lawmakers and prison officials in the late 1950s to ease the tensions at Deer Lodge, the riot of 1959 is a stain on Montana's history. After four decades of neglect by political leaders the prison had deteriorated beyond the point of good intentions or modest reform. The abrupt introduction of enlightened penological principles by Warden Powell threatened the inmate status quo and acted as a catalyst for the insane escape attempt by Jerry Myles, a desperate man mentally conditioned by twenty-five years of prison life.

On the surface it appeared that the 1959 riot had not been a direct consequence of deteriorating prison conditions. Yet the threat to Myles's stature among the inmates was an immediate result of internal reform instituted in the wake of the protracted disintegration of the prison. Above all, the 1959 riot succeeded in arousing the state from its long slumber and forced the issue of prison reform into the public spectrum.[43]

NOTES

1. Statements by August Byers, Clyde Sonet, Marvin Wallace, and Erwin Seiler, 1959, folders 7–9, box 61, Record Series 76 (hereafter RS 76), Montana Attorney General Records, Montana Historical Society Archives, Helena (hereafter MHS).

2. Statements by Charles Brown and Ralph Knudsen, folder 7, box 61, RS 76, MHS; Everett Felix, interview by author, August 10, 1988.

3. Statements by Charles Brown, Lawrence Backman, Fred Dawson, folders 7 and 9, box 61, RS 76, MHS.

4. Statements by William Cox, Deforest Thompson, and James Jones, folders 8 and 9, box 61, RS 76, MHS; William Cox, interview by author, September 7, 1988;

"Transcript on Appeal," *State of Montana v. George E. Alton,* 1960, docket 10191, Record Series 114, Montana Supreme Court Records, MHS (hereafter *Montana v. Alton*).

5. Floyd Powell, interview by author, September 7, 1988. For official reports and studies, see *Report of Special Joint Committee of the Twenty-Second Legislative Assembly of the State of Montana on State Institutions at Deer Lodge, Galen, and Warm Springs, 1931,* copy in folder 2, box 155, Manuscript Collection 35, Montana Governors' Papers, MHS (hereafter MC 35); "Report of the Joint Investigating Committee to Investigate the Montana State Prison at Deer Lodge, February 15, 1953," in *House Journal,* 33d Montana Legislative Assembly (Helena, Mont., 1953), 351–57; *Report and Recommendations of the Montana State Penal Institutions Survey Committee, March 15, 1957,* copy in folder 8, box 4, Record Series 196, Montana State Board of Examiners' Records, MHS (hereafter RS 196); *A Report by Mr. Kenyon J. Scudder, Director of Field Services, Osborne Assoc., Inc., September 15, 1957,* copy in folder 1, box 13, Record Series 319, Montana Legislative Council Records, MHS (hereafter RS 319); Board of Prison Commissioners, August 7, 1957, folder 6, box 61, RS 76, MHS; *Evaluation Report, Montana State Prison, December 16, 1957,* by R. L. Wham, copy in folders 1 and 5, box 61, RS 76, MHS; *Montana State Prison, A Report to the Thirty-Sixth Legislative Assembly by the Montana Legislative Council, December 1958;* "Transcript of Meeting of the House of Representatives' Special Investigating Committee of the Montana Pardons and Parole Board," February 4–6, 1959, folder 41, box 1, Record Series 11, 36th Montana Legislative Assembly Records, MHS (hereafter RS 11). For inmate accounts see "Nobody Cares," *Montana Opinion,* 1 (June 1957), 1–14.

6. Judith Johnson, "For Any Good at All: A Comparative Study of State Penitentiaries in Arizona, Nevada, New Mexico, and Utah from 1900 to 1980" (Ph.D. diss., University of New Mexico, 1987), 217.

7. James R. McDonald, *Historic Structures Report, Montana State Prison* (Deer Lodge, Mont., 1981); Jules Karlin, Joseph M. Dixon of Montana (Missoula, Mont., 1974), 2:87–93, 105–77.

8. "An Act Prohibiting the Sale or Exchange in the Open Market of Goods, Wares and Merchandise Produced, Manufactured or Minted by Convicts or Prisoners . . . ," in *Laws, Resolutions and Memorials of the State of Montana Passed by the Twenty-Third Legislative Assembly in Regular Session* (Helena, Mont., 1933), chap. 172.

9. "Nobody Cares," 2; folder 6, box 61, RS 76, MHS; *Report of Special Joint Committee of the Twenty-Second Legislative Assembly,* copy in folder 2, box 155, MC 35, MHS.

10. "Transcript of Hearing, Board of Prison Commissioners," September 25, 1957, folder 9, box 72, Record Series 197, Montana State Prison Records, MHS (hereafter RS 197); Minutes of Board of Prison Commissioners, 1952–1958, folder 17, box 72, RS 197, MHS; Minutes of State Board of Examiners, Minute Book 63, RS 196, MHS; *Evaluation Report, Montana State Prison,* R. L. Wham, copy in folders 1 and 5, box 61, RS 76, MHS; William T. Crowley, interview by author; Average Inmate Population from 1927–1957, folder 2, box 13, RS 319, MHS.

11. *Evaluation Report, Montana State Prison,* R. L. Wham; *Correction Benevolent Association Inc. of the City of New York Report,* copy in folder 11, box 114, MC 35, MHS; Report by Kenyon J. Scudder, 2; *Report of Eugene Tidball,* February 3, 1958, copy in

folder 2, box 13, RS 319, MHS; *Montana State Prison, A Report to the Thirty-Sixth Legislative Assembly,* 9.

12. "Nobody Cares," 13; *Report and Recommendations of the Montana State Penal Institutions Survey Committee,* copy in folder 8, box 4, RS 196, MHS.

13. Carl Frodsham, interview by author, August 29, 1988; William Rose, interview by author, November 6, 1988; "Nobody Cares," 4; "The True Facts Leading up to the Recent Uprising at the State Prison at Deer Lodge, Montana, July 30, 1957, as Seen by an Observer and Written by Him," September 1957, folder 2, box 13, RS 319, MHS.

14. Prisoner Demands for July 30, 1957, Montana State Prison, folder 8, box 4, RS 196, MHS.

15. *Deer Lodge (Mont.) Silver State Post,* August 2, 16, 1957; *Kalispell (Mont.) Daily Interlake,* February 2, 1958; Elaine Warner to Attorney General Forrest H. Anderson, October 29, 1957, folder 1, box 61, RS 76, MHS; Gladys Swindland to Attorney General Forrest H. Anderson, September 26, 1957, folder 1, box 61, RS 76, MHS; O. L. Timer to Attorney General Forrest H. Anderson, November 2, 1957, folder 1, box 61, RS 76, MHS.

16. Statement by Attorney General Forrest H. Anderson to Board of Examiners, November 3, 1958, folder 5, box 1, RS 196, MHS; Attorney General Forrest H. Anderson to Governor J. Hugo Aronson, November 1, 1957, January 23, 1958, folder 1, box 61, RS 76, MHS.

17. Powell's initial zeal is detailed in Floyd Powell, "Memoirs," 60–67, in collection of author; Floyd Powell to Board of Prison Commissioners, December 6, 1958, MC 35, MHS; Floyd Powell, *Preliminary Long Range Planning, Montana State Prison, September 23, 1958,* copy in folder 1, box 13, RS 319, MHS.

18. Powell, interview.

19. Rose, interview.

20. *Deer Lodge (Mont.) Silver State Post,* December 26, 1958, January 9, 16, February 13, 1959.

21. Descriptive List of the Prisoner, folder 5, box 30, RS 197, MHS; *Butte Montana Standard,* June 25, 1958; Walter Jones, "How We Broke the Montana Prison Riot," *Saturday Evening Post,* June 13, 1959; *Montana v. Alton.*

22. Descriptive List of the Prisoner, folder 3, box 38, RS 197, MHS; *Montana v. Alton,* 768.

23. Crowley, interview; *Revised Code of Montana* (1947), 10–611.

24. "Record of Prisoners," vol. 15, RS 197, MHS; statement by Bo Sherman, folder 7, box 61, RS 76, MHS.

25. Statements by John Simonsen and Floyd Powell, folders 9 and 7, box 61, RS 76, MHS; Powell, "Memoirs," 78–88.

26. Statements by Floyd Powell, folder 7, box 61, RS 76, MHS; Powell, interview.

27. Statement by Floyd Powell, folder 7, box 61, RS 76, MHS.

28. Ibid.; testimony of Floyd Powell, *Montana v. Alton;* Powell, interview.

29. Powell, "Memoirs," 85–86; statement by James Gaines, folder 7, box 61, RS 76, MHS.

30. Rose, interview; Felix, interview; Clyde Sollars, folders 7 and 9, box 61, RS 76, MHS.

31. Statements by Lawrence Backman, George Axtell, John Simonsen, and Robert Wyant, folders 7 and 9, box 61, RS 76, MHS.

32. Rose, interview; Frodsham, interview; statements by James Gaines, Charles Brown, and John Ahilbin, folder 7, box 61, RS 76, MHS.

33. *Great Falls (Mont.) Tribune,* April 19, 1959; statement by Walter Jones, folder 8, box 61, RS 76, MHS; Jones, "How We Broke the Montana Prison Riot," 80; Powell, "Memoirs," 90–93; Powell, interview.

34. Powell, interview.

35. "Transcript of Meeting of the House of Representatives' Special Investigating Committee of the Montana Pardons and Parole Board, February 4–6, 1959," folder 41, box 1, RS 11, MHS; Powell, "Memoirs," 58, 71–72; *Great Falls (Mont.) Tribune,* April 18, 20, 1959.

36. Powell, "Memoirs," 93–94; Powell, interview; statement by Carl Frodsham, folder 9, box 61, RS 76, MHS; Frodsham, interview; testimony of Edward Ellsworth, *Montana v. Alton,* 627.

37. Powell, "Memoirs," 97; Felix, interview; Powell, interview.

38. Frodsham, interview; testimony of Edward Ellsworth, *Montana v. Alton,* 633–35.

39. Mike Mansfield to Montana State Board of Prison Commissioners, telegram, October 30, 1959, folder 4, box 4, RS 196, MHS.

40. *Helena (Mont.) People's Voice,* November 4, 1960; Ellis L. Waldron and Paul B. Wilson, *Atlas of Montana Elections, 1889–1976* (Missoula, Mont., 1978), 221; *Kalispell (Mont.) Daily Interlake,* October 30, 1960; *Missoula (Mont.) Daily Missoulian,* November 1, 1960; *Deer Lodge (Mont.) Silver State Post,* October 28, 1960.

41. J. Hugo Aronson and L. O. Brockman, *The Galloping Swede* (Missoula, Mont., 1970), 122.

42. Crowley, interview.

43. For the impact on prison reform of riots in other penitentiaries during the 1950s, see Judy Johnson, "For Any Good at All," 217. For twentieth-century prison reform movements, see Larry E. Sullivan, *The Prison Reform Movement: Forlorn Hope* (Boston, 1990).

Janine Windy Boy, lead plaintiff in Windy Boy v. Big Horn County

JOHN WARNER, PHOTOGRAPHER, BILLINGS GAZETTE

Jim Crow, Indian Style

ORLAN J. SVINGEN

Montana history cannot be understood without a close examination of Native American history. Too often, perhaps, historians have tended to focus their attention on the nineteenth century while overlooking the important role of Native Americans in Montana's history over the past century.

Orlan J. Svingen, a professor of history at Washington State University in Pullman, examines with passion the struggles that Native Americans have faced in efforts to participate in Montana's political process, particularly at the local level. In reading this polemical essay, students of Montana history might consider some of the following questions: Do the conditions that Svingen described as existing in the 1980s still exist today? How relevant would the author's case study be to the large number of Native Americans who live in Montana's urban communities? How do the sources that the author employs influence his historical interpretation? And, finally, how does Montana's 1972 state constitution—which mandates equal representation in state elections and stresses the unique contributions of Native Americans to Montana's historical evolution—challenge some of the basic assumptions of Svingen's essay?

IN JUNE 1986 JUDGE EDWARD RAFEEDIE RULED THAT "OFFICIAL ACTS OF discrimination . . . have interfered with the rights of Indian citizens [of Big Horn County, Montana] to register and vote." Civil rights expert and American Civil Liberties Union attorney Laughlin McDonald later observed in the *San Francisco Examiner* that racism against Indian people in Montana was even worse than he had expected. "I thought I'd stepped into the last century," McDonald explained, "Whites were doing to Indians what people in the South stopped doing to blacks twenty years ago." Big Horn County Commissioner and area rancher Ed Miller "longs for the good old days" when Indians remained on the reservation. Angered by Rafeedie's ruling, Miller threatened to appeal the decision to the Supreme Court. "The Voting Rights Act is a bad thing," Miller complained. "I don't see no comparison with Negroes in the South." Before Janine Windy Boy and other plaintiffs filed suit against Big Horn County, "things were fine around here," Miller lamented. "Now they [Indians] want to vote," he exclaimed. "What next?"[1]

On June 13, 1986, United States District Judge Edward Rafeedie ordered that "at-large elections in Big Horn County violate Section 2 of the Voting Rights Act . . . [and] that a new system of election must be adopted." Judge Rafeedie's decision culminated a three-year process begun in Big Horn County by Crow and Northern Cheyenne voters who refused any longer to accept second-class voting rights.[2]

The case began its way into court in August 1983, when Jeff Renz and Laughlin McDonald, ACLU attorneys for the plaintiffs, submitted a "Motion for Preliminary Injunction" preventing the defendants, Big Horn County, from holding a general election on November 6, 1983. The motion called for a hearing before federal judge James Battin in Billings, Montana. The motion and subsequent suit against Big Horn County charged that the at-large system in county commissioner and school board elections in Big Horn County diluted the Indian vote so as to disenfranchise American Indian voters.

The plaintiffs in *Windy Boy v. Big Horn County* argued that the at-large scheme denied the plaintiffs' rights to participate in elections and to elect representatives of their choice to county and school board offices. In Big Horn County, where non-Indians constitute 52 percent of the population and American Indians form 46 percent, at-large elections violated the Fourteenth and Fifteenth Amendments and Section 2 of the 1965 Voting Rights Act. They asked the court to bar further at-large elections until new districts could be apportioned for the Board of Commissioners and School Districts 17H and I.[3]

The case turned on the 1982 amendment of Section 2 of the 1965 Voting Rights Act. Amended Section 2 declares unlawful any election procedure or voting law that "results" in discrimination because of race, color, or membership in a language minority.[4] In an earlier decision the Supreme Court had held that Section 2 violations required proof of purposeful discrimination.[5] Recognizing that intentional discrimination is difficult to prove, Congress amended Section 2 stating that no voting procedure can be imposed by a "State or political subdivision in a manner which results in a denial or abridgement of the right of any citizen . . . to vote."[6]

Centuries of conflict dominate Indian-white relations and created the setting wherein late nineteenth- and twentieth-century civil rights violations began. By the time Congress passed the Indian Citizenship Act in 1924, a sophisticated structure of anti-Indian policies was clearly already in place. Just as passage of the Fifteenth Amendment precipitated countless barriers for the freedmen, the Indian Citizenship Act also failed to elevate American Indian civil rights on an equal footing with non-Indians.

Until 1924 the various states ignored Native Americans and passed numerous unchallenged laws eliminating Indian people from the political process. In 1924, however, non-Indians harboring anti-Indian attitudes now confronted Indian people armed with the protection of the Fourteenth and Fifteenth Amendments.[7]

In addition to federal Indian policies of dispossession, wardship, and concentration, specific territorial and state laws affected Indian people. In 1871 Montana Territory denied voting rights to persons under "guardianship" and outlawed voting precincts at Indian agencies, trading posts in Indian Country, or "on any Indian reservation whatever."[8] In 1884 *Elk v. Wilkins* held that Indians were not made citizens under the Fourteenth Amendment because they were not persons born subject to United States jurisdiction.[9] As such Montana was not obliged to allow Indians to register to vote in state and county elections. The Montana Enabling Act of 1889 opened voting rights to all male citizens without regard to race or color with the exception of Indians not taxed.[10] At the turn of the century two more Montana laws restricted voting rights to taxpayers only and to resident freeholders listed on city or county tax rolls. Although certain American Indians could become citizens under the Dawes and Burke Acts of 1887 and 1906, Montana systemically denied voting rights to Indian people. The State denied residency to Indian citizens living on reservations and excluded those from voting who maintained relations with a tribe. In 1911 the State Legislative Assembly declared that anyone living on an Indian or military reservation who had not previously acquired residency in a Montana county before moving to a reservation would not be regarded as a Montana resident.[11]

By 1916 Robert Yellowtail, a leader in Crow politics, compared racism against American Indians with the policies used against black Americans. Singling out discriminatory practices in public accommodation and schools, Yellowtail charged that Hardin, Wyola, Lodge Grass, and Crow Agency had drafted their own "Jim Crow" laws in Montana. Just as emancipation and Reconstruction had failed to elevate freemen into the mainstream of America, the Indian Citizenship Act fell short of incorporating Indian people into the larger society. Instead a pattern of separation emerged, widened by state laws diluting the effect of citizenship.[12]

In 1924 Congress extended citizenship to all Indians born in the United States. Application of the Fourteenth Amendment meant, moreover, that they were citizens of the United States "and of the State wherein they resided."[13] Having given Indians all the basic political hardware, congressmen could say, just as was said after Reconstruction, that Indians had all the "tools" for political equality; now they were on their own. But historians recognize that black Americans did not achieve equality with southern whites after Reconstruction. What followed emancipation and the Reconstruction amendments was the white response to the abolition of slavery—segregation. In addition to facing a closed society, black Americans confronted an alien electoral system. Many lacked an understanding of political issues. Large numbers were illiterate or semi-illiterate; and, as Joel Williamson has explained, some even sought relief in withdrawal from associations with the white race."[14]

Was the 1924 Indian Citizenship Act an Indian emancipation proclamation? After that legislation formally ended the "wardship" status for Indian people, did non-Indians respond by creating a de facto form of segregation in its place? The reservation system certainly lent itself to separating Indian people from non-Indians. Instead of fearing the Africanization of southern society, did Big Horn County and other Indian counties in the north fear an "Indianization" of the political process? Did non-Indians redefine their relationships with Indian people by creating an Indian version of the Black Code or Mississippi Plan? Were Indian voting rights afforded the same consideration as non-Indians? Did Indian children receive an educational experience on a par with non-Indian children? Were Indian people summoned for jury duty? And what accounts for signs appearing in Hardin businesses declaring "No Indians or dogs allowed,"[15] or public outhouses with "Whites" and "Indians" scrawled over the separate doors?[16] Although Indian people had won legal and political rights a pattern of separation had become firmly entrenched in the minds of non-Indians—a mind-set fostered by years of acceptance of the ideology of white racial superiority.

Shortly after the passage of the Indian Citizenship Act, the *Hardin Tribune* focused on newly won Indian voting rights. News accounts and editorials drew front-page attention to Indian voting potential and pondered its impact on upcoming elections. Robert Yellowtail attracted a great deal of news coverage when he ran for state office in fall 1924. The *Tribune* estimated five thousand and then nine thousand Montana Indians would vote in the 1924 elections, and it closely monitored the number of Indian people who registered in Big Horn County. Clearly, Big Horn County's non-Indian population dreaded the possibility of an Indian being voted into county or state office.[17]

Three years later state machinery hobbled Indian voting potential when the Montana legislative assembly passed a law in 1927 dividing Montana counties into three-commissioner districts. The law established at-large elections for county commissioners who were elected to six-year terms on a two-year staggered basis. In order to be elected each candidate had to win a countywide election.[18] On the surface, and in counties with a homogeneous population, at-large elections appeared to make county-elected officials more responsive to the wider needs of a county. It can be argued, moreover, that at-large elections were progressive responses to the call for greater democracy in the United States. To ethnic minorities, however, Indian people included, at-large elections erased their chances for minority representation because it required a majority vote in a countywide election. As of October 1986 no American Indian had been elected to the Board of County Commissioners in Big Horn County.

Who is to say what the motives were for instituting the at-large election process? Did some support it to genuinely enhance the democratic process while others saw the plan as a subtle method for diluting the "political efficacy" of American Indians in counties with large Indian populations? Or was the at-large election scheme originally a racially neutral phenomenon that was subsequently corrupted for invidious purposes?

The legislative history of Senate Bill 17 establishing at-large elections reveals no overt anti-Indian bias, but its sponsorship by three senators, two of whom were from Indian counties, suggests more than coincidental ties. Senator Christian F. Gilboe from Valier, Montana, represented Pondera County, which included a portion of the Blackfeet Indian Reservation. Senator Seymour H. Porter, another sponsor to the bill, from Big Sandy, represented Choteau County, which embraced the Rocky Boy Indian Reservation. The motives behind Senate Bill 17 may remain debatable, but the results of the at-large election scheme promoted by Senators Gilboe and Porter are eminently clear to Indian people in Big Horn County.[19]

Ten years later more state actions crippled Indian voting in Montana. In 1937 the state mandated that all deputy voter registrars must be qualified taxpaying residents of their respective precincts. Because American Indians were exempt from certain local taxes, the state's action excluded Indian people from serving as voter registrars, thereby undermining Indian voter registration on the reservation. In the same year Montana canceled all voter registration and required the re-registration of all voters. Indian registration had risen steadily, but after the 1937 cancellation process Indian voting numbers remained depressed, not returning to the pre-1937 levels until the 1980s.[20]

The events of 1924 did not inaugurate an enlightened period of goodwill between Indian and non-Indian voters. Between 1924 and 1934 Indian candidates ran for state and county offices, but none won. The at-large election scheme and subsequent state actions had effectively disenfranchised American Indians in Big Horn County.

After 1937 it was clear that non-Indians had not welcomed Indian people into the political fold of state and county politics in Big Horn County. Despite the 1924 citizenship legislation, attitudes about Indians and about their political participation had changed very little. Comparing Indians elected to office before and after 1924, absolutely nothing had changed.

Indian voters did not even enjoy the personal satisfaction of being sought out on a coalition basis by non-Indian candidates. Through racially polarized voting, Indian candidates were systemically defeated by non-Indian voters who elected non-Indian candidates. To Indian people in Big Horn County voting rights conferred by citizenship were meaningless.

Comparing Indian voting rights problems with the black historical model offers dramatic parallels with Jim Crowism and segregation. Both groups confronted the separation of races and second-class treatment. The black experience is useful because it dramatizes the seriousness and the pervasiveness of Indian discrimination. Throughout southern society black Americans had interacted with whites, but on rural reservations Indian people confronted fewer non-Indians. The relative isolation of the reservation and its inhabitants allowed racial tensions and discrimination to go unnoticed within American society.

The black experience also draws needed attention to Indian voting issues because it invites society to conclude that Indian people have suffered indignities no longer tolerated by the courts or black Americans. Nonetheless the black model has a narrow application to the American Indian experience because blacks and American Indians represent different cultural patterns. Many distinct factors affect Indian voting patterns in ways peculiar to Indian people. For example, illiteracy and semi-illiteracy rates among Indian people make it difficult to participate in elections based on the English language. Dale Old Horn, department head of Crow Studies at Little Big Horn College, explains that Crow is the primary language of his people. Political and social events at Crow Agency, moreover, are conducted in Crow and English to guarantee the widest understanding. So when it comes to voting, rather than seek assistance from non-Indians in getting ballots interpreted, some Indian people simply avoid the polls.[21]

Old Horn and Mark Small, a Northern Cheyenne rancher in Big Horn and Rosebud counties, identified Bureau of Indian Affairs paternalism as another peculiar Indian problem. State laws that all but denied the constitutionality of the 1924 citizenship act left Indian people traditionally dependent on the federal government and its agent, the BIA. The BIA, Small noted, created a "false sense of security" among Indians and persuaded many to believe it would take care of their concerns. This action, in effect, promoted dependence, helplessness, and statewide voting inactivity among American Indians. By ignoring the question of Indian civil rights, the BIA retarded the development of full citizenship for Indian people, according to Old Horn and Small.[22] The question needs to be asked: If the government is guilty of fostering federal paternalism among Indian tribes and thereby promoting state voting inactivity is the federal government guilty of violating its trust responsibilities in the area of Indian civil rights?

Another cultural expression affecting the voting rights question is the matter of tribal sovereignty. Some Indian people avoid confronting state and county voting rights issues because involvement with the state might be seen as inviting state jurisdiction over tribal politics. Demanding equal rights in Montana county and state elections might touch off a new round of termination discussions. Non-Indians promote these fears, Small explained, by challenging Indian people with the question: "We don't vote in your tribal elections, so why are you trying to vote in ours?"[23]

Another far-reaching issue involving voting rights is the avoidance of bigotry and racism. Janine Windy Boy, the lead plaintiff in the Big Horn County suit and president of Little Big Horn College in Crow Agency, explains that it is a foregone conclusion: "You just don't go where you aren't wanted."[24] Being branded a "pagan, heathen, savage, or a blanket-assed Indian" is reason enough, Old Horn observed, for some Indian people to avoid the election process.[25] Gail Small, an attorney in Lame Deer and an enrolled member of the Northern Cheyenne, explains that Indian people have been "put down" by non-Indians so frequently that some actually internalize the criticism. "After you are told you are incompetent long enough," Small said, "some [Indian people] start believing it." These attitudes, which have historically opposed Indian political participation, have created a deep sense of alienation among Indian people towards state government.[26]

What, then, accounts for the political wasteland for Indian people in Big Horn County extending up to the 1980s? I have argued that the historical relationship between Indians and non-Indians in the pre- and post-1924 period created a setting hostile to Indian participation in federal, state, and county elections. The post-1924 years inherited the wardship concept and perpetuated a system, which, whether by design or not, excluded Indian people from participation. Despite being struck down by laws, the historical barriers and stereotypes against Indian voting rights among non-Indians promote the attitude that it is inappropriate for Indian people to vote in state and county elections.

Voting rights cases involving American Indians are not new. Ample case law beginning in the mid-1970s demonstrates that Indian people meeting age and residency requirements cannot be denied voting rights. Exemptions from certain taxes no longer limit their right to vote, and election districts must be apportioned under the "one person, one vote" principle. The 1975 amendment to the Voting Rights Act requires voter registration facilities in Indian communities, and it affords special language arrangements for language minorities.[27] Fred Ragsdale, Jr., an Indian law specialist at the University of New Mexico Law School, explains that Indian voting rights are not matters of Indian law. Ample case law precedents make this a simple citizenship question under federal law. Referring to previous voting rights cases, Ragsdale believes that "the easy ones are over with," and henceforth decisions will turn on the quality of factual questions, proof, and statistics.[28]

If case law supporting Indian voting rights is so clearly defined by the courts, what accounts for violations of the Voting Rights Act in Big Horn County? The clearest answer is the at-large election scheme, described by Jeff Renz, co-counsel for the plaintiffs, as a form of reverse-gerrymandering in Indian counties. One might expect that Indians who comprise 46.2 percent of Big Horn County population would have elected at least one Indian to county or state office sometime in the past sixty-two years. In response to this disturbing statistic and to the case in general, the defendants—non-Indian officials of Big Horn County—offer curious responses: (1) past problems cannot be blamed on us today, (2) nothing in Big Horn County hinders Indian voting rights, and (3) no official discrimination against Indians exists in Big Horn County.[29]

The cumulative impact of nineteenth- and twentieth-century federal Indian policies, state legislation, and racial tensions have created a cultural setting intolerant of American Indian voting rights. What else accounts for the defendants' responses to the plaintiff's charges? The skeptic, however, may argue away each separate example cited, dismissing them as the results of pre-1924 citizenship laws, pre-1965 voting procedures, or unenlightened racial attitudes. But when considered within a historical chronology—the way Indian people consider them—their impact is staggering.

Let us next turn, then, to some of the current and specific problems Crow and Northern Cheyenne people confront in Big Horn County. In terms of county employment, for example, out of 249 employees, the highest number of Indians employed by Big Horn County totaled six in 1985—or 2.4 percent of the county workforce.[30] Of the 100 members on twenty county citizen boards, only two Indians have ever been appointed.[31] Membership on these boards is significant because they promote programs and provide valuable experience and countywide name recognition for their members. Despite offers from tribal police to serve subpoenas against Indian jurors, only three Indians served on coroner's juries in Big Horn County between 1966 and 1983.[32]

During the 1970s and 1980s, Indian people in Big Horn County became more vote conscious, and a voter registration drive produced as many as two thousand Indian registrants. At first county officials cooperated, but as the numbers grew officials began rejecting registration cards continuing minor mistakes previously overlooked. This was followed by a refusal to provide Indian people with additional blank forms with the excuse that new ones were being printed—even though information on old and new forms were identical. Another excuse from the clerk and recorder's office was that the office had already given out large numbers of registration cards to Indians and that no more would be forthcoming until those already given out were returned.[33]

Then in 1982 four Indian and pro-Indian candidates entered the Democratic primary election and defeated their non-Indian opponents. The outcome shocked non-Indians in Big Horn County and prompted immediate anti-Indian sentiment. Little league baseball teams from Crow Agency, for example, encountered racial hostility just after the election, and non-Indian Democrats charged the organizers of the voter registration drive with fraud and accused them of stealing the election.[34] The chairman of the county Democratic Party admitted that "we sort of got caught with our pants down."[35] Disgruntled non-Indian Democrats left the party and formed the Bipartisan Campaign Committee (BCC), the sole purpose of which was to challenge Indian candidates from outside the Democratic Party. The BCC had no Indian membership, it supported no Indian or "pro-Indian" candidates, and opposed only Indian and "pro-Indian" candidates. Its campaign literature informed readers that the Democratic candidates elected in the 1982 primary were not "qualified" and that they did not "reflect the majority opinion of the voters in this County." The Democratic Indian and "pro-Indian" candidates won but only after narrowly surviving a BCC write-in campaign.[36]

In 1984 Gail Small, a Lame Deer attorney and a graduate of the University of Oregon Law School, ran for state representative in House District 100. Small later described her campaign as one characterized by race. For example, while campaigning east of Tongue River on Otter Creek, she knocked on the door of an area rancher and introduced herself as a candidate for state representative. She explained that she was particularly interested in natural resources and water issues—both vital to this coal-rich region. The rancher responded by pointing off in the distance where the ruins lay of a blockhouse fortress used in the so-called "Cheyenne Outbreak" of 1897. "It was just yesterday that we were fighting you off," he replied to Small, "and now you want me to vote for you?" His response typified Small's reception by non-Indian voters and persuaded her never again to run for office.[37]

In both 1982 and 1984 elections many Indian people who had registered to vote came to the polls only to learn that their names were not on the list of registered voters. Despite showing proof of registration, election judges refused to allow them to vote. Others who had voted in primary elections found their names removed from the general election registration list. Clo Small, a former precinct committee woman, explained that for years she and her husband, Mark Small, had voted in Busby, but for no apparent reason, in the 1982 school board election she was told that her voting precinct was in Kerby—approximately twenty miles south of Busby. Her husband's precinct remained Busby.

In a related incident, Mark and Clo Small drove from Busby to Hardin, Montana, to obtain voter registration cards. Small hoped to obtain a large number so that he could help register Northern Cheyenne Indian people living inside Big Horn County. Leaving his wife in the car outside the courthouse, Small went to the clerk and recorder's office and requested voter registration cards. The clerk handed him eleven and instructed him to sign for the numbered cards. Small explained to the clerk that he had driven considerable distance and that eleven registration cards were hardly worth the trip. The clerk responded: "We are out of them." Angry and suspicious, Small returned to the car and explained to his wife what had happened. Clo Small, a non-Indian, decided to try her luck. When she walked into the clerk and recorder's office moments later and asked for voter registration cards, the same clerk handed her a three-inch stack of cards.[38]

Windy Boy v. Big Horn County offers historians a wide range of ponderables. Despite full citizenship and recent favorable decisions, Indian people still confront official discrimination against their most fundamental civil rights—social and cultural aspects aside. Clearly the attitudes of their non-Indian counterparts have not kept pace with gains Indian people have made in the courts in recent years. Non-Indians rely on pat responses such as Indians should look to the federal government for help, or Indians don't pay taxes, so why should they vote in white elections? While these attitudes persist, counties with large Indian populations will continue to oppose, challenge, or hamstring the voting rights of Indian people.

By amending Section 2 of the Voting Rights Act to consider the "results" of voting procedures rather than requiring proof of intentional discrimination, Congress has decided that parties should not quibble over intentionality. If election practices "result" in discrimination, a violation of federal law has occurred. This sounds simple and straightforward, but it becomes complicated when applied to the reservation setting, when compared with historical Indian policies, and when considered within the context of Indian-white counties controlled by non-Indians.

It is time for historians to survey nineteenth- and twentieth-century American Indian issues with a broader perspective. Rather than applying a litmus paper test to isolated laws frozen in time and concluding that they were equally demanding to all citizens, let us ask ourselves what the cumulative, long-term impact of these policies and laws have been on a culturally distinct language minority.

In the aftermath of Judge Rafeedie's decision, civil rights prospects for Crow and Northern Cheyenne people are, at best, mixed. On the positive side, abandonment of at-large districting enabled Indian people of District 2 to elect John Doyle, Jr., as Big Horn County's first Indian county commissioner. Doyle's election reverses decades of discriminatory voting practices and illustrates the strength of Indian voting power freed from vote dilution.[39]

On the negative side, however, anti-Indian sentiment seems as strong and defiant as eve.: In the spirit of former County Commissioner Ed Miller who complained that the Voting Rights Act was "a bad thing," the defendants filed a motion of appeal in August 1986. Subsequent to that the *Hardin Herald* reported that an anti-Indian jurisdiction group known as Montanans Opposed to Discrimination (MOD) had become interested in the case. Composed primarily of white ranchers, MOD backed a local Secret Concerned Citizens Committee (SCCC), whose objective was to seek the basis for criminal prosecution of two of the plaintiffs in *Windy Boy*, Janine Windy Boy and James Ruegamer, and also Clarence Belue, a former "pro-Indian" county attorney in Big Horn County. Using a five thousand dollar donation from MOD, SCCC sought to uncover evidence of wrong-doing for prosecuting all three. These actions, however, came to center on Windy Boy and Belue. Charges against Belue resulted in his review before the Montana State Bar Association.

Also in the wake of the decision and prior to the November 1986 election, Janine Windy Boy received a telephone call from an agent of the Federal Bureau of Investigation in Billings, Montana, asking to meet with her. The FBI explained it was investigating complaints lodged against her with the United States attorney's office. The complaint alleged that Windy Boy, president of Little Big Horn Community College at Crow Agency, had misused her office by allowing Democratic candidates and tribal officials to use community college facilities rent free. The FBI concluded its inquiry after Windy Boy met with agents in Billings and delivered documentation disproving the allegations.[40]

Clearly a political setting in Big Horn County free of distrust, suspicion, and racism remains a long way off. Historical political inequality, oppression, and Indian-hating requires more than one election to usher in a period of racial harmony. One court decision such as *Windy Boy* means nothing more than non-Indians in Big Horn County can no longer "officially" ignore the county's Indian population. Rafeedie's decision may weaken racist foundations in the county, but the old patterns of distrust, suspicion, and harassment will continue until Indian people are no longer viewed and treated as political refugees in a white man's world.

NOTES

1. *San Francisco Examiner,* October 5, 1986; *New York Times,* July 5, 1986.

2. "Memorandum Opinion," *Windy Boy v. Big Horn County,* June 13, 1986, 647 F. Supp 1002 (D Mont 1986).

3. "Notice of and Motion for Preliminary Injunction," August 31, 1983, Circuit Court of the United States, Ninth Circuit, District of Montana, Billings Division.

4. Public Law 205, 97th Cong., 2d sess. (June 29, 1982); *U.S. Statutes at Large,* 96 (1982): 131.

5. *City of Mobil v. Bolden,* 446 U.S. 55 (1980) 60–74.

6. H.R. 227, 97th Cong., 1st sess.; S.R. 417, 97th Cong., 1st sess.

7. *Indian Citizenship Act, U.S. Statutes at Large,* 43 (1924): 253.

8. *Laws, Memorials, and Resolutions of the Territory of Montana Passed at the Seventh Session of the Legislative Assembly* (Deer Lodge, Mont., 1872), 460, 471.

9. Francis Paul Prucha, ed., *Documents of America Indian Policy* (Lincoln, Neb., 1975), 166–67.

10. *Montana Enabling Act of February 22, 1889, U.S. Statutes at Large,* 25 (1889): 676–84.

11. *Laws, Resolutions and Memorials of the State of Montana Passed at the Fifth Regular Session of the Legislative Assembly* (Helena, Mont., 1897), 226–28; *Laws, Resolutions and Memorials of the State of Montana Passed at the Eighth Regular Session of the Legislative Assembly* (Helena, Mont., 1903), 159; *Laws, Resolutions and Memorials of the State of Montana Passed at the Twelfth Regular Session of the Legislative Assembly* (Helena, Mont., 1911), 223.

12. Robert Yellowtail, "Why the Crow Reservation Should Not Be Opened," *Red Man Magazine,* April 1916, 265–69. See also "Exhibit 65" in "Plaintiffs' Second Request for Judicial Notice," n.d.

13. *U.S. Statutes at Large,* 43 (1924): 253.

14. Joel Williamson, *After Slavery: The Negro in South Carolina during Reconstruction, 1861–1877* (Chapel Hill, N.C., 1965), chap. 10 passim.

15. "Testimony of Dick Gregory," 1009.

16. The following citation contains two photographs illustrating segregated public outhouses for "Indians" and "Whites." Dan Whipple, "Failure of Democracy: Prejudice and the American Indian," *Northern Lights,* July-August 1986, 7.

17. *Hardin (Mont.) Tribune,* May 23, June 20, July 2, 11, 1924.

18. *Laws, Resolutions and Memorials of the State of Montana Passed by the Twentieth Legislative Assembly in Regular Session* (Helena, Mont., 1927), 226.

19. Ellis Waldron and Paul B. Wilson, *Atlas of Montana Elections* (Missoula, Mont., 1977), 113–14.

20. *Laws, Resolutions and Memorials of the State of Montana Passed by the Twenty-fifth Legislative Assembly in Regular Session* (Helena, Mont., 1937), 523, 527.

21. Dale Old Horn, interview, June 30, 1986, Crow Agency, Mont.

22. Ibid.; Mark Small, interview, July 2, 1986, Billings, Mont.; Clo Small, interview, July 2, 1986, Billings, Mont.

23. Ibid.; South Dakota Advisory Committee to the United States Commission on Civil Rights, "Barriers to Political Participation," in *Native American Participation in South Dakota's Political System* (n.p., 1981), 20.

24. Janine Windy Boy, interview, July 1, 1986, Crow Agency, Mont.

25. Old Horn, interview.

26. Gail Small, interview, July 7, 1986, Lame Deer, Mont.

27. See cases—*Goodluck v. Apache County* (1975), *Apache County v. U.S.* (1976), *Little Thunder v. South Dakota* (1975), *U.S. v. County of San Juan* (1980)—referred to in Stephen L. Pevar, *The Rights of Indians and Tribes* (New York, 1983), 212–16.

28. Fred Ragsdale, Jr., telephone interview, August 15, 1986.

29. Jeff Renz, interviews, June 23, 24, 25, 1986, Billings, Mont.

30. "Plaintiffs' Amended Proposed Findings of Fact and Conclusions of Law," 37.

31. "Testimony of Dick Gregory," 295; "Testimony of James Ruegamer," 383–85.

32. "Testimony of Robert Little Light," 586; "Testimony of Clarence Belue," 174–93.

33. "Testimony of Leo Hudetz," 611–12.

34. Ibid., 615; "Testimony of James Ruegamer," 340.

35. Ibid., 361.

36. "Attention! Voters!" Bipartisan Campaign Committee advertisement, n.d.; "Thank you Big Horn County," Bipartisan Campaign Committee advertisement, n.d.; "Testimony of Leo Hudetz," 616; "Testimony of James Ruegamer," 340–45, 361.

37. Gail Small, interview.

38. Mark Small, interview; Clo Small, interview.

39. Jacque Ruegamer to the author, November 20, 1986; *Hardin (Mont.) Herald,* November 5, 1986.

40. Janine Windy Boy, telephone interviews, January 7, February 18, 1987.

Rides at the Door (left) and Reuben Black Boy are seated beneath Black Boy's Thunder Medicine Pipe bundle (ninaimsskaahkoyinnimaan), which was purchased eventually by Bob Scriver and then sold to the Provincial Museum in Edmonton, Alberta.

Troubled Bundles, Troubled Blackfeet

The Travail of Cultural and Religious Renewal

WILLIAM E. FARR

In 1989 Browning, Montana, sculptor Bob Scriver sold his collection of Blackfeet
spiritual and cultural artifacts to the Provincial Museum of Alberta, Canada, for
1.1 million United States dollars. A celebrated western sculptor and inveterate
collector of Indian artifacts, Scriver was born in Browning in 1914 and in his later
life actively participated in Blackfeet spiritual practices. Until the sale, according to
William E. Farr, a professor of history at the University of Montana, Missoula, few
of Scriver's Blackfeet neighbors understood the extent of Scriver's collection or
"recognized the magnitude and degree of their communal loss" it represented.

In this award-winning essay Farr investigates the ways Blackfeet individuals and
families participated in a rich, complex cultural and religious heritage, the ways
ritual items were used in the tribe's "spiritual economy," and how, in this context,
Scriver's collection could have come to be. He also asks hard questions about
the legitimacy, implications, and legacy of the collection's sale. Exploring the
larger issues of Blackfeet spiritual and cultural identity, Farr examines how
identities are lost and reimagined while suggesting that cultural legacy can
become a platform for contemporary renewal, "a song of resurrection."

AFTER 1885 AND THE FINAL DEMISE OF THE BUFFALO ON THE GREAT PLAINS, THE
past no longer told the Blackfeet, and by extension, the Plains Indian,
what their future should be. Their earlier reliance on the shaggy beasts
they called ee-nee abruptly became a curse.[1] Theirs would be a new
dependency that included white men in greater numbers, railroads and
markets, government authority, ideas of private property, and a future

increasingly divorced from a buffalo past. Their generational task would change as well. The Blackfeet needed not only to survive but also to redefine themselves, creating in the process a usable future, and to do so with less and less. Forced onto steadily shrinking reservations, into immobility, starvation, and withering poverty, leaving the past was not easy. It never is. It could not, however, be avoided.

A new order was being imposed, one consisting of different realities and different spaces—a geography cut up now by fences and gates, latches and keys, permanent houses with rectangular rooms and square windows, with doors, tables, and wooden floors; a new time scale represented by ration days, Lord's days, days of work and days of rest, and mechanical time pieces that fragmented the natural cycle of sun and moon into abstract, precisely measured segments. Most of all there was a different authority, careless of the value of the old information and the old skills. Experience on the war trails and horse raiding, for example, were of dubious utility in the new order.

There was cultural resistance to the new order, of course, and much cultural baggage survived into the present; in these endeavors the Blackfeet had measurable success. Yet their negotiations with both past and future left them suspended—caught in between—and unable to move economically, politically, or communally. Their very immobility was resistance of a sort—inchoate and largely unspoken—yet stubborn, complicating the more general paralysis imposed by government regulations. Hunkered down, they waited. Active or passive, their resistance to the new order had limits. And the disconnections, separations, and frayings, the diminishments and dispossessions, all so alienating and so destructive of a remembered community life, in the end tended to overwhelm. Less and less could not mean more and more.

Today, on the threshold of the twenty-first century, when the cultural nadir, the irreducible minimum, has been mercifully left behind, and younger Blackfeet are seeking a religious and cultural renewal, comes what seems to many as the cruelest irony, a last major dispossession, the loss of cultural and spiritual artifacts regarded as essential for cultural continuation. Just when there is such yearning for the past to guide the future, when historical ownership and connectedness again seem possible, when the magic of supernatural grace is most needed, Bob Scriver, the celebrated western sculptor of Browning, Montana, has sold his immense and carefully protected collection of early Blackfeet spiritual and cultural artifacts to the Provincial Museum of Alberta, Canada, for $1.1 million.[2]

This delicately crafted sale embodies so many contemporary apprehensions: fear that with these last crucial losses the bridge to the thaumaturgical world of healing and safety will be denied forever; fear that these cultural losses, coming so hard on the heels of other losses, particularly of language, will finally unglue forever the wholeness of an earlier Blackfeet tradition, threatening in fact the very notion of Blackfeet identity; fear that the modern Blackfeet will be forever outnumbered by ghosts with more vitality than they have yet to which they have no access.

And the Scriver sale was so abrupt, so unexpected, so potentially traumatic because it represents in some important respects a collection of individual family tragedies, a sad social history, in which personal possessions, often spiritual items, that were formerly so cherished and defining, found no willing inheritors, and so were neglected, abandoned, lost, or sold. Stumbling repeatedly through individual crises, bewildered by both past and future, without the steadying hand of traditional cultural guides, Blackfeet families individually had to negotiate a cultural landscape that had become less and less recognizable or meaningful. Often a first step in any imaginative redefinition of self and family was a sloughing off, a kind of hollowing out to make way for something new—more powerful, more effective. Sometimes, caught up in their own contradictions, a number of Blackfeet turned their backs on their traditional religious and public rituals, lost faith and proceeded to live only in the new space of a solely secular world. Sometimes they converted to Christianity or merged with it and were told by missionaries, ministers, or priests of God's jealousy and admonished to "put off the old and put on the new"; sometimes they stubbornly developed their own pragmatic approach, running two religious tracks, parallel systems, traditional and Christian, side by side, keeping both alive, each in its own compartment. In the process, they often sold their former sacred items to whites as curios, trophies, or artwork—sometimes directly, sometimes via tribal brokers, or they entrusted them to local people like Bob Scriver whose stewardship they felt comfortable with, whose care they trusted.

There was grief and anger, of course. There were losses and losers, and too often both were hidden out of shame or explained away. Family members were not told what others in the family had done. Grandparents covered up the theft of family treasures, spiritual or cultural, by grandchildren. Wives did the same for husbands. When asked later where a sacred object was, the rueful answer too often was, "Well, we don't know, it just disappeared"; or, "It was the flood of 1964"; or, "It burned up in a fire." Often this was not the case. Items were not lost in floods or fire; they were pawned or sold. Each family thought its losses private and confined to itself—or yes, if pressed, maybe a few others were affected, too, but certainly not so many that the tribal heritage and community existence was jeopardized.

After Bob Scriver sold his collection of Blackfeet artifacts to the Canadian provincial museum in 1989, when the inventory catalogs of that collection became known, when the Alberta museum mounted its elaborate exhibition in 1991, trumpeting it as a "Repatriation of Canada's Heritage," the layers of self-deception were ripped away, publicly exposing for all to see the awful cultural crisis that had been privately nurtured and tolerated for too long.[3] The sale created a fire storm of criticism and controversy among Blackfeet on both sides of the United States–Canadian border. It forced people from all over the reservation, the reserves, and beyond to recognize the magnitude and degree of their communal loss.

Some Indian people accepted the losses as inevitable or even desirable. Others saw a chance, a so-called last chance, to recover from the shared responsibility of this latest cultural trauma, this final dispossession, by getting the collection back. They would take back what had been taken away and thereby recover the means to creating a recentered equilibrium, a spiritual or physic center, so that now, finally, in the 1990s the past could be again joined to the present. That is what was at stake, and that is why rarely have the issues, large and small, that plague Indian country today—from questions of cultural identity, of possession and ownership of the past, and of cultural reformation, to the sacredness of ritual and artifact and the problems of repatriation—been brought into clearer focus than with the circumstances and controversy surrounding Bob Scriver's collection, its international sale, and its final conveyance out of the United States.

Segments of the American Blackfeet, as was to be expected, were particularly critical of the Scriver sale. After all, the most comprehensive collection of Blackfeet materials in private hands had now left Browning, Montana, and it represented more of a loss to them than to their Canadian tribesmen. Not only was this a traumatic cultural blow, they argued, but in surreptitiously selling this irreplaceable treasury, Bob Scriver, their long-time friend and neighbor, had betrayed their personal trust and that of their parents and grandparents.

Aroused to high drama young traditionalists, many affiliated with Blackfeet Community College, and the tribe in general held strategy sessions, public meetings, and issued invitations to Scriver to come and discuss the sale. Ironically even religious leaders such as Mike Swims Under and George Kicking Woman, who had been so helpful to Scriver over the years in his own religious quests, were upset and would participate later in recovery efforts in Canada. Loyalties tugged, jerked, and sometimes divided. Stung and defensive, Bob Scriver's response, at least in part, was to publish *The Blackfeet: Artists of the Northern Plains*.[4] The book constitutes among other things a very personal reply, an effort to justify his actions, an explanation from his side as to why he had sought so diligently to preserve a record of the Blackfeet past—and then sell it.

The book hardly looks like an apology. It looks like an absolutely beautiful, if not marvelous, museum publication, a photographic catalog of the Scriver collection representing a family interest, if not passion, pursued over almost a century by two generations of Scrivers. Yet appearances can be deceiving. Although *The Blackfeet: Artists of the Northern Plains* with its photographs and text looks familiar enough, and while it certainly documents, salvages, and even consecrates the fragile memory of Blackfeet tribal life, this is more, much, much more, than a conventional museum catalog or inventory. Deeper, more turbulent waters are flowing here.

An internationally renowned western artist, Robert Scriver was born in Browning, Montana, in 1914, the second son of Thaddeus E. and Ellison MacFie Scriver. T. E. Scriver was an early licensed trader to the Blackfeet. Following the example of his former employer and friend, J. H. Sherburne, he established a mercantile operation called Willets and Scriver in 1907. Scriver and Sherburne were competitors at Browning, site of the relocated

Blackfeet agency, hub of the American Blackfeet Reservation, and important railroad stop on the Great Northern line.

Just how much of what eventually became the Scriver collection was acquired by Thaddeus Scriver remains unclear. Equally unclear is how much Thaddeus Scriver relied on C. P. Carberry, another and even earlier trader-collector, for obtaining Blackfeet artifacts. Certainly T. E. Scriver frequently collected artifacts from Indian and white as he pursued his business. And certainly he did so not only with the Southern Piegan but also with Canadian Blackfoot as they trailed south to visit, race horses, and celebrate. In time T. E. Scriver's oldest son, Harold, took over the Browning Mercantile and continued with Robert Scriver to share their father's interest in collecting.[5] Both the amassed collection and the book, then, reflect the sustained efforts of a white reservation trading family that was attracted to the passing historical and cultural richness of the Indian community that surrounded it.

But that is not all. Bob Scriver's role in compiling the collection was never simply that of a knowledgeable and well-connected local who appreciated the vitality of reservation craftwork with the eye of the artist he was to become. Although he obtained a master's degree in music from Vander Cook School of Music in Chicago and taught music in Browning and Malta, Montana, leaving the management of the Browning Mercantile to his brother, Harold, he was always an eager student of what he perceived as the vanishing West.[6]

Later, still in Browning but in his mature years, Bob Scriver edged closer and closer to active participation in the fragmented cultural and spiritual life of the Blackfeet as they struggled to persevere in the long period of cultural disarray following World War II and the 1950s. He was not, in other words, a mere collector of things Blackfeet. He was curious, sympathetic, and alive to the dream-like local past. Consequently, the book, the collection, and the Blackfeet benefit from Scriver's intimate commentary as it draws upon more than fifty years of devoted local experience. This is, therefore, at once a very personal remembering of the Blackfeet past and one deeply respectful of its cultural life as Scriver understands it.

Bob Scriver crossed a significant threshold in 1969. During an elaborate three-day public ceremony with hundreds of guests, and at great financial expense to Bob Scriver, Richard Little Dog transferred his Thunder Medicine Pipe and gave his father's name of Sik-Poke-Sah-Mah-Pee to the Browning artist and rancher. The following year Scriver had a heart attack. With mortality already weighing heavily there came the death of his father. Then, disgusted with "the cant of Christianity," Scriver reached even deeper into Blackfeet spiritualism encountering his own supernatural or medicine dream.[7] With the transfer of the Little Dog Medicine Pipe, followed by his own dream encounter and its subsequent interpretation and recognition by neighboring elders, Scriver became an accepted cultural holy man and pipeholder. Among the American Blackfeet this was and remains without precedent. Other white men around the turn of the century—George Bird Grinnell, Walter McClintock, and James Willard Schultz—were adopted into the tribe, married into the tribe, and participated in or recorded religious ceremonies. And there have been other white men who have possessed religious items capable of spiritual power and activity, but they did so without cultural acceptance and without a legitimate transfer.

Scriver is different; he actually became an active holy man, and he has long been accepted as such. Scriver remains a late convert, of course, and his ritual grasp is weak, but Blackfeet spiritual tradition has long provided for such situations through assistants and prompters.[8] So, turning to former keepers and assistants like George and Molly Kicking Woman, Mike Swims Under, and others, to officiate, to supply the necessary ritual, song, or sequence of words, Scriver has honored his spiritual obligations with some considerable fidelity.

The Blackfeet: Artists of the Northern Plains is by no means only a vindication for a contested international sale; it is informed as well by an elder's wisdom and an egoist's self-promotion. And there is a lot of Bob Scriver here. Nowhere is this more apparent than in the biographical accountings and photographic essays validating his vision dream and in the family photographs and portraits of the then seventy-six-year old man, still rugged, aggressive, and quintessentially western. In the final biographical piece there is an intriguing update on the state of the collection, now lodged in Edmonton, Alberta, as well as a personal analysis of why he felt compelled to sell the collection to the provincial museum in the first place. Smuggled into the piece as well is a ringing assertion

*In 1971 Bob Scriver had a dream instructing him to create a
Badger Lodge bundle, which included a painted tepee.
Pictured here with George Kicking Woman, Scriver attaches the badger
tail to the lodge cover in the ceremonial fulfillment of his dream.*

that the sale, besides being an act of cultural rescue and caring, was really a repatriation. The "collection went home," he says defiantly. "So be it."⁹

Again, this is not a simple book, and it is certainly not a simple story. Nor is the complexity limited to the Blackfeet, their art, and their material culture. It also reveals the crusty personality of Bob Scriver and the complex relationship of his own highly successful sculptures about the Blackfeet, the Blackfeet themselves, and their world. That world, as does his, rests in the interplay of mountains, basins, and plains, where the Milk River, Cut Bank Creek, Two Medicine Creek, Little Birch Creek, and Big Badger Creek cut watery lines of orientation through a shortgrass landscape. Along these waters the Blackfeet bands, after the buffalo disappeared and following confinement, had slowly settled down like a few beads on a long string. The very setting was complex. It was the 1880s and the reservation Blackfeet were being born.

Earlier, using such common natural elements as hide, feathers, shell, horn, teeth, wood, and bone, the Blackfeet, without pretension or undue self-consciousness, had developed a form of spiritual praise and spiritual pleading that did honor to a warrior society as it sought balance with the creative spirits. Later, with the introduction of white trade goods— beads, brass tacks, mirrors, trade cloth, bells, and steel—came an even grander florescence of craft activity. Still later, reservation confinement and settlement actually intensified artistic creation. There was more time and less travel. The result was not only accumulation and more art but also a greater cultural intertwining.¹⁰ How uniquely the Blackfeet blended the two, making the white commodities their own, stealing them away to become something unique to themselves. Witness the guns, belts, and knife sheaths decorated with patterns of brass tacks, the Hudson's Bay blanket capotes, the hats that became distinctive reservation statements, the beaded vests or thimble bespangled dresses, all transformed through a different cultural prism. The Blackfeet brought artistry to the simplest items in their daily lives. How beautiful these artifacts are and how achingly human. Whites have grown used to responding this way. Spreading tides of museum catalogs, traveling exhibits, and the acceptability and fashionableness of Indian art have conditioned us. From toney Santa Fe art auctions to Ralph Lauren's slick nostalgia, we are inundated with Native American design, and so, somehow, we are altogether too prepared for the beauty, the craft, and the powerful artistic expression represented in *The Blackfeet: Artists of the Northern Plains.* What we are not prepared for, at least what I was not, was the page after page of spiritual artifacts, or what Scriver rather neutrally labels "ritualistic materials," that constitute the last half of the volume.[11] That is what really sets this collection apart and gives it its dynamism, its force. Suddenly we are no longer dealing with just an exhibit catalog, an art book, where cultural remains of a life-style long absent appear or where horse trappings, household goods, spoons, lodge rests, and belts prevail. Readers, even casual observers, now sense an intrusion into a different dimension, a spiritual interstice, a supernatural world of vision and belief, of enormity and smallness, of cohesion and connection, of enchantment and value. It is at this point that the collection really comes alive.

Arriving at this inner sanctum, Scriver in his unstinting book lays open the holiest, most private, most powerful spiritual objects of the Blackfeet to the full, unblinking scrutiny of the camera and then the unsuspecting reader. The glossy pages brighten up the soft patina of countless handlings as, one after the other, the pages reveal the private secrets of personal bundles, society bundles, healing bundles, and the immense, complicated beaver bundles of the Southern Piegan that once belonged to Home Gun and to Chief White Calf. There are three natoas (Holy Turnip Headdress) bundles, so sacred and so central to the Medicine Lodge of the Sun Dance. They are detailed and compared. Thunder Medicine Pipes are there as well, outstretched, crackling with intensity, and still brilliant in their exotic, long-hidden color. Among them is Scriver's own Little Dog Thunder Medicine Pipe bundle. All are opened, unbundled—the significant ritual activity of the Blackfeet holy order—without ceremony or song, and spread out on their original wrappings, systematically photographed, cataloged, numbered, keyed, and described in minute clinical detail.[12]

There is in this a kind of violation, a sense that you are seeing something you should not—that you are out of place—something akin to a prying voyeur, who both wants to look and does not want to. You try to avert your eyes, to look away from these sacred, powerful items, but try as you might, you cannot. They are there. So, furtively, your eyes turn back to them and to their secrets, seeking the energy, the mystery you know is there or at least once was.

Bob Scriver introduces this most important segment with a welcome but highly abbreviated treatment of Blackfeet religious rituals and ceremonies. This complex ritual order emerged from a deep sense of inadeqacy and fear, of uncertainty and incomprehension. The Blackfeet world possessed an extra dimension, for amid the visible world, was an invisible one, another magnitude, a spiritual one that is more powerful, more meaningful, more lasting. It was a universe alive with spirits, good and bad, of every shape and description. The greatest of these Percy Bullchild has translated as "Mother Earth and Creator Sun," but there were many others including all the creatures of water, mountain, and plain, from dragonfly to grizzly bear. To face their uncertain and hostile world of endemic intertribal wars, constant danger, and incomprehensible sickness and misery, the Blackfeet cried out for pity, pleading for help and supernatural intervention. And while there were a variety of channels to access these periodic infusions of grace so necessary for a proper balance, the most certain way was a dream experience where transcendental power would be given.

In these dreams of power, working in fields of higher perception, an enchanted encounter would ensue in which a spirit animal or force, a bird or insect, transforming itself, would become momentarily a talking person, a spirit helper. Such an experience became known as the individual's dream (Nits-o'-kan). As animals became guardians or parents of the dreamer, often they revealed a mechanism, a ritual, through which their supernatural help could be channeled. These revelations included purification instructions through the use of smudges with sweetgrass, sage, sweet pine, and balsam fir, disclosures of specific songs, painting patterns, altar designs, hairstyles, and clothing as well as unique prayers—all precise directions for triggering and aiming the magical power. Percy Bullchild, for example, had Creator Sun saying:

> Now, my son, I'll give you some of my power that can cure anything if you use it the way I teach you. Listen good, this is a song that goes with my power. . . . The song, the feather of a red-winged woodpecker, and the red earth paint, along with a prayer to me, will help the sick or the injured get well, especially if you use the red earth paint to annoint [sic] their face. This is my power.[13]

Such commanding power was not without cost; the person empowered understood that such gifts came with definite sacrifices, obligations, and taboos, restrictive and onerous. This arrangement can be thought of as a kind of gift, trust, and contract all rolled into one—a reciprocal agreement allowing spirit helper and recipient to stay in touch—and while the transferred power had a public dimension, the discovery remained essentially private and individual.[14]

The final, most material part of the gift/contract was the actual bundle, which was made up according to the dream's instructions. Mountain Chief's father, for example, as a result of such a dream, "made up a big bunch of feathers, taking one from all the different birds, a drum, and a red flannel coat trimmed with otterskins and brass buttons." There were rattles, too, and some fourteen songs.[15] In the more elaborate and more public dreams belonging to the age-graded societies or to the tribe itself there would be many more elements—loon skins, a lynx tail, the neck of a swan, or perhaps paint bags, unusually shaped fossils that look like miniature buffalo, an eagle-bone whistle, or a lock of human hair. These were not the exotic offerings of the three biblical kings, not frankincense and myrrh, these were elements that the Blackfeet found around themselves that represented a dialogue between landscape and people. Neither symbol nor solely mnemonic device, these holy objects and songs contained in the bundle worked together to uncover for the celebrants the power and meaning of the original spiritual meeting and protocol.

Blended evocatively, these dreams, instructions, songs, and their physical reminders were of enormous sacramental significance to their possessors. They threw open the otherwise tightly closed gates, allowing a miraculous commanding power to suddenly transform or help an individual, his band, or even the tribe itself. Confirming and radiating mysterious power, capable of bringing destruction or blessing, sickness or health, glory or ignominy, poverty or wealth, these items were a throbbing powerhouse of spiritual aid, empowering and critical for those who were pitied. The new kinship made a difference. By wearing a particular and personal medicine bonnet in battle, for example, Mountain Chief (Big Brave) miraculously escaped many deadly bullets and arrows, coming away completely unscathed.[16]

Once secured, these revered, energizing powers exacted duties and obligations. They had to be guarded and protected, cared for daily like children; in fact, their owners are usually referred to as father and mother. Yet these same ritual wards were greatly feared. No one lived with them casually. Because they were housed in numerous skin or cloth wrappings, bundled up when they were not in actual use, and their privacy respected, they were referred to as bundles or, more properly because they frequently had therapeutic ability to heal and to deliver cosmic aid, medicine bundles.

Within the larger Blackfoot Confederacy, made up of the Northern Blackfoot (Siksika), the Northern Piegan, the Blood (Kainai) and the Southern Piegan (Pikuni or Blackfeet),[17] these sacred items and the transcendent power they embodied would often be transferred from the original dreamer or recipient to a second and third person, in fact to a whole sequence of individuals. In theory the one person substituted for the other, becoming the other, and with the transfer of the tangible pipe, bonnet, or bundle went all the original oral obligations, ceremonies, songs, and rituals and all the original spiritual power—a construct not unlike apostolic succession in Catholicism in which the original connection between the divine and the subsequent, thickening wall of generations was maintained for the spiritual benefit of all.[18]

Individuals other than the dreamers who needed specialized help for war, health, or love often sought the reputed or well-tested power of a specific charm, amulet, medicine shield, horse charm, lodge, or pipe. They did so by initiating a transfer of those blessed items to themselves via a mediator or negotiator. It was possible, of course, to seek your own supernatural contact, but as early anthropologist Clark Wissler and others have noted, the majority of the Blackfeet did not dream themselves, but rather relied upon "the few who do or on the large stock of medicine items readily available for transfer."[19] In earlier times that often meant the supplicant gave—literally sacrificed—horses, buffalo robes, blankets or blanket coats, and weapons for spiritual help. It was hard, however, to keep the formal distinction of offering and sacrifice intact, and in time people came to think of these actions as essentially payments or a purchase and spoke of buying or selling.

The cumulative effect was to introduce into the ideological structure of Blackfeet life a sacred economy, a feature where for generations, bundles, dream materials, and inspired rituals were bought and sold, circulating freely throughout the whole of the Blackfoot Confederacy.[20] Steadily moving from family to family, from band to band, traded and re-traded, marketed and invested, bundles and song cycles, sacred altar patterns and prayers were passed around and around. Seldom kept for very long, large inventories of items would pass through the hands of the spiritually restless or ambitious by the time they reached prominence in middle age. A single pipe-bundle may have had thirty or more owners.[21] Sometimes an individual would own a famed bonnet or pipe two or three times in his life. Those owning warshirts, tepees, bundles, and medicines of every sort enjoyed a high degree of prestige and esteem, in part because of their willingness to assume the religious burdens that benefited the tribe as a whole, in part because they were willing to sponsor expensive public ceremonies. Such possessions were also considered an investment, spiritual and economic; and, while the selling price could fluctuate depending upon changing levels of perceived effectiveness, a gradual inflation, often encouraged and enforced by the tribe, usually prevailed.[22]

There were two reasons for this wide dispersal of sacred objects. First, in a dangerous and uncertain world, it was important that the spiritual treasury of the Blackfeet be widely dispersed—that everyone, men and women alike, know the stories and rituals and understand the available mysterious powers so necessary for tribal survival. Concentration would have been reckless. Second, the Blackfeet were a semi-nomadic people, steadily moving their camps, seeking game or pasture for their ever-increasing horse herds. One person or even one band could not be expected to carry all the bundles and religious paraphernalia, however portable.[23] By the time they were forced onto a reservation here, and onto reserves in Alberta, this second, more practical consideration, counted for little. But the first continued to reflect the Blackfeet sense of themselves as constituting a religious community.

These spiritual investments were wonderfully impervious to most kinds of losses. If stolen in war, destroyed, worn out or somehow ruined, the bundles, lodges, and horse and war medicines could be easily reconstructed, duplicated, with no serious spiritual damage. In a sense they were indestructible because what really counted was the owner's ritual rights, and those he never lost.[24] An additional advantage was the way in which they could be converted quickly through sale and transfer back into horses, blankets, and guns, the other dimension of the sacred economy.

Nor were those of moderate means left out of this economy. Family and friends frequently pooled their marginal resources to allow one of their own who needed help to acquire the specific spiritual object that offered relief. And later, after the crisis had passed, after the article was resold, these same investors would share the probable profits. It amounted to spiritual insurance. In other cases an owner would loan out a powerful war item, say the Never-Sits-Down shield, and temporarily transfer its power in return for a share in any possible booty.[25]

With each formal transfer another individual, another family was introduced and habituated to another segment of the rich, developing religious heritage. The result historically was an ever wider circle of tribal involvement augmented periodically by newer individual dreams and rituals. Such spiritual and cultural cycling, then, was a powerful, integrating device, allowing everyone to participate in what amounted to a Blackfeet cosmology, intact and entire.

This spiritual system presupposed, however, that these holy packages would be kept moving throughout the Blackfoot Confederacy, that spiritual responsibilities would be shared mutually, and that they would not be accumulated or hoarded by an overzealous individual. Moreover, to keep spiritual losses to a minimum, the spiritual system would be essentially a closed economy, a participating circle in which only insiders, tribesmen and believers, would be included. In the twentieth century both presumptions would be challenged by whites and Indians alike, and Bob Scriver, working from within and without this notable ritual scheme, employed many of the arcane exchange traditions as he aggressively enlarged his growing collection. He knew many of the rules.[26]

The sale of the Scriver collection to the Provincial Museum of Alberta in 1989 came as a jolting surprise to many among the Southern Piegan on the Blackfeet reservation. Part of that surprise had to do with the sheer size of Scriver's collection. The sale was surprising also because, with the exception of a few select pieces, the collection had never been on display in Scriver's taxidermist's private museum, the Museum of Montana Wildlife, nor apparently had the community had any indication that he was willing to negotiate a sale for his rumored fabulous collection. Only after the sale was completed did the American Blackfeet, and particularly the young traditionalists, stir themselves to determined activity, and in so doing they bitterly contested three critical issues.

First, Scriver, using his spiritual authority as a "holy man," denied that the sacred bundles in the collection were "alive," and he further asserted that there was no possibility for them to be resurrected. Second, he argued that the collection was being "repatriated" or returned to Canada where purportedly most of the collection had come from. Finally, there were Browning Blackfeet who were incensed with the denial on the part of Scriver (and to some degree the provincial museum) that the tribe had any legitimate interest in the collection.[27]

Bob Scriver has contended in numerous newspaper interviews and in *The Blackfeet: Artists of the Northern Plains* that the powerful spiritual objects in his collection have become inoperative, have lost their sacred character, and are, however culturally interesting, little more than empty husks.[28] That is why he can sell them and why he can now open them to the casual glances of a wider world. The reason they are dead, he asserts, is that the rituals or ceremonials have been forgotten, and, as he puts it, "once a bundle is sold with no transfer taking place and no power root being transferred, it loses its power and becomes an inactive object, therefore merely an artifact."[29] Not only are they silent and dead, but the implication is that a museum is a proper place for them along with other dead elements of the past, whether spiritual or cultural. This proposition, that sacred bundles can be alive or dead is a necessary distinction for Scriver, almost a precondition for any ethical sale away from the Blackfeet. Dead bundles or spiritual objects have no life force and no ties, he would argue, cosmic or tribal.

There are, however, two bundles for which Scriver is personally and spiritually responsible, namely, the Richard Little Dog Medicine Pipe, acquired through legitimate transfer, and the Badger Lodge bundle, the result of Scriver's own 1972 medicine encounter.[30] These were not a part of the sale although both are depicted in Scriver's book. Both are "still active," he writes and, he promises, both "will be kept alive."[31] The Browning community has taken that vague promise to mean that at some future time Scriver will formally transfer both bundles to a worthy recipient, that is, to a member of the local Blackfeet community.

Having pronounced the numerous medicine bundles in the collection to be dead, Scriver tackles a more difficult problem, maintaining that no one can bring a bundle back to life. Traditional practice, he says, would preclude any "true believers breaking this taboo." Without proper transfer the bundle's "power is vacated."[32]

Sacrilege is the stealing of sacredness, and that is precisely what is at stake here. Having been declared dead and their power vacated, Scriver unilaterally removes from the bundles whatever grace or sanctification they may have had in the sacred economy. Now truly they become just another piece of property, just a thing to be possessed. Disposed of, they are subject to white notions of private property, of "mine and thine," where the individual has power over the object, not the other way around. When asked by *Great Falls Tribune* reporter Richard Ecke if Blackfeet tribal members could be angered by the sale, Scriver answered, "Why should they be? *They didn't own them*" (emphasis added).[33]

This has about it the character of a self-fulfilling prophecy, for when Bob Scriver declares the sacred bundles dead and inactive and then has them photographed and published for all the world to see in their nakedness, without the insulation of belief, ritual, or song, they, in fact, are robbed of their power. When we look at them directly, there on the page, so still and quiet, so undeniably ordinary, we become dead to their voices and they become dead to us.

Are the bundles in Scriver's collection dead? Is Scriver right? That depends upon when and with whom you are talking. Rarely has there been cultural unanimity regarding medicine bundles. Robert N. Wilson (1890s), Clark Wissler (1903), and Walter McClintock (1900), using numerous informants from all parts of the Blackfoot Confederacy, certainly found a normative pattern of use and agreement. So too did Edward S. Curtis (1921), Madge Hardin Walters (1930s), and Adolf Hungry Wolf (1970s). But each also learned of innovations, substitutions, subtractions, deviations, and differences. Many of these examples of flexibility date from the early reservation years after 1900 when new experiences and intertribal contact introduced a dynamic spirituality at once plastic and forceful. Blackfeet spiritual life then ran deep, was widespread and well. A detailed, seamless daily ritual life could be pursued without undue self-consciousness. Then a pious, yet informed attitude prevailed, accepting of shortcomings such as songs unlearned with the transfer of sacred objects, of words forgotten, or misplaced, of stumbled sequences. Practitioners could "get rough with the bundle" precisely because they were so comfortable and so secure within their integrating tradition.

In the late twentieth century such security and flexibility became attitudes of the past. Now there are so many opinions and so many contradictions. Have the sacred and ceremonial items and bundles depicted in the book lost their power? It is hard to say. Certainly they have not for Reg Crowshoe, a Piegan spiritual leader from Brocket, Alberta. In an interview with the *Great Falls Tribune* Crowshoe reported that the Blackfoot tribes in Canada "want to borrow the artifacts [from the museum] to resume ancient ceremonial rites and to teach their rituals to a new generation."[34] Rebirth in other words is possible, restoration desirable. Robert Rides At the Door said, "Those bundles are still alive, but need treatment." Floyd (Tiny Man) Heavy Runner, however, thought that "without a knowledge of the language, some bundles could not be brought back into use."[35]

Members of Crowshoe's band were decidedly fearful of the bundles' continued religious force. Trying to protect against the release of "malicious energy" when the collection of Scriver bundles arrived at the Edmonton museum, the Northern Piegans schooled white museum workers on how to handle the sacred objects. Crowshoe himself prayed to the Sun and Thunder to forgive museum staff members for any accident. In his mind they were clearly in jeopardy, "at risk," he said. "I asked for protection for the workers because they don't know what they are doing. If you don't show the proper respect," he revealed, "something might take retaliation."[36]

Another indication of the vitality of the bundles came following the arrival of some twenty-five Montana Blackfeet who had caravanned to the Alberta Provincial Museum seeking the return of at least the Southern Piegan parts of the Scriver Collection.[37] Negotiations ended in a confrontation, however, when George G. Kipp, a Thunder Medicine Pipe holder from Browning, tried to seize the Last Star bundle. When museum officials and armed museum guards forced Kipp to relinquish the bundle, Kipp retaliated by cursing the museum director, Dr. Philip Stepney. Stepney reported that Kipp told him, "I will outlive you," while making an up-and-down motion with his fist. Then, turning to a museum guard who blocked his way, he said, "I will live to see your ashes," and made the same gesture again. Immediately Blood Indian elders from Standoff, Alberta, some of whom had accompanied the Browning contingent in support of their claims, tried to protect the spiritually threatened director from the "strong words" by blessing Stepney, by painting his face and wrists a red-brown ocher.[38] Again, without belaboring the point, many members of the Blackfoot Confederacy, American and Canadian, do not agree with Scriver's assessment, feeling it is not only self-serving, but just plain wrong.

The second major issue, and one of the more interesting aspects of the contested sale of the Scriver collection, is the matter of repatriation. Literally repatriation means to return to a fatherland or native country, that is, a place of origin, and the term has long been used in the field of international art where, as a result of the spoils of war or theft, artistic works have been torn out of their original surroundings and carted off or sold to a foreign country. Recently the term has been applied to Native Americans when referring to the return or repatriation of Indian human remains that have been robbed from their graves, disinterred for scientific study, or removed as a result of great building projects such as railroads, dams, and highways and sent away to federal agencies or museums.

Since the late 1980s a number of individual states and the federal government have begun to seriously consider the need to enact state and federal legislation that would protect Indian graves and would include returning human remains as well as specific cultural material found in federal museums to appropriate tribes. Repatriation became a national concern in 1989, when in the 101st Congress Senators John McCain and Daniel Inouye as well as Representatives Morris Udall and Charles Bennett each introduced bills dealing with various aspects of Native American graves protection and repatriation.[39]

Repatriation is a key to the sale of the Scriver collection for two reasons. First, it was the pending United States legislation, Scriver says, that forced him to sell his beloved collection. Second, Canadians were also concerned with cultural repatriation, although of a different sort, and had developed a federal fund, the Canadian Cultural Property Export Review Board, to "buy back" lost cultural items. It was this fund that provided the $1.1 million to buy the Scriver collection. Scriver felt threatened. Reacting to what he termed the proposed "federal confiscatory legislation," he said, "I had no choice but to remove the Scriver Collection from such a possibility by repatriating it to a foreign country."[40]

In fact, by the time President George Bush signed into law the Native American Graves Protection and Repatriation Act (NAGPRA) in November 1990, the legislation only applied to federal agencies and federally funded museums.[41] Private collections were not threatened and in no way did the act imperil Scriver's continued ownership or a future sale. Nevertheless, federal legislation was most definitely a concern as well as a rationalization for the actual timing of the sale. If the sale was to be done prior to successful legislation it would have to be done quickly. "So on Oct. 13, 1989, the collection was transported via an official Canadian government vehicle under fully bonded export permits to the Provincial Museum of Alberta . . . where it is safe from threats of fire, theft, vandalism, and U.S. government confiscation."[42] Scriver might well have added that it is safe from his neighbors, American Blackfeet traditionalists, who might have retrieved their religious items from any major museum in the United States under NAGPRA. In his mind they seemingly constituted a danger to his collection that was every bit as threatening as fire or theft. By selling to the Canadians one year prior to NAGPRA, Scriver protected not only his purchase price but the integrity of the collection as well.

Did the collection go home, as Scriver puts it? Was this a taking back on the part of the Canadian tribes or a taking away as seen from the perspective of the American Blackfeet? These questions introduce another Latin word, provenance, meaning to come from or origin, a word always of importance to cultural historians, but particularly to lawyers. To answer whether the collection items went home, we have to know where they came from. The great majority of the Scriver collection originated with the American Blackfeet and that is not where it is now. It was not returned or repatriated to its origins, the Southern Piegan. It went for a considerable sum of money to a white provincial museum in Edmonton, Alberta, from a wealthy white sculptor in Browning, Montana. That is hardly repatriation.

In more specific terms, actual origin or ownership within the Blackfoot Confederacy is seldom represented in *The Blackfeet: Artists of the Northern Plains,* let alone provenance or an extensive record of past genealogy. In many cases origin and ownership simply may not have been available.

The famous Blood "Long-Time Pipe," for example, seemingly has no date of origin. It was always among the Blood people and was therefore beyond the collective memory. In other cases the medicine bundles were sold or pawned secretly outside the tribal circle by an owner who had lost his faith, transferred his allegiance to Christianity, or who was simply desperate for cash. In still others the bundles have been passed back and forth among families and bands, among Piegans, Bloods, and Northern Blackfoot. Bundles have been buried with their owners and not made up again, or they have been broken up and scattered. Duplicates and even triplicates existed. It is therefore not always easy or even possible to determine origin or ownership, past or present.[43] Still, beyond the confines of this book, remarkable pedigrees have been remembered by elders, bundle genealogies that go back through thirty owners. Anthropologists, museums, and historians have assembled lengthy histories of sacred items, and Scriver himself, with the Little Dog Thunder Medicine Pipe, relates a six-person record.[44]

That is not to say there is no documentation or attribution in the Scriver collection. There is, and its message is not what "Canadian repatriation" would lead you to believe, for a significant amount comes from the Southern Piegans, from Montana—Fish Wolf Robe's dance bustle, Bird Earring's paraphernalia, or the major medicine bundles such as White Calf's Beaver bundle, Home Gun's Beaver bundle, the Heavy Runner Natoas bundle, and the Last Star Thunder Medicine Pipe bundle, to name a few. These attributed ownerships certainly give credence to many American Blackfeet who hold that the Scriver sale was not a repatriation at all. Those holy articles were already at home.

The general lack of detailed documentation found in *The Blackfeet: Artists of the Northern Plains,* moreover, given the experience and enthusiasm of the Scriver family, and particularly Bob Scriver, strains the imagination. We should encounter dates of acquisition, person or persons from whom the items were obtained, circumstances of sale, previous owners—in other words, some history.[45] Was this simply an oversight, compounded by the involvement of two or three family members, or was it rather a cautious legal safeguard by a shrewd collector?

In a sense there is a religious and cultural war going on out there. Young traditionalists on both sides of the forty-ninth parallel, the "medicine line," are attempting to recover and reclaim an attenuated spiritual and cultural legacy amid language loss, shop-till-you-drop materialism, appalling alcoholism, unemployment, and apathy. Surprisingly, many older Indian people have misgivings or are openly hostile. They have long since abandoned traditional beliefs for Christianity as either Catholics or Pentacostals. Intolerant of restoration, these older Indians still hold enough latent Indian belief that their sentiment is basically: "Don't fool around with what you don't know"; or, "If you can't do it right, just right, don't do it!"

With the traditional religious hold so tenuous, the tendency is to concentrate upon a strict liturgical construction—one where ritualistic practice becomes certain and mechanical, and deviation for whatever reason, suspect. Opinions fly. Nor is there an accepted religious or cultural authority to adjudicate or instill a normative pattern. And there is a real reluctance in the current stage of the spiritual renaissance for leaders or elders to identify for others what is right or wrong. Without the wholeness of a public understanding there is rampant skepticism or apathy regarding belief or ritual. There are efforts, of course, to reclaim a centering set of practices. There are efforts at generating a spiritual revival, but too often they remain individual visions, not unlike the unleashing of so much personal individualism following Martin Luther when everyone became his or her own priest and biblical interpreter.

For those who know or care, the Scriver collection, its Canadian sale, and Scriver's haunting book will be forever linked to a cultural crisis. So many disturbing questions come back into view after slipping just over the edge of the contemporary historical horizon. When are these spiritual objects dead? Are they still culturally alive? Was repatriation justified? Long after you have closed the back cover of *The Blackfeet: Artists of the Northern Plains,* after you stare blankly at the glossy colored photograph of Bob Scriver's personal Badger Lodge flying its sacred badger flag— after all of that—you know something is irretrievably gone: the elders as people, yes, of course, but more important the thick swirls of life that circled the buffalo, the dusty, bustling, communal camp life, the freedom from dependence, and the connectedness that a shared religion provided.

And while two generations of Scrivers have salvaged something of the art and culture of that time, squirreling it away in a dark, hidden recess in

Browning, where the bundles were fed tobacco (why feed dead bundles?) as both a spiritual offering and insect repellant, the old way of life is still gone. Still gone even though now a museum in Edmonton, Alberta, will open the collection to the public, will lend the bundles on occasion to individual bands, Southern Piegans included, even though the collection will be visually preserved on the pages of this book now being pawed over by shoppers in malls throughout Montana and the West.

No matter. Something is still gone, lost somewhere between what has been and what is, lost in the alchemy of time. You cannot help but have the feeling that both Scriver's collection and his book constitute a muted dirge of remembrance. This is something of the story even if it is not the whole. But inheritances seldom come whole. They come instead in bits and pieces. And while legacies are always saddled with losses, if timely, legacies can also transform themselves into significant platforms for future renewals. In this sense the sale and the book may constitute not just an elegy, but a song of resurrection, for now a number of Blackfeet spiritualists are finding the courage to build upon the past, to make their own way up difficult narrow paths, up into the high places, up into their own "dream beds," rather than relying solely on the historical dreams of their elders. Will they go individually and alone or will they be able to pull others with them, forging a collective community of belief? No question is more crucial to the religious community. The traditional belief system of the elders allowed for both, permitting new dreams by solitary new dreamers and sanctifying communal efforts as well.

Inhabiting those dreams collectively, however, will require common practice and years of patient, shared veneration, as it once did. It will take years for the new dreamers to acquire the same degree of spiritual legitimacy as that which surrounds the historical bundles. But it can happen. A living inheritance, a culture still capable of scolding, has to be the goal. The young revivalists, of course, want it both ways and are both anachronistic and anxious for the future. They want a past that is usable and one that can be linked to the future. They want to reappropriate, reassemble, and reinhabit a spiritual world using rules never simple and never rigid, and they want it now.

The tribal codes or manuals to do this are still remarkably alive. The means are there. And when the spiritual authority that the new dreamers desire comes, it will be in the form of practices, cultural and religious, old and new. Practice made Blackfeet belief what it was, and practice will do so again. And if by chance some of the medicines sold to Canada or now resting in museums elsewhere can regain something of their sacred character by drawing upon a wider untapped or unknown reservoir of re-interested Blackfeet religious practitioners who know more than Scriver anticipates, or if historical research can turn up more of the original dreams, songs, sequences, and patterns—in other words the spiritual syntax—than The Blackfeet: Artists of the Northern Plains reveals, then the lost bundles are not only spiritually alive, they can be critical guides to the renewal underway.

Indeed, in this perspective, what matters most in constructing a sustaining and sustainable future may not be the spiritual artifacts themselves, however tangible and inspiring, but the ritual history—that is the stories, oral and written, of visions and quests, of songs and bundles, of their creation, use, and transfer, which together provide such a reassuring grasp of the rules, of the code to the whole Blackfeet spiritual economy. These tracks of transmission will provide further evidence of the regenerative flexibility of the entire process when it was fully alive, and by such means a culture not fully alive, but certainly not dead, can be revived.

Unintentional and inadvertent as it may be, Bob Scriver's collection, its sale, and the publication of The Blackfeet: Artists of the Northern Plains together have sparked a disturbing generational debate about questions having to do with religious vitality and cultural ownership and with self-identity, cultural persistence, and cultural creation. Reinvention seems to be the modern task. The Scriver case is an instructive reminder that contemporary people, Blackfeet or otherwise, must be open to a spiritual vision of their own time. Only then will they be able to knit themselves and their previous world back together.

NOTES

1. Donald G. Frantz and Norma Jean Russell, *Blackfoot Dictionary of Stems, Roots, and Affixes* (Toronto, Ontario, 1989), 337, give "einii." See also Walter McClintock, *The Old North Trail, or Life, Legends and Religion of the Blackfeet Indians* (London, 1910), 401, where "Ee-neu-ah" appears.

2. On newspaper coverage in Montana and Alberta, Canada, see *Edmonton (Alberta) Journal,* May 22, 1990; *Calgary (Alberta) Herald,* May 22, 1990; *Great Falls (Mont.) Tribune,* (seven articles) May 23–June 23, 1990; and *Browning (Mont.) Glacier Reporter,* June 28, 1990.

3. Philip H. R. Stepney and David J. Goa, eds., *The Scriver Blackfoot Collection: Repatriation of Canada's Heritage* (Edmonton, Alberta, 1990), vi.

4. Bob Scriver, *The Blackfeet: Artists of the Northern Plains, The Scriver Collection of Blackfeet Indian Artifacts and Related Objects, 1894–1990* (Kansas City, Mo., 1990).

5. Ibid., xv–xvi. See also Philip H. R. Stepney, "Bob Scriver: The Man and the Collection," in Stepney and Goa, eds., *Scriver Blackfoot Collection,* 6–9.

6. Stepney and Goa, eds., *Scriver Blackfoot Collection,* 6.

7. For Alice Kehoe's notes taken during the Badger Lodge ceremony in summer 1971, see Scriver, *Blackfeet,* 140.

8. Clark Wissler, *Ceremonial Bundles of the Blackfoot Indians,* vol. 7, pt. 2, *Anthropological Papers of the American Museum of Natural History* (New York, 1912), 140, 276.

9. Scriver, *Blackfeet,* 291.

10. See Richard Conn, "Blackfoot Clothing Style," in Stepney and Goa, eds., *Scriver Blackfoot Collection,* 96; and, especially, Royal B. Hassrick, "After the Buffalo Were Gone," in Ann T. Walton, John C. Ewers, and Royal B. Hassrick, *After the Buffalo Were Gone: The Louis Warren Hill, Sr., Collection of Indian Art* (St. Paul, Minn., 1985), 51.

11. Scriver, *Blackfeet,* 171–284.

12. Older Blackfeet noted the critical importance of song in uncovering the sacred bundles, "every knot and cord is *sung off* the bundle," carefully allowing the contents to come into view, in sequence and with respect, so as not to arouse the wrath of the spirit world. See Wissler, *Ceremonial Bundles,* 250, 262–63, 265.

13. On Creator Sun, see Percy Bullchild, *The Sun Came Down: The History of the World as My Blackfeet Elders Told It* (San Francisco, 1985), 77–81, 267. On dreams and transfer of sacred articles, see Wissler, *Ceremonial Bundles,* 71–106; Adolf Hungry Wolf, *The Blood People: A Division of the Blackfoot Confederacy* (New York, 1977), 79–89; George Bird Grinnell, *Blackfoot Lodge Tales: The Story of a Prairie People* (New York, 1920), 191–92, 250, 263; McClintock, Old North Trail, 352–53; and Howard L. Harrod, *Renewing the World, Plains Indian Religion and Morality* (Tucson, Ariz., 1987), 22–37.

14. Wissler, *Ceremonial Bundles,* 103.

15. Ibid., 274. Mountain Chief (Big Brave) was a cherished informant of Clark Wissler and D. C. Duvall. Many of his medicine items are enumerated and described in considerable detail in Wissler, *Ceremonial Bundles.*

16. Ibid., 116. See also Harrod, *Renewing the World,* 89–90.

17. Hugh A. Dempsey, "The Blackfoot Nation," in Stepney and Goa, eds., *Scriver Blackfoot Collection,* 331. See also Hana Samek, *The Blackfeet Confederacy, 1880–1920: A Comparative Study of Canadian and U.S. Indian Policy* (Albuquerque, N.M., 1987), 11–13; and John C. Ewers, *The Blackfeet: Raiders of the Northwestern Plains* (Norman, Okla., 1958), 5.

18. Wissler, *Ceremonial Bundles,* 103.

19. Ibid., 104.

20. Ibid., 119. The Never-Sits-Down Shield, for example, originated with the Northern Blackfoot, migrated to Curly Bear of the Southern Piegan, and was later transferred to Many Mules, a Blood Indian, sometime prior to 1912.

21. Ibid., 273–76. Mountain Chief remembered owning some twenty individual medicines from the time he was nineteen years old, sometimes selling them within five days before he had a chance to learn their songs or rituals. For corroboration, see Hungry Wolf, *Blood People,* 126–31.

22. Hungry Wolf, *Blood People,* 135.

23. A single medicine pipe, the Elk-Tongue Pipe owned by Many-Tailfeathers, for example, "was a load for a horse." The beaver bundles were even larger. James Willard Schultz (Apikuni), *Blackfeet and Buffalo: Memories of Life among the Indians* (Norman, Okla., 1962), 14, 277.

24. Ibid., 277.

25. Ibid., 100.

26. Ibid., 155–56, 277. On ritual stealings and forced sales, see also Hungry Wolf, *Blood People,* 137–39; and McClintock, *Old North Trail,* 252–53.

27. Major medicine pipe bundles, beaver bundles, and other bundles have had a public and communal character. See Grinnell, *Blackfoot Lodge Tales,* 277, 281; Hungry Wolf, *Blood People,* 30, 125–31; McClintock, *Old North Trail,* 90–92; and Wissler, *Ceremonial Bundles,* 147–52, 204–9.

28. Scriver, *Blackfeet,* vii, 171, 212, 266. For a discussion of how evocative symbols, i.e., Blackfeet bundles, can lose their connection with transcendent meaning and return to the ordinary world, or how religious symbols live in a culture and die there, see Harrod, *Renewing the World,* 67–68, 86–92.

29. Scriver, *Blackfeet,* 171, 212.

30. Ibid., 138.

31. Ibid., 212.

32. Ibid., 171.

33. *Great Falls (Mont.) Tribune,* May 25, 1990.

34. Ibid., May 23, 1990.

35. Ibid., June 21, 1990.

36. *Calgary (Alberta) Herald,* May 22, 1990.

37. The Blackfeet Tribal Business Council authorized and sanctioned these tribal members to negotiate for return of cultural and religious items in Resolution 268–90, on file with the Blackfeet Tribal Business Council, Browning, Montana.

38. *Great Falls (Mont.) Tribune,* June 21, 23, 1990. Cynthia Kipp, mother of G. G. Kipp, a medicine-pipe keeper, denies that her son put a curse on museum director Philip Stepney. See Cynthia Kipp's eyewitness account, *Browning (Mont.) Glacier Reporter,* June 28, 1990.

39. On Public Law 101–601, see Jack F. Trope and Walter Echo-Hawk, "The Native American Graves and Repatriation Act: Background and Legislative History," in "Symposium: The Native American Graves and Repatriation Act of 1990 and State Repatriation-Related Legislation," *Arizona State Law Journal,* 24 (Summer 1992), 54–71.

40. Scriver, *Blackfeet,* 291.

41. Public Law 601, 101st Cong., 2d sess. (November 16, 1990). See also *New York Times,* November 4, 1990; and *Christian Science Monitor,* January 3, 1991, as quoted in Andrew Gulliford, "Curation and Repatriation of Sacred and Tribal Objects," *Public Historian,* 14 (Summer 1992), 26.

42. Scriver, *Blackfeet,* 291.

43. Wissler, *Ceremonial Bundles,* 135–36.

44. Scriver, *Blackfeet,* 260. On bundle genealogies, see Hungry Wolf, *Blood People,* 143.

45. See, for example, an exquisite Crane's Head Whistle for which Scriver gives no information on when, where, or under what circumstances the item was purchased and added to the Scriver collection. Scriver simply says "the seller of this whistle undoubtedly got it through barter of some kind." Scriver, *Blackfeet,* 282.

*After nearly three decades of incredibly rich, environmentally devastating copper
mining, the Berkeley Pit, shown here in 1958, was closed in 1983 by ARCO,
parent corporation to the Anaconda Company.
Shortly after the mine closed the Pit began to fill with toxic water.*

MONTANA HISTORICAL SOCIETY PHOTOGRAPH ARCHIVES, HELENA

Pennies From Hell

In Montana, the Bill for America's Copper Comes Due

EDWIN DOBB

There are thirty billion gallons of toxic wastewater in the Berkeley Pit and another thirty-five billion gallons in Butte's thirty-five hundred miles of mine tunnels. At the head of the largest Superfund site in America, and of the entire Columbia River drainage, the country's biggest mine flood is currently contained. What does it represent?

A problem? It is, potentially, an environmental catastrophe. A challenge? There are over half a billion dollars of dissolved metals in the pit. A symbol? "Like Concord, Gettysburg, and Wounded Knee, Butte is one of the places America came from," according to writer and Butte native Edwin Dobb. Certainly the Pit represents the unintended consequences of over a century of hard-rock mining, of natural resource extractive industry, in Montana. But does it symbolize an end to the only economy besides agriculture the state has ever known, or a new beginning?

RUST-COLORED, REEKING OF SULFUR, AND SURROUNDED BY CORRODED EARTHEN terraces so sterile they appear incandescent in strong light, the six-hundred-acre lake that rests within the man-made cavity known as the Berkeley Pit looks nothing like a refuge, though it must have seemed so to the ill-starred flock of snow geese that stopped there while passing through southwestern Montana in November 1995. It is uncertain how many birds eventually rose from that bitter pool and flew over the rooftops of Butte, the town that borders and embraces this former copper mine, continuing their winter migration from Arctic Canada to California, but at least 342 of them did not. That is the number of carcasses Pit monitors found drifting in the lake and washed ashore in the weeks following the flock's stopover. Postmortems conducted under the auspices of the University of Wyoming later revealed what most people immediately suspected: that the geese had succumbed to the water, which is acidic enough to liquify a motorboat's steel propeller, and to its poisonous mineral contents, principally copper, cadmium, and arsenic. In each bird autopsied the oral cavity, trachea, and esophagus, as well as digestive organs like the gizzard and intestines, were lined with burns and festering sores. To even so much as sip from the Pit, it seems, is to risk being eaten alive from the inside out.

A few days after the first dead snow geese were discovered, Steve Blodgett, a friend and neighbor, suggested that we visit the Pit ourselves to see the unprecedented kill at close range, and looking for any opportunity, no matter how oblique, to get reacquainted with my hometown, I eagerly accepted. Besides possessing a talent for grasping situations whole and summing them up in striking ways, at the time Steve happened to be a reclamation specialist with the local city-county planning department, making him the ideal Virgil to lead this unusual descent. "The Pit is the receptacle of all our sins," he offered, half seriously, as we edged down the fearsome receptacle's back wall, foothold by handhold, one at a time. To be sure, there is a hellish air about the place. In 1982, after operating for twenty-seven years, the Berkeley Pit fell silent. It was then a yawning hole one mile wide, a mile and a half long, and more than a quarter-mile deep. About the same time mine officials shut down the pumps that had removed groundwater from the huge excavation and the labyrinth of older, inactive shafts and tunnels adjoining it, inaugurating what may turn out to be the most extensive mine flood in the world and precipitating a staggering environmental problem that will haunt Butte long into the future.

On the Hill—the term locals use for the fifteen-square-mile slope that forms the north end of Summit Valley where the mining district is located, as well as what remains of Butte's original neighborhoods and business district—sulfur permeates the bedrock. When exposed to air and water, long-buried sulfide minerals produce sulfuric acid, a highly caustic compound that, given enough time, can dissolve almost any metal with which it comes into contact. Once the pumps were silenced and water began migrating back into the mine works, the Pit in effect became a mammoth chemical transformer, a highly dynamic, self-perpetuating machine yielding ever-increasing amounts of hazardous soup. Today, at about 30 billion gallons and rising millions more daily, it is without equal in the United States, threatening the alluvial aquifer beneath Summit Valley as well as the Flat—the central and southern parts of the valley where at least half of the town's 33,500 residents now live—along with the upper reaches of the Clark Fork River Basin, from Silver Bow Creek, which flows along the base of the Hill, to Milltown Dam, more than a hundred miles downstream of Butte. Already considerably contaminated after 130 years of mine waste runoff and smelter fallout, the entire floodplain from the Hill to the dam has been included on the federal Superfund list and is the largest such complex in the country.

"That's Horseshoe Bend," Steve said, pointing toward a frayed ribbon of silver draped from the northeast corner of the Pit and down a steep, partially staircased slope to the lake several hundred feet below. Through binoculars the ribbon, about a mile away, resolved itself into a raging cataract, the confluence of long-buried creeks and seepages that surface at a nearby horseshoe-shaped waste dump and spill two to three million gallons of surface water into the Pit every twenty-four hours. Like the ribbon, the terraces that form the walls of the Pit are much larger than they at first appear. Built to accommodate the comings and goings of house-sized 170-ton haul trucks, each step is forty feet wide and at least that many feet high. The steps also are eerily lifeless, bleached of all color save the palest shades of yellow, gray, and red, and, more than any other part of the mining district, they are haunted by the odor of brimstone. My guide and I had by then clambered down a half-dozen of these infernal terraces, but we could descend no farther, the next cliff being too precipitous, too unstable. Still high above the water, we scanned the Pit for traces of the birds. "If we can clean up this," Steve said, "we can clean up anything." Two cloud-white bodies floated near the east shore, upside down in a reflected sky.

The snow geese were instantly canonized as martyrs to copper mining, yet another sacrifice demanded by the gods of extractive industry. The symbolism was easy to grasp and even easier to exploit, but it was nonetheless misleading because it suggested that innocence died in Summit Valley in the late 1990s though in fact it had expired many generations earlier, when the mining camp was settled and its fallen character firmly and permanently cast. Whatever the West has stood for in the popular imagination, Butte has always stood for something else, splendid exception and tragic aberration all at once. Encircled by tremendous and more or less unspoiled natural beauty, in a state that today some residents, no more troubled by modesty than they are by irony, call the last best place, it was from the start a place apart, far gone and then some, so much so that in 1943 the journalist Joseph Kinsey Howard considered it "the black heart of Montana," and this despite a stubborn affection for the people of Butte and their way of life. Summit Valley earned this distinction after the United States entered the age of electricity, the age of house lights, telephones, and plug-in appliances, motors and generators, to say nothing of the machinery and armaments required to prosecute two world wars, all of which were made with copper. Next to iron, the principal constituent of steel, no metal was more important to the economic growth of the country, and the enriched veins beneath Butte were thick with it. From the late 1800s through the first part of this century, the so-called Mining City yielded about 13.25 billion pounds of copper, which was a third of the total used in the United States during the period and a sixth of the world supply—all from a mining district covering only four square miles. Overall the Hill has produced about 20 billion pounds of copper.

Now that the United States is fast developing a so-called postindustrial economy, increasingly trading in such abstractions as service and information while leaving it to the rest of the world to extract, process, and render raw materials into tangible products, the history and fate of Butte may appear irrelevant to the world outside Summit Valley. But they are not, and precisely because we are so eager to shed our industrial past, well in advance of grasping the extent to which industry's shadow is still with us—indeed, is the very stuff of which we are made. The mines, mills, and factories upon which twentieth-century America was founded receive scant attention in the popular stories we tell about the period, and when they are acknowledged, it is usually from the perspective of heroic valorization or naive disdain. Especially regarding the use of such limited resources as timber, energy, and metals, public debate has become so fragmented that it obscures the connections that tie all Americans to places like the Berkley Pit, thereby precluding well-considered, honest responses to the uncomfortable questions they raise about desire and complicity, capitalism and modern culture.

Butte also deserves the close attention of anyone concerned about attempts by the Republicans in Congress, abetted by key western Democrats, to weaken the pioneering environmental legislation of the past three decades, in particular the 1980 Superfund law, which established mechanisms for reclaiming the country's most hazardous waste sites. Especially alarming have been proposed bills that would in effect absolve corporate polluters of responsibility for cleaning up most of the approximately 1,200 sites now on the federal Superfund list, including Summit Valley. And although it is true that since the 1994 midterm elections the most extreme members of the majority party have been forced into retreat, environmentalists and corporate executives alike believe that the original Superfund law is deeply flawed, certain of its liability provisions having provoked an enormous amount of expensive and time-consuming litigation and precious little reclamation since its passage. Reform, then, is likely sooner or later. Whether this effort will accurately reflect the many complexities and persistent ambivalence that inhere in our relationship with the natural world is probably too much to hope for.

Meanwhile the Hill, set apart from the West yet intimately tied to the country as a whole, provides an ideal vantage point from which to view this relationship, to look beneath the surface of an extractive industry that has been both immensely beneficial and immensely destructive. Like Concord, Gettysburg, and Wounded Knee, Butte is one of the places America came from. Indeed it can be looked upon as a national laboratory, in which the inner workings of a crucial kind of economic activity are laid bare and United States environmental policy is being put to one of its most severe tests. Butte is where we must return, in the manner of a pilgrimage, if we wish to grasp in full the implications of our appetite for metals—for everything from cars and computers to building materials and batteries—an appetite that remains unabated even as we grow more dependent on imports to satisfy it, conveniently displacing the costs and consequences overseas, beyond the reach of conscience.

"THE HILL'S HAD A HELLUVA RUN," Steve said, before we began our ascent
back to the rim of the Pit. Most mines are short-lived, encouraging a
short-run outlook best expressed today in the hundreds of ghost towns
that lie between the Great Plains and the Pacific Ocean. In Summit Valley,
by contrast, mining has persisted, one run after another, considerably
longer than almost anywhere else. Since 1864, when gold was discovered
along Silver Bow Creek, the Hill has been the native home of hard-rock
mining in the West, a place where hope favored nomadic gamblers, fickle
speculators, and, in the end, financiers and entrepreneurs who would
not dream of living here. Though the gold played out within a few years
and the silver era that followed lasted little longer, beneath the ramshackle
camp and beyond its boom-and-bust start-up lay something of far more
enduring value: the largest known deposit of copper ore in the world.
The vein that Marcus Daly, an uneducated but shrewd prospector, found
at the three-hundred-foot level of his Anaconda mine in 1882 ranged in
width from fifty to one hundred feet and in places was as much as 50
percent pure, and that was merely the high-grade tip of a subterranean
iceberg extending at least a mile below the surface and containing more
than 4 billion tons of copper ore. "The world does not know it yet," Daly
is reputed to have said, "but I have its richest mine." He was right, and
from his historic strike forward geology was destiny in the place that
came to be known as the "Richest Hill on Earth."

The social, economic, and political effects of the ensuing "red harvest,"
the term Dashiell Hammett used in his novel of the same name, which
was set in the area, are difficult to overstate. In a region dominated by
haystacks and cow towns, Butte soon became a boisterous island of urban
depravity and unbridled industrial capitalism, in its heyday home to
between 75,000 and 90,000 people, the only mining camp in the West to
undergo such a drastic transformation. There was nothing in New York
or San Francisco that could not also be found in this remote corner of the
mountainous West. The Hill produced staggering fortunes for a handful
of ambitious, frequently ruthless capitalists, Daly among them, who are
collectively remembered and sometimes reviled as the copper kings, and
a consortium of bankers and investors on the East Coast and in Europe,
including the Rockefellers of Standard Oil. It also undergirded a community
of great ethnic breadth, a decidedly unwestern cosmopolitanism that

drew from every wave of immigrant—Welsh, French, and German, Chinese, Lebanese, and Greek—to reach United States shores in the late nineteenth and early twentieth centuries; helped immensely to turn the labor movement into a progressive force in American life; and, finally, gave rise to one of the most powerful mining firms in the world—the Anaconda Copper Mining Company.

The Company. To the extent that Butte is an archetypal American town, it is so because many of the forces that shaped the country existed here in an undisguised and frequently extreme form, and in no instance was this more true than in the case of corporate power, whose center was the Hill but whose reach extended far beyond Summit Valley. As the late historian K. Ross Toole used to argue, Anaconda maintained a more comprehensive hold on Montana's natural resources, government, and people than any other corporation in any other state. One of the most egregious examples of the Company's willingness to wield this power with thoroughgoing ruthlessness occurred in 1903. Unable to obtain a favorable decision from local judges in a violent conflict over the ownership of certain ore veins, it shut down all of its operations on the Hill. Without warning, sixty-five hundred men were thrown out of work. The Company then announced on the front page of Montana's major newspapers that if the governor were to convene a special session of the state legislature, and if the legislature were to pass a "fair trial" bill that allowed the Company to transfer its legal dispute to a more favorable court, then it would reopen the mines. The governor complied, as did the legislature.

To understand why the governor buckled so easily it helps to know that Butte was not the only town that suffered because of the shutdown. At the time the Company employed three quarters of the wage earners in Montana, and all of them lost their jobs as well. It also helps to know that the Company owned all but one of the state's major dailies. Thus, when it came to coverage of issues pertaining to mining interests—the shutdown, for instance—it owned the allegiance of most mainstream journalists. By the end of the First World War the Company had taken control of the entire Hill. It owned the world's largest nonferrous smelter complex in the neighboring town of Anaconda, twenty-three miles west of Butte, as well as numerous lumber mills and millions of acres of timber. City water systems, stores, hotels, banks, railroads—the Company reached into every realm of Montana life, including the capital, where it bought elected officials with suitcases full of cash, liquor by the caseload, women, whatever kind of "hospitality" it might take to swing policy and legislation its way. During boom times union miners made good money in Butte, it is true, but that also served the Company's purposes by concealing the larger, alarming economic pattern: almost all of the wealth extracted from the Hill—some $25 billion worth—left the state.

The Company's influence notwithstanding, geology had always been the final arbiter of events in Butte, and eventually geology was the undoing of Anaconda's corporate empire. As early as the 1920s the labor-intensive underground mines in places like the Hill, where the copper sulfide might be located more than a mile below the surface, started to lose their competitive edge to the open-pit mines of corporations such as Kennecott and Phelps Dodge. In 1923 Anaconda purchased a controlling share of the Chile Copper Company, which by then owned the world's most extensive deposits. By that time Anaconda executives knew that if the Butte operations were to stay profitable they would soon have to switch to pit mining on the Hill; there remained only enough high-grade ore to last another thirty years or so. But it was a decision Company officials were reluctant to make, because it called for the destruction of most of the town's original neighborhoods, which had grown up around the mines and directly atop the ore body. Finally, in 1955, the Company announced to the people of the Mining City that it could continue to guarantee them a living wage only if it destroyed a large portion of the place where they lived. There was little anyone could do but get out of the way.

Thus began the final and nearly fatal stage of large-scale hard-rock mining in Butte. One by one the underground operations closed down. By 1975, when the sheave wheels ceased turning atop the last active headframe—the Mountain Consolidated, or Con, whose shaft was 5,291 feet deep—the workings included about 4 miles of vertical shafts, 2,500 miles of tunnels, and 7,000 miles of stopes, for a total of almost 10,000 miles of passageways. Meanwhile the Berkeley Pit had come into being— rather, nonbeing—an ever-expanding void on the east side of the Hill that had swallowed the Irish neighborhood known as Dublin Gulch; Meaderville, where the Italians lived; and most of Finntown; along with the sections where the Serbs, Croats, Montenegrins, and Albanians had settled; as well as the McQueen Addition, whose original residents were Austrian and Hungarian. In all about one third of the Hill was depopulated. Destroyed, too, were the Columbia Gardens, a seventy-acre refuge of shade trees, flower displays, and broad lawns that included a large dance pavilion, Ferris wheel, merry-go-round, and elaborate wooden roller coaster— Butte's versions of Central Park and Coney Island joined together and treasured no less.

The town might have continued to consume itself in this fashion, the entire Hill turned inside out, were it not for a historic election in Chile, by that time the location of the Company's most productive holdings. In the early 1970s, shortly after taking office, President Salvador Allende nationalized the country's foreign-owned mines, pushing Anaconda to the brink of bankruptcy. By 1977 Anaconda, to its relief, had found a buyer for its Montana holdings, the Atlantic Richfield Company, although the purchase turned out to be a regrettable decision for ARCO, an oil and gas enterprise that had grown fat during the energy crisis but possessed neither the savvy nor the stomach for hard-rock mining. Add to that a sudden drop in the price of copper to sixty-odd cents a pound, the lowest in years. By summer 1983 ARCO had lost all of the money it cared to lose and suspended operations in Butte. The western edge of the Berkeley Pit then lay only a few blocks from the heart of Butte's old business district, called Uptown, all of which had been slated for destruction. For the first time in more than a hundred years the Hill was completely idle.

Too busy digging ore to worry about appearances, Butte has never fit well in the gallery of wholesome outdoor portraits that makes up the postcard version of Montana. This is how Dashiell Hammett described the town, which in *Red Harvest* he called Poisonville: "An ugly city . . . set in an ugly notch between two ugly mountains that had been all dirtied up by mining. Spread over this was a grimy sky that looked as if it had come out of the smelters' stacks." The sky is clear now, and, given the mile-high altitude and quicksilver climate of Summit Valley, it frequently undergoes astonishing transformations. More days than not the sun makes an appearance, perhaps briefly but almost always dramatically, whereupon the expanses of air that lie between the Hill and the mountain ranges lining the horizon grow immense with light, creating an acute, nearly tangible impression of volume. Sometimes the weather is especially

Meaderville's Top Hat bar (circa 1950) offers foreground to the headframe of the Leonard Mine. Both bar and mine, and Meaderville itself, succumbed to the expanding Berkeley Pit.

Montana Historical Society Photograph Archives, Helena

restless, bringing to the valley swift-moving processions of broken clouds, and to such painterly effect that the spectacle overhead surpasses the landscape itself. The Hill, though, where the past is made of stone, not air and light, remains "all dirtied up."

While the Berkeley Pit may be Butte's most forbidding aspect, it is only one of many elements in an extensive and complex mining heritage. Because the acidic, lead-laden soil is in many places virtually devoid of organic matter, little vegetation grows in the mining district, nor does it fare so well on nearby mountainsides, which are largely barren after exposure to decades of smelter fallout. Scattered across the area are piles of waste rock, ranging from truckload heaps to a pyramid-size mound, the Alice Dump, that rests, truncated, at the top of the Hill, behind the old village of Walkerville. Interspersed among the dumps are glory holes— gouges in the surface that once inspired dreams of overnight riches but never yielded enough ore to justify sinking a shaft. Add to this somber portrait the Yankee Doodle Tailings Pond, built to accommodate the waste produced by the processing of ore from the Pit and hanging immediately behind and above it. Well over one thousand acres and at least six hundred feet deep, this pond is not really a pond but a slate-gray sea of toxic sand and evaporating water, one of the most extensive dumps in the world. And consider Silver Bow Creek, which by skirting the Hill divides it from the Flat, and might run yellow or bronze or burnt orange, anything but the color of clean water, anything but a current for the living. As a youngster I knew the stream only as Shit Creek. For many who live here the outstanding feature of the Hill is the mine yards, or rather the ruins they have become, especially the iconic headframes that straddle the flooded, crumbling shafts. Thirteen have survived—lamp-black skeletons, five to fourteen stories high, brooding over the mining district. Locals call them gallows, and with more reverence than irony.

What may most surprise the visitor to Butte, however, given the environmental damage already wrought, is the presence of a second mine, the East Continental Pit, located between the Berkeley Pit and the mountain range, part of the Continental Divide, that forms the eastern boundary of Summit Valley. Now the only active mine here, the East Pit was inaugurated in 1980, shut down along with everything else on the Hill three years later, and revived in late 1985, when ARCO, poised to scrap everything it owned, sold the former Anaconda properties to Dennis Washington, a prosperous entrepreneur from nearby Missoula. Washington also had been thinking of the Hill as a salvage operation, until Frank Gardner, a third-generation miner and old Anaconda hand, devised a plan to streamline the East Pit that came to rely on a much smaller force of nonunion laborers. At the same time Don Peoples, then chief executive of the Butte–Silver Bow local consolidated government, arranged a number of critical concessions: a three-year tax break, reduced power and freight costs, exclusion of the East Pit and the Yankee Doodle Tailings Pond from the Superfund site. The mine, it seemed, could once again turn a profit. A small one, to be sure, but a profit nonetheless. Not long after Washington purchased the East Pit, the copper market rebounded, and it has remained above, sometimes well above, the mine's break-even point ever since (although a sudden spike in electricity prices has caused a temporary closure), so much so that a few years ago Forbes magazine estimated Dennis Washington's net worth at more than $1 billion, the bulk of which he made in Butte, on an investment of only $18 million, the fire-sale price ARCO accepted for the Richest Hill on Earth.

Reopening the East Pit put a partial brake on Butte's decline by providing good incomes for the more than three hundred men who work in the mine and mill, or concentrator, which translated into additional jobs throughout the community, and by generating tax revenues, which have come to represent a sizable portion of the city-county budget. But even under the best of circumstances the minable reserves in the East Pit will be exhausted in about twenty-five years. As was true during Anaconda's reign, the threat of shutdown is omnipresent, never mentioned, of course, but always implied during disputes with regulatory agencies and a certainty if market conditions were to change drastically. The lasting physical legacy of Washington's Montana Resources will be the same as that of every mining company that has opened in Summit Valley—a landscape "all dirtied up." True, Washington's firm, working within a more demanding regulatory climate, has begun to cap and revegetate the waste rock and tailings it is producing and, as required, has posted a multi-million bond with the state, a kind of environmental insurance policy, though a woefully inadequate one. But the mine itself will not be reclaimed. Given present market conditions and the state of excavation technology, the restoration of large hard-rock pit mines is prohibitively expensive, so it is simply not done.

When the East Pit ceases operation it, too, will begin filling with groundwater, not as toxic as that in the Berkeley but, when the level rises high enough, in need of treatment all the same. What is more, the East Pit will rival the Berkeley as the most prominent man-made feature in Summit Valley. If, as Montana Resources officials hope, the excavation continues for another two to three decades, the East Pit's eventual footprint will be roughly half as large as that of the Berkeley. The two cavities are separated by the Continental Fault, however, the eastern, uplifted section forming the Continental Divide while the western section serves as the valley floor. Thus the bedrock and ore body on the Divide side of the fault are elevated by 3,500 feet, making the mine's terraced back walls considerably more visible. From some parts of the valley the two pits and the intervening waste seem to merge into a single colossal wound, fully occupying not only a third of the Hill but the lower half of the Continental Divide.

Wherever one may stand on the difficult issues raised by extractive industry, it is fair, I think, to say that the juxtaposition of these two holes, one the uppermost section of the largest Superfund site in the country, the other a productive mine whose fruits—molybdenum, used in lightweight alloy products such as surgical instruments, airplane parts, and mountain bikes, and, of course, copper—are today enjoyed by the residents of Missoula and Manhattan no less than by those of Butte, reflects the schizophrenic attitude the United States has adopted toward an appetite whose consequences it cannot yet face forthrightly. And like much else about Butte, what is transparent here tends to be obscured elsewhere, though it is no less problematic. Pit mining, mostly for gold, increased throughout the West during the 1980s—in Alaska, British Columbia, Nevada, even Montana. Fifteen years ago United States mines produced about one million ounces of gold. The total in 1995 approached 11 million, a tenfold increase. The rush was driven by consistently high prices for the metal and a new technology, cyanide heap-leaching, which enables mines to extract microscopic amounts of gold yet creates extraordinary volumes of hazardous waste rock. Almost three tons of ore is needed to produce enough gold for one small wedding band, and

76 percent of the gold refined throughout the world in 1995 was used to make exactly that—jewelry.

OUTSIDE THE UNITED STATES, in countries that lack conservation laws or the will to enforce them, pit mining has become the preferred method for extracting metals of all kinds, in some cases leading to ecological destruction on a scale that makes the scars on the Hill look like the backyard scratchings of children. A typical example is the Grasberg Mine, in Irian Jaya, Indonesia, the world's largest-known deposit of gold and the third-largest of copper. Creating acidic tailings at the rate of 120,000 tons per day, Grasberg has already produced more than 400 million tons, and plans call for the generation of another 2.8 billion. Members of the Amungme tribe have repeatedly protested the clogging and contamination of streams and flooding of rain forest and agricultural lands. In March 1996 several thousand villagers rioted, closing the mine for two days; Indonesian President Suharto responded by flying in soldiers. At about the same time an Australian human-rights group released a report contending that dozens of local people had been murdered or disappeared during the previous year. Such are the environmental and social legacies of large-scale pit mining in the international arena.

It has been a long time since anyone died in clashes with mining interests in Summit Valley or since troops were called in to quell riots, but it did happen, and often. Ever a place of extremes, Butte was the site of one of the longest, costliest, and most influential battles in the modern American struggle between labor and industry. On June 8, 1917, an underground city labored day and night to provide copper for the American war machine, newly arrived in Europe. It was 11:45 P.M. At the adjoining Granite Mountain and Speculator Mines, on the east end of the camp, a shift boss had descended to the twenty-four-hundred-foot level of the main shaft to help untangle an electric cable that a rope crew had been trying to lower since late afternoon. Somehow his hand-held carbide light touched a frayed and oily edge of insulation, setting it on fire. With the cable serving as a fuse and the updraft acting like a chimney, flames shot toward the surface igniting the surrounding timber and transforming the shaft into a three-thousand-foot inferno. That night 168 men perished in what turned out to be the worst hard-rock mining disaster in United States history.

Just three years earlier a fight for control of the American Federation of Labor–backed Butte Local No. 1 had broken out between factions representing the militant Industrial Workers of the World, or Wobblies, and the moderate Western Federation of Miners. It led to ten days of mayhem during which Miners' Union Hall was obliterated by dynamite, Butte's socialist mayor was forced out of office, and Montana's governor declared martial law, sending the National Guard to enforce order in Summit Valley. Following the Granite Mountain–Spectulator fire, a new union, the Metal Mine Workers, immediately demanded additional safety measures. Rebuked by the Company the union called a strike, and in response more than 15,000 men walked off the job. Once again martial law was invoked.

For the next sixteen months Butte was ruled by National Guard troops, surreptitious Pinkerton detectives (of which Dashiell Hammett was one), and gun-wielding Anaconda thugs. In the early hours of August 1, 1917, Frank Little, an especially persuasive IWW leader, was abducted from his boarding house by a half-dozen vigilantes, dragged behind a car until his kneecaps were scraped off, and hanged from a railroad trestle. Seven thousand mourners joined the funeral procession. A year later, alarmed by the increasing unrest and impatient with civil liberties, particularly when exercised by immigrant Sinn Feiners and Finnish anarchists who had no desire to fight the Germans and said so, the state legislature outlawed the IWW and passed the Montana Sedition Act, which banned, among other things, "disloyal, profane or scurrilous" antigovernment writing and speech and legalized summary deportations. The act was considered such a sterling display of patriotic fervor that the United States Congress adopted similar terms in the federal version it passed later that year. The strikes and provocations continued. On April 21, 1920, Company guards opened fire with machine guns on IWW pickets gathered along Anaconda Road at the gates of the Neversweat mine yard. One man was killed, thirteen others wounded, all shot in the back. This time the governor called in a contingent of regular United States Army troops to patrol the streets while work resumed on the Hill.

The inscription on Frank Little's headstone reads, "Slain by capitalist interests for organizing and inspiring his fellow men." Although some may quarrel with that verdict, there is no question that the IWW organizer's death was an unusually violent instance of the sacrifice that ordinary men, under much less dramatic circumstances, made every day in Butte. Those killed in the Granite Mountain fire were among an estimated twenty-five hundred whose lives ended underground before the Berkeley Pit came into existence. At least ten times that number were seriously injured and disabled, and it is anyone's guess how many tens of thousands died prematurely from miner's lung and other occupational illnesses, to say nothing of the nonmining residents whose lives were shortened due to exposure to heavily polluted air. To honor the fire victims, along with all those the victims have come to represent, a memorial plaza, the Granite Mountain Overlook, was constructed recently, some eighty years after it was authorized. A prow-shaped battlement of concrete and brick, the Overlook is perched on the eastern-most edge of the Hill, between the Berkeley Pit and the Yankee Doodle Tailings Pond, offering a bird's-eye view of the Granite Mountain headframe.

The day before I descended into the Pit in search of dead snow geese, I visited the Overlook with Mark Reavis, Butte–Silver Bow historic preservation officer. "Here we can tell the whole story of hard-rock mining in America," he said, explaining that the Overlook anchors a project known as the Anaconda-Butte Heritage Corridor. The idea, reduced to essentials, is this: In 1962 Uptown Butte, a six-square-mile district that contains several thousand structures, was designated a National Historic Landmark, the second largest in the country. In the 1980s, when the mining district, which overlaps Uptown, was added to the Superfund list, that designation took on unexpected significance; cleanup projects would now have to meet federal guidelines regarding the maintenance of historic resources. Instead of simply reducing the risks of waste dumps by converting them with a layer of clean soil, say, and planting hardy grasses, or erecting chain-link fences around mine yards, the dumps and mine yards would have to be made safe without doing damage to their historic character.

Not all of the tailings and headframes fall within this dual jurisdiction, to be sure, but the fact that some of them do has led Reavis and other community activists to an unusual vision of environmental reclamation, one that assumes that clean does not always mean pretty and that pretty is not always attractive. Butte's heart may indeed be black, but it would forfeit whatever heart it has if its mining past were erased or replaced by a sanitized theme park full of virtual mines and signs that explain away everything forbidding and controversial about the place. This is why a good part of the waste that lies before the Granite Mountain Overlook will not be reclaimed or, viewed from a historic angle, already has been reclaimed, but as a memorial to what actually happened here. This is also why, if the Anaconda-Butte corridor is acknowledged as a Labor History Landmark—the National Park Service recently added the area to its short list—the Wobblies and the gun-toting goons and Anaconda's century-long stranglehold on the community will be included in the official story of the Hill. And it is why some mine yards will be preserved as they are or restored to their original condition whereas others will be made to serve the social needs of the community; the Belmont hoist house, for example, which once contained the motors that raised and lowered cages into the Belmont mine shaft, has been converted into a senior citizen center—a building inside a building, the present abiding within the past.

"History has to be usable," Reavis said, nodding toward the ravaged landscape below the Overlook. "If it's not usable, it's forgotten."

Mining the past is a theme that is almost as pervasive in Butte as the threat of shutdown, and no holdover from the past is more in need of attention than the water. The condition of streams, lakes, and aquifers is the surest gauge of the meaning we actually assign—through what we consume, not what we say we value—to the metals we extract from the ground, yet it is the only element in the mining equation that we literally cannot live without.

Water in the upper Clark Fork River basin, as in most hard-rock mining districts throughout the world, is everywhere contaminated, and where there is no water—in dumps, along stream banks, around the downwind of smelter sites—there is rainfall, and thus contaminated runoff, which eventually winds its way to existing streams. Follow the flow: the bedrock aquifer, lying some distance below the alluvial aquifer in Summit Valley, contains highly elevated levels of arsenic, lead, and cadmium, as well as copper. Although no one has ever devised a successful method for controlling the migration of groundwater through bedrock, much less for purifying it, the cost of merely trying to do so here has been estimated at between $7 billion and $10 billion. For all practical purposes, then, the aquifer is polluted beyond repair. (Having ruined all local sources, Butte early on built a pumping and diversion system that carries drinking water from a neighboring, undisturbed valley.) As for surface water, until 1911, when the Company constructed the first of three sedimentation ponds near Warm Springs, about twenty-five miles downstream of Butte, mine-waste runoff that flowed into Silver Bow Creek migrated as far as Milltown Dam, just outside Missoula. During spring floods, contaminated water often breached the pond dams anyway. It still does. Consequently, all of Silver Bow Creek is an industrial sewer. The Clark Fork River from Warm Springs to Missoula is laced with arsenic, manganese, lead, copper, and zinc, and some six million cubic yards of toxic-metal sediment rest at the bottom of Milltown Reservoir, behind the dam.

The site that best exemplifies the sorry condition of water in Summit Valley is, of course, the Berkeley Pit, and it always will, though only partly because of the size of its lake and the nature of its contaminants. More alarming still are the dynamics of the flooding; whereas the surface water entering from above, about half of the total flow, can be controlled, the groundwater seeping in from below cannot, not ever. Imagine that. Water will always migrate into the Pit from the highly fractured and heavily mined bedrock that surrounds it; the infernal receptacle will always be cursed. Not for a hundred years, not for a thousand, but always.

That is why Butte residents like Fritz Daily, school counselor, former state representative, and all-around gadfly, have been losing sleep since the pumps were shut down fourteen years ago. "Mine flooding could easily destroy the town, environmentally, economically, and socially," he says, envisioning a catastrophe that would force the evacuation of a good part of the valley. Daily also insists on the following: "The most valuable resource in the Pit is the water, once you figure out how to make it water again." What he means is that the copper, iron, and other minerals are present in such large quantities that they would be worth something, perhaps a great deal, if extracted in a cost-effective manner—if, in other words, the mine water could be mined. Of all the schemes to repair the environmental damage in Summit Valley this is by far the most intriguing, because it holds out the hope that the biggest liability on the Hill might be transmuted directly into an asset, which is as close to realizing the alchemical dream of medieval times as we are likely to get in the late twentieth century. Whether this modern version of the dream can be fulfilled is far from certain, however.

In 1993 a Canadian firm, Metanetix, declared amid much fanfare that it was going to extract dissolved metals from the water in the Kelley shaft, west of the Pit. "What is perceived by everybody as a major disaster, we see as being a major opportunity," one official boasted to the local newspaper, while pledging to invest $10 million in the facility and predicting that it would employ as many as two hundred workers and turn an annual profit of $50 million or more. But after only two years precious little metal had been shipped, all operations had been curtailed, and the firm was busy salvaging part of the Kelley headframe. More hopeful are the waste treatment studies being conducted at several new businesses in the area. One of these is MSE, Inc. (formerly Mountain States Energy), a research-and-development firm headed by Don Peoples, now out of local government and determined to help the Mining City overcome its dependence on mining through the encouragement of businesses that specialize in innovative technologies. Butte would seem to be an ideal location for such an effort, not least because it is home to Montana Tech of the University of Montana, long one of the outstanding engineering institutions in the world. But the most fitting new arena into which the local economy might expand is environmental cleanup. What better place to design and test reclamation strategies than the Hill? Under contract with the Department of Energy, MSE has to date studied six mineral-recovery technologies and is scheduled to examine several more, though no approach has yet proved capable of separating dissolved metals from mine water at anywhere near a profitable cost.

That the concept of mining water remains less a promise than a prayer could not have been more evident than in fall 1994, when the Environmental Protection Agency and the Montana Department of Health and Environmental Sciences (now the Montana Department of Environmental Quality) decided on a remedy for the flooding of the Berkeley Pit and other mines on the Hill. The plan calls for the diversion of surface water at Horseshoe Bend, between the back wall of the Pit and the rock impoundment that holds in place the Yankee Doodle Tailings Pond. Assuming that the water within the Pit will not pose a threat to human health or the environment until it rises to an elevation of 5,410 feet, 50 feet below where the EPA projects pit water could seep back into the groundwater system, the agency also ordered a pumping and treatment

plant to be constructed by 2021, four years before the critical level likely
will be reached. Although the plan allows for the use of the new treatment
technologies, should one ever prove feasible, the only method now
available is considerably less than ideal: adding lime to the water to
neutralize its acid content and draw out metals en masse, a process that,
ironically enough, would yield vast amounts of hazardous sludge—
between five hundred and a thousand tons daily—that would have no
economic value. Where the sludge would be disposed of, whether back
into the Pit or in a nearby repository, would be determined later as well.

Having waited since 1987, the year the Pit was added to the federal
Superfund list, everyone in Butte was pleased that the EPA and the state
had finally selected a remedy, though many interpreted the plan as a
decision not so much to take action as to postpone it. Granted, starting
in spring 1996 and continuing until the recent East Pit closure, ARCO
and Montana Resources diverted water at Horseshoe Bend, reducing
pit flooding by about half. On April 15, 1996, Jack Lynch, the current
chief executive of Butte–Silver Bow, pushed the button at a new pumping
station, diverting the stream through an eighteen-inch pipe to the Yankee
Doodle Tailings Pond, where lime was added to remove metal and reduce
acidity. The water was then discharged into the pool at the far end of
the impoundment, to be recycled through the concentrator, and this
will resume when the East Pit reopens. But the more incorrigible and
unpredictable source of flooding, groundwater—about 2.5 million
gallons of it every day—will not be addressed for some thirty years.
This is what disturbs Daily, who is skeptical of all forecasts of water
behavior on the Hill, especially those based on the assumption that the
hydrologic system in Summit Valley is now returning to a natural, pre-
mining state. "Everything underground has been altered," he says.
"Nature's gone." In this view, allowing the flooding to continue—
specifically, allowing the Pit water, already more than seven hundred
feet deep, to rise another three hundred feet, as the EPA proposes—is
to gamble with the future of Butte in a way that is more reckless, because
potentially more ruinous, than Anaconda ever did. If the water were to
enter the alluvium, the layer of soil that rests on top of the bedrock, it
would tend to flow downward, off the Hill, toward the eastern side of
the Flat, percolating into basements; making former wetlands, now

neighborhoods, wet again; and eventually contaminating the alluvial aquifer and the headwaters of the Clark Fork River.

Risks aside, this much is certain: once the new pumps start they can never be stopped. The Pit was excavated in one generation, the dozens of underground mines that surround it in five or so, but the aftereffects of these engineering feats will be felt for hundreds of generations, until the next ice age or geologic cataclysm, a perpetual problem in need of a perpetual solution. Just as there is no foreseeable end to the flow of toxic water, there is, under the EPA remedy, no end to the production of toxic sludge. Holding this image in mind may be unsettling for the residents of Summit Valley, but it is now the backdrop to everything that happens here.

NOVELIST LAWRENCE DURRELL has written that a place expresses itself through the people who inhabit it, that a community bears the impress of the land no less than the land is molded by human ambition. If he is right, and in matters of geography Durrell's instincts seem to me unerring, then as hopeless as the Hill may sometimes appear, there could scarcely exist a better place to find something more valuable than hope—clarity. For it is those whose lives begin and end in Summit Valley, whose dead are buried here, who are in the best position to take the full measure of hard-rock mining—by virtue of their long intimacy with it. When the bills come due for the metals the country consumes, the costs are not apportioned according to use; they are paid in Butte, and in places like Butte. The Hill is unique among such sites in that it is both a mining district and a town, a culture as well as a highly disturbed geological formation, and the two are inseparable. Larger hard-rock pit mines certainly exist—Bingham Canyon, southwest of Salt Lake City, is more than twice as large as the Berkeley—but none so dangerous rests so near the heart of an urban center.

For Butte the chief implication of this precarious arrangement concerns how it might continue to live, and even flourish, in the presence of a legacy that could well betray it, and at any time, for as long as anyone dares imagine. As Jack Lynch put it, "Butte not only has to live with the problem, it has to live with the solution." For those who live outside Summit Valley but nonetheless benefit from mining, the implications of Butte's twofold nature revolve around recognition—acknowledging that the Hill also is America's unsettling backdrop, that we all live on the edge of the Pit, and taking that often overlooked connection into account when rendering judgment of extractive industry. Almost everyone who resides here today either worked underground or knows someone who did. There is nothing quite like the hair-raising tension that gathers in a bar full of Anaconda retirees, say, when someone, outside or not, glibly states that the Hill is an abomination. You cannot long survive as an environmentalist in Summit Valley without arriving with or coming to a respect for mining and miners, and not only because you may be ostracized but, more important, because it is so transparently hypocritical not to admit your indebtedness.

For those who do acknowledge that indebtedness and wish to grasp what it means in human terms, the challenge lies not in finding people willing to talk freely about themselves, but in sorting through the welter of tales, fables, and downright lies they tell about the place. As the longtime residents of Butte continue to mine history, reworking their memories for images of themselves and of the town, the past remains ever on the verge of revealing itself, but without fully and finally doing so. This is surely true in the Silver Dollar Saloon, a haven of easy conviviality and large tolerance located at the corner of Main and Mercury, in the center of Butte's Uptown. Since its construction in 1894, the Dollar Building, a handsome two-story structure of red brick and forest-green wood trim, has housed several bars, a carriage works, Chinese retailers, and a brothel, called the Lucky Seven after its address, 7 West Mercury, the notorious street that still served as Butte's red-light district when I attended high school, only a few blocks away. One evening in the mid-1990s, I found myself on a stool there, accompanied by half-glimpsed ghosts, listening to Dan Price, an eighty-year-old resident, who paused now and again, squinting, as if to assay each stone he had quarried from his life before revealing it to the stranger beside him. "I was a ten-day man," he said. "I'm not proud of it, but that's how it was." Whenever he was broke, Dan rustled a job on the Hill, usually underground, worked through his first payday, then went on a binge until the money ran out again.

Dan's self-induced boom-and-bust habits afforded him the opportunity to see the insides of more mines than most of his contemporaries; it also gave him the leisure to explore the insides of a great many books. Well acquainted with western literature and always poised to recite favorite passages, Dan evidently read, and continues to read, as enthusiastically as he once drank. He reserves a particular fondness for deceased writers who shared his double passion for the alcoholic and verbal arts and who, more often than not, were undone by it, Thomas Wolfe most fondly and most tragically. "You know that Baudelaire poem, Ed, the one about drinking?" Sorry to say, I had not committed the lines of "Get Drunk" to memory, but somehow I unloosed a couple of hobbled fragments, enough to satisfy his wish to revisit the poem's meaning, if not its music: "It is Time to get drunk! If you are not to be martyred slaves of Time, be perpetually drunk! With wine, with poetry or with virtue, as you please."

Baudelaire's advice seemed at home in the Silver Dollar Saloon, or, for that matter, Butte as a whole. Though now considerably less rambunctious than it once was, the town has little use for the neo-puritanism that periodically sweeps across the country. And that tolerance is of a piece with the wide-open atmosphere of its early years, when Butte not only exercised exceptional leniency in the matter of debauchery and dissipation among its citizens, but openly promoted them, as Carry Nation learned when she brought her temperance crusade here in 1910. Nation chose Mae Malloy's Irish World, located at 9 East Mercury, as her starting point, a decision whose consequences everyone in the Mining City but she could foresee, and surely would see, such entertainment being too rich to miss. A rowdy crowd fell in step behind Nation as she marched along Mercury to the brothel, where Madame Malloy, informed that the patron saint of sobriety was headed her way, stood waiting atop the front stairway. Ignoring Malloy's repeated warnings to take her crusade elsewhere, Nation marched up the stairs and straight into the arms of a conviction more formidable than her own. Malloy ripped the habit from Nation's head, then slammed her against a wall and pummeled her with her fists. The crowd cheered. When Nation collapsed to the floor the crowd roared again. Just as Malloy was about to demonstrate an exceedingly painful two-step called the Mercury Street Stomp the police arrived to escort the battered missionary back to her hotel. For Nation, who was sixty-three years old at the time, the incident marked the end of a colorful if bizarre career; she never again set foot in a saloon. For the people outside the Irish World, the thrashing of the country's leading advocate of abstinence was a delicious moment, one that warranted immediate celebration— with drinks all around.

The encounter between Nation and Malloy is nothing to be proud of, certainly, but that is how it was on the Hill—flamboyant, promiscuous, grotesque, cruel, the heart revolving ever blacker and turn by turn ever harder in a crucible of copper ore. Mining made it so, historians agree, by forging a bond between corporate self-interest and a certain kind of human temperament. The ready availability of bars, gambling halls, and whorehouses served Anaconda's needs by distracting miners from the manifold hazards of their labor and keeping them in financial circumstances so precarious that quitting to find safer, more reliable work was unthinkable. By the same token, underground hard-rock mining tended to attract men with a high tolerance for uncertainty, physical danger, and uprootedness, men for whom the prospect of disabling injury or crushing indigence was always present, instilling in them an almost religious devotion to the pleasures of the moment. While timbering a shaft or dynamiting a drift somewhere in the oppressive recesses of the Con, Lexington, or Neversweat, the miner may have been time's martyred slave, but not after the shift whistle blew.

Although active and retired miners now make up only 2 percent of the population, people here still answer the call of the mine whistle, and it is good that they do, because, like the revelry at an old-fashioned Irish wake, such spirited celebration helps dispel the demons that would otherwise plunder the soul—dispel them only temporarily, of course, but long enough to enable one to face the morning, when the clock starts again. It is no accident that in a town where for decades the communal dream was striking it rich but more often than not the reality was impoverishment, there still exists, on the one hand, a degree of levity and romanticism out of proportion to circumstances, and, on the other, a fatalism so thorough it induces passivity, even paralysis, especially in the face of large, outside entities capable of delivering the ultimate threat: shutdown. When the tendencies are combined, however, something very different emerges—a talent for fully recognizing a troublesome situation while at the same time not being bested by it—and it is the most promising example of mining's impress on the Mining City.

"My biggest fear is that cleanup will go undone," Jack Lynch told me. We were sitting in his spacious office in the county courthouse, discussing the many different bills that have been proposed in Congress since the Superfund law came up for reauthorization years ago. Lynch, a slender, energetic man in his late forties, knew full well that Butte was once again facing the threat of shutdown—in this instance, the sudden end of reclamation projects—but he and his staff were determined to stay in the high-stakes poker game that goes by the name Superfund, as long as the game lasted.

Included at the table with Lynch were ARCO, Montana Resources, the EPA, the Montana Department of Environmental Quality, businessmen and business developers, and an array of city-county officials. One game, several conflicting interests and competing loyalties. For ARCO and Montana Resources the risks are largely economic; after years of disputing overlapping liabilities, they wish most to settle their differences and meet federal requirements while losing as little money as possible. The regulatory agencies have a different aim: to fulfill the mandate of the Superfund law—to protect "human health and the environment." And the entrepreneurs, for their part, are betting on any form of reclamation they believe will make Summit Valley more attractive to new business and, in some instances, on specific remedies that might benefit them directly, through construction contracts, for example, or the leasing of waste-treatment technologies. The gamble was by far the most perilous for Lynch and his staff, because they represented the people who have the most to lose—the residents of Butte, those alive today and those who will be living here long after ARCO and the EPA have departed.

Further complicating the Superfund game are the plays made away from the table. To take the most significant example, ARCO, which in its local publications and advertisements calls itself a "partner in responsible reclamation," tried mightily to dissolve that very partnership by lobbying for changes to the original Superfund legislation that, taken together and in their most extreme form, would have allowed the corporation to walk away from Montana without having to spend another dime on reclamation. Three features of the law that ARCO has always found particularly objectionable are "retroactive liability," by which a corporation can be forced to pay for pollution that occurred prior to the passage of a law forbidding it; "joint and several liability," which stipulates that all responsible parties, regardless of the size of their contribution to an environmental problem, must share cleanup costs; and "successor liability," by which the purchaser of a site is required to assume the liabilities associated with that site. When Sandy Stash, ARCO general manager in Montana, says "Superfund's been a failure," she is referring to the practical results of these provisions—a muddle of suits and countersuits that has consumed corporate resources while stalling reclamation efforts throughout the country. Stash believes that ARCO, having taken control of the Hill in 1977, three years before Superfund was enacted and following a hundred years of intensive mining, should not be held liable for the actions of Anaconda. The EPA's position, by contrast, is that in an imperfect world the only way to guarantee that big polluters pay for the environmental damage they cause is to make them pay for the costs of reclaiming any damaged site they own. Buy an asset, in this view, and you buy all associated liabilities.

ARCO's position may be unpopular, but the corporation is far from alone in its dissatisfaction with the Superfund law. For several years critics of all persuasions have been charging that the program has produced little beyond the enrichment of lawyers and technical consultants. As frustrated as anyone else, Montana senator Max Baucus, a Democrat, led an effort in 1993 and 1994, when he was chairman of the Environment and Public Works Committee, to amend the act by exempting from liability small businesses and municipalities, setting up a more equitable allocation system to resolve multiparty disputes, and allowing local communities a larger role in the selection of remedies. Stash was a member of the advisory group that had worked for more than a year to reach agreement on these compromises, as were other industry leaders, along with insurance company representatives, EPA scientists, and local government officials, including Jon Sesso, director of the Butte–Silver Bow Planning Department. But anticipating the outcome of the midterm elections, Republicans refused to entertain Democratic initiatives of any kind, merit be damned. In September 1994, when Baucus's carefully crafted reauthorization bill finally made it out of committee, Bob Dole, soon to become Senate Majority Leader and later the Republican presidential candidate, prevented it from reaching the floor for debate.

The reauthorization bill that Republican John Chaffee, Baucus's successor to the chair of the Environment and Public Works Committee, and Bob Smith introduced in April 1996 envisioned a very different solution to the problem of costly, protracted litigation—eliminating all sites contaminated prior to December 11, 1980, when the original Superfund law was enacted. Fewer sites, fewer disputes, a proposition of impeachable logic and disastrous implication. Here in Summit Valley the Chaffee-Smith bill would have absolved ARCO of all responsibility for areas it had not already signed agreements with the EPA to clean up, including the metal-laden sediment behind the Milltown Dam, all of the upper Clark Fork River, and, most worrisome to Lynch, the contaminated soils on the Hill. ARCO had promised to honor decisions already reached regarding mine flooding, the tailings alongside and pollution within the stretch of Silver Bow Creek in Summit Valley and within the creek floodplain between Butte and Warm Springs Ponds. But if Congress were to open the door by deleting the retroactive liability provision, ARCO might have the grounds to contest the decisions in court, since they, too, address environmental problems created before 1980. Estimated costs of remedies already negotiated or presently under design are well in excess of $250 million and likely will climb much higher in the coming years. "The country doesn't have the money," Lynch told me in a moment of extreme understatement, "nor does the state."

Under no illusions about the motives of the other players at the Superfund table, Lynch hoped only that the game would continue long enough to allow him to negotiate lasting solutions to the valley's problems. He and his staff had already managed to gain a measure of control over the decision-making process, in particular persuading the EPA and ARCO that land use should be taken into account in cleanup remedies. In keeping with the philosophy behind the Anaconda-Butte Heritage Corridor, Lynch tried to merge reclamation and economic development into a single ambition, in the hope that the remedies would produce outcomes a good deal more useful to the community than fields of weeds and locked mine yards, especially on the Hill, where the targeted fields and yards are of a piece with the old parts of town.

But "lasting" no longer means what it did when Congress enacted the original Superfund law. Later that day I met with Jon Sesso, Lynch's point man in the Superfund negotiations. "What everyone is starting to realize," he told me, a slightly pained look on his face, "is that most cleanups will need long-term maintenance of some kind." The Pit remedy—pumping and treating ever-rising toxic water—is not the only one that will continue long after ARCO and the EPA have forgotten the Hill. So will several of the others, requiring a range of responses, from neutralizing the aftermath of unexpected erosion to filling in and securing cave-ins, a problem that can only get worse over time, given the thousands of miles of failing shafts and tunnels beneath the Hill. Thus, Lynch and Sesso argue, Summit Valley needs an insurance policy, in the form of a trust fund, say, large enough to provide the county with the staff, equipment, and other resources it requires to oversee the remedies—in perpetuity. This is another reason why Lynch insisted on a place at the Superfund table and was willing to run the risk that the local government's give-and-take style of advocacy would be viewed by environmentalists as capitulation. The truth is that without ARCO's financial help neither "responsible reclamation" nor an insurance policy to maintain reclamation measures is even remotely possible. ARCO may be a reluctant partner in the Superfund program and, at times, a manipulative one, but it has been willing to compromise, repeatedly, it has already spent a great deal of money, and it will continue to do so as long as the Superfund process remains intact. The gamblers in the courthouse, both Lynch and his staff and the people who have succeeded them, know better than to turn away a player with such deep pockets.

As in any game, it must be remembered, chance, too, may assume a critical role, and it is increasingly likely to do so as time passes. What if Fritz Daily is right, and water leaves the Pit before it reaches the level the EPA and ARCO deem critical? And what impact would an earthquake have? The continental fault, which runs underneath the Yankee Doodle Tailings Pond, has been silent for as long as anyone can remember. To some seismologists that means Summit Valley is very stable. To others it means that the area is long overdue for a nasty tremor. Would the impoundment hold? The engineers at Montana Resources say yes, unequivocally, and doubtless they believe it. This is their home, too. But if Dennis Washington lived in Butte, within sight of his mine, might there now be in place some kind of early warning system and evacuation plan, as has been recommended by at least two consulting firms? Were the dam to collapse, some of the fine-grained waste would behave like a liquid, surging into the Berkeley Pit, possibly displacing a toxic tidal wave, while the rest slid down the Hill. If either the water or the sand reached the Flat, the damage to property could be catastrophic. If either arrived without warning, in the middle of the night, say, people could be injured or killed. Failure may indeed be unlikely, but the enormity of the consequences would seem to call for extraordinary protective measures. My guess is that if those who really benefit from mining, not just stockholders but consumers, lived beside the pits, waste piles, and contaminated water, like the people of Butte, there would be more enthusiasm for erring on the side of caution in this and all other environmental matters in Summit Valley.

Since moving back to Butte nines and a half years ago, I have lived near the top of the Hill, in one of the frontier zones where mine ruins adjoin the remnants of mine-side neighborhoods, headframes towering above rooftops, tailings lapping at back doors. From my three-room shanty in Walkerville it is less than a quarter mile to the Granite Mountain Overlook. I go there often, following my crooked, one-lane street, past a row of empty lots, all but two of the original houses having been destroyed to make room for the Berkeley Pit. I walk through the expanse of rolling dumps that separates Walkerville from the back wall of the Pit, toward the Granite Mountain mine, the fire-darkened axis of the mining district. All that can be seen today is the top half of its headframe, resting within a recess in a randomly stepped cascade of waste rock. To the north, where the waves of tailings crest, lies the high berm of the Yankee Doodle pond, a constantly expanding delta of hardened slurry, and beyond that Sunflower Hill, often sunlit but rarely in flower. Visible to the south are the uppermost levels of the Berkeley Pit, the concentrator, and the back wall of the East Pit, where the ore zone resembles a massive blue-gray stain on the flesh-colored foundation of the Continental Divide and the mammoth trucks that creep along the terraces newly carved in its side seem in the distance like toys. Only after several visits to the Overlook did I notice midway between the Berkeley and East pits an acre or less of flat, mostly undisturbed land where a few scrawny pine trees yet grow, all that remains of the east-side neighborhood known as McQueen. If the earth has ends, this surely is one of them.

Sometimes a crow will appear, bold and raucous, angling across the bow of the Overlook, then gliding over the waste sea that stretches to the Divide. The crow, I have come to believe, is to the Hill what the albatross is to the ocean—bearer of omens, the essence of the place embodied, black heart aloft. Making its home on the Hill year-round, living well in a dangerous landscape, the crow is much more emblematic of Butte than the snow goose, a migratory bird that passes through the valley twice a year, rarely stopping and, rarer still, staying, not unlike the tourists who travel Interstate 90 all summer long, in search of innocence and prettiness. Western Montana has of late induced a kind of lightheadedness in people long gone from wild places, and the romance is not misplaced. Raw natural beauty is here in abundance and on an overwhelming scale, and it can sweep one away. But every moon has its dark side, and Butte is Montana's dark side, as necessary as night, as necessary as the nocturnal work that took place here.

Like whiskey straight, the Hill is an acquired taste, but it is well worth cultivating, even if one goes no further than to contemplate the American landscape from the perspective of the Granite Mountain Overlook. Today, bearing the social and physical scars of one of the most long-lasting and lucrative mining runs in the world, a run that is not yet over, the Hill contradicts some of our most cherished beliefs: that history is necessarily progressive; that any problem is fixable, given enough goodwill and technical ingenuity; and, closest to home, that it is possible to consume immense quantities of raw materials without creating ethical and environmental dilemmas of immense consequence. Not one of these notions will survive the corrosive waters of the Berkeley Pit.

Montana in the Twenty-first Century

Harry W. Fritz

The present, someone once said, is the point where the future pauses and becomes the past. For historians this means that the contemporary era is no less important and, in fact, no less historical than the distant past. The purpose of history, after all, is to explain who we are, how we got that way, and where we are going. Our contemporaries, especially students, are at least as interested in the here and now as the there and then.

The following article by Harry Fritz, a professor of history at the University of Montana, holds that contemporary Montana is just as important, as transformational, as more intensively studied eras of the distant past. History is the study of the past, but not for the past's own sake. Only if we use the past to comprehend the present and engage the future is its study worthwhile. Today, as always, Montana is poised at the present, between past and future. A sense of history, especially contemporary history, can help chart an achievable future.

THE TURN OF THE MILLENNIUM IS AN APPROPRIATE TIME FOR SUMMING UP THE past, assessing the present, and predicting the future. The time is perhaps more appropriate in Montana than elsewhere because long-term transformational changes have suddenly culminated in a new Montana, a state fundamentally and significantly different than its past. Without the past as a steady compass, however, foreseeing the future is difficult. The intensity of current debate and reactionary politics are sure signs of confusion and uncertainty. Without knowing what is ahead, Montana grasps at elusive straws.

In particular, four major developments have occurred almost simultaneously in Montana. Two were predictable in 2000: the quadrennial elections and the decennial census. Two others are works in progress: the impact of electrical power deregulation and the convulsive death rattle of a natural-resource-based economy. Montana is rapidly losing, at best marginalizing, its traditional economic pursuits, yet, seemingly incongruously, people are moving here in great numbers. The economy, the environment, politics, demography, and development are the ingredients of twenty-first-century Montana political culture.

Montana's traditional economy has been in steep decline for twenty years. The 1980s was truly a depression decade. Mines, mills, and smelters closed; drought and other afflictions beset agriculture; the 1970s energy boom went bust. These grim downturns continued in the 1990s,

Holter Dam—shown here in 1918, the year it was completed by the Montana Power Company—was purchase by Pennsylvania Power and Light Resources, Inc., in 1998. It is now included in an initiative to give Montana citizens the option to "Buy Back the Dams."

MONTANA HISTORICAL SOCIETY PHOTOGRAPH ARCHIVES, HELENA

exacerbating several long-term adverse trends—the loss of high-paying jobs in the natural resource economy, low per-capita and per-family income, high numbers of multiple-job families. By some measurements Montana ranks dead last in the nation in these statistical categories.

Yet each industry had its moments in the 1990s—flashes of prosperity providing respite from bad tidings and hope for the future. Dennis Washington's Montana Resources, Inc., mined copper and molybdenum in Butte's East Pit. Stillwater Mining produced platinum and palladium. Gold mines employing a cyanide heap-leaching process operated near Whitehall and in the Little Rockies. But at decade's end there were only 1,936 metal mining jobs in Montana—just one-half of 1 percent of the total number of jobs in the state. The Montana Mining Association, the industry's cheerleader, could not collect enough money to keep its office in Helena open.

Shakedown in the timber industry continues. Mill closures and consolidations have cost jobs and reduced income. The state's annual timber cut is down by more than a third, from 1.4 billion board feet in the mid-1980s to just over 900 million in 1998. Most of the decline comes from reduced harvests on national forests, 60 percent of Montana's timberlands. The federal government is the villain in Montana logging circles—they believe it pegs prices too high to sell while reducing the allowable cut. Timber prices fell from $325 per thousand board feet in 1999 to $180 in 2000. The break-even figure is $280. The North American Free Trade Agreement (NAFTA), beneficial to eastern finance, hurts Montana loggers. Most of the log-home manufacturers in the state import lodgepole pine from Canada even though Montana grows more lodgepole pine than any other state.

Yet in the mid 1990s the dwindling supply of sawlogs ironically produced a positive benefit. Timber prices shot up and imparted a temporary stability and even prosperity to the wood-products industry. High prices impelled private landowners to log their holdings; even the State of Montana increased the cut on state forests. Employment in the industry, despite shifts among loggers, millworkers, truck drivers, log-home builders, and furniture manufacturers, remained fairly steady at slightly less than eleven thousand. These workers represent less than 2 percent of the Montana workforce. Montana grows 1.3 billion board feet annually; that fact assures a permanent timber industry.

Montana farmers and ranchers do fine when rain falls and commodity prices are high. Since the early 1990s neither has been the case. In recent years the federal government has paid more to Montana farmers than they have earned from sales. The average age of a farmer in Montana is rapidly approaching sixty. Red meat is high in fat, calories, and cholesterol. International markets are shrinking. Genetically modified products frighten agriculturalists. The Conservation Resource Program takes land out of cultivation. "There comes a time," says Norman Sullivan of the Farmers' Union, "when it's no longer feasible to farm."

A few farm corporations have gone modern, with specialized products and targeted customers. Wheat Montana, near Three Forks, produces high-quality, chemical-free wheat that consumers can mill themselves. Big Sky Beef, near Malta, pays up to 15 percent above market for top-quality Angus, which it sells over the internet. Organic farmers thrive at places like the Missoula Farmers' Market. Small family farmers are in trouble, but agriculture survives.

Montana's energy industry has stagnated since the price of oil plummeted after 1983. Only recent power shortages indicate that it may still have life. Coal production, the boom industry of the 1970s, has increased only incrementally since then. One promising new development is coal-bed methane, a natural gas. Drilling into coal seams and pumping out water releases pressure-trapped methane. Montana has proven resources of one trillion cubic feet in the Powder River Basin alone. So far only 165 wells operate near Decker; there is a potential for 9,500. Unfortunately, the process depletes aquifers and discharges salty water into the Tongue River. Researchers hope to find new uses for the water or maybe pump it back into the ground.

Despite recurrent booms and brief periods of prosperity, the natural resource extractive industries of Montana have been declining, relatively, for more than eighty years. Technological improvements in every one of the state's bedrock industries have enhanced labor productivity and corporate profits at the expense of jobs and income. Structural changes in international manufacturing and commerce—globalization—have placed Montana at a permanent disadvantage. Once there were fifteen thousand underground hard-rock miners in Butte. In 2001 there were none. In a sense Montana is Butte, writ large. Like the rest of America,

Montana has transmogrified into a sales-and-service society. Economic growth in 2001 centers on retail trade, transportation, travel and recreation, education, medical care, banks, legal and insurance services, retirement. The Treasure State has become Big Sky Country.

Yet many Montanans have not internalized these profound transformations. The state's mindset, particularly among politicians, remains firmly in the nineteenth century. "Logging, mining and oil and gas drilling are today a tiny and declining part of Montana's economy," proclaimed the *Missoulian* in December 2000, touching off an angry debate.[1] For the first time in two centuries of development one can argue that extractive industries are not the wave of the future in Montana. It is truly a new millennium.

Montana's environmental movement retains strong popular support, but it has been unable to transform that approval into political strength. The environmental era, born in the 1970s, died in the 1990s. In an effort to encourage industry the legislature, beginning in 1993, persistently weakened water and siting standards. "Twenty-five years of environmental progress was wiped out in ninety days" in 1995, charged one critic.[2] A citizen initiative in 1996, I-122, to restore water testing standards went down under an onslaught of mining money. Another initiative, to ban cyanide heap-leach mining, is entangled in litigation. The Major Facility Siting Act, which required environmental assessments before undertaking large-scale construction, was an environmental cornerstone in 1975; it suffered legislative evisceration in 2001.

Montana has more than its share of environmental hazards and threats. The State has sued Pegasus Gold's Little Rockies operation over pollution of streams with arsenic, cadmium, and acid. The company filed for bankruptcy, leaving Montanans holding the cleanup bag. W. R. Grace and Co., which ran a vermiculite mine near Libby until 1991, has been found liable for poisoning its workers with asbestos; 192 people have died. Grace also declared bankruptcy without providing medical costs. The largest Superfund site in the nation, the Clark Fork Operational Unit, stretches 120 miles from Warm Springs Ponds to the Milltown Dam. All of these pale before the potential danger of the Berkeley Pit.

When Atlantic Richfield pulled the plug on the pumps that kept the Butte mines dry (April 22, 1982, Earth Day), the Berkeley Pit began filling with toxic wastewater. As of November 2001 water in the Butte mines had risen 3,084 feet; water in the Berkeley Pit was 948 feet deep. Seven to eight million gallons per day flow into the pit; the water table rises about two feet per month. There are approximately 35 billion gallons in the pit. Currently the water is within five feet of contacting the alluvial bedrock interface, in danger of seeping into the Silver Bow Creek drainage, at the uttermost reach of the Columbia River Basin. Spillage, landslides, earthquakes, or simply time (a "Critical Water Level" will hit in 2012) will create an unprecedented environmental disaster. The legacy of the past persists.

In the 1990s Montana became a firmly Republican state. Conrad Burns began the process in 1988 when he unseated two-term Democratic senator John Melcher. Burns has since been re-elected twice—the first Republican in the state's history of popular elections to serve more than one term. Republican Stan Stephens won the governorship in 1988. His successor, the popular Marc Racicot, defeated Dorothy Bradley in a close race in 1992, then won reelection in 1996 with an astonishing 80 percent of the vote. (His Democratic opponent, liberal Chet Blaylock, died during the campaign.) Term-limited out in 2000, Racicot became Republican national party chairman in 2001. His successor, Republican Judy Martz, won a surprise victory over state auditor Mark O'Keefe in 2000, with a campaign that promised to reduce taxes and encourage industry.

Following the census of 1990 Montana lost one of the two United States congressional seats it had enjoyed since 1912. The 1992 House race pitted two long-term incumbents in a race for the lone office. Democrat Pat Williams from the west narrowly defeated Republican Ron Marlenee. When Williams retired in 1996, the seat went to Republican Rick Hill (1997–2001), and then to former lieutenant governor Dennis Rehberg of Billings, also a Republican. Rehberg represents the second-largest (after Alaska) congressional district in America, and more people than any congressman in the history of the American republic.

Republicans also captured the State House of Representatives in 1992; the Senate followed in 1994. Democrats have not retaken either chamber. One-party Republican government was the rule as Montana entered the twenty-first century although Democrats did maintain control over three lesser statewide offices: attorney general (Mike McGrath), superintendent of public instruction (Linda McCulloch), and state auditor (John Morrison).

Montana's emerging permanent Republican majority places it politically in line with other Rocky Mountain states. Organized labor and independent farmers, two sources of past Democratic strength, have declined in numbers and power. Democrats have not discovered the issues to return to office, while Montanans respond positively to national Republican positions on guns, government, taxes, and abortion. Recent migrants vote conservatively. Destination counties like Flathead and Ravalli have become Republican strongholds. The party has survived term limits, depression, deregulation, and a poor environmental record. It appears to have a lock on the immediate future.

Despite economic inertia people moved to Montana in great numbers in the 1990s. On March 21, 2001, when the United States Census Bureau released its county-by-county population figures, the numbers were surprising, even shocking. The total population topped 900,000—an increase, at 902,195, of 103,130 people since the 1990 census. The 12.91 percent jump was large (in the 1980s, the state's population increased by only 12,475, or 1.6 percent) but not large enough to regain the congressional seat lost after 1990. Montana grew rapidly, but not as rapidly as the rest of America (13.15 percent). Montana's seat went to Georgia. (In the early 1990s the Census Bureau's estimates of Montana's population growth had been high—high enough, at 15,000 newcomers per year, to reach nearly 950,000 by 2000 and lock up a second congressional seat. But the numbers tailed off in the last half of the decade, falling below 2,000 people two years running. Economic doldrums in California had fueled an exodus to Montana and other western states; a popular telephone number there was 1-800-OUTOFLA. But when the California economy righted itself, the outflow dwindled.)

Who *were* the newcomers? About 20 percent were Californians, fleeing the fast lane. (We know this by counting surrendered driver's licenses. The rest, it is said, were Oregonians fleeing arriving Californians.) Other suppositions include retirees, students, survivalists, granolas, fly fishermen. About one-third of the increase was natural (births over deaths and departures); two-thirds represented migration from other states. Some 60 percent of those who moved to Montana had ties to the state—they had lived here once, had family here, or vacationed here. Some were "Hummingbirds"—upscale types who flew into Montana and bought twenty-acre ranchettes to visit twice a year. Some were "Equity Refugees"—people who sold their out-of-state homes for a bundle and rolled the money over into Montana spreads to avoid tax penalties. And some were "Lone Eagles"—professionals who abandoned city life and set up home offices in Montana. For the first time in human history, one can separate one's residence from one's workplace. "There really are no geographic restrictions," said one recent transplant from Tacoma. "With a fax and a modem, you can be anywhere."[3]

Why did they come? Traditionally, economics—the search for better jobs, better chances—has fueled American migrations. But the Montana economy has not been creating new, high-paying jobs. The state is losing quality jobs and is at the bottom of the income barrel. So the 1990s migration into Montana was noneconomic, nontraditional. Newcomers sought amenities: recreation, education, privacy, security. "In fact," the *Missoulian* noted, "people are moving to Montana from the very states that pay higher wages. Why?" The answer: "For the Montana lifestyle. For the fishing and hunting and other recreation. For the wide-open spaces and beauty. For the chance to live at the end of a road, or to have a house on five acres with a horse and two goats. For the opportunity to escape the rat-race, to live without fear of crime, or to raise a family in a family-friendly setting."[4]

Where did they go? To the destination counties: Flathead, Lake, Ravalli, Gallatin. To the "dominant" counties, where natural increase was also important: Missoula, Lewis and Clark, Yellowstone. To the adjacent counties of small populations but high growth rates, where spillover has created bedroom communities: Broadwater, Jefferson, Park, Carbon, Musselshell. Above all to western or mountainous Montana, creating the most serious demographic problem facing Montana in the early twenty-first century.

Montana has fifty-six counties, but twenty-three of them (41 percent) actually lost population in the 1990s. In the midst of a statewide population boom, these counties suffered a net decline. With a single exception (Deer Lodge County, where the city of Anaconda has not yet recovered from the closure of its smelter in 1980), all of the counties that lost population are in central and eastern Montana. They are rural, agricultural counties, small to begin with. Some of these counties have been losing population ever since they were created in the Homestead Era, 1900–1920. These twenty-three counties are home to a combined total of 128,320 people (14.2 percent of the state), down 8,851 residents (6.4 percent) since 1990.

Another seventeen counties (30 percent) gained ground, but only incrementally. Their population increased, but not as fast as the state rate (12.91 percent). Again, with four exceptions (Granite, Lincoln, Powell, and Silver Bow counties), all of these stand-pat counties are the rural and agricultural counties of central and eastern Montana. These seventeen counties contain 230,332 people (25.5 percent of the state), up just 11,657 residents (5.3 percent) since 1990.

Just sixteen counties grew faster than the state as a whole. These contiguous counties curve across western and south central Montana in a sweeping arc, from Flathead County on the Canadian border in the northwest to Yellowstone and Carbon counties, the latter adjacent to Wyoming. These were the fastest-growing counties in Montana. Some contain major urban centers (Yellowstone, Missoula, Gallatin, Lewis and Clark, Flathead); some house spillover communities (Broadwater, Carbon, Golden Valley, Jefferson, Madison, Mineral, Sweet Grass). Astonishingly, these sixteen counties added 100,298 new residents in the 1990s. Montana added 103,130. In these sixteen counties live 543,543 people (60.2 percent of the state), up 100,298 residents (22.6 percent) since 1990.

The implications of this statistical biformity are troubling. Rural and agricultural Montana, particularly in the central and eastern parts of the state, is suffering serious depopulation. People are moving out or staying and growing older; there are few if any in-migrants. Forty-one counties, with 39.7 percent of the state's population, netted just 2,806 new residents in the 1990s. Farms are not passed on, businesses close, towns atrophy, schools consolidate. Politically this population aggregate lost nearly eleven representatives to state government after the 2000 reapportionment. The great divide has never been greater.

More than a century ago the historian Frederick Jackson Turner proclaimed the end of the frontier in American history. The United States no longer featured an advancing line of settlement. A population density of two people per square mile, Turner reasoned, constituted a community. By these lights twenty-four of Montana's fifty-six counties are statistically unsettled. Only one, Granite County, is west of the Continental Divide. Garfield County, where tax delinquents calling themselves "freemen" holed up in 1996, has a population density of 0.3 people per square mile. The demographers Frank and Deborah Popper of Rutgers University have documented the Great Plains exodus. They claim the land should never have been settled in the first place. Their solution has the federal government stepping in, buying up private holdings, ripping out the fences, and restoring the "Buffalo Commons." This is not the solution advocated in Garfield County. There is no apparent solution.[5]

These economic, environmental, political, and demographic transformations are pretty much done deals in early twenty-first-century Montana. But the future has never been more problematic. The consequences of these profound changes are unclear. Moreover, new developments in energy, education, the environment, and economic development spell uncertainty. Prime among these x-factors is deregulation.

In spring 1997 the Fifty-fifth Montana Legislature passed a bill, Senate Bill 390, deregulating the generation and sale of electrical power in the state. Transmission, distribution, and other services were not included. The bill passed at the behest of the Montana Power Company, Governor Marc Racicot, and the Republican legislative majority. Major industrial customers of Montana Power, who believed they could buy cheaper power on an open market and wanted freedom from mandatory regulation, also pressed for the bill's passage. Montana Power claimed that total federal deregulation was imminent. Governor Racicot and the Republicans, adherents of a free-market ideology, believed that competition among producers would lower energy costs.

The Montana Power Company was founded in 1912 by consolidating numerous small power producers in the state. Its president, John D. Ryan, also headed the giant Anaconda Copper Company (with an interlocking directorate and a shared president, the two powerful corporations were the "Montana Twins"). Anaconda was, in fact, the largest single power consumer in the United States. The Milwaukee Road, the first long-distance (438 miles) electrified railroad in America, was another big customer. Montana Power bought or built thirteen hydroelectric dams on Montana rivers and in the 1970s constructed four mine-mouth, coal-fired electrical generation plants at Colstrip. These facilities provided Montanans with the sixth-lowest power rates in the nation. As of July 1, 1997, 750 kilowatt hours of electricity (the average monthly residential use) cost homeowners $46.17. The national average was $65.37. Hawaiians paid $143.70.[6]

Montana Power was from the beginning a regulated monopoly. The Public Service Commission granted the company a monopoly to shield it from competition. In return Montana Power provided cheap electrical power to businesses and residents. It was a cozy arrangement. Montanans complained when they received their winter power bills or when the company asked the service commission for a rate increase, but in reality they had little to cry about. The regulated Montana market produced and controlled a power supply more than twice the local demand. In 1997 this cheap industrial and residential power seemed available for the foreseeable future.

Deregulation had no immediate impact upon passage in 1997. Even Montana Power Company professed no intention to implement the measure. Just eight months later, however, in December 1997, Montana Power announced that its hydroelectric dams and coal-fired power plants were up for sale. The company would still transmit and distribute electricity and natural gas, but 1,543 megawatts of power were on the market. Almost a year later, in November 1998, Montana Power found a buyer. Pennsylvania Power and Light Resources, Inc., (PPL) of Allentown, Pennsylvania, agreed to pay $988 million for the company's generating facilities, including the out-of-state generating capacity at Montana Power's Colstrip plants. At the same time, it bought those parts of the Colstrip plants not owned by Montana Power from Portland General Electric and Puget Sound Energy. The package deal totaled $1.586 billion for more than 2,600 megawatts of power. Montana Power then arranged to sell its transmission and distribution facilities—its wires, poles, and pipelines— to NorthWestern Energy and Communications Solutions of Sioux Falls, South Dakota. The price was $1.1 billion. The Public Service Commission approved the deal in January 2002.

At first deregulation seemed to work. Montana Power's large industrial customers—Montana Resources, Exxon, Stone Container, Columbia Falls Aluminum (which alone consumed almost one-eighth of Montana's power capacity)—left the shelter of regulation on July 1, 1998, and for a year or two found cheaper competitive power rates. But in 2000 the energy market disappeared. Escalating demand, drought, power shortages in California, and transmission difficulties exploded market rates. Companies faced price increases of 1,000 to 1,500 percent. Skyrocketing power rates literally priced many corporations out of business.

Deregulation, at least temporarily, cost Montana much of its industrial base. (Ironically these victims of SB 390 actually led the fight for its passage.) Montana Resources in Butte, despite a long-term contract for inexpensive power, suspended operations in June 2000, laid off 320 workers, and sold its excess power for a profit on the spot market. Smurfit-Stone Container in Frenchtown furloughed 150 of its 600 employees and bought power at ten times the regulated price. "We cannot afford to buy electricity on the open market," said manager Pat Clevenger. For Conoco, Inc., according to its manager John Bennett, "The early results have been catastrophic." Advanced Silicon Materials, Inc., moved to Butte in 1996. "We use a huge amount of power, and that's why we located in Montana in the first place," explained manager Dave Keck. "Market prices would be devastating to us." Columbia Falls Aluminum found it more profitable to cease production, pay its employees for a year, and sell its unused power (pre-contracted at a low price) on the boom market. American Smelter in East Helena closed. By early 2001 over 2,800 Montana job losses were attributable to the energy crisis, and 4,500 more were jeopardized. Already suffering from market contractions, Montana industry could ill-afford deregulation.[7]

Residential and small commercial users avoided the crisis brought on by deregulation for a time. The 1997 deregulation bill froze power prices for 288,000 consumers at 2.225 cents per kilowatt hour until June 30, 2002. The 2001 legislature brokered a deal whereby PPL would sell Montana Power 500 megawatts of electricity at four cents per kilowatt hour (forty dollars per megawatt hour) for five years beginning July 1, 2002. But demand for power is generally greater than 500 megawatts. The deal, House Bill 374, would have forced Montana Power to buy the rest of the necessary power on the open market at considerably higher rates. Montana Power grimly predicted that residential rates would rise by "only" 50 percent on July 1, 2002. Schools, businesses, government itself shuddered.

Yet hardly was the ink dry on HB 374 when it became a dead letter. The Democratic Party launched a successful petition drive to refer the measure to the people. The energy crunch eased somewhat. Conservation and delayed usage of electricity helped. Eight new power plants appeared on Montana drawing boards. A Las Vegas company announced plans to build a $2.7 billion complex of four 500-megawatt generating plants near Red Lodge. Rocky Mountain Power, Inc., proposed a coal gasification plant and 110-megawatt generating facility in the old Holly sugar factory in Hardin. A Montana/North Dakota firm planned two 80-to-100-megawatt coal-fired plants near Broadview. NorthWestern Corps selected Great Falls as the site of three 80-megawatt gas-fired turbines. Great Northern Power Development and Kiewit Mining Group announced a joint venture to develop lignite holdings in eastern Montana for one or more 500-megawatt plants. Continental Energy Services of Butte planned a 500-megawatt gas-fired power plant southwest of the city. Suddenly Montana's future seemed awash in surplus electricity. Down came the market price, and down came Montana Power's estimate of rate increases from 50 percent to 29, 20, and finally 12.8 percent (in the first year). Although Montana prices were still the highest in the region, market economics (and repealed siting standards) seemed to be working.

Montana is not yet out of trouble. The market is capricious, volatile. Business and industry prefer a regular, predictable universe. The proposed plants would increase the state's capacity by 2,400 megawatts, but there are no present customers for this extra power and no way to ship it elsewhere. "There is no market in Montana, and you cannot get it out," said Will Rosquist of the Public Service Commission. The state does not have the transmission capacity to move the proposed new megawatts. "Building more transmission lines is more important than new generation," agreed Joel Cook of PPL.[8] But high-voltage power lines cost at least $1 million per mile, and Montana has many miles. Montana power mainly flows west, because Montana is in the electrical power grid of the Western Systems Coordinating Council. Bottlenecks exist at connection points near Spokane, the Idaho border, and Miles City.

In late 2001 a citizen's group launched a petition drive to qualify an initiative for the 2002 ballot to give Montanans a chance to buy PPL's Montana dams and run them as public power utilities. "Montanans should not have to pay exorbitant prices for Montana electricity produced from Montana water from Montana mountains," said Paul Edwards of Helena.[9] Though the measure faces legal and constitutional challenges, it makes PPL executives nervous.

This "fiber hotel," located on the third floor of the Billings Granite Tower, provides a secure, temperature-controlled environment for high-tech equipment used by a variety of Montana businesses.

COURTESY I CONNECT MONTANA

Montana's power deals had their critics, and they were vociferous. "Deregulatory legislation has done more, in less time, to destroy major Montana industries than the combined acts of the massed army of all environmentalists since the beginning of time," said one businessman. Former Congressman Pat Williams exclaimed that "Montana held the four aces of cheap power, and a corporate-lackey legislature demanded a new deck of cards." Defenders claimed, without much evidence, that deregulation was bound to happen and that in the long run a competitive market would stabilize and even lower Montana's energy costs. This was a faith-based enterprise. "Given time, deregulation will be good for Montana, the company, the investors, and the public," promised a Montana Power Company spokesman. Good or bad, Cal Sweet of Kalispell Electric summed up: "In modern Montana history there is one defining moment, and that defining moment is deregulation."[10]

And what of the future? Perhaps the State of Montana should take a leaf from the Montana Power Company's book. In 1997 Montana Power was a long-standing, small market, somewhat traditional, even fusty old energy company. It used Montana's coal and water to generate electrical power, and transmitted that power cheaply and efficiently to the state's businesses and homeowners. Five years later, in 2002, not even the name "Montana Power" remained. In its place was a new-fangled telecommunications company, Touch America.

Bob Gannon, CEO of both Montana Power and Touch America, straddled the great divide. Touch America was originally a tiny microwave firm called Telecommunications Resources, Inc. (TRI), part of a Montana Power subsidiary called Entech. TRI upgraded its wire cables to fiber optics. As Michael Jamison put it, "Where Montana Power had once laid copper lines to carry electricity, it now laid fiber optics to carry information."[11] In 1990 TRI expanded, buying a small long-distance provider, Touch America. The Public Service Commission did not regulate the new acquisition. Suddenly, in the Age of the Internet, the Age of IT (information technology), Touch America became Montana Power's biggest money-maker. The tail wagged the dog.

Montana Power's transformation from energy to high-tech symbolizes modern Montana. The state itself is painfully undergoing a similar transformation. "The industrial age is over. The information age is here," said Gannon.[12] Mining, logging, agriculture, and energy yield to telecommunications, e-commerce, streaming solutions, and fiber optics. The new Montana struggles to be born. Information technology is not yet a recognized industry in Montana; it has no occupational licensing association; it employs no lobbyist. But, like it or not, it is the wave of the future, in America, in the world, and, last of all, in Montana.

The new economy requires massive investment in infrastructure—not just roads, rail lines, and sewers but fiber-optic cables, satellite-based telecommunications, and educational training. "The new logic of economic nationalism," argues former United States Secretary of Labor Robert Reich, consists of "the skills and insights of a nation's work force, and the quality of its transportation and communication links to the world (its infrastructure). . . . Increasingly, educated brainpower—along with roads, airports, computers, and fiber-optic cables connecting it up—determines a nation's standard of living."[13] Today the new technology requires that every house, school, business, and community be wired, "connected," accessible to the Internet and all information sources and communication capabilities. It is not just desirable, it is necessary. Instant access must be as common as running water, as light at the flip of a switch.

Montana has done little to facilitate the new economy. The economic development plans and public policies of the Racicot and Martz administrations show little IT awareness. Below the level of state government, however, there is a flurry of activity. Regional telephone cooperatives, especially, are deploying ADSL (Asynchronous Digital Subscriber Line) service to their growing number of subscribers. ADSL is a high-speed data service that operates six times faster (high band width) than do current capabilities. It offers hope for the future, perhaps the only hope, to rural communities and small-town Montana.

Nor can Montana permit the kinds of environmental and ecological devastation symbolized by the Berkeley Pit. A Phelps Dodge/Canyon Resources, Inc., proposed cyanide heap-leach gold mine near Lincoln threatens the Big Blackfoot River, "the river that runs through it." The largest proposed gold mine in Montana history, at 6,000 feet long and 1,200 feet deep, the "Seven-Up Pete Joint Venture" would move 980 million tons of ore to obtain 3.7 million ounces of gold over fifteen years. Elsewhere the Sterling Mining Company's plans for an approved but unrealized copper/silver operation in the Cabinet Mountains calls for the discharge of three million gallons of wastewater daily into the Clark Fork River and a one-hndred-million-ton tailings pile. These projects are part of industry's ideal future.

One reason these developments are still on hold, aside from environmental challenges, is low commodity prices. Gold is hovering at $279 per ounce, copper at 70 cents per pound. Energy costs are uncertain. A smoldering national recession in the wake of the 2001 terrorist attacks hinders capital formation. As always, Montana's fate is dependent on outside factors.

Montana must also shore up its system of higher education after twenty years of substandard support. The state ranks last in the nation in dollars invested in education—less than $8 per $1,000 of per capita income in

2001 as compared to $13.50 in 1985. We are 44 percent below the average of seven peer states. States that have invested in higher education have fared well in the new, competitive, conceptual economy. There is a direct relationship between investment in education and *average* annual income. The university system has done its part with substantial increases in funded research. "We can't hope to create more high-paying jobs in this information-intensive economy," said Regent Mark Semmons in 2001, "unless and until we make a serious investment in education."[14]

Montana's future, America's future, rests on the skills and abilities of its work force, on the quality of life in its cities and towns, and on its high-tech infrastructure. A program to "cut more trees, dig more copper ore and mine more gold as a way to improve Montana's economy," argued a former Republican state senator George Darrow, "does not appear to carry the promise of expanding job opportunities and a prosperous future."[15] Educated brainpower, clean and safe communities, and high-speed hookups will speed the transition, as Federal Reserve Board Chairman Alan Greenspan says, "from the manufacturing to the conceptual economy," from primary extractive industries to tertiary, high-technology pursuits. "To make Montana attractive to businesses and entrepreneurs," says Dave Lyman, who runs a small business in northwestern Montana that employs thirty people, we must "concentrate on the quality of life, the school and university system, maintaining the wildlands and the clean air and water we still have, and the rich treasure of the arts in Montana."[16] As always, education, environment, and a healthy economy go together. Montanans, especially politicians, take note.

NOTES

1. *Missoula (Mont.) Missoulian,* December 14, 2000.

2. John B. Wright, *Montana Ghost Dance: Essays on Land and Life* (Austin, Tex., 1998), 120.

3. *Missoula (Mont.) Missoulian,* September 29, 1991.

4. Ibid., September 7, 1988.

5. Deborah Epstein Popper and Frank J. Popper, "The Great Plains: From Dust to Dust," *Planning* (December 1987), 12–18.

6. *Montana Energy,* 18 (January 1998).

7. *Missoula (Mont.) Missoulian,* February 18, 2001.

8. Ibid., January 20, 2002.

9. Ibid., November 21, 2001.

10. Ibid., February 18, 2001.

11. Ibid.

12. Ibid.

13. Robert B. Reich, "The REAL Economy," *Atlantic Monthly,* February 1991, 36–37.

14. Mark Semmens, "Investing in Higher Ed Helps Economies Grow," *Main Hall to Main Street,* 7 (March 2001), 6.

15. *Missoula (Mont.) Missoulian,* December 19, 2000.

16. Ibid., January 20, 2002.

Bibliographic Essay

This bibliographical essay is not meant to be exhaustive. Rather we have attempted to include major secondary works that will enable students of Montana history to pursue topics that might interest them after having read *Montana Legacy*.

The most comprehensive survey of Montana history is Michael P. Malone, Richard B. Roeder, and William L. Lang, *Montana: A History of Two Centuries*, revised ed. (Seattle, 1991). As president of Montana State University, Bozeman, Mike Malone was deeply interested in how Montana's past affected its present, and in 1996 he penned the short volume, *Montana: A Contemporary Profile* (Helena, Mont., 1996), which examined social and economic developments in the state through the mid-1990s. His last work before his untimely death in 1999 was the edited volume, *Montana Century: 100 Years in Pictures and Words*, (Helena, Mont., 1999), a lavishly illustrated book with essays by historians and writers assessing the twentieth-century histories of everything from agriculture to art.

Two older synthetic studies that have had a major influence on Montana historiography are Joseph Kinsey Howard, *Montana: High, Wide, and Handsome* (New Haven, Conn., 1943), and K. Ross Toole, *Montana: An Uncommon Land* (Norman, Okla., 1959). Clark C. Spence's *Montana: A History* (New York, 1978) is also well worth reading.

Several anthologies contain important essays on a variety of topics in Montana history. Among these are William L. Lang, *Stories from an Open Country: Essays on the Yellowstone River Valley* (Billings, Mont., 1995); Rex C. Myers and Harry W. Fritz, eds., *Montana and the West: Essays in Honor of K. Ross Toole* (Boulder, Colo., 1984); Robert R. Swartout, Jr., ed., *Montana Vistas: Selected Historical Essays* (Landam, Md., 1982); and Michael P. Malone and Richard B. Roeder, eds., The Montana Past: An Anthology (Missoula, Mont., 1969). Dave Walter collected the proceedings of some of the Montana History Conference's most popular sessions in *Speaking Ill of the Dead: Jerks in Montana History* (Helena, Mont., 2000). Many of Walter's own essays, covering a wide array of historical topics, are found in Dave Walter, *Montana Campfire Tales: Fourteen Historical Narratives* (Helena, Mont., 1997). An important collection of primary source materials is *Not in Precious Metals Alone: A Manuscript History of Montana* (Helena, Mont., 1976), and an excellent collection of maps is found in Robert L. Taylor et al., *Montana in Maps, 1974* (Bozeman, 1974).

The literature on the fur trade and the exploration of the West is voluminous. The most famous pair of Euro-American explorers to traverse Montana were Meriwether Lewis and William Clark. A good place to start reading about their expedition is James P. Ronda, ed., *Voyages of Discovery: Essays on the Lewis and Clark Expedition* (Helena, Mont., 1998). Ronda's *Lewis and Clark Among the Indians* (Lincoln, Neb., 1984) offers an important new point of view on the expedition, and the collection of his own essays in Ronda, *Finding the West: Explorations with Lewis and Clark* (Albuquerque, N.M., 2001) presents the perspective of a scholar who has studied the expedition for decades. Ronda himself was inspired by John Logan Allen's *Passage through the Garden:*

Lewis and Clark and the Image of the American Northwest (Urbana, Ill., 1975). In 2001
Gary Moulton completed a new edition of thirteen volumes of *The Journals of the Lewis
and Clark Expedition* (Lincoln, Neb., 1983–2001). Stephen Ambrose's *Undaunted
Courage: Meriwether Lewis, Thomas Jefferson, and the Opening of the American West* (New
York, 1996) has brought unparalleled interest to the expedition; a very good general
account of the journey is David Lavender, *The Way to the Western Sea: Lewis and Clark
Across the Continent* (New York, 1988). For a luscious presentation of Karl Bodmer's
exquisite drawings and paintings from Maximilian's expedition, see Karl Bodmer,
David C. Hunt, and Martha V. Gallagher, *Karl Bodmer's America* (Lincoln, Neb., 1984).

A. B. Guthrie's historical novel, *The Big Sky* (New York, 1947) ignited many
Montanans' fascination with mountain men and the fur trade. Guthrie's work and its
impact are considered in William E. Farr and William W. Bevis, eds. *Fifty Years After
The Big Sky: New Perspectives on the Fiction and Films of A. B. Guthrie, Jr.* (Helena, Mont.,
2001). Montana literature has always had a strong historical tradition. In the 1980s and
1990s dozens of authors have followed in the wake of A. B. Guthrie, Dorothy Johnson,
Darcy McNickle, and Mildred Walker to write powerful texts using Montana's
landscape and history as integral characters. William Kittredge and Annick Smith,
eds., compiled a mammoth anthology to introduce readers to Montana literature
through the 1980s in *The Last Best Place: A Montana Anthology* (Helena, Mont., 1988).
William W. Bevis's *Ten Tough Trips: Montana Writers and the West* (Seattle, 1990) and
Rick Newby and Suzanne Hunger, eds., *Writing Montana: Literature under the Big Sky*
(Helena, Mont., 1996) analyze the work of other important Montana writers and
provide many suggestions for further reading.

Two events that have drawn dozens of historians' attention to Montana are the Battle
of the Little Bighorn and the campaign against the Nez Perce. Again, the literature on
these topics is vast, but two recent anthologies collect a variety of perspectives on
Custer's encounter with the Sioux and Cheyenne: Charles E. Rankin, ed., *Legacy: New
Perspectives on the Battle of the Little Bighorn* (Helena, Mont., 1996) and Paul L. Hedren,
ed., *The Great Sioux War, 1876–77* (Helena, Mont., 1990). James Welch, with Paul Stekler,
tells the story from the Native American point of view in *Killing Custer: The Battle of the
Little Bighorn and the Fate of the Plains Indians* (New York, 1994). Jerome A. Green's *Nez
Perce Summer, 1877: The U.S. Army and the Nee-Me-Poo Crisis* (Helena, Mont., 2001) is an
exhaustive study of the flight and final capture of the Nez Perce.

Montana's borders contain seven Indian reservations and many tribes. William L.
Bryan, Jr., introduces the reservations, tribal groups, and significant individuals in
Montana's Indians Yesterday and Today, 2d. ed. (Helena, Mont., 1996). Studies of specific
tribes and reservations include Frederick E. Hoxie, *Parading Through History: The
Making of the Crow Nation in America, 1805–1935* (New York, 1995); Rodney Frey, *The
World of the Crow Indians: As Driftwood Lodges* (Norman, Okla., 1987); Joseph Medicine
Crow, *From the Heart of the Crow Country: The Crow Indians' Own Stories* (Lincoln,
Neb., 2000); John Fahey, *The Flathead Indians* (Norman, Okla., 1974); Robert Bigart, *In
the Name of the Salish and Kootenai Nation: The 1855 Hell Gate Treaty and the Origin of the
Flathead Indian Reservation* (Pablo, Mont., 1996); Bon I. Whealdon et al., *"I Will Be
Meat for My Salish": The Montana Writers Project and the Buffalo of the Flathead Indian*

Reservation (Pablo, Mont., 2002); Paul C. Rosier, *Rebirth of the Blackfeet Nation, 1912–1954* (Lincoln, Neb., 2001); John C. Ewers, *The Blackfeet: Raiders on the Northwestern Plains* (Norman, Okla., 1958); Thomas R. Wessel, *A History of the Rocky Boy's Indian Reservation* (Bozeman, Mont., 1974); Loretta Fowler, *Shared Symbols, Contested Meanings: Gros Ventre Culture and History, 1778–1984* (Ithaca, N.Y., 1987); Edward A. Barry, Jr., *The Fort Belknap Indian Reservation: The First One Hundred Years, 1855–1955* (Bozeman, Mont., 1974); Orlan J. Svingen, *The Northern Cheyenne Indian Reservation, 1877–1900* (Niwot, Colo., 1997); and John Stands in Timber and Margot Liberty, *Cheyenne Memories* (New Haven, Conn., 1967).

There are no book-length studies to date that focus exclusively on the Chinese experience in Montana, but valuable studies with a more national focus include Jack Chen, *The Chinese in America* (San Francisco, 1981); Shih-shan Henry Tsai, *The Chinese Experience in America* (Bloomington, Ind., 1986); and Roger Daniels, *Asian America: Chinese and Japanese in the United States since 1850* (Seattle, 1988). The most important single account dealing with nineteenth-century American-Chinese relations is Michael H. Hunt, *The Making of a Special Relationship: The United States and China to 1914* (New York, 1983). Two of the best case studies on the Chinese experience in America are Judy Yung, *Unbound Feet: A Social History of Chinese Women in San Francisco* (Berkeley, Calif., 1995) and Liping Zhu, *A Chinaman's Chance: The Chinese on the Rocky Mountain Mining Frontier* (Niwot, Colo., 1997).

Transportation, labor, and settlement go hand in hand in western history. Susan Badger Doyle's two-volume compendium, *Journeys to the Land of Gold: Emigrant Diaries from the Bozeman Trail, 1863–1866* (Helena, Mont., 2000) collects all the surviving diaries and reminiscences of civilian travelers on the Bozeman Trail. Carlos A. Schwantes's *Railroad Signatures Across the Pacific Northwest* (Seattle, 1993) and *Long Day's Journey: The Steamboat and Stagecoach Era in the Northern West* (Seattle, 1999) further examine the transportation history of the region. Michael P. Malone probes the life of the man responsible for drawing thousands of homesteaders to eastern Montana in *James J. Hill: Empire Builder of the Northwest* (Norman, Okla., 1996). The best study of Hill's railroad, the Great Northern, is Ralph W. Hidy et al., *The Great Northern Railway: A History* (Boston, Mass., 1988). Mary Hargreaves, in her two studies, *Dry Farming in the Northern Great Plains, 1900–1925* (Cambridge, Mass., 1957) and *Dry Farming in the Northern Great Plains: Years of Readjustment, 1920–1925* (Lawrence, Kans., 1993) analyses the conditions farmers faced in eastern Montana. In *Bad Land: An American Romance* (New York, 1996) Jonathan Raban describes the homesteaders' culture. Beth LaDow's *The Medicine Line: Life and Death on a North American Borderland* (New York, 2001) is a study of settlement in the borderlands straddling Montana and Saskatchewan. John W. Bennett and Seena B. Kohl expand the study of northern settlement from Minnesota to Montana and Manitoba to Alberta in *Settling the Canadian–American West, 1890–1915: Pioneer Adaptation and Community Building* (Lincoln, Neb., 1995).

The field of social history can encompass a wide array of topics: ethnicity and immigration, town building and political movements, religion and cultural expression, gender and race relations. Many books overlap these categories, but two works address specific issues in Montana's social history. Lawrence F. Small edited a two-volume collection of essays, *Religion in Montana: Pathways to the Present* (Billings, Mont., 1995), which presents useful short histories of the many religious groups and churches in Montana. Laura Wilson's *Hutterites of Montana* (New Haven, Conn., 2000) is a lavishly illustrated portrait of Montana's Hutterite colonies. One particular ethnic group is featured in Rob Kroes, *The Persistence of Ethnicity: Dutch Calvinist Pioneers in Amsterdam, Montana* (Urbana, Ill., 1992). Robert A. Harvie's *Keeping the Peace: Police Reform in Montana, 1889 to 1918* (Helena, Mont., 1994) is an analysis of one of the Progressive Era's major concerns, social control and order, and a window onto several little-studied Montana small towns.

The dramatic events of the late nineteenth and early twentieth centuries that led to the rise of industrialization in Montana continue to capture the attention of numerous historians. Most recently Janet L. Finn, Donald MacMillian, Laurie Mercier, and Mary Murphy have added books to the existing literature on Anaconda and Butte. Mercier, in *Anaconda: Labor, Community, and Culture in Montana's Smelter City* (Urbana, Ill., 2001) makes a significant contribution by focusing on the much neglected post–World War II period of Montana's history. MacMillan's posthumously published *Smoke Wars: Anaconda Copper, Montana Air Pollution, and the Courts, 1890–1924* (Helena, Mont., 2000) examines the early legal and political struggles over industrial pollution. Finn's *Tracing the Veins: Of Copper, Culture, and Community from Butte to Chuquicamata* (Berkeley, Calif., 1998) is an invaluable comparative study of copper communities in Montana and Chile. Murphy's *Mining Cultures: Men, Women, and Leisure in Butte, 1914–41* (Urbana, Ill,, 1997) looks at social and cultural life in Butte once the boom that made it the "world's greatest mining town" was over and analyzes the persistence of community.

Three earlier studies remain central to the study of industrial Montana: Michael P. Malone's *The Battle for Butte: Mining and Politics on the Northern Frontier, 1864–1906* (Seattle, 1981); Jerry W. Calvert, *The Gibraltar: Socialism and Labor in Butte, Montana, 1895–1920* (Helena, Mont., 1988); and David M. Emmons, *The Butte Irish: Class and Ethnicity in an American Mining Town, 1875–1925* (Urbana, Ill., 1990). A good work on the technological aspects of Montana's coppr industry is Brian Shovers et al., *Butte and Anaconda Revisited: An Overview of Early-Day Mining and Smelting in Montana* (Butte, Mont., 1991).

The field of western women's history has generated new studies of women's lives across the spectrum of agricultural and industrial societies. Finn, Mercier, and Murphy's books all pay close attention to gender relations. Paula Petrik's *No Step Backward: Women and Family on the Rocky Mountain Mining Frontier, Helena, Montana, 1825–1915* (Helena, Mont., 1987) and Linda Peavy and Ursula Smith's *The Gold Rush Widows of Little Falls: A Story Drawn from the Letters of Pamelia and James Fergus* (St. Paul, Minn., 1990) investigate frontier life from the point of view of women. In *Photographing Montana, 1894–1928: The Life and Work of Evelyn Cameron* (New York, 1990) Donna Lucey published the photographs and story of an English woman who made eastern Montana her home and documented the life of her family and neighbors through photography. Fred W. Voget, with Mary K. Mee, *They Call Me Agnes: A Crow Narrative Based on the Life of Agnes Yellowtail Deernose* (Norman, Okla., 1995) and Alma

Hogan Snell, with Becky Matthews, *Grandmother's Grandchild: My Crow Indian Life* (Lincoln, Neb., 2000) recount the lives of two extraordinary Native American women.

Jeannette Rankin, a woman who made history in myriad ways, is the subject of several biographies: Norma Smith, *Jeannette Rankin, America's Conscience* (Helena, Mont., 2002); Kevin S. Giles, *Flight of the Dove: The Story of Jeannette Rankin* (Beaverton, Ore., 1980); and Hannah Josephson, *Jeannette Rankin: First Lady in Congress* (New York, 1974). Rankin was only one of many significant Montana politicians who have become the subjects of biography and memoir. There is as yet no good biography of Burton K. Wheeler, but his daughter Elizabeth Wheeler Colman penned a memoir of her mother's years as wife of Senator Wheeler in *Mrs. Wheeler Goes to Washington* (Helena, Mont., 1989). Three other books document the lives and political careers of formidable Montana senators. J. Leonard Bates's *Senator Thomas J. Walsh of Montana: Law and Public Affairs from TR to FDR* (Urbana, Ill., 1999) is a magisterial biography of an early-twentieth-century senator, while Francis R. Valeo covers a portion of *Mike Mansfield's career in Mike Mansfield Majority Leader: A Different Kind of Senate, 1961–1976* (Armonk, N.Y., 1999). Donald E. Spritzer is the biographer for another of Montana's powerful Democratic senators in *The New Dealer from Montana: The Senate Career of James E. Murray* (New York, 1986). Clark Spence covers the early years of Montana's political development in *Territorial Politics and Government in Montana, 1864–1889* (Urbana, Ill., 1975). The tumultuous period surrounding World War I is dealt with in Arnon Gutfeld, *Montana's Agony: Years of War and Hysteria, 1917–1921* (Gainesville, Fla., 1979). Ellis Waldron's and Paul B. Wilson's *Atlas of Montana Elections, 1889–1976* (Missoula, Mont., 1978) is an indispensable source for charting political trends in the state. For a popular account of many of Montana's most influential politicians, see John Morrison and Catherine Wright Morrison, *Mavericks: The Lives and Battles of Montana's Political Legends* (Moscow, Idaho, 1997).

Montanans have long enjoyed the pleasures of Glacier and Yellowstone National Parks and enjoyed reading about their histories. There are studies of every aspect of the parks from their organization to their flora, fauna, and architecture. A few books that look at the big picture are Richard Sellars, *Preserving Nature in the National Parks: A History* (New Haven, Conn., 1997); Mark David Spence, *Dispossessing the Wilderness: Indian Removal and the Making of the National Parks* (New York, 1999); Chris J. Madoc, *Yellowstone: The Creation and Selling of an American Landscape, 1870–1903* (Albuquerque, N.M., 1999); and Paul Schullery, *Searching for Yellowstone: Ecology and Wonder in the Last Wilderness* (Boston, 1997).

Contemporary environmental concerns have generated passionate books. Jim Robbins's *Last Refuge: The Environmental Showdown in the American West* (San Francisco, 1994) introduces many of the contemporary struggles over land use in Montana and the Rocky Mountain region. Two of Richard Manning's books also deal with contemporary land use controversies: *Last Stand: Logging, Journalism, and the Case for Humility* (Salt Lake City, 1991) and *One Round River: The Curse of Gold and the Fight for the Big Blackfoot* (New York, 1998). David Stiller scrutinizes the environmental history of a hard-rock mine in *Wounding the West: Montana, Mining, and the Environment* (Lincoln, Neb., 2000). Earlier works on environmental issues include K. Ross Toole, *The Rape of the*

Great Plains: Northwest America, Cattle, and Coal (Boston, 1976) and Michael Parfit, *Last Stand at Rosebud Creek: Coal, Power, and People* (New York, 1980).

This review has mentioned only published books, but there is a wealth of articles on Montana history, the best source of which is *Montana The Magazine of Western History*. The *Great Plains Quarterly* also regularly publishes essays about Montana history. Excellent masters' theses generated at the state universities, senior honors theses from Carroll College, and an increasing number of dissertations from graduate students at universities around the country are another superb source. Clearly Montana and its rich past continue to provoke thoughtful analysis, good writing, and good reading.

Credits

Colin G. Calloway, "Army Allies or Tribal Survival? The 'Other Indians' in the 1876 Campaign," *Legacy: New Perspectives on the Battle of the Little Bighorn* (Helena, Mont., 1996), 63–82

Edwin Dobb, "Pennies from Hell: In Montana, the Bill for America's Copper Comes Due," *Harper's*, 293 (October 1996), 39–54

Keith Edgerton, " 'A Tough Place to Live': The 1959 Montana State Prison Riot," *Montana The Magazine of Western History*, 42 (Winter 1992), 56–69

David Emmons, "The Orange and the Green in Montana: A Reconsideration of the Clark-Daly Feud," *Arizona and the West* (now *Journal of the Southwest*), 28 (Autumn 1986), 225–45

William E. Farr, "Troubled Bundles, Troubled Blackfeet: The Travail of Cultural and Religious Renewal," *Montana The Magazine of Western History*, 43 (Autumn 1993), 2–17

Harry W. Fritz, "Montana in the Twenty-first Century," written for this collection

William J. Furdell, "The Great Falls Home Front during World War II," *Montana The Magazine of Western History*, 48 (Winter 1998), 63–73

Verlaine Stoner McDonald, "A Paper of, by and for the People': The *Producers News* and the Farmers' Movement in Northeastern Montana, 1918–1937," *Montana The Magazine of Western History*, 48 (Winter 1998), 63–73

Mary Melcher, " 'Women's Matters': Birth Control, Prenatal Care, and Childbirth in Rural Montana, 1910–1940," *Montana The Magazine of Western History*, 41 (Spring 1991), 47–56

Laurie Mercier, "Creating a New Community in the North: Mexican Americans of the Yellowstone Valley," *Stories from an Open Country: Essays on the Yellowstone River Valley*. Ed., William Lang (Billings, Mont., 1995), 127–47

Mary Murphy, "Bootlegging Mothers and Drinking Daughters: Gender and Prohibition in Butte, Montana," *American Quarterly*, 46 (June 1994), 174–94

Joseph C. Porter, "Marvelous Figures, Astonished Travelers: The Montana Expedition of Maximilian, Prince of Wied," *Montana The Magazine of Western History*, 41 (Autumn 1991), 36–54

Mark David Spence, "Crown of the Continent, Backbone of the World: The American Wilderness Ideal and Blackfeet Exclusion from Glacier National Park," *Environmental History*, 1 (July 1996), 29–49

Orlan J. Svingen, "Jim Crow, Indian Style," *American Indian Quarterly*, 11 (Fall 1987), 275–86 . Copyright © 1987

Robert R. Swartout, Jr., "From Kwangtung to the Big Sky: The Chinese Experience in Frontier Montana," *Montana The Magazine of Western History*, 38 (Winter 1988), 42–53

Dave Walter, "Hogan's Army: 'A Petition with Boots on'," *Montana Campfire Tales: Fourteen Historical Narratives* (Helena, Mont., 1996), 103–13

Index

McCain, John, 301
McClintock, Walter, 289, 299
McCulloch, Linda, 346
McDermott, William, 68–69, 70, 72
McDonald, Laughlin, 267–68
McGrath, Mike, 346
McKenzie, Kenneth, 6, 15–16
McKinnon, Edna Rankin, 136, 137
McNelis, Mike, 183
Meaderville, 188, 189, 192, 193, 318
Medicine Crow, 35, 38, 40
Medicine Crow, Joe (historian), cited, 40
Melcher, John, 346
Metal Mine Workers' Industrial Union, 325
Metanetix, 329
Mexican Americans, in Yellowstone valley, 221–43; and community building, 234–39, 243; discrimination against, 225, 230, 232; and education, 321–33, 241; and generational changes, 233–34, 239–41
Mexican American Community Organization (MACO), 234
Mex-keh-mah-uastan, 10
midwives, 142–46
Miles, Nelson, 31
Miller, Alfred, 170–71
Miller, Ed, 268, 279
mining: and Berkeley Pit, 311–40; and Chinese, 47–49; decline of, 343, 344–45; and Populist movement, 68; and repeal of Sherman Silver Purchase Act, 66–67
Minneconjou, 31
Missoula Farmers' Market, 344
Missoulian, 345, 348
Mitchell, David D., 6–7, 9, 10, 11, 16–18, 21
Montana Migrant Council, 242
Montana Mining Association, 343
Montana National Guard: and 1959 state prison riot, 258, 260; and labor strife in Butte, 325
Montana Power Company, 350–51, 352, 354, 355
Montana Resources, Inc., 322, 323, 330, 335, 338, 343, 352

Montana Sedition Act (1918), 325
Montana State Prison riot (1959): causes of, 249–56; consequences of, 261–62; description of, 247–49, 256–61
Montanans Opposed to Discrimination (MOD), 279
Montes, Juan, 243
Moon festival (Chinese), 56
Moran, Michael, 88
Morrison, John, 346
Mountain Chief, 294
Mountain Pocket, 36
Mountain States Energy (MSE), 329
Mountain View Mine, 90
Muentzer, Alma. See Hileman, Alma Muentzer
Muentzer, Lillie, 185
Muir, John, 112
Muir Tunnel, 70
Mullan Road, 45
Mullan Tunnel, 51
Murphy, Catherine Hayes, 143
Murphy, Helena Bradbury, 146
Murray, Frank, 254
Murray, Mrs. Michael, 189
Myles, Jerry, 248–49, 255–56, 257, 258–59, 260–61, 262

Naaki, 34
Napi (Old Man), 106
Nation, Carry, 333–34
Native American Graves Protection and Repatriation Act (NAGPRA), 302
Newton, Isaac, 3
Nonpartisan League, 153, 154, 155, 156, 157, 161
North American Free Trade Agreement (NAFTA), 343
Northern Cheyenne Indians, 32, 34, 268, 273, 274, 276, 277, 278. See also Cheyenne Indians
Northern Pacific Railroad, 40, 65, 66, 230; and Chinese workers, 50–52, 60; and "Hogan's Army," 68–74
NorthWestern Energy and Communications Solutions, 351

O'Bannon, Ed, 88

O'Connor, Maurice, 84
O'Connor, Sara, 146
O'Daly, Hugh, 87–88
O'Donnell, I. D., 222
O'Fallon, Benjamin, 6
O'Farell, John J., 88
O'Hara, Pat, 189
O'Keefe, Mark, 346
Old Crow, 36, 40
Old Horn, Dale, 273–74
O'Leary, Pat, 183
O'Neill, "Rimmer," 88
Other Magpie, 38
Our Lady of Guadalupe Catholic
    Church, 236–38, 242

Page, John B., 72–73
Panic of 1893, 65, 66
Paradise, Viola, 139–40
Parkman, Francis, 28
Parnell, Charles Stewart, 87
Parrot Mine, 90
Patriotic Order, Sons of America, 92, 94
Pawnee Indians, 29, 32, 33–34, 41
Pegasus Gold, 345
Pennsylvania Power and Light
    Resources, Inc. (PPL), 351
Penrose, William J., 90, 91–92, 94–95
Peoples, Don, 322, 329
Peoples Publishing Company, 156
Peralez, Esther, 231, 233, 234, 236, 237,
    241
Phelps Dodge/Canyon Resources, Inc.,
    356
Piegan Indians, 12, 13, 14, 15, 16–22, 109,
    292, 303
Pierce Packing Company, 230–31
Pinchot, Gifford, 112
Pioneer (town), 49
Plenty Coups, 31, 39–40, 41
Plentywood Herald, 153, 157, 162–65, 168–
    69, 170, 171
Polk, Harry, 163
Popper, Deborah, 350
Popper, Frank, 350
Populist movement, in Montana, 65,
    66–75
Porter, Seymour H., 272

Portland General Electric (PGE), 351
Powell, Floyd, 249–50, 254–55, 256–58,
    259, 260, 261, 262
Pretty Eagle, 40
Pretty Shield, 38
Price, Dan, 332–33
prison riot. See Montana State Prison
    riot
Producers News, 153–72
Prohibition, and Montana, 163, 177–94
Provincial Museum of Alberta, 283, 285,
    286, 297, 300–301, 302
Puget Sound Energy, 351
Pulliam, Francis, 260
Puro, Henry, 168
Puutio, Aino Hamalainen, as midwife,
    145–46

Quarnberg, Josie Torres, 239

Racicot, Marc, 346, 350, 356
Rafeedie, Edward, 267–68, 278, 279
Ragsdale, Fred, Jr., 275
Rainier Press, 172
Ramsey, James, 71
Randall, James, 256, 258
Rankin, Jeannette, 133, 136
Rankin, Wellington, 137
Raymond, Helen, 187
Reavis, Mark (historian), cited, 326–27
Red Cloud, 41
Red Harvest, 316, 319
Red Lodge, 145
Rehberg, Dennis, 346
Reich, Robert, 355–56
Renz, Jeff, 268, 275
Rides at the Door, Robert, 300
Riggs, Merle, 242
Rinehart, Mary Roberts, 115
Rivera, Esther, 224, 226, 227, 230, 231,
    236, 237, 239, 240, 242
Rivera, Robert, 225–26, 229, 230, 231, 236,
    238, 242
Robert Emmet Literary Association
    (RELA), 87, 88, 89, 92
Rock Springs, Wyo., riot against
    Chinese, 57
Rocky Boy Indian reservation, 272